THE BIBLE IN THE MAKING

Books by Geddes MacGregor

The Bible in the Making
Introduction to Religious Philosophy
Corpus Christi
The Thundering Scot
The Tichborne Impostor
The Vatican Revolution
From a Christian Ghetto
Les Frontières de la morale et de la religion
Christian Doubt
Aesthetic Experience in Religion

THE BIBLE
IN THE
MAKING

BY GEDDES MacGREGOR

J. B. LIPPINCOTT COMPANY
PHILADELPHIA & NEW YORK

In gratitude to him who on my fifth birthday
Gave me my first Bible
As a prize for reading the shortest verse

CONTENTS

PREFACE

This book is designed for people who want to know something about the Bible as a book. How was it put together? How has it been handed down from one generation to another? What and where are the oldest manuscripts? How was it first translated, and what, precisely, is its place in literature? These are questions demanding factual answers, whether we approach the Bible as a book entirely apart—the very handiwork of God—or as but one literature among many.

It is a pleasure to take the opportunity of thanking Dr Norman Cockburn, General Secretary of the British and Foreign Bible Society, for generously granting me permission to quote statistical tables from his society's annual report, and Dr William C. Somerville, General Secretary of the National Bible Society of Scotland, for providing information, including some unobtainable from published sources. Acknowledgment is due for helpful materials provided by the American Bible Society, the New York Bible Society and not least the Division of Christian Education of the National Council of the Churches of Christ in the United States of America, which has been generous in allowing me to quote copyright materials. I am grateful also to the Very Reverend Dr Pitt Watson, ex-Moderator of the General Assembly of the

Church of Scotland and Honorary Chaplain to Her Majesty Queen Elizabeth II, and Professor J. K. S. Reid of the University of Leeds, England, for their courtesy in answering questions. Permission to reproduce copyright passages has been kindly granted by several publishers to whom acknowledgment is made in footnotes.

I wish to record my thanks to Dr Henry J. Cadbury, Professor Emeritus of Harvard University and a distinguished Biblical scholar, for his kindness in reading the proofs and in drawing my attention to errors. For any that remain I hold myself, of course, responsible. To Dr Gerald Larue, Associate Professor in the University of Southern California, I tender thanks for some useful suggestions and much helpfulness in the later stages of the work. It is a special pleasure to thank one of my graduate students, Rabbi Gottschalk, Dean of Hebrew Union College, Los Angeles, who made valuable suggestions for the chapter on Jewish translations.

GEDDES MACGREGOR

Ard Choille
Kennedy Lane
Bryn Mawr
Pennsylvania

THE BIBLE IN THE MAKING

I

INTRODUCTION

THE BIBLE, whether approached with skepticism or faith, is certainly the most astonishing book in the world.

Many factors contribute to its uniqueness. It is not age that makes the Bible unique, for there are other ancient literatures that could claim considerably greater antiquity. Nor does its distinction lie in the fact that it may be said to have taken over a thousand years to write. More startling, perhaps, is its present circulation: the Bible is so unrivalled as today's top best-seller that it is not even counted in the lists. Its distribution is enormous. Over twenty-five million copies, complete or in part, are distributed every year by the Bible societies alone. Included in the 1,688 tons of goods dispatched in the year 1957 by the oldest of these, the British and Foreign Bible Society, founded in London in 1804, were nearly two million copies of the entire Bible. This distribution, now increasing, has for long been immense. For example, the American Bible Society, since its establishment in 1816, has distributed nearly half a billion copies of the Scriptures. To the work of these societies, and that of the twenty-two others now organized together with them, is chiefly due the translation of the entire Bible into over two hundred—parts of it into over eleven hundred—languages. Of the Revised Standard Version published in 1952, seven million copies were sold in the first seven years.

Yet the immense popularity of the Bible today is less remarkable than the fact that it was the world's best-seller for centuries before the term "best-seller" was invented. And long before that, long before the invention of printing made it possible to produce such a very large book in any considerable quantities, manuscript copies were more eagerly sought after than any printed book is likely to be. The story of how the Bible was transmitted to us, eventually in its present form, is indeed exciting. It also helps to answer the question: What is this book which, having been accounted so precious by Christians in the days of the Emperor Diocletian that they suffered the most cruel tortures rather than give up copies of it to the Roman authorities, now has a demand exceeding the most popular novel of the year?

The first Bible ever to be printed appeared over five hundred years ago. It was a Latin edition published at Mainz, Germany, not later than the middle of August, 1456. Printed in double columns, forty-two lines to a column, and in two folio volumes, it was the greatest printing achievement of its day. About forty copies of this edition now exist. One of these, purchased for about $400,000, is in the Library of Congress, Washington, D.C. The Henry E. Huntington Library, San Marino, California, also has a fine copy whose fifteenth-century binding of stamped leather and metal bosses over heavy wooden boards has enabled it to escape the "cropping" of pages that has been the fate of many precious old books. This Latin edition is commonly called the Gutenberg Bible, being attributed to Henne Gensfleisch, a printer who assumed the name Johann Gutenberg. He is widely credited with the invention of printing by movable type. For this distinction there may be, however, other claimants. Lourens

Janszoon Coster of Harlem, Holland, for instance, appears to
have printed a Latin grammar about a decade or so earlier.
It is also probable that the type for the famous Bible was cut
by another printer, Peter Schoeffer.

The Gutenberg Bible is technically designated the "42-line
Bible." It has also been called the Mazarin Bible from its
having been first drawn to the attention of experts in the library of Jules Mazarin, which is now incorporated in the
Bibliothèque Nationale in Paris. Mazarin was a remarkable
seventeenth-century Italian who, after taking his degree in
law and serving as a captain in the army of the Colonna,
became a naturalized Frenchman and entered the service of
Louis XIV. At the instigation of the latter, Mazarin, who had
never been ordained even sub-deacon, let alone priest, was
created a Roman cardinal. Out of the enormous revenues he
collected from various rich ecclesiastical offices, he amassed a
huge fortune, part of which he devoted to the famous library
that included a copy of this rare and extremely beautiful
first printed edition of the Bible.

The Latin version printed in that edition had already,
however, been circulating in Europe for more than a thousand years, in copies each laboriously written out by hand.
Completed in the year 404, by St Jerome, this version came to
be known as the Vulgate, because it was adopted, in western
Europe, as the "vulgar" or common edition. It was a good
translation in its day, for Jerome was an extremely able man
who worked from the Hebrew and Greek originals.

Jerome was born about the year 340 at Strido, a town on
the border of Dalmatia. His parents were Christian and he
received his early education at home. Then he went to Rome,
where he received the equivalent of a modern liberal education. He learned grammar and rhetoric; he listened to the
advocates in the law-courts; he attended lectures on Plato
and other Greek philosophers whose works had by then ac-

quired the status of a dead but respectable tradition. On Sundays he went on expeditions to the Catacombs where he applied himself to the study of the inscriptions over the martyrs' graves. In 360 he was baptized by Liberius, Bishop of Rome. Later, after periods of residence in Gaul and elsewhere, he travelled in the East. A dangerous illness was the occasion of his determination to devote himself exclusively to Christian scholarship. He had cherished an ambition, in his youth, to become a great literary stylist, and his inclinations were still directed to the study of pagan literature. One night at Antioch, however, in or about the year A.D. 374, he dreamt that an accusing voice addressed him in the words: "You are a Ciceronian, not a Christian!" Shortly afterwards he became a hermit at Chalcis in the Syrian desert and applied himself to the study of Hebrew. Eventually he gained the repute of being the greatest Biblical scholar the Christian Church had ever produced. He died at Bethlehem in 420.

The three oldest, fairly complete, manuscripts of the Bible known to be in existence now are in Greek. Two of them were written probably at least two generations before Jerome was making his Latin translation; the third was written a little later. One of these manuscripts, the property of the Vatican Library in Rome for at least five hundred years, though for long jealously guarded from the public, is known as the Codex Vaticanus. It is on vellum—said to be antelope skin— with three columns to the page. It lacks, however, all the New Testament from Hebrews ix.15 onwards. The other two manuscripts are both in the British Museum. One of them, the Codex Alexandrinus, latest of the three in date, came to England in 1627 and was put into the British Museum in 1757.

The other has had more recent and very exciting adventures. Known to scholars as the Codex Sinaiticus, it is so called because it was discovered, in 1844, in the monastery of

St Catherine, on Mount Sinai. It was found in that monastery —a great gaunt building, walled in like a Norman keep—by a German scholar, Constantin Tischendorf, who was visiting there in May, 1844, in search of any manuscript fragments he might chance to find. He actually found 129 leaves of the manuscript in the trash-basket, and was told by the monks that they were about to be burned; and that two other similar basketfuls of "rubbish" had already been so destroyed. In the long run,[1] after a series of very involved yet quite honorable transactions, the assembled manuscript was presented, in 1867, to the Tsar of Russia and placed in the Imperial Library. The monks received from the Tsar the sum of 9,000 roubles (very roughly, about $7,000 at that time), besides having the Archbishopric of Sinai secured for their nominee by the Tsar's influence. At the Bolshevik Revolution the manuscript passed into the hands of the Soviet Government, who sold it, in 1933, to the British Museum for the sum of £100,-000. Though defective in some other respects, it contains the New Testament in complete form. It may be seen without fuss by anyone in London who cares to go to the British Museum, where it is exhibited in a glass case in one of the main halls. While it is, of course, one of the most important and valuable manuscripts in the world, it has been catalogued in the ordinary way and bears the mark: "B. Mus. Addit. MS. 43725." It is written on vellum, four columns to the page, by three scribes, two of whom were bad spellers and one of these so bad that modern scholars have wondered how he ever came to be entrusted with the work. However, when we are dealing with writings of such extreme rarity, we cannot afford to grumble at the inexpertness of one of the team of scribes.

By the time these manuscripts were being written, the Bible had already had a very long history. The earliest parts

[1] It was not till a later visit in 1859 that Tischendorf discovered enough of the manuscript to reveal its full value.

of the New Testament, one or two of the Epistles, were written about twenty years after the crucifixion; the Gospels, in the form in which we now have them, later still. (Some explanation of this will be given in another chapter.) As a collection of Christian literature with special authority of its own, the New Testament was not, however, recognized and set apart till about the year 200. It was written in Greek, which at the time of its writing was widely used as an international means of communication. The Bible that Jesus and his disciples knew was the Old Testament, written in Hebrew, though it had by then been translated into Greek for the benefit of the many Jews who lived beyond Palestine. The Greek version of the Old Testament was done at Alexandria in Egypt, a very cosmopolitan city that was a sort of New York of the ancient world. The Hebrew Scriptures, as we shall see, were put together over the course of many centuries. Probably the oldest passage in them is the Song of Deborah, which is to be found in the fifth chapter of the Book of Judges. Experts have dated that passage at about twelve hundred years before the birth of Christ. Other parts of the Old Testament, however, were written not very long before he was born.

   The Old Testament was completed in roughly its present form by the time of Christ. But this statement needs to be amplified, for it depends on what is meant by "completed." In the first place, books consisting of sheets folded and cut, as in the book you are now reading, were unknown at that time. Books consisted of scrolls, sometimes done up with rods or handles at either end for the purpose of winding and unwinding. Various materials including animal skins were employed; but the most conventional material was papyrus, which had been used in Egypt from remote antiquity, even before Biblical times. Papyrus was produced by the Egyptians from a reed that grew in the region of the river Nile. The Hebrews may have imported their supplies of this material from Egypt; but it is likely that they produced some of their own, for papyrus grows in northern Palestine at the present day.

Strips of the stem of the reed were first laid out in a row covering an area corresponding to the size of sheet desired, and they were then overlaid with cross strips. Moisture was applied to the two layers, which were then hammered out flat and put in the sunshine to dry. The result was an off-white, rough surface which was later buffed smooth with some hard substance such as a piece of ivory. Such a sheet would be less than a quarter the size of a page of the *New York Times;* but sheets could be sewn or glued together to make up a scroll, say, thirty feet long.

Finding the place you wanted in such a scroll was by no means easy. Not only was the scroll an awkward thing to handle, as you will easily imagine if you have ever tried your hand at wallpapering; there were neither chapter nor page numbers to help you. The text just went on and on. When we read (Luke iv.17) that Jesus, in the synagogue, was handed the scroll of the Book of Isaiah and found his place in it, we ought to bear in mind that finding your place in such a scroll demanded a great deal more skill and much more thorough acquaintance with the book than would now be required to look up a passage in a modern copy of the Bible. Moreover, physically, one book of the Bible was enough to handle; for this reason alone there could be no question of a "complete" Old Testament, in the sense of a single scroll containing all the books that are now in it.

There was, however, another reason. What present-day Christians call the Old Testament was divided into three parts which had, in Jewish eyes, unequal status. The first part, the Torah (the Law), consisted of the Pentateuch (Genesis, Exodus, Leviticus, Numbers, Deuteronomy), and was held in tremendous esteem. Placed in an "ark"—a sort of

wooden coffer—in the synagogue, as it is to this day, the scrolls
of the Law were treated as though the very material of which
they were composed was sacred. The second part was a literature called "the Prophets." This literature, which we
shall consider later, included books such as Isaiah, Amos and
Jeremiah. It acquired an important position, yet one that was
subordinate to that of the Torah. A third literature, called
"the Writings," included, for instance, Job and the Psalms.
By the time of Christ this third part of the Hebrew Scriptures
had largely taken shape. The Psalms served as a sort of hymn-
book, the contents of which must have evoked many and
varied memories. Not the least memorable perhaps would be
those designated in modern Bibles "A Song of Degrees," [2] for,
according to some scholars, these were marching songs sung
by pilgrims on their way to Jerusalem. The Psalms, some of
which were probably based on ancient, traditional songs of
the Hebrews, were destined to play a very special role in the
devotional life, public and private, of Christians. But though
all the third literature, which included books ranging in diversity from Ruth to Proverbs, from Chronicles to the Song
of Solomon, had taken shape by Christ's time, it was not by
then officially settled as part of the sacred literature. Among
the many things to be explained later on is how the books
now collectively known as the Apocrypha are to be fitted
into the picture that has here been sketched only in the most
general way as a preliminary to our story.

Fragments of the Hebrew text of this great ancient literature that we call the Old Testament were, till about twelve
years ago, singularly scarce. There was nothing at all to
compare, for instance, in antiquity and extensiveness, with
the Greek manuscripts that have been described. The damp
soil of Palestine precluded the survival of papyrus rolls.

---

[2] Psalms cxx-cxxxiv. "Degree" (*gradus*) means a "step." Jerome entitled
each of these psalms *canticum graduum*.

Egypt, on the other hand, had for long yielded a great many manuscripts and fragments of all sorts. Over twenty years ago, fragments of a Greek papyrus of Deuteronomy, written about a hundred and fifty years before the birth of Christ, were discovered and published by the Rylands Library, Manchester, England. The discovery, in 1947, of a whole scroll of the Book of Isaiah in Hebrew, in a cave near the Dead Sea was much more exciting. There were further finds of a similar sort, shortly afterwards. Much of the significance of these finds lies in the fact that the manuscripts are in Hebrew, for before then no extensive manuscripts of the Hebrew Scriptures were known to exist that could be dated earlier than about A.D. 900. The Dead Sea Scroll of the Book of Isaiah is certainly much older than that, and although experts are not agreed on the exact date, it may well be of the century before Christ.

So rare were even fragments of Hebrew manuscripts that adventurers were tempted to enterprising frauds. One of the most audacious of these was perpetrated in 1893, when, in August of that year, a tremendous stir was caused by the alleged discovery of a manuscript of Deuteronomy with considerable variations from the received text. This manuscript, if genuine, would have been of far more revolutionary importance than the discovery of the Dead Sea Scrolls has been. Eleven, not ten, commandments were set forth, and there were many other equally interesting differences that would have discredited the results of all the patient labors of Biblical scholars up to that date. The manuscript was owned by a Jew called Shapiro, who affirmed that he had obtained it several years previously from some Arabs. It purported to have been written about 800 B.C., and the writing, in characters similar to those of a stone inscription that had been found in 1868 and was known to date from about 850 B.C., was on strips of old leather. Among the evidences of forgery that rapidly came to light was the fact that the old leather strips had been cut from the margins of an ordinary synagogue scroll.

Why are there so few surviving manuscripts of the Hebrew Bible? There are several reasons besides the dampness of the Palestinian soil to explain why there is such a dearth of Hebrew manuscripts till more than eight centuries after the dispersion of the Jews in A.D. 70. With the fall of the Temple at Jerusalem in that year, the ritual worship with its animal sacrifices was at an end, and the dispersed Jews had nothing to take with them on their wanderings but their Bibles. To the copying out of these they devoted immense care. The regulations for making a copy of the Scriptures are set forth in the Talmud (the great post-Biblical collection of Jewish law and legend) and show how scrupulously careful the scribes had to be. The scroll of the Law for use in a synagogue has to be fastened, for instance, with strings made from the skins of "clean" animals. The length of each column was prescribed: not more than sixty nor fewer than forty-eight lines were permitted. Lines had to be drawn before the writing was done, and if a scribe inadvertently wrote more than three words without first lining his copy, the whole thing was rendered worthless. He had to see that the space of a thread lay between each two consecutive letters that he wrote, and he was not allowed to write even a single letter from memory, without first looking at the approved text from which he was making his copy. He had to see that he never began the sacred name of God with a pen newly dipped in ink, lest he spatter this. The ink had to be black, made exactly according to a carefully delineated prescription. Throughout the whole of his work, the scribe was required to sit in full Jewish dress, and he was forbidden to speak to anyone, even a king. Any copies that did not entirely conform to this exacting standard had to be destroyed. What chiefly accounts for the absence of early Hebrew manuscripts, however, is the fact that as soon as any scroll became worn out it had to be put in a special room called the Geniza, adjoining the synagogue, the contents of which room were periodically cleared out and destroyed. The Jews had no interest in preserving tattered old copies of the Scriptures for the sake of their antiquity: what they wanted were accurate copies, and so long as accuracy of current copies was insured by the rigid regulations, old ones could be discarded. From all this it is not surprising to learn that the comparatively early copy of the Book of Isaiah discovered near the Dead Sea twelve years ago revealed no vitally important deviations from the text previously available to scholars.

On the other hand, it is not to be expected, without extreme ritualistic care such as the Jewish scribes brought to their task, that a book as enormous as the Bible could be copied out by hand in the course of many centuries and translated from one language into another without the introduction of a great many errors. As we know it today, the Bible contains 31,173 verses and must be read at the rate of twenty-three chapters a week by anyone who wishes to complete it in a year. For all the care that scribes often devoted to their task, a great many errors inevitably crept in. Deviations occur even among the most reliable of the ancient Greek manuscripts.

Before the invention of printing, the difficulty of reproducing the Bible did not consist solely in the labor of copying it by hand. Parchment was scarce, so that contractions were very freely used. Sometimes a valuable manuscript, such as the Codex Ephraemi, a fifth-century Bible now in the Bibliothèque Nationale, Paris, was treated so that, the writing having been erased by scraping and pumicing, the pages might be used over again for making another book. The lower writing was not usually quite obliterated, however, though it was extremely difficult to decipher it until chemical means were found to revive what had been rubbed out. Such a book, with one set of writing superimposed upon another, is called a palimpsest. Again, manuscripts were often corrected by later copyists who scraped out with a knife what seemed to them incorrect, and modern scholars know that in many cases it was the corrector, not the manuscript, that was at fault. Sometimes a note would be made in the margin which a subsequent copyist would take to be part of the text. The hazards of inaccuracy in copying out the Bible by hand in the circumstances that prevailed in those days were so great that it is indeed astonishing that a text has been preserved which, despite technical problems it presents to the learned, may be taken as generally not straying very far from the sense of the original. Translation, we shall see, is another matter.

What has been said makes it plain enough that the full story of the Bible, from the time a Hebrew first wrote, some three thousand years ago, the Song of Deborah that is now embedded in the Book of Judges, down to the present decade when the latest American translation, the Revised Standard Version, first appeared in print, would make an exceedingly lengthy and technical study. Here we engage in no such undertaking, but confine ourselves to such facts as will sufficiently show why the Bible commands the respect of even the most skeptical of those of its readers who approach it intelligently. Others who, loving the Bible with a devotion that inspires them to regard it with a much deeper reverence, should need no invitation to behold the mystery of its making revealed to them in history. For it is a truism that "they seek to understand who truly love."

II

THE SETTING OF
THE OLD TESTAMENT

THE ANCESTORS of the men who wrote the Old Testament were nomadic tribesmen in western Asia. It is fairly certain that the word "Hebrew" is closely connected with the name "Habiru" which, as tablets of the period show, was given disparagingly by the settled communities to the wandering bandits who for centuries engaged in raiding the desert fringes of northwestern Mesopotamia some four thousand years ago. Sometimes they settled down for a time, becoming mercenaries, hiring themselves out as laborers, or even selling themselves as slaves to the settled families. But they were a restless people. Whether they were restless because they were landless or landless because they were restless it is not possible to say. What is certain is that while some of them continued a nomadic or semi-nomadic life, others eventually settled in the fertile eastern part of the Nile Delta, "the land of Goshen," where for a long time (four hundred years, according to tradition) they lived in comparative contentment until they were reduced to slavery by the Egyptians. The date of this change in their fortunes is obscure: according to one theory, it probably occurred between 1319 and

1301 B.C., during the reign of Sethos I, an Egyptian Pharaoh whose ambition to rebuild his cities drove him to conscript the Hebrews as slaves in his brickyards.

One of these captive Hebrews raised a rebellion. Under his inspiration the Hebrews made a desperate bid for freedom. The Egyptians, pursuing hotly, were drowned, while the fleeing Hebrews, after their trek across the desert, reached Mount Sinai in safety. The escape is commemorated in one of the most joyful songs in the Old Testament [1] and its leader was, of course, Moses. At Mount Sinai, under the inspiration of Moses, the people entered into a covenant with Yahweh, their God. At this time the Hebrews' conception of God was very different from what it was to become centuries later. In common with all primitive peoples, they were still thinking of the universe as directed by many gods. The gods of the Egyptians, for example, were very real, very powerful. But Yahweh, the Hebrews believed, had helped them against the Egyptians. Yahweh would be their God. They would enter into an agreement with Yahweh, pledging themselves to obey him as, they believed, Yahweh pledged himself to protect and succor them. They would be faithful to Yahweh, who, Moses told them, demanded complete fidelity. There must be no philandering with other gods: they would be henceforth one people under one God. "Thou shalt have no other gods before Me," was the commandment.

It may be said that the people of Israel came into being at Mount Sinai; yet not even a Moses could turn a lawless band of recently emancipated tribesmen into a law-abiding and settled community overnight. The Israelites were far behind their neighbors in the arts of both war and peace. They were unskilled immigrants who retained their tribal organization with its old clan loyalties and divisive feuds.

[1] Exodus xv.

But they were quick to adapt themselves to their changed way of life, and within about two hundred years they had established themselves as a unified people. They were extremely proud of their own history and achievements and seem to have quickly come to regard themselves as a very special people, a people set apart from all others, a people who were different from their neighbors. Almost all that is distinctive about the Old Testament, which is the literature of this people, springs from an awareness of their peculiarity. Nevertheless, because they were also in process of being nationalized and civilized, they naturally sought to copy the institutions of their better-established neighbors; hence, after a period of rule by tribal leaders ("the Judges"), the adoption about 1020 B.C. of a monarchical system of government.

The land the Hebrews had made their own was a small one, though extremely varied in climate and contour. Palestine, west of the Jordan, is larger than Connecticut but considerably smaller than Vermont. The area of its cities was astonishingly small. For instance, the capital, Jerusalem, covered at one time only eight acres [2]—no more than the building-lot an American businessman might buy for a large family house. The fortification of the cities was, however, often very impressive, especially the great double gate which was the site of much public business. Every day it would be crowded with all sorts of people. Haggling tradesmen would jostle with filthy beggars; scribes would stand around offering to write letters for a fee; laborers would loiter in hope of being hired for the day; travellers would arrive inquiring for lodging for the night. In the greater cities there were shopping quarters— rows of untidy bazaars displaying their wares on shaky stands or on the ground. The congestion, dirt and odor of the ex-

[2] Even by the time of Christ it was still only about a quarter of a square mile in area.

tremely narrow streets must have been horrible, for there was, of course, almost no sanitation. They were no doubt also exceedingly noisy, and by far the most desirable dwellings would be those on the upper floors adjoining the city walls, where at least one side of the house would be free from the uproar of the city. Yet for all the chaos of these noisy, dung-strewn alleys, and for all the incessant pandemonium around the gate, the cities were full of energy and no doubt often irresistibly interesting.

Saul was the first King of the Hebrews under the new system of monarchical government. He was followed by David, under whom Israel was considerably extended by foreign conquest. Jerusalem became the capital. David's ambitions for the centralization of authority and the neat organization of the whole people exceeded his achievements; but his son Solomon, continuing his father's work, divided the country into twelve administrative districts and sent out officers to collect taxes from all subjects. Solomon also engaged in elaborate building projects, making Jerusalem an important city with a grand new Temple, a palace and administrative offices in the latest Phoenician style, and setting up also other cities as garrison for the royal chariotry. To further his scheme, Solomon exploited copper mines, built a merchant navy, and generally developed trade and commerce.

His reign was spectacular; but it was followed by civil war that sundered the northern kingdom, Israel, from the southern kingdom, Judah. In the end, the north won. With the expansion of commerce that followed, the country seemed by the eighth century B.C. to have attained great prosperity. But, as usual, only the few enjoyed it. The prophets of this period, not least Amos, testify to the irresponsible greed of the *nouveaux riches,* the "fancy" religion they affected, and the misery of the little farmers whom corruption in high places forced into debt and even slavery. With vehement denunciation of that corruption, Amos and others warned the people that Yahweh would not let unrighteousness reign forever in the land, for it was Yahweh's land, and Yahweh, he said, was a righteous God.

The northern kingdom eventually fell, in 721 B.C., to the Assyrians. Over twenty-seven thousand prisoners were taken and deported. The southern kingdom, Judah, which had been less prosperous and less corrupt, continued for a time in precarious independence. In 701 B.C., however, came an Assyrian invasion that robbed it of forty-six cities and almost lost Jerusalem to the invaders. Judah now seemed to be in abject dependence upon Assyria; but after 640 B.C. Assyrian power waned and eventually collapsed under the growing power of Babylon. Babylonian rule, which the Hebrew prophet Jeremiah urged his people to accept, was fanatically resisted. The resistance entailed great hardship for the Judeans, whose cities were again taken one by one, culminating in an eighteen-month siege of Jerusalem, whose inevitable fall in 586 B.C. sent thousands into exile in Babylon.

It was out of the experience of the Babylonian exile that the Hebrew people received their greatest religious insights. Their prophet Jeremiah had interpreted their misfortunes as Yahweh's punishment upon them for their infidelity to their covenant with him. Jeremiah's message was not pleasant to hear; but though he sounded a gloomy prophet he was not entirely pessimistic. He believed and taught that Yahweh, having chastised the nation for its waywardness, would enter into a new covenant. This new covenant would not, however, be like that which had been made in the time of Moses, a covenant between Yahweh and the whole people: the new covenant would be between Yahweh and individuals who would be responsible to him in a personal relationship.

When the Hebrews found themselves in Babylon they suffered the intense perplexities of the homesick exile, expressed

in the mixture of nostalgia and rage of one of the most exciting psalms in their literature:

> By the waters of Babylon,
> There we sat and wept,
> When we remembered Zion.
> In the willows in the midst thereof
> We hanged up our harps,
> For there our captors asked of us
> Words of song,
> And our plunderers, mirth:
> "Sing to us
> Of the songs of Zion."
>
> How should we sing Yahweh-songs
>   in a foreign land?
> If I forget thee, Jerusalem,
>   may my right hand fail me;
> May my tongue cleave to my palate,
>   if I remember thee not,
> If I exalt not Jerusalem
>   above my greatest joy.
>
> Remember, Yahweh,
> the sons of Edom—
> the day of Jerusalem!
> Who said: "Rase it, rase it to its very foundation."
> O daughter of Babylon, thou devastator,
>   blessed be he that requiteth thee,
> Blessed be he that seizeth and dasheth
>   thy little ones against the rock! [3]

The sentiments of the captives in the land of their captors
were not such as could be expressed in the latter's presence.

[3] Psalm cxxxvii, as translated by W. O. E. Oesterley, *The Psalms* (London,
Society for Promoting Christian Knowledge, 1939), vol. ii, pp. 545 f. Reproduced by kind permission of the publishers. This psalm is sung in Jewish
homes to this day, after dinner, on the Sabbath.

The psalmist recalls and records, therefore, the inward feelings of all as they were forced to sing their songs, the holy songs of Yahweh's people, for the entertainment of foreigners in a foreign land. Yet the interior rage of the Hebrews was mingled with other feelings too, for the Babylonians treated them fairly well, and they knew considerable freedom in exile. Indeed, they enjoyed economic advantages far superior to anything they had known in Palestine. In a rich, well-irrigated plain lying between two of the greatest cities in the ancient world, Babylon and Nippur, the exiled Hebrews had immense opportunities of which many were glad, after the first agony of homesickness was past, to take full advantage. Some harvested huge crops; others entered government service or turned to commerce. Their success in the latter activity was so great that even at that remote date can be found some indications of that anti-Semitic jealousy which the Jews have since so generally evoked in the hearts of the peoples among whom they have settled. Some, intoxicated by their prosperity under an alien sky, repudiated Yahweh and accepted the gods of their captors, which meant, in those days, that they renounced their old citizenship and sought naturalization. Others, however, wished to be faithful to their religion.

These found, at first, a paradox in their situation. In the ancient world, a people and its god, a land and its religion, were inseparable. You could no more take your religion with you than you can take Independence Hall with you on a visit to Venice. You could no more take your god with you than a Londoner can take Westminster Abbey with him on a trip to San Francisco. In the early days the Hebrews had carried a box or "ark" with them as they moved from place to place in semi-nomadic fashion, and they had believed that wherever the ark went Yahweh went. But that was when they were moving together as a tribe. Now they were scattered in various places far from their now ruined Temple at Jerusalem.

The question: "How should we sing Yahweh-songs in a foreign land?" was to them a very pointed one. Theoretically, it
seemed to them, it should be impossible to do so. Yet they
discovered that in fact Yahweh, far from being confined to
Palestine, seemed to be nearer to them in their exile than ever
he had been before. So they found a fresh and deeper significance in the literature that was then in process of forma-
tion and was eventually to be transmitted to us as the Old
Testament. For while they could not take the Temple with
them from Jerusalem, they could carry with them the Word
of Yahweh in their hearts. They could no longer go to the
Temple to offer the appointed sacrifices; but in gathering together as they did on the Sabbath in their homes they could
read the sacred scrolls and other writings. Out of these in-
formal gatherings eventually was developed the synagogue of
later times, whose service, with its Bible reading and exposi-
tory sermon, had much influence on early Christian liturgy.

In 538 B.C. Cyrus the Great took Babylon. Through his
generous policy towards the Hebrew captives he found there,
the latter were enabled to return to Jerusalem. Some of them,
taking advantage of the offer, did return and erect an altar on
the site of the ruined Temple where they resumed the regular sacrifices. The conditions of the ravaged city were not
attractive, however. Nor were the returning exiles encouraged by the attitude of those who, in the meantime, had
"stayed put" and taken possession of the best surviving dwellings. To the homecomers it seemed that these were profiteers
who had moved far from the old Hebrew ideals, intermarry-
ing with Samaritans, Edomites and other neighboring peoples. The ill-feeling between the non-exiles and the returning
exiles delayed the rebuilding of the Temple for fifteen years;
but under the influence of the prophets Haggai and Zechariah
it was at length undertaken. Excited by the hope of the
divine favor that they expected this enterprise to bring, the

Hebrews rebuilt the Temple in fitting style, though not on Solomon's scale. The divine favor that was expected included, of course, the restoration of their national independence. When this hope grew dim the faith of many failed, while others grew more punctilious than ever in their religious observances. Some shared the vision of the prophets, the vision of one God who has "the whole world in his hands," and who can direct the activities of all men.

It was in this period that many of the features characteristic of later Judaism took shape. Regular observances marked the course of the year: the Passover, the Day of Atonement (Yom Kippur), and the rest. The Jews became more and more a closed society, a theocracy with a hereditary priesthood and a high priest who was believed to be descended from Aaron, the brother of Moses. At the same time, the profession of the scribe, from which the rabbis came to be recruited, acquired great importance. By then Aramaic was displacing Hebrew as the spoken language, and the need of a class of learned men to expound the ancient writings to the common people who could no longer well understand them was obvious. It is to this period, too, that belongs much of the elaborate editing and compiling of the documents that eventually gave them the form with which we are familiar in the Old Testament: more than two-thirds of these documents had by then come into being. Of this editing process, very important for an understanding of the structure of the Bible, more will be said in the next chapter.

This increasingly theocratic society came under yet another foreign rule in 332 B.C., when Alexander the Great, having expelled the Persian armies from Asia Minor and Syria, took Palestine on his way to Egypt where he founded the city of Alexandria, which he hoped would become a world center for the spread of Hellenistic culture and the Greek way of life. Alexander treated the Jews with considerable respect, and these, though probably at first aloof in their attitude towards the Hellenistic colonists who came to Palestine, fell very much under their influence. Within a few generations Palestinian Jews of the upper class, including the priests, were considerably affected by Greek ways of thought, while thousands migrated to Alexandria, where they became of course even more thoroughly Hellenized.

It was in Alexandria that was begun, in the third century B.C., the Greek translation of the Hebrew Scriptures now known as the Septuagint. This translation has acquired great importance for scholars because of the lack, already noted, of ancient manuscripts of the Hebrew Bible and the relatively much greater antiquity of manuscripts of this Greek translation. The Septuagint is so called from the tradition that seventy translators were engaged upon it.[4] For reasons that will be considered later, the contents of the Septuagint may be seen from any modern Roman Catholic version of the Old Testament.[5] Included are all the books found in the King James Version of the Old Testament and certain other books such as Ecclesiasticus, Wisdom and Tobit.

But while the aristocratic ranks of Jewish society found the attractions of Greek culture irresistible, the common people, who often constitute the hard core of conservatism in a nation, remained comparatively unaffected. In this they were supported by the scribes and rabbinic teachers among whom there arose learned schools. One of these was that of the Pharisees, who upheld a rigorous insistence on the minutiae of the law of Moses which they developed from a comparatively simple form into a highly complicated system requiring prolonged study and inviting learned controversy.

Palestine suffered a great deal of invasion after the death of Alexander; now by the Seleucids of Syria, now by the Ptole-

---

4 Scholars often refer to it as LXX.
5 Books of the Septuagint are listed in Appendix XIV.

mies of Egypt. It was a Seleucid king, Antiochus, who, in a foolish attempt to interfere with the religion of the Jews and force upon them a religion they detested, provoked them to the spectacular feat of rising against their overlords in 165 B.C. This uprising, because of the leading part played in it by Judas Maccabeus, is known as the Maccabean Revolt. The period of national independence that followed (the last the Jews were to enjoy till the recent founding of the State of Israel) continued until Palestine became, in 63 B.C., a Roman province.[6] During these later centuries B.C., Greek and Persian influences upon the literature of the Jews were very strong. It is to this period that belongs what is generally called the Wisdom literature, a group of books exhibiting in many ways the extent to which the Jews had by this time assimilated foreign ideas.[7] Some of the books that constitute this literature are now in the Bible, namely, Proverbs, and Ecclesiastes. Others, as we shall see, are in the Apocrypha. Daniel, the last book of the Old Testament to be written, also shows much foreign influence, including even the occurrence of Greek words. Scholars believe it to have been written, at any rate for the most part, as late as about 165 B.C., and in encouragement of the Maccabean Revolt.

This brief glance at the history of the Jews before the time of Christ tells us something about the sort of people they were; but it is certainly very far from telling us all, not least because it is in great part an account of the circumstances the Hebrews faced rather than of their reaction to these circumstances in the ordinary affairs of life. From the point of view of a modern, urban American, perhaps the most striking feature of their life was the enormous influence and peculiar

6 Not a province in the strict, constitutional sense, being territory subject to Roman control through the province of Syria.

7 This "Wisdom" literature contains, however, ideas that go back to Solomon's time and was characteristic of the pre-Hebrew empires in Egypt and Babylonia. *Infra*, Chapter III.

importance of the family. The extreme hardships endured by
the Hebrews in their very early days, when the desert constantly threatened every man's bare existence, taught them
the value of family loyalty and co-operation as a condition of
individual survival. As individuals, they never entirely forgot
that lesson, even when it was less urgently necessary for them
to remember it. Marriage was an absolute duty for all men:
there was no place in Hebrew society for bachelors. Polygamy
was for long generally approved and was not, indeed, formally
discountenanced by Jews till many centuries after the time of
Christ. Theoretically, a Hebrew could have as many wives as
he pleased; in practice few men could afford more than two,
while many, for either economic or other reasons, contented
themselves with one. Even two wives made for a complicated
family. It was less complicated, however, than it would seem
to a modern American or European accustomed to a different
conception of family relationships. The family depended for
its security on the absolute authority of the father, who ex-
acted unquestioning obedience both from his wives and from
his children. Disobedient children might even be put to
death. Daughters could be sold into slavery, for they were the
father's property. A wife had almost no rights at all, for she
also was owned by her husband. All this sounds, however,
much more despotic than it was. Hebrew women worked very
hard; but they were in practice held in high honor as mothers
or potential mothers of the next generation. Many modern
women might well envy the respect they enjoyed. For similar
reasons, a wedding, though it involved the payment by the
bridegroom of a sum of money that was almost if not entirely
a purchase price, was the occasion of profound rejoicing as
well as hilarious festivities, for it betokened the perpetuation
of the family upon which the hopes of all were focused.

There is almost nothing to be said in favor of living conditions. The vast majority of people lived in very simple,

one-roomed houses in which the entire family had to live, eat, and sleep. In front was a small yard where many of the daily chores were done, and the roof of the house formed a deck on which you could take the air and shout the latest gossip across to your neighbors. There could have been little opportunity for privacy, rest or quiet inside or outside the dark, mud-floored box that was the average Hebrew home. The interior was dark because it had to protect its inhabitants from the blazing summer sun as well as the winter rain, and of course there were no glass windows, but only little slits in the wall. A crude lamp burned dimly all day and night, partly to keep away evil spirits, partly because there were no matches. In bad weather even the sheep and goats were brought in from the yard to share the protection afforded by the family's leaking roof and walls of mud. Even the simplest furnishings were accounted the privileges of the rich: most families ate sitting on a mat on the floor and slept on a rug with their coat as their only blanket. Only the very rich enjoyed such luxuries as mattresses or simple divans, or storerooms for oil and wine. Probably few homes had the coveted second story to be seen in the houses of the wealthier citizens.

To some modern readers it may seem surprising that people living so long in such primitive conditions should have been able to produce a literature such as the Old Testament. Indeed, perhaps we might not expect such a people to have many thoughts beyond the next meal. It is true that the cultural attainments of the Hebrews, as measured in terms of music, pottery, and other such arts and crafts, were modest. Nor were the Hebrews in any sense a bookish people. Literacy was uncommon, probably very exceptional. How then did they produce such a literature? How did they come to be known, after the Exile, as the "People of the Book"? It is fairly certain that most of the actual writing was done by professional scribes. Some of these were exalted government officials; others were humble, hard-working men eking out a living by means of their only skill. The fact is that much if not most of the Old Testament had its origin in oft-repeated narratives and songs handed down orally from one generation to another and only later committed to writing. When the oral tradition did begin to take shape as a literature, it necessarily remained inaccessible as such to most people. Even as a literature, therefore, it was designed to be read aloud so that the many could hear what only the few could read.

What is there in the Bible of the Hebrews to make it, even from the most "un-supernatural" point of view, the great literature that has captivated the hearts and stimulated the minds of men and women throughout the ages down to our own day? Apart from some of the later passages in it, it contains no philosophical reflection to compare, for instance, with that of the *Dialogues* of Plato or the Upanishads. Its scientific conceptions are strikingly crude. Of course we should not expect them to conform to our modern standards; but they are crude even in comparison with those of the Greeks who engaged in scientific speculation before the time of Socrates. Nor has the literary style of most of the Hebrew Bible any elegance or precision that would commend it to those who love literary excellence for its own sake. Hebrew has a relatively modest vocabulary and is essentially a language of verbs. Herein is indeed a clue to the extraordinary vitality of its literature and its appeal. Whatever may be said against the Hebrew Bible from the point of view of a literary critic or one who, like Jerome before his conversion, thinks only in terms of its stylistic qualities, it cannot be said that it lacks action. There is action in every chapter; almost in every verse. While comparatively little discussion of even the simplest ideas is to be found, personalities abound and their vividness makes the Hebrew Bible fascinatingly human and absorbing. You never lose sight of the fact that you are

reading about very real people. It is not simply a faith in
their God that makes their Bible the distinctive book it is,
for all ancient peoples believed, in one way or another, in
their gods. What gives the Old Testament its peculiar and
abiding flavor is, rather, the sense it conveys of a divine purpose being ever unfolded to a growing people. The acuteness
and intensity of their experience evokes in them a uniquely
vivacious faith, so that their God, who is first encountered as
a mere tribal deity, is eventually seen and depicted as the
author of all things, the One who "in the beginning . . . created the heaven and the earth," [8] and to whom "righteousness
belongeth." [9] Never in the Hebrew Bible is there discussed
any "spiritual" philosophy disconnected with ordinary life.
It is always a fiercely human book about a fiercely human
people. The only God it knows is the One who is revealed
through the toil and hardship, the sweat and tears, of a life
lived precariously on the edge of the death-dealing desert.
The Bible so produced is the story of life so lived and of the
kind of faith that such living engenders. Whether it is also
much else besides, the reader will judge for himself.

[8] Genesis i.1.
[9] Daniel ix.7.

III

THE WRITING OF
THE OLD TESTAMENT

ALL YOU have to do to see that the Old Testament as we know it did not come straight from the pen of its several authors, is to look at the first three chapters of Genesis. There you will find two quite distinct accounts of the creation of man. The account in the first chapter is startlingly different from the account in the second and third. The tone of the first is loftier and grander; it is also more restrained. After God finished the creation of everything else and "saw that it was good," he "created man in his own image . . . male and female created he them." Having so created them he blessed them, told them to "be fruitful, and multiply," and gave them dominion over the rest of creation.

Now if you turn to the second and third chapters you will find an entirely different story. Here God is depicted as having made the earth; but "there was not a man to till" it. Then we are told that the Lord God took dust or earth and formed a man out of it as a modern child does with play dough. Having done so, the Lord God then breathed into the nostrils of the man he had formed out of the dust, whereupon the "man became a living soul." The Lord God then went forth, planted a garden in Eden, and put the man in it. After instructing the man on the subject of what fruit he might and what fruit he might not eat, the Lord God *then* decides that it was not good for the man to be alone. He looks at the beasts but can find no suitable companion among them for the man. He therefore puts the man to sleep, "took one of his ribs, and closed up the flesh," and out of the rib he has extracted the Lord God constructs a woman. We then learn that the man and the woman are untroubled by the fact that they are both nude until, tempted by the serpent to eat the forbidden fruit, they suddenly become aware and ashamed of their nudity and remedy it by making aprons for themselves out of fig leaves sewn together. After this we even find the Lord God taking a walk in the garden "in the cool of the day." The man and the woman hear the Lord God's voice and, stricken with guilt, seek cover among the trees, presumably hoping that the Lord God will be unable to find them in the dense foliage. At length, however, the Lord God asks the man point blank, "Where art thou?" and the man explains that it was because he did not dare to appear before the Lord God in a state of nudity that he had hidden himself. (Apparently he either accounts the apron insufficient or else has by this time decided to discard it.) The Lord God then remarks that the man must have eaten the forbidden fruit, for otherwise how should he even notice his nudity? The man admits the eating but blames the woman for plucking and providing the fruit of the forbidden tree. The Lord God is very angry and distributes punishments all round. But before expelling them from the garden, the Lord God himself tailors "coats of skins" for them, being apparently dissatisfied with their own attempts at dressmaking.

There is no doubt that these two stories of the creation of man which have been set down together in the opening chapters of Genesis belong to very different periods. The second is by far the more primitive one, and between the writing of the two narratives about as much time elapsed as has elapsed between the day of Christopher Columbus and our own. The disparity is obvious from the character of the stories themselves: you can detect it in reading them alongside each other in an English Bible. If you were reading them in Hebrew you would be struck by the fact that throughout the first account the word used for "God" is "Elohim," while in the second the name assigned is that of "Yahweh."

The use of the term "Elohim" goes further back, however, than the date of the passages in Genesis in which it is used. A study of various passages in the Hebrew Bible shows that there must have been originally two documents, of which the author of the more primitive one used the name Yahweh in referring to God, while the author of the other used the name Elohim. Scholars call the first document J, from "Jahveh" ("Yahweh"), and the second document E, from "Elohim."

Both these documents served as sources for the later compilers who put them together in constructing the first six books of the Hebrew Bible as it has come down to us. Both dealt with the same general material but in a different fashion. In the earlier document, J, God was depicted more crudely and in a more picturesque fashion. He was a war god, and the moral and religious sentiments that J expresses are vivid, robust, and sometimes, to modern ears, vindictive. The writer of the other source, E, is more subtle in his interpretations and attitudes. In contrast to J, who interprets the founding of the national Hebrew monarchy as a divine act, E regards it as a regrettable decline from the less autocratic form of government that had prevailed in the preceding period, the age of "the Judges." His treatment of character is more delicate than that of J. The reader who wishes to compare these sources for himself may consult the following passages by way of example:

J: Genesis xii, xiii, xviii, xix, xxiv, xxvii.1-45, xxxii, xliii, xliv; most of Exodus iv-v; Numbers x.29-36; most of Numbers xi.

E: Genesis xv (in part), xx.1-17, xxi.8-32, xxii.1-14, xl, xli, xlii, xlv; Exodus xviii.20-23, xxxii, xxxiii.7-11; Numbers xii; most of Numbers xxii-xxiv.

J was a product of the southern, E of the northern kingdom. It seems that not long after the fall of the latter in 721 B.C., the two documents fell into the hands of a writer in the southern kingdom who put them together with additions of his own. The result of his labors formed another ancestor of the Bible as we know it, called by modern scholars JE. (An example is Exodus xv.22-27.) He seems to have tried to preserve, and to have succeeded in preserving, the vivid, picturesque style of J while treating the narrative that he presents from the more prophetic view of the later age to which he belonged.

Then came the enlargement of the JE document, probably in the following century, by the addition of the discourses of Deuteronomy. These purport to be addresses delivered by Moses shortly before his death, and indeed they were no doubt based on an oral tradition of a farewell address given by that great leader of the early Hebrews. The writer of Deuteronomy incorporated older materials in his work such as the "Blessing"; [1] but the ideals and sentiments he expressed are those of his own age, not that of Moses. They are also of a very lofty moral character and lively religious insight, so that the result of the editorial process up to this point gives us a work whose contents vary from the early, picturesque folklore story in the J account of the creation to the exhortations to love God and one's neighbor that were later to be cited from these Deuteronomic passages by Jesus himself and commended by him as the essence or "sum" of the Law. So

[1] Deuteronomy xxxiii.

beautiful, indeed, was the tone of Deuteronomy that it inspired other writers to imitate it, and it is evident that one or
more of these expanded and revised certain sections of the JE
document in the spirit of the Deuteronomic work. Later still,
around 500 B.C., there was further editorial revision by a
school of priests who, after the destruction of the Temple,
codified the existing pre-exilic ceremonial regulations. Finally, in the fifth century B.C., this codification of priestly
ritual laws was incorporated with JE as revised and expanded
by the Deuteronomic editor. The first of the two creation
narratives in Genesis, as these now stand in our Bible, belongs
to the latest period of these revisions.

The revision process may be expressed diagrammatically [2]
as follows:

J (*c.* 850 B.C.) + E (*c.* 750 B.C.)   = JE (*c.* 650 B.C.)
JE + D (621 B.C.) (including most of the
   work now called Deuteronomy and the
   editing of JE)   = JED (*c.* 550 B.C.)
JED + P (500-450 B.C.) (including some an-
   cient liturgical material and the priestly
   editing of JED)   = JEDP (*c.* 400 B.C.)
JEDP   = the Pentateuch as
                                                              we now know it

So was produced, in the form in which it has come down to
us, the Hexateuch: Genesis, Exodus, Leviticus, Numbers,
Deuteronomy, and Joshua. Of these the first five constitute
the Pentateuch, which is the literature the Jews came to ven-
erate as the Law of Moses, the Torah. So persistent has been
the tradition attributing its authorship to Moses that these
books are ascribed to him even in our familiar English translations such as the King James and even the Revised Standard

[2] It is here presented in as simple a form as possible, and according to the
most generally accepted theory. The revision process was probably more complicated; but the general pattern was as presented here.

versions. It was not till the seventeenth century A.D. that scholars began to detect the composite character of the Pentateuch and not till the nineteenth that modern critical methods established the nature of the editorial process in such a way as to dispose entirely of the long tradition ascribing it to Moses. Yet doubts must have occurred to many careful readers before then, if only because among the reasons for repudiating the Mosaic authorship is the singularly obvious one that in one of the books attributed to Moses his own death is recounted.[3] There are, indeed, probably echoes in the Old Testament itself of dissatisfaction with the revisions. Jeremiah, for instance, having questioned whether his compatriots are justified in their confidence in possessing the Law of God revealed to Moses, warns them: "Behold, the false pen of the scribes hath wrought falsely." [4]

In commending the Deuteronomic summary of the Law, Jesus said that upon it hung all the Law *and the Prophets*.[5] By "the Prophets" his hearers would understand, as of course he intended, a definite body of sacred literature that had by the time of Jesus acquired a prestige second only to the Law itself. This literature was divided into two parts, "the Former Prophets" and "the Latter Prophets" respectively, and according to the Jewish computing there were four books in each part, for besides reckoning Samuel and Kings each as a single book, they counted the following twelve books of our Bible as a single book: Hosea, Joel, Amos, Obadiah, Jonah, Micah, Nahum, Habakkuk, Zephaniah, Haggai, Zechariah and Malachi. (These twelve books are now known as the Minor Prophets or Little Prophets, though they are minor or little

---

3 Deuteronomy xxxiv.5-end. Post-Biblical Jewish writers got out of this difficulty by attributing these verses to Joshua, while ascribing all the rest to Moses.

4 Jeremiah viii.9 (ASV).

5 Matthew xxii.40.

only in respect of length, by no means in respect of importance.)

The four books constituting the Former Prophets were, then: (1) Joshua, (2) Judges, (3) I Samuel, II Samuel, (4) I Kings, II Kings.

The Latter Prophets included (1) Isaiah, (2) Jeremiah, (3) Ezekiel, and (4) the twelve Little Prophets just mentioned.

This literature was fully recognized by the Jews, probably by about 250 to 200 B.C., as worthy of reverence next to the Torah. Like the latter, it had undergone much editing and revision. The line of prophets went back to the remote past. Hebrew prophecy no doubt began with the soothsayers and magicians that are to be found among all primitive peoples. What is remarkable about it, however, is that from such pedestrian beginnings it developed into a much nobler and grander movement that became a great moral force in the history of the people and bequeathed to posterity a literature of unique dignity and power. Between the earlier prophets such as Elijah, of whom we read in Kings, and Amos, who flourished in the northern kingdom about 750 B.C., there is a tremendous difference of outlook as well as distance in time. Some of the other prophets, for example Jonah, do not come on the scene till about four hundred years later still. Modern critical methods have revealed that the book of Isaiah is really the work of several very different prophets living in quite separate periods. Some think there was a *school* of prophets in the tradition of Isaiah. In Samuel there are passages that seem to be contemporaneous with the events they recount while others are plainly much later in date.

In the Law and the Prophets we have accounted for twenty-six of the thirty-nine books of the Old Testament in its present form. The other thirteen books were grouped together by the Jews as "the Writings," being the third and last of the literatures of which the Hebrew Bible was eventually composed. The Writings had acquired recognition more than a century before the birth of Christ though not officially included in the Hebrew Bible. The status of this literature was and remained till about the end of the first century A.D. subordinate to that of the Law and the Prophets. In the Writings were reckoned three groups, (1) the poetical books, consisting of Psalms, Proverbs and Job, (2) the Rolls (Megilloth), read in the synagogues at five sacred seasons and consisting of the Song of Solomon, Ruth, Lamentations, Ecclesiastes and Esther, and (3) the books of Ezra and Nehemiah (reckoned by the Jews as one book), the two books of Chronicles (likewise reckoned as one), and the book of Daniel.

The books that formed this third literature are of the most varied character. Though older materials were used, all this literature is comparatively late. The Psalms, for instance, attributed to David, are on the whole strikingly post-exilic in sentiment and expression. They were not completed till at least the third century B.C., probably even later. Proverbs, attributed to Solomon, likewise contains at the most only a few of his sayings and is substantially a collection representing the wisdom of many centuries, and including some materials that probably came from Egypt. No doubt many aphorisms of remote antiquity are included or echoed in it—there are certainly counterparts in Egyptian literature—though the book did not reach its present form till about the fourth century B.C.

Job also may be based on an old story which had been adapted by a comparatively late poet for the expression of his answer to a question that had arisen in the minds of thoughtful Jews: Why do the wicked prosper and the righteous suffer? Traditionally, the Hebrews had given little attention to the notion of a future life; their concern was with life on earth. If God was the righteous God that the prophets proclaimed him to be, he ought, it seemed, to reward the righteous with "length of days" and prosperity to fill them, and to withhold these blessings from the wicked. Experience, however, seemed often to indicate just the reverse, and the book of Job, which deals with this puzzle, is perhaps the most profound book in the Old Testament.

The Song of Solomon, which has probably nothing to do with him, is a collection of love songs. Though a highly mystical significance came to be given to it in much later times, it was no doubt frankly erotic in conception and intent. The songs, which were probably used at wedding feasts, are very beautiful. Once again, traditional elements were probably used in a compilation of comparatively late date.

Ecclesiastes is one of the latest Old Testament books, dating perhaps from about only two hundred years before the birth of Christ. Its view of life is sad and tempered with a wistful doubt about many things. This puts it in sharp contrast to the lively faith of the earlier passages in the Old Testament. Together with Proverbs and Job it represents that part of the Wisdom literature, already mentioned in the preceding chapter, that found a place in the Old Testament. Daniel, latest of all the Writings, was written, as also already noted, mainly about 165 B.C.

We saw in our opening chapter what extreme care the scribes were required to exercise in copying the sacred text. It is reported in the Talmud that the Rabbi Ishmael counselled a prospective copyist in these words: "My son, be careful in thy work, for it is a heavenly work, lest thou err in omitting or in adding one jot, and so cause the destruction of the whole world." Jesus himself is recorded, in the Sermon on the Mount, as saying that not "one jot or tittle" should "pass from the law, till all be fulfilled." [6] This reference to the "jot" and the "tittle" becomes more meaningful if we know to what it refers in the Hebrew alphabet. We are fa-

6 Matthew v.18.

miliar with the saying, "mind your p's and q's," which refers originally to the process of learning the English alphabet, in the course of which a child must beware of confusing these two letters; but no one beyond kindergarten is in danger of mistaking one for the other. Even the most experienced Jewish scribe, however, had good reason to heed the warning to watch his tittles, for the tittle [6a] is all that distinguishes the Hebrew letter *beth* (pronounced *b*) from the Hebrew letter *kaph* (pronounced *k*), and the minuteness of the tittle may be seen from the following transcription of these two Hebrew letters, alongside which is also transcribed a "jot" (*yodh*), the smallest letter in the Hebrew alphabet:

ב (*beth*)   כ (*kaph*)   י (*yodh*)

Not even the most perfect copyist could insure an unambiguous text, for Hebrew was written entirely without vowels, which the reader had to supply for himself. Since there was also no distinction between capital letters and others, no punctuation, and practically no greater space between words than between letters, the sentence which you are now reading would, if printed according to the ancient Hebrew fashion, appear as follows:

S N C T H R W S L S N D S T N C T N B T W N C P T L L
T T R S N D T H R S N P N C T T N N D P R C T C L L
Y N G R T R S P C B T W N W R D S T H N B T W N
L T T R S T H S N T N C W H C H Y R N W R D N G W L
D F P R N T D C C R D N G T T H N C N T H B R W F S
H N P P R S F L L W S [7]

[6a] On the subject of the tittle, Hebrew scholars should consider, however, the idea expressed by Professor Henry J. Cadbury in *The Peril of Modernizing Jesus*, p. 57. See also Strack Billerbeck, *Kommentar Zum N. T.* (on Matt. v. 18), I, pp. 248 f.

[7] This makes no provision for the fact that Hebrew is read from right to left.

Competent Hebraists, without as much difficulty as one might suppose, read manuscripts written in this way; but ambiguities were inevitable. To help in the elimination of these ambiguities, a school of Jewish scholars, the Massoretes, invented, probably about the sixth century A.D., a system of "pointing"—dots and dashes placed under the Hebrew letters to indicate the vowel sounds. The Massoretes naturally vocalized the text according to the practice of their own day. From this Massoretic text, in "pointed" Hebrew, we can know fairly well how Hebrew sounded when it was solemnly chanted in a synagogue as long ago as, say, the time of Mohammed. But we have no such clear knowledge of how it may have been pronounced by David or Solomon. The Massoretes halted the corruption that the passage of centuries had inevitably introduced; but they came on the scene much too late to preserve for us an entirely pure, unambiguous Old Testament text. They also compiled a set of notes, called Massorah, and offered variant readings.

There can be no doubt that even as early as the Jewish Synod of Jamnia [8] at which, about the end of the first century A.D., the contents of the Old Testament were discussed and, it is likely, officially settled, there were considerable textual variations among the existing manuscripts. The problem of later determining what, in a doubtful case, was the original reading, is obviously a difficult and highly technical one demanding, for its solution, great learning and skill. Textual critics, in dealing with such matters, know what errors to look out for. Among these the most commonplace are three, known to scholars as haplography, dittography and metathesis. The first of these occurs when the scribe inadvertently leaves out a letter, word or phrase, the second when he accidentally repeats some such element, and the third when he

[8] Jamnia (or Jabneh), a city in Judaea (Lat. 31°, 52″ N., Long. 34°, 45″ E.), is once mentioned in the Bible: II Chronicles xxvi.6.

erroneously inverts something. These are, of course, familiar errors among typists today. Their detection is often quite easy. In other cases, however, it is by no means so, and it is just in these cases that the most significant errors are likely to be overlooked. If we remember that besides such textual disparities there are also, in unpointed Hebrew, great possibilities of ambiguity, and that the Massoretes themselves frequently misled posterity by faulty vocalization that changed the meaning, we shall have some notion of the complexity of the task of trying to recover, as far as may be possible, the original Old Testament text.

Let one example illustrate this. Job is recorded [9] as referring to death as the common fate of two sharply contrasted types of man. Of one of these, according to the King James Version, Job says that "his breasts are full of milk." [10] This reading is plainly absurd. In the Massoretic text the word for milk is clearly given; the word designating the container of the milk is, however, very obscure, and translators from ancient times onwards have made wild guesses at it. For certain reasons it seems to be a part of the human body, and the Greek Septuagint ventured a word that means "entrails," while the Latin Vulgate rendered it *viscera*. These readings do not sound very convincing, and the absurdity of them is not lessened in the Douai (English Roman Catholic) Version, which has "bowels." In the King James Version the translators were apparently eager to have the appropriate part of the human anatomy as the milk-container, regardless of the appropriateness of the sex of its owner. Milk belongs to breasts, so breasts it had to be, even though the breasts were male ones. Other English translators (for example, in the American Standard Version) tried "pails" as a way of escape from the biological impossibility of "breasts." All these wild attempts sprang

9 Job xxi.22-26.
10 Job xxi.24.

from acceptance of "milk," plainly given in the pointed Hebrew of the Massoretic text. This word, in unpointed Hebrew, is identical, however, with the Hebrew word for "fat"
which of course might go with almost any part of the anatomy
and make sense. A much more likely hypothesis, therefore, is
that the Massoretes incorrectly vocalized the Hebrew to make
it read "milk" where it should have read "fat." On this hypothesis we may proceed according to the suggestion of a
modern scholar who offers us the rendering: "his legs are full
of fat." This makes perfect sense, and even if the obscure
word is not correctly rendered by "legs" we still have, if the
hypothesis is correct, the fundamental sense of the affirmation,
which is essentially that the man is fat, and this accords perfectly with the context.[11]

In view of the range of ambiguities and errors to which the
Hebrew text was subject, it could hardly have come down to
us with any accuracy at all had it not been treated with reverence and scrupulous care. Thanks to this reverence and
care for the text, the Old Testament has been transmitted to
us with remarkable fidelity. This may be verified in various
ways. For instance, the Samaritan Pentateuch, preserved by
the Samaritan community (with which, readers of the Fourth
Gospel will recall, the Jews had no dealings) [12] since the time
of Nehemiah [13] about the middle of the fifth century B.C.,
attests the substantial correctness of the text that has been
transmitted throughout the ages, first by Jews and then by
both Jews and Christians. The Samaritans claimed descent
from the patriarchs. What is certain is that from the time of
the rebuilding of the Temple there was enmity between them
and the Jews, and the breach was complete when the Samaritans set up a rival priesthood. Extremely conservative in

11 The Revised Standard Version has "his body full of fat," with a note
alluding to the uncertainty of the word translated "body."
12 John iv.9.
13 Nehemiah xiii.23-31.

spirit, they adhered to the Pentateuch, repudiating the later Hebrew literature. The fact of their conservatism and their estrangement from the Jews, makes the fact that their text accords with that of the Jewish Pentateuch an excellent corroboration of the purity of the latter. But there are many other attestations of a similar kind. When, not long before the time of Christ, Aramaic superseded Hebrew as the spoken language of the Jews, paraphrases in that language of the books of the Old Testament were designed to meet the needs of the people. These, called Targums, were not mere translations, but expositions, and for this reason they help modern scholars to understand the way the ancient Hebrew mind worked as well as provide corroboration of the text itself. The text they supply is practically identical with the Hebrew one. The Greek Septuagint, being of great antiquity, is of course of first-rate importance in the process of verifying the text, and there are also Syriac, Old Latin and other Greek versions which contribute in various ways. So, despite puzzling words and phrases, modern critical scholars have been able to reconstruct a text which, closely following yet emending the traditional one, may be taken as remarkably reliable.

IV

HOW THE NEW TESTAMENT
TOOK SHAPE

THE PALESTINE into which Jesus was born had been a Roman province for about sixty years. The Romans, whose administrative policy was wiser than that of the Seleucid king who by his interference in the religion of his Jewish subjects had invited the Maccabean Revolt, took care to allow the Jews as much freedom as possible in the practice of their religion, and permitted them to conduct much of their local government according to their own laws. It was under this relatively benevolent dispensation that Jesus lived as a Jew in Palestine. His ethical teaching was in no way radically different from the loftiest traditions of the Judaism into which he was born. This is plain from a careful reading of the Old Testament itself; the recently discovered Dead Sea Scrolls corroborate the already well established fact that as an ethical teacher Jesus gave his hearers a message which, however powerfully presented and convincingly demonstrated, was not so distinctive as to be accounted novel. In his ethical teaching Jesus was in many ways highly conservative. True, he emphasized certain elements in the now rich Jewish tradition and disapproved of certain tendencies he noted in its development; but this would be true of any teacher worth listening to. He drew attention to elements that many people found it convenient to forget, so that his ethical teaching would be often uncomfortable to many. But not only would this be true of the teaching of other rabbis of his day; it is in some sense true of every good sermon in any age. There is no reason at all to suppose that anything in his ethical teaching could have in itself so antagonized even the most hostile among his hearers as to bring down upon him the exceedingly ignominious sentence of death by crucifixion. Only what he claimed to *be* could have had such a result. To the Jews, any claim to divinity would certainly have seemed blasphemous. It is also to be noted that the disciples of Jesus were so scandalized by the crucifixion that when it was impending they "forsook him and fled." [1] It is therefore hardly an exaggeration to say, as has been said, that on Good Friday it seemed as though there were but one Christian in the world and he dead.

Whatever happened on Easter, it is noteworthy that the faith the disciples had abruptly lost in their Master was spectacularly revived. Within about twenty years of the crucifixion we find Paul, a convert to the Christian way, writing to apparently fairly well established communities of Christians in Asia Minor and Macedonia—very remote in those days from Jerusalem, the scene of the crucifixion. Since Jesus, like other famous teachers in the ancient world, left no writings, the letters of Paul are the earliest Christian literature we have. They were written between approximately A.D. 50 and 65. Scholars are not agreed on the exact order in which they were written; but Thessalonians and almost certainly Galatians were among the earliest. The Epistle to the Hebrews, later erroneously attributed to Paul, is known for certain to be the work of another writer with

1 Mark xiv.50.

an entirely different style. The purpose of all such letters was to instruct and succor young communities of Christians scattered throughout the Mediterranean world. Conveyed to such communities by hand, they were read by them at their assemblies of worship, and at first no one, probably, thought of publishing these letters any more than a modern congregation would think of publishing a letter from a beloved and respected minister who happened to be writing them from another part of the world. Such a congregation today would be content to hear the letter read once from the pulpit. In those days, however, letters were much rarer commodities than they are among us, and so the Epistles that now form part of the New Testament were read over and over again. Sometimes a letter would be shared with another Church [2]—Paul at least once requested this [3]—and of course his letters would be preserved by every Christian community that received them. They would be in the form of scrolls, and often beside them would be a scroll or two of books of the Old Testament which the Christian community might be fortunate enough to possess. Letters from an apostle such as Paul would be much treasured. After Paul's martyrdom, about A.D. 65, his letters would of course be even more lovingly cherished and copied. The central message of Paul's letters is that Christian faith hangs upon recognition of Jesus as the Messiah, God made manifest in the flesh: unless it is true that Christ had really risen from the dead and triumphed over sin and death, then, wrote Paul, they were wasting their time. [4] So was the faith of the first generation of Christians nourished by Paul who

[2] Some readers may need to be reminded that "Church" refers here to a community, not a building. The term is also used of the whole "society of the faithful," the "Body of Christ."
[3] Colossians iv.16.
[4] I Cor. xv.14.

of course, like most of the earliest converts, was a Jew by birth.

Paul and the other early Christian letter-writers wrote in Greek. The reason was a practical one. Greek was in their day an international language, used by traders and others as a common means of communication. As English is widely used throughout the world today, and as French was used in diplomatic and other circles in Europe last century, so Greek was used internationally in Paul's day. It was the language of the great cities of the world, the language of the people whom Paul and his associates specially wanted to reach. It had even penetrated Syria and Palestine. The language of the latter country was Aramaic, which Jesus spoke: a few phrases in this language are indeed preserved in the Gospels in the form in which he uttered them; for example, *"Talitha cumi"* ("Damsel, arise")[5] and *"Eloi, Eloi, lama sabachthani"* ("My God, my God, why hast thou forsaken me").[6] Paul also spoke Aramaic.[7] Nevertheless, even at Jerusalem Greek had come to be used to a considerable extent, and Paul had no difficulty in writing or speaking it. Like a modern Welshman who speaks English fluently though he delights to speak Welsh with his compatriots, Paul and many others like him, though they cherished their own language and culture, communicated with ease in Greek and probably thought in it too. So it was as natural that all the literature of the early Christians should have been written in this language, for there would have been no reason for them to write in any other unless they had wished to restrict their audience to a limited group, which they certainly did not.

It was only after Paul's death that the Gospels as we know

5 Mark v.41.
6 Mark xv.34.
7 Acts xxi.40.

them were written. There is a fairly general, though not
universal, agreement among scholars on the approximate
dates of writing. The most commonly accepted view is
that Mark was written at Rome about the time of the Fall
of Jerusalem in A.D. 70; Matthew at Antioch ten years
later; and Luke and Acts ten years later still.[8] It is a pity
that Luke and Acts are not placed together in the New
Testament, since they were written by the same author,
who apparently intended them to form together the first
complete account of the story of Christianity from the birth
of Christ down to the more recent adventures of the apostles
in their missionary enterprises abroad. Most scholars think
John was written considerably later—probably about A.D.
110. By this time it had become plain that the Gentile
world was to be more and more the sphere of missionary
labor, and it was necessary, therefore, to couch the Christian
message in Gentile rather than Jewish terms. This meant
taking into account the prevailing fashion in philosophy
in the Greek world of that day. So, it is argued, John boldly
and in a style of incomparable beauty and power presented
his account with this in mind. Shortly afterwards, the four
Gospels seem to have been grouped together, partly, perhaps, with a view to promoting John or even exhibiting
its superiority, and partly, no doubt, to take account of
individual preferences that had by this time been developed.

Such, at any rate, are the lines on which most modern
scholars have argued. The details of the reasoning are
very complicated, and a discussion of them would be either
lamentably inadequate or else would take us much too
far out of our way. There was, however, in any case another reason for the grouping of the four Gospels together.
Christian literature was growing and there were various
books coming into circulation besides the ones now in-

8 Some, however, think Luke is slightly earlier than Matthew.

corporated in the New Testament. There was, of course, nothing to prevent anyone from contributing to this growing literature, of which we shall have more to say in the next chapter. Some of it was fanciful and much of it was, for one reason or another, plainly inferior in quality to the now older documents, the Epistles and the four Gospels. These latter were so impressive that novel presentations of the Gospel story could hardly compete with them. They formed, indeed, a very striking collection of testimony: Mark written from the standpoint of Peter; Matthew from that of a Jewish Christian able to take more into his sights; Luke from that of a cultivated friend of Paul; John from that of someone who, besides knowing of the events recorded, has pondered them well enough to interpret them to the Gentile mind. Together with the Acts, in which we see their message in action, they present the "good news" (this is what the Greek word for "gospel" means) with tremendous conviction and power.

The Christians of the first three centuries often suffered very cruel persecution, not least, in the first century, under the Emperor Nero and the Emperor Domitian. The book called Revelation or the Apocalypse reflects this, being written probably about A.D. 95, towards the end of Domitian's reign. Its author is called John. Whoever he was, he was certainly not the author of the Gospel bearing the name, for the style of the two books is entirely different. The author of Revelation wrote Greek with very marked Hebraisms, and he must have been a man of a very different temper and outlook from the one who wrote the Gospel.

Though the books now in the New Testament were mostly written by A.D. 120,[9] they had by no means been collected by that date in their present form, nor had they acquired

[9] An exception is II Peter, which is probably to be dated between A.D. 150 and 175.

anything like their present status among Christians. They were read alongside of many other books of a similar kind. But the books now in the New Testament were rising steadily in public esteem, especially the four Gospels which by A.D. 150, and probably much earlier, were being read with joyous solemnity as part of the Christian liturgy.

Christianity spread with great rapidity, persecution notwithstanding. It was international in character and spirit. But the features which helped to make it attractive to many earnest seekers in the Gentile world also attracted to it many people who wanted to adapt it to fit their own wild fancies. There is evidence of the existence of such elements in Christian congregations from a very early date, and by A.D. 150 they had become a source of grave unrest and a real danger to the solidarity of the young and growing Christian Church. Humanly speaking, it looked as though troublemaking within the Church might wreak such havoc upon it as eventually to destroy it. Yet there was also solid attachment to a tradition that was believed to have been handed down by the apostles. The tension between those whose Christian faith was continually held to this touchstone which they prized and those who wanted to mold that tradition to their own religious fancies was acute. There was, for instance, a man called Marcion, who wanted to repudiate entirely all connection with Judaism, and another called Montanus, who proclaimed himself to be the very mouthpiece of the Holy Ghost. Such men had great followings and those who valued the apostolic tradition either had to succumb to the prospect of seeing the tradition lost in a wilderness of whimsical ideas or else had to develop a much more rigorous organization such as the Christians of the first generation or two had not needed. Prominent in the measures taken to safeguard the Church against the dangers that beset it was the attempt to provide a body of Scripture that could be set side by side with the Old Testament and have, for Christians, a comparable status. But this movement to limit the Christian Scriptures to a fixed number of books was much stronger among some Christian communities than among others. It was very much stronger at Rome, for instance, than in Egypt, where there was, among Christians, a marked reluctance so to limit Scripture, and a notable tendency to accept as Scripture any literature, however novel, that seemed to contain anything of even the vaguest interest to Christians.

Towards the end of the second century A.D. most of the Churches in the West, notably the one at Rome, had accepted a list of books as authoritative, were calling them the New Testament, and were reading them liturgically along with the Septuagint or Greek version of the Old Testament. The body of writing that was thus recognized consisted of the four Gospels, the Acts, and thirteen letters of Paul. Other books, notably Revelation, the Epistle to the Hebrews, II Peter, II and III John, and Jude, were regarded as less authoritative. Other works, however, which were eventually excluded from the New Testament, were regarded by certain Churches as of Scriptural or quasi-Scriptural authority. Notable among these was a work called the Epistle of Barnabas and another known as the Shepherd of Hermas.[10]

In the Eastern Church the tendency was towards a New Testament containing a more ample collection of books. The great Alexandrian scholar Origen (c. 185-c. 254), who probably knew more about the technicalities of the subject than anyone else in his day, drew up a list of books that he considered to be generally accepted by all Christians, and a list of those which, though acknowledged in some places, had no such universal status. In the first of these

[10] Extracts from both these works are quoted in Appendix IX.

two lists he put the four Gospels, fourteen letters which he attributed to St Paul—one of these was Hebrews, now known to be certainly not Paul's letter—the Acts, I Peter, I John, and Revelation. In the second list he placed James, II Peter, II and III John, Jude, Barnabas, and the Shepherd. Origen himself was disposed to acknowledge both lists, which, taken together, give us exactly what is now contained in the New Testament, plus Barnabas and the Shepherd. These two last books were very widely esteemed, and in the Codex Sinaiticus, already mentioned in the first chapter, they are to be found at the end, after the other books of the New Testament that are familiar to us as such. Eusebius of Caesarea, another great scholar of the early Church, born about A.D. 260, preferred to omit both Barnabas and the Shepherd, so his list was similar to the one in our modern editions of the New Testament. But Revelation, long felt to be a very doubtful book for inclusion, was only squeezed in. Indeed in the Eastern Church in the Middle Ages it was more often omitted from than included in manuscripts of the New Testament.

Though the Western or Latin view of what ought to be the contents of the New Testament had been substantially formulated and expressed by A.D. 200, there was no such fixed or universal opinion on the subject in the Eastern Church. Among the Eastern or Greek Fathers in the fourth century there was considerable difference of opinion. For instance, the lists of Athanasius, John Chrysostom, and Gregory of Nazianzus—all highly influential men in the history of the Christian Church—differed greatly. That of Athanasius was most like the list of books we recognize today as canonical; but it was the list of Gregory of Nazianzus that won widest acceptance in the East. His list included the four Gospels, the Acts, fourteen letters attributed to Paul, and seven other letters; it excluded Revelation.

It was about this time that St Jerome undertook his translation of the Bible into Latin, in the "Vulgate" that was to have an enormous influence on Christianity in the West. Jerome was a most diligent scholar. It will be remembered that he travelled in the East, staying for long in Palestine. Though he knew well that the Epistle to the Hebrews enjoyed less favor in the Western Church than it did among Christians in the East, he decided to include it and ascribe it to St Paul, though he took care to acknowledge that this was not according to Western custom. He also included Revelation. Even in the West slight departures from Jerome's list were not unknown; but on the whole it may be said that he finally determined for Western Christians what books the New Testament would contain.

Books had been made according to the modern format (that is, in bound pages, as in the book you are now reading) from at least the first century A.D. A book in this form was known as a codex. The Roman writer Martial remarks on how much a book in this format could hold in comparison with a scroll of similar bulk. But these codices were rare and the change from scroll to codex form was very gradual. It is interesting to note that Western Christians appear to have been very progressive, favoring the codex form in its earlier days. "From the second century, when ninety-seven per cent of the non-Christian Biblical papyri were in the roll form, we now have eight Christian Biblical papyri, and all of these are in the form of the codex. In the entire period extending to shortly after the end of the fourth century, we have 111 Biblical manuscripts or fragments from Egypt, of which ninety-nine are codices." [11] By Jerome's time, however, the codex had become quite

<hr />

[11] Jack Finegan, "The Original Form of the Pauline Collection" in *Harvard Theological Review* (April 1956), vol. xlix, 2, p. 87.

common in the West, and the fact that his Latin Vulgate New Testament was generally made up into one volume —a practice that did not generally prevail in the East— probably helped to promote the common acceptance of his choice of books in compiling it.

It would be false to suppose, however, that the choice of the books that have been handed down to us in the New Testament depended entirely upon Jerome or any other individual. For though the inclusion or exclusion of a few of the books might have been to some extent accidental or arbitrary, there was never any grave doubt about the majority of the books eventually included. The four Gospels had rivals, as we shall see. But none of these ever had much likelihood of attaining a permanent place in the Christian Scriptures. It must be borne in mind, however, that, of the books that did achieve such a place, the Gospels were among the last to be written.

The vast majority of modern scholars consider that there were, however, earlier documents, now lost, which were used in the writing of the first three Gospels, Mark, Matthew and Luke. Of these hypothetical sources, the one designated Q has been most widely discussed. It is argued by some critics that Q itself may have been based on still earlier sources. On the other hand, at least one distinguished contemporary Oxford scholar, Austin Farrer, has argued with vivacity in favor of a very different theory. The questions involved are extremely intricate: the Gospels present modern critical scholars with more difficult and more fascinating problems than do any other sections of the Bible. The diligence of scholars in tackling these problems reflects, of course, belief in their importance.

It will be remembered that the oldest existing manuscripts of the Bible, the Codex Sinaiticus and the Codex Vaticanus, both dating from the fourth century A.D., are written on vellum. Had it been the general practice to use material of this sort in the first century, perhaps a few very early copies of New Testament books might have survived. Indeed it is not entirely impossible that we might even have inherited or discovered an authentic letter in Paul's own hand. For though persecution and other troubles played a part in the destruction or disappearance of many Christian manuscripts, the most important factor in their loss was the impermanency of the writing materials commonly used in those days. Papyrus, we have seen, was very perishable, and only under favorable conditions have even fragments been preserved. Papyrus scrolls were extensively copied and there was a very flourishing book-trade in the ancient world. The great libraries of Alexandria had probably about half a million manuscripts among them. Seneca, Nero's tutor, comments disdainfully upon the rage for book buying on the part of people who, though they might not read the books they bought, loved to own them. It was fashionable to have a library. Apparently there were Roman precursors of James Barrie's character who spoke with pride of owning "five yards of books," and of Ring Lardner's tycoon who "loved to dine among his books, of which he had a complete set." A rich Roman or Athenian merchant might have boasted a private library of perhaps fifteen or twenty thousand scrolls. It is said that some owned even larger collections. Booksellers would sometimes produce as many as five hundred copies of a manuscript. If scrolls were so extensively copied as a commercial enterprise, it is highly probable that a very large number of copies of the New Testament books was in circulation in the first and second centuries, each lovingly copied out by hand. None has survived, so far as is known.

Fragments of pottery with a verse or two of the New Testament written upon them have been discovered. Pottery and other similar materials were often used for scribbling notes, reminders, receipts, and the like. These *ostraka,* as they are called, were the cheapest writing materials in use, corresponding roughly in status to our modern jotting pad. But they were awkward and quite unfashionable for anything more than a casual scribble. Wax tablets were also used for such purposes, but of course the writing on them was impermanent: they were designed to be used over and over again. As in every age, people wrote on walls and the like, and in the catacombs and elsewhere many Christian inscriptions have been found. Despite the perishability of papyri, a great many fragments of Christian documents have been recovered; but the possibility of recovering anything so extraordinarily interesting as, say, an original letter of Paul is indeed exceedingly remote. However, very interesting finds have been made. Thousands of fragments of papyri came to light about the turn of the present century, for instance, at Oxyrhynchus, about ten miles west of the Nile, near the modern Behnesa. Among these are fragments setting forth sayings attributed to Jesus which, though they sometimes recall sayings recorded in the Gospels, are not to be found in the Bible.[12] More recently, in 1952, manuscripts of parts of the New Testament turned up at Khirbet Mird in the region of the Dead Sea.

We are fortunate that manuscripts as ancient as Sinaiticus and Vaticanus have survived. It may seem that, dated at, say, A.D. 350, they are very far removed in time from the original books, which were mostly written between two hundred and fifty and three hundred years earlier. The present writer likes to recall, however, that, though he is only in his forties, his great-grandfather was born in the

---

[12] These non-Biblical sayings of Jesus are set forth in Appendix VIII. Manuscripts that have since come to light have in turn given scholars a better understanding of the Oxyrhynchus papyri.

eighteenth century, before the death of George Washington in 1799. To one whose great-grandfather was a contemporary of the first President of the United States, the War of Independence does not seem very long ago. Thinking along such lines we may go on to reflect that if one of the scribes who wrote the Codex Sinaiticus was an elderly man, it is conceivable that his grandfather might have been the grandson of St Peter.

V

APOCRYPHAL BOOKS

THE GREAT SANHEDRIN, which passed sentence of crucifixion on Jesus Christ, was the Supreme Court of Justice at Jerusalem.[1] It consisted, in its original form, of seventy-one members, composed predominantly of the priestly aristocracy but including learned laymen—Pharisees, for instance—who were probably co-opted for life. Besides its judicial functions, which included those of a court of first instance at Jerusalem, it collected taxes and acted as a Supreme Council to review the problems of the whole Jewish world. After the final destruction of the Temple at Jerusalem in A.D. 70, its character was inevitably altered; but at Jamnia, and later at Tiberias, it contrived to continue the exercise of a spiritual jurisdiction over all Jewry. It was at Jamnia, we have seen, that, about A.D. 90, it met and discussed the question of the contents of the Hebrew Bible. It has been generally supposed that it was this rabbinical synod that finally settled what the contents of the Hebrew Bible should be.

This did not mean, however, that the books which it declined to include ceased to have any importance. Some of these books had for long been treated with great rever

---

[1] It probably had the right to try capital cases. *See* Josephus, *Antiq.*, XIV, ix.3 f; also Matthew xxvi.3 f., Acts iv.5 f, vi.12, xxii.30. But cf. John xviii.31.

ence, being numbered among the Writings which, however, it will be remembered, had not attained the status of
the Law or the Prophets. Beyond Palestine, the Jews who
used the Greek Septuagint Version had been accustomed
to include these books, for they had been included in that
widely used version of the Bible since the translation into
Greek had been made.

It is important to bear in mind that the Christians of
the first century inherited what is now called the Old Testament and, having only a slowly growing literature of their
own, regarded it as their Bible. Neither St Paul nor the
flourishing Christian communities to which he addressed
his letters knew any other Scriptures: the Gospels, as we
have seen, had not by then been written. If we could open
the treasure-chest of one of these early Christian communities, we might find in it perhaps one or two scrolls consisting
of copies of books of the Hebrew Bible; but we should
probably find a good many more scrolls of these books in
the Greek version, for this was the most widely known in
such circles and the only one that their Gentile members,
and even some of those of Jewish extraction, could read.
These Christians read the Old Testament in Greek with
no less devotion than that with which their Jewish fathers
had read it. The only effect their conversion to Christianity
had on their attitude towards that Bible was to encourage
them to read it even more diligently, for it contained, it
seemed to them, evidence that it was Jesus to whom the
prophets alluded as the expected Messiah. The attitude
of these Christians who had been brought up under Jewish
influence easily passed over to their Gentile brethren. So
the Old Testament was the standard reading of the first-
century Christians generally. Only the lack of a sufficient
number of copies prevented its being more widely read in
private by all who could read, and this very lack would

make it all the more necessary for it to be read, as, indeed, it was, in public worship. The New Testament writers themselves not only quoted the Greek Version of the Bible (that is, by the way, why some of their quotations slightly depart from those familiar to us in English translations that have been made directly from the Hebrew); they imitated its style.

Here is an example of the difference between the quoted version and the original version of a passage as they are reproduced in translation in the Revised Standard Version. Christ is represented as reading out of the book of Isaiah as follows:

> The Spirit of the Lord is upon me,
> because he has anointed me to preach good news to the poor.
> He has sent me to proclaim release to the captives
> and recovering of sight to the blind,
> to set at liberty those who are oppressed,
> to proclaim the acceptable year of the Lord.[2]

The original passage as it appears in Isaiah in the same Revised Standard Version reads as follows:

> The Spirit of the Lord GOD is upon me,
>   because the LORD has anointed me
> to bring good tidings to the afflicted;
>   he has sent me to bind up the brokenhearted,
> to proclaim liberty to the captives,
>   and the opening of the prison to those who are bound;
> to proclaim the year of the LORD's favor, . . .[3]

The difference is due to the fact that the passage as it appears in Isaiah is English translation from the Hebrew, while as it appears in Luke it is an English translation of a Greek (Septuagint) translation of the Hebrew.

2 Luke iv.18-19.
3 Isaiah lxi.1-2.

Besides the books of the Hebrew Scriptures already noted, the Greek Septuagint Version of the Old Testament also included the following: Esdras,[4] Tobit, Judith, several additional chapters of Esther, Wisdom of Solomon, Ecclesiasticus, Baruch, Song of the Three Children, History of Susanna, Bel and the Dragon, I and II Maccabees.[5] It seems natural that this Jewish literature should have been included in the Greek translation of the Hebrew Bible begun in Alexandria. It consisted mostly of books which, many scholars have thought, had their origin abroad, in Babylonia, Egypt and perhaps elsewhere. The Alexandrian Jews were more cosmopolitan in their outlook than were most of their Palestinian brethren. Most of this literature is later than 300 B.C.; some of it was written after the death of Christ. It is all of great value and importance for an understanding of the New Testament, for though Jewish in spirit it is affected by Greek ideas and so forms a link with the New Testament which was addressed to the Greek-speaking world.

Especially interesting to a student of the New Testament are the two books of Maccabees, which tell the story of the Maccabean Revolt, one from the point of view of a Sadducee, the other from that of a Pharisee. In the latter we find expressed a narrow and vindictive Jewish nationalism that accords neither with the teaching of Jesus nor with the spirit of Deuteronomy. By command of Judas, the hero of the story, Nicanor, the Syrian general, had been slain: "And when he had cut out the tongue of that ungodly Nicanor, he commanded that they should give it by pieces unto the fowls, and hang up the reward of his madness before the

---

[4] Esdras presents special difficulties. For an explanation, see Appendix XIV.

[5] This collection of writings may be found, in English, in various forms. Convenient editions are published of the Apocrypha in English, both in the King James Version (Oxford University Press) and the Revised Standard Version (Thomas Nelson). See also Appendix XIV.

temple. So every man praised towards the heaven the glorious Lord, saying, Blessed is he that hath kept his own place undefiled. He hanged also Nicanor's head upon the tower, an evident and manifest sign unto all of the help of the Lord." [6] Judith is a tale in which the heroine, though imprisoned in the tents of an enemy general whom she is ruthlessly planning to slay, scrupulously observes the dietary and other laws before the killing.

In the book of Tobit we have a well-written short story: Tobit, a pious Jew, goes regularly to Jerusalem for the appointed feasts, resists idolatry, pays his tithes, gives alms generously and observes the details of the Law with great punctiliousness. For all that, he is overtaken by great misfortunes. He becomes blind, impoverished, despised. In the end, however, his fidelity is abundantly rewarded. Tobit is an appealing character, and some of his sayings recall notions that are familiar to Christians; for example, his injunction not to be afraid to give a small amount if that is all you can afford,[7] brings at once to mind what Christ said about the widow's mite.

Some of the books in this literature, for instance, Ecclesiasticus, were really translations of old Hebrew works refurbished for the Greek-speaking Jew. Others gave to a novel story the name of a hero of the past. The Wisdom of Solomon, for example, could not have been written before the time of Alexander, who died in 323 B.C. According to some modern scholars it was written much later—perhaps about a decade after the crucifixion of Christ and during the reign of Caligula, when the Alexandrian Jews were suffering persecution. At any rate, it had no more to do with Solomon than had the Song of Solomon that has found a place in the Hebrew Bible. It seems, nevertheless, that it influenced Paul,

6 II Maccabees xv.33-35.
7 Tobit iv.8.

and perhaps the famous opening sentences of John owe something to an idea expressed in it: "In the beginning was the Word, and the Word was with God, and the Word was God. He was in the beginning with God; all things were made through him, and without him was not anything made that was made." [8] In the Wisdom of Solomon we read:

God of the fathers and Lord of mercy,
Who madest all things by thy word,
And through thy wisdom thou formedst man,
That he should have dominion over the creatures made by thee,
And rule the world in sanctity and righteousness,
And execute judgment in uprightness of soul. [9]

Though it happens that no direct quotation from any of this literature occurs among the quotations from Scripture that the New Testament writers make,[10] the first-century Christians not only used it but considered it to be as much a part of Scripture as were books such as Proverbs or Job. Indeed, down to at least A.D. 300, all the books of the Greek Septuagint Bible were generally accounted Scripture by Christians. Neither the Greek nor the Latin Fathers of the Church before that date make any distinction in citing from these books. In the fourth century, however, a distinction begins to appear. Fathers of the Church of this later period, such as Eusebius, Athanasius, Cyril of Jerusalem, Epiphanius, and Gregory of Nazianzus —all of the Eastern Church—came to recognize a difference between the books that were in the Hebrew Bible and those that were not. Jerome, because of his diligent Hebrew studies and his personal contacts with Christians and Jews

---

8 John i.1-3 (R.S.V.).
9 Wisdom of Solomon ix.1-3 (Joseph Reider, *The Book of Wisdom*, published for Dropsie College; New York, Harper, 1957).
10 There is, however, a quotation in the New Testament from the Book of Enoch, which forms part of another, similar literature. *Infra,* p. 76.

in the East, made a distinction between books that were to be accounted "apocryphal" and those that were to be accepted as "canonical." The meaning of these terms should be carefully noted. "Apocrypha" comes from the Greek and means "hidden," that is, the books that are to be kept hidden, in contradistinction to those which, being "canonical," that is, regular, are to be generally used. Jerome sometimes called the apocryphal books the "ecclesiastical books": he apparently thought that they should be regarded as books of ecclesiastical or scholarly interest, but not books for ordinary use in the worshipping life of the Church. The term "apocrypha" was not originally intended as in any sense a reproach. Indeed, some of these apocryphal books actually proclaim themselves as such in the title; for instance, "A Holy and Secret Book of Moses."

Though Jerome distinguished between apocryphal and canonical books, he included the books of the Septuagint in the Vulgate, and the tradition of the Roman Church, maintained to this day, is to regard as canonical all books contained in the Septuagint [11] with the exception of the Prayer of Manasses and III and IV Esdras.[12] The tradition that has prevailed with the Reformation heritage, on the other hand, has been to exclude from the canon all books that were not to be found in the Hebrew Bible. This is not to say that the Reformers disdained the apocryphal books. Luther, for instance, did not disparage them: he included most of the books in an appendix to the translation of the Bible that he published in 1534, and he said they were good books to read. The Reformers generally recommended such books for edification but declined to

11 For a list of the books of the Septuagint and of the Hebrew Bible respectively, and the order in which they appear (not followed in modern Bibles), see Appendix XIV.

12 For an explanation of the place of these books, see Appendix XIV.

use them as a warrant for determining any point of Christian teaching.

The Apocrypha has always been included in the copy of the Bible presented to British sovereigns at their coronation. For while the Church of England has since the Reformation traditionally held a characteristically moderate position on the status of the Apocrypha, Anglican churchmen have jealously resisted tendencies to minimize its importance. For instance, at the coronation of King Edward VII, the British and Foreign Bible Society had prepared a sumptuous copy of the Bible for use in the solemnities; but when it was discovered that it did not contain the Apocrypha it was refused and another copy which did was substituted for it. At the coronation of Queen Elizabeth II a curious situation arose. Then for the first time in history the Moderator of the General Assembly of the Church of Scotland (which, established by law and Presbyterian in government, the sovereign solemnly promises on accession to protect) took part in the coronation solemnities. Immediately after the Queen had taken the coronation oath, "laying her hand upon the Gospel in the Great Bible," she kissed the Book. When she had signed the oath the Bible was then delivered to the Dean of Westminster who handed it to the Moderator (the Right Reverend Dr Pitt Watson) for presentation to Her Majesty. The Moderator, in presenting the Bible, made a brief speech in which, referring to the Book, he said: "Herein is wisdom. This is the Royal Law. These are the lively oracles of God." Since the copy of the Bible contained the Apocrypha,[13] the propriety of its being described by the official representative of a Church committed to a Confession of Faith that expressly excludes the Apocrypha, is open to question. It is possible, of course, to hold that in so designating the Book "the

13 Dr Pitt Watson has kindly assured me that this was so.

lively oracles of God" the Moderator excluded the Apocrypha as he excluded the title-page and other non-canonical writings within the covers of the volume; but not all persons would be satisfied with such an explanation.

The tradition of the Eastern Church on the subject of the Apocrypha has been different from all the traditions of the West. Throughout the Middle Ages, in the East, there was great latitude in the use of the apocryphal books. The lines drawn between the canonical and the non-canonical books were never sharp. But in 1672, at the Synod of Jerusalem, the Eastern Church decided that of the books not appearing in the Hebrew canon only Tobit, Judith, Ecclesiasticus and the Wisdom of Solomon should be accounted among the canonical books of the Old Testament.

It is not to be imagined that the canonical books of the Hebrew Bible together with the Apocrypha exhaust ancient Hebrew literature. There were other works which did not acquire sufficient repute to make them likely candidates for inclusion in the list of canonical books. Among such other literature is to be reckoned what is nowadays called by scholars the Pseudepigrapha, that is, writings ascribed to an author other than the real one. In the narrower, technical sense, the Pseudepigrapha includes only certain Jewish writings that are roughly of the same period as the Apocrypha, but which, unlike it, were not included in the Septuagintal Greek Version. Examples of such works are: the Assumption of Moses, the Psalms of Solomon, the Book of Jubilees and the Book of Enoch. This last is actually mentioned and quoted in the New Testament.[14] The whole extant literature known as the Pseudepigrapha is useful in helping us to understand the New Testament better, especially in its relation to the Old.

The term "Apocyrpha" is used primarily to designate the

14 Jude 14 f.

Jewish books included in the Greek Septuagint of the Alexandrian Jews but excluded from the Hebrew canon. But the term—used, as we shall see, in a different sense—has also a more extensive application to the Bible as we know this today. The literary fecundity of those who came under the influence of Christian ideas was tremendous. It resulted in a literature which, apart from the New Testament canon itself, ranged from works embodying a fairly sober, traditional expression of the Christian faith (Barnabas, the Shepherd of Hermas, and the First Epistle of Clement are examples) to writings of the most worthless kind that give rein to mere idle chatter and are sometimes even blatantly immoral in tendency.[15]

This extensive literature was poured forth for centuries; indeed, it may be said that it never stopped, for there was certainly an abundance of fancy and fable in the Middle Ages, and surely religious trash is published as much today as ever it was. Egypt appears to have been a fruitful soil for the more fanciful productions. There is a story, for example, of Christ having appeared to the apostles and to Mary when the latter was weeping at the prospect of her own death. Death himself then appeared, and when Mary saw him her soul leapt from her body into the arms of Christ. Peter and John, in obedience to the command of Christ, lifted up Mary's body, while the other apostles sang, keeping watch for three and a half days. Then Christ returned in a chariot of light, drawn by cherubim, and put the soul of Mary back into her body again, before setting her, "wearing the flesh," at his side in the chariot. Finally, preceded by singing angels, Christ and Mary ascended into heaven in glory. This is typical of the many stories of the corporeal assumption of Mary.

[15] A few examples of this literature are provided in Appendix IX. There is an excellent modern edition by Montague Rhodes James: *The Apocryphal New Testament*, Oxford, 1924.

It seems that curiosity was widely felt about the infancy of Jesus: there are many legends designed to satisfy this. According to an Arabic one, commonly known as the Arabic Gospel of the Infancy, Jesus, at the age of seven, is engaged in the childish pastime of making mud animals. Unlike the other children, however, he is able to make his animals walk and his birds fly. In this same manuscript, Joseph is represented as being not a very good carpenter, so that Jesus, while still a child, has to help him by shortening or (a more remarkable accomplishment) lengthening the beams wrongly cut by him.

It is noteworthy here that the appetite for such fanciful legends has by no means been sated in modern times. Bold forgeries claiming to be old gospels have been perpetrated quite recently. A remarkable one was published in Paris in 1894. It was in Latin and purported to be the work of St Peter. A French translation was provided by one Catulle Mendès, who would no doubt also be entitled to be designated author of the Latin but for the fact that most of it is borrowed from Latin translations of various old apocryphal Gospels, all well known to Christian scholars, including the Arabic Gospel that has just been mentioned. It was claimed that the Latin manuscript had been discovered in an abbey in the Salzkammergut. The English-speaking world was not for long deprived of the fruits of the "discovery": ten years later a translation was published by the Scott-Thaw Company, New York, and by Burns and Oates, London, "Publishers to the Holy See."

The apocryphal Christian Scriptures included fanciful accounts of the doings of the apostles (Acts) as well as those of Christ (Gospels). Probably to the latter part of the second century A.D. belong works entitled the Acts of Peter, the Acts of Paul, the Acts of John, the Acts of Andrew, the Acts of Thomas. Some writings were definitely motivated by the desire to promulgate heretical views: the Gospel of Philip and the Gospel of Thomas, for instance, are of this class.[16] The extension of the term "apocryphal" to the other sort of literature that grew up in Christian circles is misleading, for here it is being used in a very different sense indeed, more akin to that in which it is popularly used in ordinary conversation nowadays when, in calling a story "apocryphal," we mean to say it is a tall tale. By this we do not necessarily imply, of course, that it is calculated to deceive; only that what truth there is in it, if any, is poetic truth, not the truth of historical narrative. Because the use of the term "apocryphal" to cover both senses tends to blur an important distinction, some scholars prefer that it should not be applied at all to a literature that is not being designated "hidden" or "secret" but is being dubbed, rather, "spurious" or "not to be taken seriously." This objection should be carefully borne in mind.

There are, however, a few cases of Christian books that were held in such esteem that they almost won a place in the New Testament, as there are also one or two books, such as Revelation, which, though they did eventually win such a place, seem to have come close to exclusion. The vital point is that the New Testament we have is not composed of books selected by any synod, council, or other counterpart of the Jewish Synod of Jamnia that is generally supposed to have selected the Hebrew canon.[17] With the exception of one or two marginal cases on both sides, the books in the New Testament have their place there because an overwhelming body of opinion in the Christian Church of the first two centuries caused the faithful, under the guidance of their teachers, to revere them so much that they naturally came to be placed

[16] Recent research casts some doubt on the *extent* to which such books were consciously designed to support heretical doctrine. A recently discovered Coptic text of the Gospel of Thomas appears to show that this book was not consistently heretical.

[17] Even the Synod of Jamnia did not do much more than ratify existing custom.

beside the Scriptures that were to become, for Christians, the "Old Testament." By A.D. 200 there was little doubt about most of the books that were eventually included in the New Testament. Later synods and councils of the Christian Church, in setting forth lists of canonical books, did not do much more than put their seal to what had been already established in practice.

The motives of ancient authors in attributing their own works to an admired or distinguished personage should not be misunderstood. It is true that some resorted to the practice for monetary gain; but there was certainly no question of this among the early Christian writers. It was accounted quite natural and honorable in the ancient world among Jews and Gentiles alike for a writer to suppress his own name in favor of that of an admired master to whom he felt he owed the inspiration. So to Demosthenes was attributed the Fourth Philippic, though this work was very probably written after Demosthenes' death by an admirer who perhaps worked from some of the famous orator's notes which he used as the basis for a composition in the style of Demosthenes. Generally speaking, no forgery was intended in such cases. A disciple simply felt constrained to present in his own language the ideas of his master; yet modesty forbade that he should borrow the ideas and put to them his own name. He might misinterpret the ideas, of course, and it did not seem to trouble consciences that to a deceased author should be ascribed the writings of any imitator who might try, however clumsily, to use his ideas and his style. Was the work done in the spirit of David? Were the sentiments characteristic of him? Were the words that were put into his mouth words that David might have spoken? If so it seemed fitting to give it David's name and proper to suppress one's own. Several of the New Testament books themselves are pseudonymous: a certain case is II Peter. On the other hand, this did not mean that for a work of this kind to gain acceptance a writer had only to churn out something with a vague resemblance to the tone of the author whose name he pleased to give to it. No doubt the unsuccessful attempts at this literary enterprise were more numerous than the successful ones. For success you had to carry conviction, and in the case of writings on a subject that so deeply concerned the minds and moved the hearts of men as did the story of Christ and the apostles, success was comparatively rare, as the enormous bulk of the non-canonical literature of early Christianity abundantly attests.

VI

HANDING DOWN THE BIBLE
IN THE ANCIENT CHURCH

I T IS VERY difficult to guess how many Christians in the ancient world could read or write. The Roman educational system was rigidly uniform in character, and a good deal is known about it. Less is known about the educational methods and attainments of the Jewish minority, which, for the most part, held aloof from the system, continuing its traditional educational program, which was focused upon the synagogue. Converts to Christianity would of course bring with them whatever sort of education they had received, and this would vary in kind according to whether they were Gentiles or Jews, and in extent according to their economic and social status. It is impossible to determine what proportion of Christians came from this or that rank in society. Some were slaves or belonged to the poorest class of citizens; but there were certainly many others who were well-to-do and some who were quite rich. The regulations devised for the help of the Christian poor by their economically more fortunate brethren—a practice that was taken for granted as an essential feature of the life of the Christian community— prove that there must have been a considerable number of converts in favorable economic circumstances while others were very needy. There was a similar variation in literacy. It must be remembered that literacy did not depend on rank: some slaves were better educated than their masters. In A.D. 348, Cyril, who became Bishop of Jerusalem about that time, explained why the essence of the Christian faith had been summed up in the Creed which he enjoined his hearers to commit to memory. "For," he said, "since all cannot read the Scriptures, some being hindered as to the knowledge of them by want of learning, and others by want of leisure, in order that the soul may not perish from ignorance, we comprise the whole doctrine of the faith in a few lines."

There is no doubt that the Bible played an enormous part in the education of Christians in the ancient Church, whether they could read or not. By the "ancient Church" is meant the Christian Church before the beginning of the period of a thousand years that is commonly called the Middle Ages. There is, of course, no sharp dividing line between either the ancient and medieval period, or the medieval and modern period. The transition was gradual. We may say, however, arbitrarily but conveniently, that the Middle Ages begin with the fall of the Western Empire in A.D. 476 and end with the printing of the first Bible in 1456. In the present chapter we are concerned, therefore, with the handing down of the Bible among Christians throughout the period ending in A.D. 476. It was during this period that Christianity, after undergoing persecution of great but sporadic severity, acquired in A.D. 313, under the Emperor Constantine, toleration and imperial favor. It was a period of immense vitality and controversy in the Christian Church, in which the most characteristic doctrines of Christian orthodoxy were formulated, notably at the Council of Nicaea in 325 and at the Council of Chalcedon in 451.

The New Testament books, widely circulated in Greek,

were translated at a very early date into other languages. These early versions are of great interest to scholars, because they were made long before the oldest Greek manuscripts now in existence. As early as about A.D. 150 the New Testament was translated into Syriac and into Latin, and about A.D. 200 came a translation into Coptic, the language of Egypt. Of these early versions copies exist which help the scholar to check the Greek texts and get behind them to a more exact knowledge of the original words of the writers of the New Testament, for in so far as the original text of these old versions can be ascertained, scholars can usually reconstruct the Greek text that the translators had before them. So can be set forth with greater accuracy than would otherwise be possible the words that would be found in a Greek manuscript of the New Testament written early in the second century, which is not very long after the date of the first writing of the books.

Syriac is a dialect of Aramaic, Christ's native tongue, and was the language of Mesopotamia and Syria. It is known that in Edessa, in the valley of the Euphrates, between about A.D. 150 and 175, a work was circulating known as the Diatessaron. The title was taken from a Greek phrase which means "harmony of four." A harmony of the four Gospels, it was the work of a scholar called Tatian who was a native of the Euphrates Valley where he was born about A.D. 110. The story of his Diatessaron is a romantic one. Tatian, after travelling in many lands, was converted to Christianity. His work was probably written in Rome and taken to Syria, where it was translated into Syriac, and it is known that this translation was the chief form in which the Gospel story was circulated in Syria till the fourth century. In the sixth century, Bishop Victor of Capua found a Latin copy of it, which he edited. Unfortunately, he corrupted the text. His edition is extant in a manuscript known as Codex

Fuldensis. This and a manuscript that turned up many centuries later in the Netherlands, which seems to have preserved a better text, were all that were known of the Diatessaron till last century. In its original Greek form it appeared to have been entirely lost.

In 1836, however, the Fathers of an Armenian community in Venice published an Armenian version of the works of Ephraem of Syria, a fourth-century writer, among which was a commentary on the Diatessaron. Armenian was a language little known at that time, so that no one much heeded this publication. But even when, in 1876, the Armenian Fathers put out a Latin version of it, little notice was taken till 1880, when Ezra Abbot, an American scholar, drew attention to it. Because the commentary included considerable sections of the original work, it was of much interest to scholars.

But the most remarkable part of the story is to come. The publicity given to this publication prompted scholars to search the Vatican Library, where they found an Arabic translation of the Diatessaron. This manuscript was shown to a Coptic ecclesiastic visiting Rome, who said he had seen a similar one in Egypt. This, which turned out to be a better manuscript, was edited and, together with the Vatican manuscript, published in 1888. A vellum fragment was later discovered which, when examined at Yale in 1933, was found to contain fourteen imperfect lines of Tatian's Diatessaron in Greek. This manuscript is believed to belong to the first half of the third century.

The Diatessaron is of special interest because of its very early date. Almost as early, however, is the version of the Gospels known to scholars as the Old Syriac, whose existence, even, was not suspected till 1842, when the British Museum received, after long negotiations, a collection of manuscripts from a monastery in the Nitrian Desert in

Egypt. Among them were eighty leaves of a copy of the Gospels in Syriac which experts at the British Museum recognized as presenting a text different from that of any other known version. These leaves were found to be a fifth-century manuscript. Then in 1892, two Englishwomen from Cambridge visited the monastery on Mount Sinai where the German scholar Tischendorf had discovered the Codex Sinaiticus. There they photographed several manuscripts, including a Syriac palimpsest which, as they observed, contained a Gospel text. Returning to England, they showed their photographs to two Cambridge scholars who recognized the palimpsest as containing the whole of the Old Syriac Version. The outcome was that scholars soon had access to an ancient version that has been of considerable importance in arriving at a better knowledge of what the writers of the New Testament actually wrote.

Much better known throughout the ages has been another Syriac version, also of great antiquity, known as the Peshitta. Though the date of this version is uncertain, it was in all likelihood done between 411 and 435.

The Bohairic Version (Bohairic was the literary dialect of Coptic which eventually superseded other dialects) is the only Coptic version that contains the whole of the New Testament. Probably dating from the first half of the third century, it has also been of much value to scholars. Fragments of a Sahidic version (another Coptic dialect) dating from the fourth century have also come to light, and there were other ancient Eastern versions of the New Testament.

The most interesting of all the versions is the Old Latin, known to have been made long before St Jerome's Vulgate which superseded it, and believed to date from as early as about A.D. 150. It seems likely that it originated in Africa, and it is supposed that another version, seemingly independent, later appeared in Europe. It also seems that because of the divergences between these rival translations, a revision was produced. At any rate, St Augustine (354-430) praised a certain version, accounting it better than its predecessors. It is very difficult to ascertain any information about the details of the history of these families or groups of manuscripts of the Latin New Testament before Jerome's day. What is certain is that they existed, were numerous, and varied greatly in text. Jerome himself complained of this. Though no complete copy of any of these pre-Vulgate versions exists, there are thirty-eight manuscripts which together give scholars a great deal of information about the Latin texts of the New Testament that were circulating in the ancient Church before Jerome's Vulgate superseded all others and became the official Bible of the Roman Church.

The Bible, including the Old Testament and, as far as it had taken shape, the New, was read by a large number of Christians from the first century onwards. There is no evidence that anyone was ever discouraged from reading the Bible, and there is much to indicate all literate Christians were being strongly recommended to search the Scriptures so as to discover for themselves the truth of what their teachers taught them. Books were not unduly expensive, in terms of the spending power of the well-to-do, and no doubt the houses of such Christians, where the brethren at first foregathered, would contain, in a cupboard or chest, at least a few scrolls. Scholars, being often impecunious, were no doubt frequently handicapped for want of an adequate private library: it would be very annoying to lack just the particular book of the Bible you wanted to consult. But that there was a great deal of private Bible reading is attested in many ways, and you could do a lot of Bible reading even though you had access to only a limited number of books of the Bible. Almost all the early

Christian writers show that they knew the Scriptures well, and some of them praise the amount of Bible reading done by their readers. "Ye know the Holy Scriptures," wrote Clement of Rome in the first century, "yea, your knowledge is laudable, and ye have deep insight into the oracles of God." Nearly all the early writers not only assume that their readers are accustomed to read the Bible, but also seem to imply that even the illiterate Christians to whose ears the contents of their writings may come will have heard the Bible extensively read to them, both at worship and perhaps also in private meetings with a literate friend. Several writers indicate that it was by reading the Bible that they became Christians.

It would be entirely wrong to suppose, however, that Bible reading was the essential expression of the life of the Church. The Bible was accounted a study. What constituted the life of the Church was the living presence of Christ who was, they loved to remember, "known of them in the breaking of bread." [1] But the Christ whose presence they recognized in the Eucharist or Holy Supper was held to be the same Christ of whom the disciples, reflecting on what had happened on the road to Emmaus, had said: "Did not our heart burn within us, while he talked with us by the way, and while he opened to us the scriptures?" [2] The Christians of the immediately succeeding generations vivaciously believed that it was life in the Christian community that made the Bible come to life for them. But it could not come to life if they did not read it.

By the end of the second century, however, the Bible had been much used not only for the upbuilding of Christian piety, but by the adversaries of the Christian way and those standing hesitantly on the fringe of it. It had by

[1] Luke xxiv.35.
[2] Luke xxiv.32.

then become, indeed, a stick for hitting the Christians as much as a staff for supporting these in their earthly pilgrimage. So Tertullian, the great late second-century Christian writer, for instance, while recommending the reading of the Bible, indicates his awareness that in itself it must not be expected to convert people. Likewise, Irenaeus, another second-century Christian writer, seeks other ways of exhibiting the truth of the Christian faith. But, for all that, the Bible continued to be regarded as the Church's supremely precious document. "Let a man take refuge in the Church," Irenaeus writes; "let him be educated in her bosom and be nourished by the Scriptures of the Lord." Tertullian and others recommend that literate married couples should read the Bible together, and so Bible reading became a prominent feature in the lives of devout Christian families, many of whom set apart certain times of the day, notably just before the principal meal. Well-to-do Christians who did not have to earn their daily bread were enjoined to visit the homes of their brethren and read the Bible to them. Indeed, the practice of visitation for the purpose of reading the Bible to those who could not read or did not own any books was so common by the end of the second century that we even hear of people using it as cover for some less edifying aim.

On the other hand, while piety dictated much Bible reading, there is no doubt that grave difficulties attended the promotion of the practice. The Bible was not entirely without literary merit; but it could not compete with the great classical models upon whose work the taste of cultivated people in the Graeco-Roman world was founded. The fact that the literary style of much of the Bible offended cultivated persons was, however, of little practical account on the whole, for it is not the function of a religion to produce masterpieces of style. Of much greater consequence was the fact that, even as long ago as, say, A.D. 200, the Old Testament presented a great many difficulties to the ordinary reader. Perhaps people were then more aware of the difficulties than they were to be fourteen hundred years later when ordinary folk had taken up daily Bible reading again. In the third century, in Egypt, the great Biblical scholar Origen made frequent allusions to the fact that many people, because of inherent difficulties in the Bible, found it boring and tried to escape from the tedium of much reading of it. This indicates that the taste for Bible reading that had been widespread among Christians in the first century or two was waning. Origen himself felt, however, that though the Bible did contain treasures that only the learned could appreciate, it was also a literature that could be read or listened to with profit by even the simplest person. So he had no thought of making the Bible a priestly preserve, and he recognized that very often an educated layman could understand it better than could many a priest. Origen himself had been required by his father to read the Bible at an early age and encouraged to prefer it to other studies, and it seems that, being a precocious boy, he plagued his father with very searching questions about it that the latter could not answer. All this demonstrates that in spite of the difficulties that Bible reading presented, the practice had taken hold and was adhered to by all who were not mere baggage in the Christian expedition.

The place of the Bible in the third century was recognized by the Roman authorities, for these, in trying to stamp out Christianity, seem to have supposed that a good way of doing this would be to have copies of books of the Bible confiscated. What the authorities were interested in confiscating were primarily the Bible chests of the Christian communities; but they often sought for private copies too, on the pretext that such literature must be always in some sense communal property among the Christians. So many people were forced to give up copies of the Scriptures and were deeply grieved at the loss. The practice of learning by heart was, however, much commoner in the ancient world than it is at the present day, and many who had had to forfeit their precious copies could still go on reciting to themselves and others long passages they had learnt. A blind Christian is said to have known many books of the Bible by heart. To some slight extent this may be a pious exaggeration. It is not unlikely, however, that there is much truth in such stories. Even in much later times people did commit enormous passages to memory.

During the times of persecution, the Church took a very severe attitude towards clergy who, under torture, revealed to the authorities the whereabouts of the community Bible chests, for the clergy were regarded as the official custodians of these copies. At first it was considered such a heinous offense so to betray this trust, even under extreme torture, that it was classed with murder and other such crimes, the commission of which entailed excommunication from the Christian fellowship with no possibility of return. Later on, a second chance was provided, if the offender exhibited signs of genuine penitence, and later still the Church grew much more lenient towards her erring children. It is interesting, by the way, to note, in this connection, that when people had the choice of appealing to either a bishop or a confessor (that is, one who had suffered torture and had come through it steadfastly confessing the faith), they generally preferred the latter, for he had the reputation of being much more generous in accepting offenders back to the fold. No doubt the confessors, knowing from experience what was the pain of being tortured, were more inclined than the bishops to leniency towards those who had weakened under it.

Education generally declined in the third century, and so the practice of Bible reading that had become part of the Christian way of life prepared the Church for the role she was to have as schoolmistress to a world that was relapsing into barbarism. By about A.D. 400, when the persecution of the Church had ceased, it seemed to many intelligent observers that for all the intellectual pride of those who had scoffed at the Bible, this had really taken the place of the writings of the great philosophers and poets who had been formerly held up for admiration. It was not denied that they had been great men; nor was it suggested that Plato and Aristotle, Pindar and Cicero, had not made contributions of great value to humanity in their day. What was increasingly felt, however, was that their day was done. Their tradition was not being carried on. Few read them any longer. The few who did loved to parade their acquaintance with the heroes of old; but they themselves had none of the creative power of the intellectual giants they admired. There was a widespread feeling that the great names in the illustrious past of Greece and Rome had been singularly lacking in lasting influence. Plato, it was noticed, had taught the immortality of the soul; but he had not even been able to persuade his own celebrated pupil Aristotle on that score. By the year 400, many thoughtful Christians had reached the conclusion that the splendor of the past was indeed a past splendor; in its very glory it revealed the puniness of even the highest of merely human enterprises. A poet might compose the most exquisite ode in the literature of the world; yet his own son might not even care to read it, or have a talent for its appreciation. A great philosopher like Socrates or Plato might arouse the interest of the learned and do much good in his way within a hothouse society of academes; but what influence had he on the world at large? What did he mean to the common man? Such reflections fostered the hope that not only would the Bible displace the ancient philosophers and poets; it would have an audience far wider than ever they had had.

By about A.D. 360, books of the Bible were already on their way to becoming best-sellers. Unscrupulous booksellers were taking advantage of their popularity by raising the price, and we even hear of publishers issuing price-lists to warn customers not to pay more than a certain amount. Christians were discouraged from selling their copies, because the Bible was to be regarded as a Christian's tools, which he ought never to sell unless so stricken by misfortune as to be quite destitute. By this time fine copies were on sale: the Codex Vaticanus and other extant manuscripts are examples of such *éditions de luxe*. The rich were reproved for reading the magnificent copies they owned less diligently than the poor read those few books they had been able to copy out in their own hand for their own use.

The most sold book is not always the most read. It must not be supposed that everybody who bought the Bible used it intelligently or tried to understand it. Magic was then, as now, a constant factor in the life of the Church. So the Bible acquired for many a physically sacrosanct character and became the object of certain vulgar superstitions. Copies of the Gospels were used as charms. Menstruating women were discouraged from touching the Bible. Such practices were, of course, reproved. Their existence is no more remarkable than the existence today of people who, though they never attend church, send a large donation every year, apparently in the hope that their check will secure a pass to heaven without the inconvenience of their having to devote time to such matters on earth. A similarly

magical view of baptism is common in our own day, when
parents call their pastor with a request to have their child
"done," as though they were talking of a magical ointment
from the witch-doctor. It is well known to churchmen
today that too many people go to the sacraments as though
they were stopping at filling-stations for another tankful
of grace. So a talismanic attitude towards the Bible can
never be entirely precluded. There was in quite recent
times—in certain circles perhaps there still is—a taboo against
placing any other book on top of the Bible. In some Jewish
circles it is still forbidden to put even the Prophets on
top of the Torah. Such an attitude, though superstitious,
is surely less reprehensible, from a religious point of view,
than that of the farmer whose son was asked by the pastor
whether they had such a thing as a Bible in the house,
and who replied, "You mean the book Pop sharpens his
razor on?" The old-fashioned leather-bound Bible served
such purposes well when razors were open in fact while
Bibles were often open only in theory. A talismanic attitude towards the Bible on the part of many people in the
fourth century is not surprising; but the existence of such
an attitude at that time does corroborate the fact to which
attention has already been drawn, that the Bible was a
difficult book even then. The lazy-minded found it easier
to revere its pages than to try to understand them.

This was much more the case in the Latin West than
in the East. In St Paul's day the Christians at Rome had
spoken Greek. As the situation changed, the old Latin
versions helped to make the Bible into the "people's book"
that all responsible churchmen felt it ought to be. But
it was not only the language that had made the Bible a
difficult book to Latin-speaking Christians. That had been
but an added barrier which the Latin versions effectively
removed. The fundamental barrier was the antique and

foreign cast of the Biblical ideas. The sound of the words was appealing; there was a grandeur in them that commanded popular respect. But sonorous words in themselves induce slumber rather than shed light, and so in the West we find an increasing tendency to treat the Bible with reverence but not to read it. In the East the gulf between Biblical notions and everyday thought was not so wide, and the situation was on the whole much better there.

In spite of the decline in Bible reading, the Bible was very far, however, from becoming an unknown book. On the contrary, parts of it, such as the Gospels and the Psalms, were constantly heard. What the faithful heard in church services no doubt often stimulated some of them to look up the Bible for themselves. But the point is: in the West at any rate, the Bible had become, towards the end of the period under consideration, a sacred treasury rather than a widely-read book. The turmoils of the fifth century —the invasions of the Goths and Vandals, and the other upheavals that were to reduce Europe to anarchy and chaos for a long time—accelerated the decline in Bible reading among ordinary people. The Psalms were, however, deeply loved, and that they should have had such a remarkable appeal to a people quite unlike the Jews, and in circumstances very different from those that prevailed when they were written, is a testimony to their universal qualities. "Of other scriptures," wrote a great theologian of Antioch about this time, "most men know nothing. But the Psalms are repeated in private houses, in streets and market-places, by those who have learned them by heart, and feel the soothing power of their divine melodies." Boatmen sang them as they sailed; metal-workers shouted them as they toiled. "Anyone possessed of his five wits ought to blush for shame," wrote St Ambrose (c. 339-397), Bishop of Milan, "if he did not begin the day with a psalm, for even the tiniest birds open and close the day with sweet songs of holy devotion." And as the barbarian hordes swept over Europe, leaving desolate waste in their train, the Psalms must have seemed for many to come to life as never before. To men who had been accustomed to the old sense of security and were being plunged into the chaos that attended Rome's downfall, the Psalms spoke as perhaps they had never spoken since the Jews, their hearts torn by their exilic tribulations, had found in these "songs of Zion" that peace that the noisy follies of the world can neither give nor take away. The image of the Hebrew shepherd had passed into the language of the war-torn West: "The Lord is my shepherd; I shall not want. He maketh me to lie down in green pastures: he leadeth me beside the still waters. He restoreth my soul: he leadeth me in the paths of righteousness for his name's sake. Yea, though I walk through the valley of the shadow of death, I will fear no evil: for thou art with me: thy rod and thy staff they comfort me. . . ." Job and Samuel and Deuteronomy might be covered with a respectful dust; but the Psalms, as well as the Gospel, lived on in the hearts of those who heard the tender words at the ambo or pulpit from which the Gospel was read: *Ego sum pastor bonus:* "I am the good shepherd: the good shepherd giveth his life for the sheep."

VII

A THOUSAND YEARS
TILL PRINTING

I T IS NOT so very long ago since it was fashionable to refer to the thousand years between the fall of the Western Empire in A.D. 476 and the discovery of America as the "Dark Ages." That a period which was known to have produced a Dante, a Giotto, a Thomas Aquinas, not to mention some of the greatest architecture in the history of mankind, should have been accounted so dark is indeed odd. There is, however, a distorted element of truth in the phrase. For though the later Middle Ages, notably the thirteenth and fourteenth centuries, were very bright indeed in many ways, the earlier centuries, especially the three hundred years before the crowning of Charlemagne on Christmas Day, A.D. 800, were in almost every way exceedingly dark in the western Europe that was to become, later on, the undoubted mistress of the world. The disintegration of the old order brought anarchy in its train, and so hopeless did the situation appear that many people took it for granted that the world was irretrievably condemned to chaos. Endless and inconclusive wars laid waste what had seemed an imperishable order. Such conditions were fatal to the development of any culture, for though intellectual life may thrive on hardship, it requires a modicum of security and peace to enable it to flower.

The influence of Christianity upon that scene of devastation was in many ways limited. It is commonly forgotten that though Christianity had acquired a special status under Constantine in the fourth century, its spread was gradual. The word "pagan" comes from a Latin word, *pagus,* a rural district, and its use by Christians reminds us that, however fashionable Christianity might have become in the urban regions, the country folk were for long unaffected by it and clung to their old gods, as country folk tend to do.

As for the remoter parts of Europe, it should also be remembered that it was not till late in the tenth century that Christianity began to make any headway at all in the Scandinavian countries, and a long time then passed before the process might be said to be in any sense complete. The chronic disorders of the dark period brought, besides political chaos, a decline in commerce and industry so disastrous that it looked as though the world were reverting to complete savagery. The fine old Roman roads fell into disrepair. It was exceedingly dangerous to undertake even comparatively short journeys. By land one's path was beset by robbers, while pirates infested the sea. Their calling was made profitable, and their retribution rendered unlikely, by the unsettled conditions that prevailed. Towns and cities, once prosperous, decayed, dwindling in population as their impoverishment diminished their appeal.

With all this came a rapid slump in literacy. The principal occupation of the vast majority of honest people was a crude agriculture. Land was, indeed, almost the only property left that was worth having, and it was in the process of holding it that the feudal system emerged, a system that diminished the authority of the little princes and other rulers whose chief occupation was fighting. War was indeed so much the exclusive occupation of the aristocracy in this period that a literate ruler was at least as much of an oddity then as would be in our day an oil magnate with a passion for writing Greek odes. Charlemagne was exceptional in his admiration for learning. When at length, after much bloodshed, the illiterate conqueror established a semblance of stability throughout a considerable part of western Europe, he invited English and other scholars to his court and even "went to school" himself. Charlemagne's patronage of learning helped to revive education, though for long afterwards the tradition died hard that letters were a monkish art and that skill in arms alone befitted a ruler. Before his time there could hardly be said to be any tradition about it, for there was little tradition about anything; only dire necessity and the urgent exigencies of the moment.

For Christians caught in such a web of disaster it was no easy task to bring the warring tribesmen into any sort of allegiance to Christianity. The Bible, which even before the fall of Rome had become, we have seen, a difficult book to most people in the West, now seemed exceedingly remote. Of what use could it be for civilizing the wild men that were pulling the world down about their own ears? The best-loved passages found their place in the liturgy of the Church; to most people the rest was indeed locked away and widely forgotten.

Yet it was not forgotten by all. Some, sharing the common opinion that the state of the world was hopeless, sought to set up, in such secluded places as they could find, ideal communities where they could live at peace and, establishing a Christian order within their own walls, keep alive the traditions and ideals that chaos was blotting out. The Celtic Church, in Ireland and Scotland, for long depended almost exclusively on such monks. But foremost among the leaders of the monastic movement was St Benedict (c. 480-c. 550), an Italian born just after the fall of the Western Empire. He is commonly accounted the "father" of monasticism in the West; but the quest for the cloister was characteristic of many thoughtful men and women before he provided a rule of life for those who sought to live as monks.

Benedict, with deep religious insight as well as a Roman genius for administration, gave to the monastic movement that was already in process of development the orderly conditions that made it what, at its best, it was to become. In his youth he had been much distressed by the vices and frivolities of Rome, whither he had gone to study. About the year 500 he went to live a hermit's life at Subiaco, near Rome. By the time he was fifty he had moved to Monte Cassino, on whose summit, after he had destroyed a pagan temple still devoted to the worship of Apollo, he established a monastery. Benedict himself was a layman; yet bishops and priests sought his guidance. The life he prescribed, though simple and by some standards austere, was not harsh, and Benedict's monks probably lived more comfortably than the majority of people in the world of their day. An orderly life, it was in many ways more rational, even from a humanistic standpoint, than either the vicious decadence of the well-to-do or the aimless misery of the poor. Food and clothing were adequate; fasting moderate. Humility was extolled. But the most striking emphasis, at any rate to the casual observer, was upon hard work—an activity that the world despised as servile—and it was this that was to lead the monks to become the custodians of the Bible.

The Benedictine life consisted from the first in a careful disposition of the entire day. Idleness was accounted the principal enemy of their purpose. A time was, of course, set aside for labor in the fields, for this was very important to a community intended to be independent of the world. Times were likewise appointed for study, for prayer, for meals, and for sleep. The rule of silence was designed both as a means of assisting the monks to devote themselves to inward reflection and of promoting a quiet and steady output of productive labor. Silence was observed even during meals, at which one of the monks read aloud to the others out of an instructive book. It was, however, the long daily round of worship that was accounted the "day's work," properly speaking, of the monk. This was the *divinum officium*, that is, the monk's duty to God, which must be put before all else. Here the Bible played a central part. The worship was so ordered that the whole Psalter should be recited each week, and in the course of the year the monks read at worship considerable portions from the Old and New Testaments.

Benedict gave his monks a Rule or constitution the provisions of which are famous for their wisdom. Much of it was based upon the Psalms: the rule of silence, for instance, recalled the text: "I said, I will take heed to my ways, that I sin not with my tongue." [1] Before and after meals, indeed almost at every turn throughout the day, a few verses of a psalm were recited. And in later centuries, when bells were cast, the brethren, as they waited by the furnace for the metal to be poured into the mold, sang Psalm cl: "Praise him upon the loud cymbals." The Psalms were the very stuff of the monastic life. As one medievalist vividly puts it, "the religious man's inner life was above all in the Psalter. . . . The very sound of the chant became part of a man's life, bench answering manfully to bench, while their breath rose in the frosty air of a midnight choir." [2]

1 Psalms xxxix.1.
2 G. G. Coulton, *Five Centuries of Religion* (Cambridge, 1936), vol. iii, p. 414.

Probably most monks came to know the entire Psalter by heart. With a psalm they had been admitted to the Order, and as they lay dying a psalm was whispered in their ears and uttered on their now feeble lips.

In the earlier days, the monks read a great deal of the rest of the Bible in the course of the year. Gradually, however, the selections became more and more abbreviated, as the reading of the lives of the saints and other such literature displaced to a considerable extent the reading of the Bible. The Lectionary or book of Bible readings began to be incorporated into a larger, omnibus work, the Breviary, which included readings from various sources, and of this the Roman Church still requires her priests and monks to read their daily stint. But though Bible reading as it had been understood in the early centuries was thus gradually ousted from the daily round of worship, the monks did not by any means entirely forsake the Bible. It was here that their tradition of industry put later ages in their debt, for to the copying out of the Bible they devoted much labor. In the scriptorium or writing room a group of monks would sit, patiently taking down to the dictation of a brother the words of the sacred text till a certain number of copies of the entire Bible had been made. The pages of these medieval Bibles were often beautifully ornamented and gilded, and sometimes elaborately illustrated with exquisitely delicate paintings depicting, as the monastic artists imagined them, the scenes the Bible describes. These painstaking embellishments made some of the medieval Bibles priceless art-treasures. But there were other Bibles too, less decorative but more suited for ordinary use. The revival of learning that came with the rise of the universities in the eleventh and twelfth centuries stimulated a demand for these among studious clerics.

A large number of the existing medieval manuscripts of

the Latin Vulgate Bible belong to the thirteenth century.[3]
These manuscripts have certain features well known to
scholars. The writing is small and compressed, arranged
in double columns and with very little of the decoration
or illumination associated with more sumptuous medieval
manuscript editions. Many of these thirteenth-century Bibles
are quite small. Their whole format and design reflect the
seriousness of the purpose for which they were intended.
They were for study, and their existence is to be attributed
to the salutary influence of St Louis (1214-1270), King of
France, and to the scholarly interests that found expression
in the founding of the Sorbonne. These Bibles were not
noteworthy for purity of text. Their historical importance
lies, rather, in the revival of scholarly interest in the Bible
that they betoken. Also to be noted, however—for it is
a point to which we must return later—is the fact that
it was at this stage that the system of chapter divisions
with which we are familiar became conventional. The
division of the Bible into passages of varying length had
for long been customary. But the now familiar chapter
division was devised by Stephen Langton, a Sorbonne doctor who became, in 1206, a cardinal and, in 1207, Archbishop of Canterbury. He took a leading part in the movement that led to Magna Charta. The division into chapters,
as he arranged it, was arbitrary but convenient in its way.

The reverence of the common people for the Bible was
immense; their knowledge of it extremely meager. Since
even to the monks it became sacrosanct but ill-understood
lore, a venerable mystery rather than a book to be read, it
could hardly have meant anything to the ordinary man or
woman who in any case was generally unable to read either

[3] Readers who seek a more extensive treatment of the medieval manuscripts should consult the best modern study available in English, *The Study
of the Bible in the Middle Ages,* by Beryl Smalley (Oxford: Blackwell, 1952).

it or any other book. Of course there were some monks who
knew the Bible remarkably well in many ways: for instance,
in the tenth century, Bernard of Clairvaux, who did all
but found the Cistercian Order, of which the much later
Trappists are a reformed congregation, probably knew his
Bible as well as Luther did. But the average priest, far
from reading the Bible, was often hardly able to cope with
the Latin of his Mass. Even the most earnest and devout
cleric was content to be familiar, as in many cases he was,
with the Psalms and those passages of the Gospels and
Epistles that were appointed to be read at Mass. The laity,
among whom Latin became little understood, and who
could follow only the most frequently recurring phrases
in the service, were for the most part as little able to read
the Bible in Latin as is the average American to read it
in Greek. Of the existence of an original text behind the
Latin the ordinary person had no notion at all. Even the
majority of scholars gave no thought to it, contenting themselves with a Latin text which was there to be interpreted
in certain traditional ways. And though it was Jerome's
Vulgate that had taken hold, it was often much mutilated.
There were many attempts to produce a standard text; but
not until the invention of printing did it become possible
to have in practice one that was even uniform.

The influence and power of the Roman Church in western
Europe grew so steadily and spread so extensively that we
often forget that it did not achieve that victory unopposed.
In the course of the thousand years we are considering
there were many movements of various kinds which, each
in its own way, threatened the Church. The threat was
almost constant; sometimes it was very grave. The Dominican Order of Preaching Friars, which played a vital part
in the later Middle Ages in the Roman attempt to put
down heresy by force, and whose greatest luminary, St

Thomas Aquinas, has been adopted as the quasi-official thinker of the Roman Church today, had its origin in the urgent need to recover to the church whole regions in the south of France and the north of Italy which in the twelfth century had practically drifted out of Christendom. These were the principal regions affected by the Albigenses, whose dualistic doctrine (a revival of an old Persian religion) cannot by any stretch of charity or indulgence be accounted Christian, yet who claimed to find in the Bible support for their beliefs. The Waldenses who, on the other hand, have sometimes been accounted precursors of the Reformation and who constitute what little there is of Italian Protestantism at the present day, being strong in Piedmont and elsewhere in Italy, also appealed to the Bible. Such movements were popular, not aristocratic, and the indiscriminate use by their leaders of the Bible as it was very imperfectly known and understood in the Middle Ages naturally led to often startling results. That the Roman Church became, in these circumstances, suspicious of and opposed to undirected Bible reading by the common people is not surprising. You can hardly entrust faulty texts to gifted but untrained sons of the people with a flair for stirring hearts, and then expect them not to add to the confusion.

In the dark period through which the continent of Europe passed before the time of Charlemagne, passages of the Bible were already being translated in England into the tongue of the people. It is not possible to tell exactly when this work began. There is a legend that about A.D. 670 there was a laborer called Caedmon working at the monastery at Whitby in the north of England. In the evenings it was the custom to call for songs; but when it came near Caedmon's turn he would leave the table, for he had no gift in that direction. One night, having so done, he lay down on his straw and fell asleep. In a vision he saw Christ who said to him, "Caedmon, sing *Me* something!" Caedmon explained he was no good at that sort of thing; but Christ encouraged him. The song Caedmon sang was written down in the Anglo-Saxon dialect. A Biblical paraphrase, it is the first native growth of English literature.

The first known *translation*, however, of any part of the Bible into Anglo-Saxon is Aldhem's version of the Psalms, probably written towards the end of the seventh century. The work was continued by Bede, a great English scholar who at the time of his death in A.D. 735 was engaged upon a translation of the Gospel according to Saint John. On the Eve of the Feast of the Ascension, as Bede lay dying, he went on dictating to his disciples, urging them to write quickly. The following morning he was reminded that a chapter remained to be done. Throughout that day the remainder of the task was prolonged by interruptions and the failing strength of the dying scholar. In the evening he was reminded that one sentence had still to be written. When it had been dictated, the scribe said, "Now it is finished," to which Bede replied, "Thou speakest truly; it is finished," and, having bidden his friends lay him on the stone floor of his cell, he died peacefully with a prayer upon his lips. In the ninth century King Alfred translated, or caused to be translated, several parts of the Bible.

So far as is known, no text of any of these translations has survived. There do exist, however, very early manuscripts which give, alongside of the Latin text of the Gospels, a paraphrase in the people's tongue—useful, no doubt, as an aid to those priests who gave their flocks little homilies on the Gospel for the day. Verses of the Psalms likewise survive, of which the following is an example. It represents the verse translated in the King James Version thus:

"Create in me a clean heart, O God; and renew a right spirit within me." [4]

> Syle me, halig God,
> heortan clæne;
> and rihtne gast
> God geniwa
> on minre gehigde
> huru, min Drihten.

The oldest manuscript presenting a translation of the Gospels apart from the Latin text is one dating from about A.D. 1000 in the library of Corpus Christi College, Cambridge. This is a copy of a text known to have been circulating in the southwest of England at least as early as about 950. Before the Norman Conquest in 1066, Aelfric had translated into the people's tongue considerable portions of the Old Testament. These were, however, really more paraphrases than translations.

For some time after the Conquest there was comparatively little activity of this kind. The language underwent much change through the incorporation of Norman words, and there were no fresh translations to take the place of the Anglo-Saxon ones that had gone out of date. The people's knowledge of the Bible was, even at the best, scanty. It was confined to what they might glean from hearing such makeshift devices as rhyming paraphrases and, if they were fortunate, perhaps an occasional homily at Mass. By the time Wyclif [5] came on the fourteenth-century English scene that Chaucer has immortalized, the Bible must have been very remote indeed from the life of the people. The average priest was in no better a case. He usually knew too little Latin to read the Bible well enough to help his flock, even if he were minded

---

[4] Psalm li.10.

[5] The name "Wyclif" is variously spelt. English spelling was not fixed till comparatively recent times.

so to do. A visitation of seventeen parishes in Berkshire in 1222 disclosed the fact that five of the clergy did not even know enough Latin to mumble their way through the Mass. Nor is it to be imagined that the better-educated priests were better educated in the Bible; they were in some respects more remote from it than were those who could only limp through a Gospel lesson.

It was John Wyclif and his associates who produced a translation of the New Testament about the year 1380, followed a year or two later by a translation of the rest of the Bible. This, the first complete translation of the Bible into English, was not without shortcomings. The style was uneven: parts were colloquial; others exceedingly stilted, with curious Latinisms. Even the modern reader would have no difficulty in recognizing, say, "boyschel" as merely an antique spelling of the word "bushel"; but "gemels" for "twins" and "spelong" for "cave" would be less obvious. Much of the Old Testament translation is ascribed to Nicholas of Hereford, an Oxford associate of Wyclif's. Here is Hereford's rendering of the opening words of the Twenty-third Psalm: "The Lord gouerneth me and no thing to me shal lacke; in the place of leswe where he me ful sette. Ouer watir of fulfilling he nurshide me; my soule he conuertide." Shortly after Wyclif's death in 1384 a revised version was made, and it was through this medium that knowledge of the English Bible was disseminated in the fifteenth century.

It is known that the circulation was remarkably wide. The Lollards or "poor preachers" as Wyclif's active supporters came to be called, went wherever they could get a hearing. In a field or a lane, with a little crowd around him, such a "poor preacher" might be heard, preparing the hearts and minds of men for the Reformation their generation would not live to see, but in which the great-grandchildren of some of his hearers might one day take part. It was a hazardous occupation in those times to preach against vested ecclesiastical interests as did Wyclif. The preaching was sometimes abruptly ended by roasting the preacher. Wyclif, thanks to his influence in court circles, had personally escaped that fate. His followers were not always so fortunate. Many of them, moreover, discouraged by a statute passed in 1401 on the subject of burning heretics, were effectively silenced, for the Lollards knew that "heretics" meant them. But the work went on in spite of sporadic persecution, and the strength of it lay in the dissemination of the English Bible in which men and women were learning to find hope for themselves and for the betterment of humanity's condition. "God graunte to us," runs the prayer in the preface to the revised edition of Wyclif's Bible, "alle grace to kunne [6] wel and kepe wel holi writ, and suffre ioiefulli sum peyne for it at the laste." Joyfully or otherwise, many did suffer pain for the English Bible with which Wyclif had provided them. Some were burned with copies of it round their necks. The demand for the book far exceeded the supply. How great was the latter is attested by the fact that, fagots notwithstanding,[7] over a hundred and fifty manuscript copies of Wyclif's Bible survive to this day. People gladly paid a good price for even only a few sheets of the much-prized book. It is said that the price for an hour's loan of it every day for a course of reading was a load of hay.

The price does not seem unreasonable, for such a manu-

[6] *know*

[7] Those who read the Wyclif Bible were liable to forfeiture of "land, cattle, life and goods." Archbishop Arundel, writing to Pope John XXIII, complained that Wyclif, having endeavored by every other means to assail the doctrine of the Church, had, "as a crowning act of wickedness, with a view to this, produced a fresh version of the Bible in the vernacular," and was "doing the work of Antichrist by the expedient of a new translation of Scripture into the mother tongue." (David Wilkins, *Concilia Magnae Britanniae et Hiberniae*, 1731.) Prominent among the causes of unrest that favored the spread of Lollardy was papal pressure on England for money. This was, of course, also by no means an unimportant factor in promoting the measures taken against the Lollards.

script represented an enormous amount of labor. Moreover, the borrower might very well be engaged in a surreptitious reproduction of considerable passages while the book was in his possession. Copyright was not easily safeguarded in those days; nor did all recognize the Irish decision on the subject laid down by Diarmad, the King at Tara, in the sixth century. The story goes that St Columba, on a visit to the aged St Finian in Ireland, had obtained permission to read the latter's copy of the Psalter. Every night, while the old saint slept, the young saint was hard at work in the chapel where by a miraculous light, it is said, he diligently copied till he had a complete edition of his own. St Finian discovered this and was furious with his guest, arguing that the copying had been unlawful, since the original labor was his. The dispute was referred to King Diarmad who gave the famous though perhaps not entirely judicious decision. "As to every cow belongs her calf," said the King, "so to every book belongs its son-book." So Columba lost his Psalter and legend has it that his anger at the royal judgment was one of the causes of his leaving Ireland. In fifteenth-century England, however, observance of the law of copyright was still far from general. At any rate, to its infringement was no doubt due the existence of a considerable number of the manuscripts whose contents brought joy to many hearts.

Wyclif had intended his Bible to be for ordinary folk, not for scholars or nobles, and at its best the Wyclif Bible is pithy and plain in style. Many of the most familiar and best loved phrases in the English Bibles we use today originated with it. "Strait is the gate and narewe is the way"; "the beame and the mote"; "the cuppe of blessing that we blessen"—these are all familiar to us. Most of us love and admire the simple beauty of the King James Version; yet some of its phrases seem almost to muffle the clear ring of their Wyclifian ancestors: "Blessed be the mylde men, for thei shuln welde the eerthe."

The role Wyclif's Bible played in England as a precursor of the Reformation was unique. Its influence extended to Scotland too, through a manuscript translation made by Murdoch Nisbet into Scots [8] about the year 1520, by which time, on the continent of Europe, Luther's words had already captivated many an aching heart. Despite the invention of printing in the middle of the previous century, there had been no printed version of the English Bible in Britain.

In continental Europe, on the other hand, the invention of printing had yielded remarkable fruits in Bible translation even before Luther was born. The "42-line Bible" attributed to Gutenberg had shown what printing could do. It is said that more than a hundred editions of the Latin Vulgate were published before the year 1500. Translations were made into most of the vernacular tongues of western Europe by that time. There were two independent versions in Italian in 1471. In 1477 the New Testament was printed in French; in 1487 the whole Bible. There was a Spanish translation in 1478, and in 1488 a translation into the Bohemian tongue. In the Netherlands, between 1480 and 1507, the Psalms were published seven times. Luther did not begin his famous translation—so important for the German language itself—till 1521, by which time there had been nineteen editions of a German version. One of these was published at Strasbourg in 1466, seventeen years before Luther's birth.

The most radical defect of all the early translations was that they were translations from the corrupt Latin text without reference to the Greek and Hebrew sources. Wyclif, for example, though a learned man in his day, and the head of an Oxford college, knew no Greek. But for the revival of interest in the ancient languages, the English Bible as we know

8 See Appendix I.

it could not have been produced. The concern for going back to the original sources was not the fruit of the Reformation but its antecedent. Indeed, the first printings of the New Testament in Greek were promoted by two men neither of whom was sympathetic to the Reformation and one of whom was a cardinal of the Roman Church and Archbishop of Toledo. An edition of the Greek New Testament was first published in 1516. It was the work of Desiderius Erasmus, who, though he satirized the ignorance and corruption of the Roman clergy, had no great liking for the Reformation. Two years earlier, another edition of the Greek New Testament had already been printed; but this edition, by Francis Ximenes, was not published till several years later, because of delays in obtaining papal permission.

Ximenes was a very remarkable man. He gave up a distinguished administrative career in the Church in order to become an Observantine friar. His life of extreme austerity attracted attention, and such large crowds flocked to consult him on spiritual questions that he retreated to a more inaccessible monastery and lived for considerable periods as a hermit. But he had not been forgotten. After some time he was called by Queen Isabella to be her confessor and, having reluctantly accepted this office, he soon found himself playing an important role in affairs of state. Convinced that a revival of discipline in the Church was necessary, he used all his great influence to reform the disorderly monasteries of Spain. It is said that more than a thousand monks and friars left the country rather than submit to the discipline he imposed. There is no doubt that under his influence the moral life and religious zeal of the Spanish clergy immensely improved. It was largely because of his work that Spain, unaffected by the Protestant Reformation, came to play the leading role in the movement to revive the Roman Church. Ximenes was not himself a very great scholar; but he had the vision to promote scholarly work, for he recognized its disciplinary value. In Italy he had encountered Renaissance influences, and he felt that if only they could be consecrated to the service of the Roman Church the decadence everywhere apparent could be checked and turned into lively zeal. He did not believe the Bible should be made available to the laity without restriction; but he thought it ought to be the principal study of the clergy. The grandest expression of this conviction took the form of a work known as the Complutensian Polyglot, which was so called from the Latin name (Complutum) for Alcalá, the famous Spanish university that Ximenes founded. This edition of the Bible contained the Old Testament in Hebrew, Greek and Latin, and the New Testament in Greek and Latin. Published in 1522, it was a noble printing achievement as well as a great landmark in the story of the Bible.

VIII

FIRST PRINTING OF
THE ENGLISH BIBLE

O N OCTOBER 6, 1536, in the little town of Vilvorde, which lies between Brussels and Malines, an Englishman was led forth from the castle prison to the stake. In a loud voice he prayed: "Lord, open the King of England's eyes." He was then strangled to death and his body burned to ashes. For eighteen months he had been imprisoned in the castle, and the only letter of his that has survived—there is a copy in the British Museum—was written from his cell there. From it we catch a glimpse not only of the character of the man who gave us the first printed edition of the English Bible, but also of the grim conditions of the jail that was the reward of his last years. The letter contains an appeal for a warmer cap, "for I suffer extremely from cold in the head, being afflicted with a perpetual catarrh, which is considerably increased in the cell; also a piece of cloth, to patch my leggings. My overcoat has been worn out. My shirts are also worn out. I also wish his [the jailer's] permission to have a candle in the evening; for it is wearisome to sit alone in the dark."

The author of this sad letter was William Tyndale, who had gone up to Oxford about the year 1510 and studied there till 1515, at Magdalen Hall. By this time the Renaissance had affected Oxford: men such as John Colet had imbibed its spirit at Florence and other continental centers of the new learning. The older scholars at Oxford had been generally content to quote the conventional medieval authorities. The new Oxford scholars quoted Plato and the New Testament. When Colet lectured on the Epistles of St Paul, those who sat at his feet were soon able to see Paul's letters with new eyes. All this was of the most lively interest to Tyndale. We are told that he read privately to groups of students and fellows of Magdalen College "some parcel of Divinity, instructing them in the knowledge and truth of the Scriptures." Later, he went to Cambridge, which Erasmus had recently left.

About the year 1522, Tyndale conceived the idea of translating the Bible into English. He would begin by translating the Greek New Testament. Erasmus had expressed the wish that the Bible should become so well known among the people that bits of it should be sung in the fields. Tyndale wanted more. He resolved that the plowboy should know his Bible better than the priest. It was hardly five years since Martin Luther had nailed his famous ninety-five theses to the church door at Wittenberg that served as the University notice-board; yet already, in Germany, the Reformation had made great headway. Tyndale's resolution was, however, an ambitious one to make in an England in which Cardinal Wolsey, having just missed the papal throne, was wielding almost royal power. High-ranking ecclesiastics often lived in great splendor in those days; even so, Wolsey's pomp was a byword. Having enjoyed the favor of both Henry VII and Henry VIII, he had become, in 1514, during the latter's reign, Archbishop of York. The following year he had been made both Lord High Chancellor of England and a Roman cardinal. His revenues from these and other sources were enormous; nor did he hesitate to use them in a lavish display, living in the style of a great monarch. On special expeditions he was attended by four thousand horsemen, including nobles, prelates and knights. At home, his ordinary establishment at Hampton Court numbered about a thousand persons. Some nine or ten nobles, each with several servants, waited upon him. To attend his table there were twelve chaplains, a physician, four legal advisers, two secretaries, a herald-at-arms, and other courtiers. It is hardly surprising to learn that he disliked the Reformation.

After leaving Cambridge, Tyndale had gone as tutor in the household of Sir John Walsh, a Gloucestershire knight. It was a comfortable position for a young scholar to hold. The manor house was beautifully situated in the Cotswolds, and duties were light, so that Tyndale had plenty of time for study. The family was hospitable to the clergy, who were frequent guests in the dining-hall. The young scholar spent a good deal of time in their company. He did not hesitate to get into arguments, and as he was already quite learned in the Bible he generally got the better of these disputes, which probably offended the other disputants. In any case, Lady Walsh remonstrated with young Tyndale about his arguments with her guests. She did not see how he could be qualified to argue with clergymen whom she accounted "better placed" than he. It was to one of these that Tyndale is supposed to have said, in the course of an argument, that if God spared his life he would cause the boy driving the plow to "know more of the Scripture than thou dost." Lady Walsh would not unnaturally take this to be a piece of unseemly youthful boasting.

Determined to go ahead with his project, Tyndale went up to London in 1524, seeking the support of ecclesiastical leaders, notably Tunstall, the Lord Bishop of London. The latter disappointed him. "Room enough there was in my Lord's house for belly-cheer, but none to translate the New Testament." Soon Tyndale reached the conclusion that there was

no room in all England for this purpose. He turned, therefore, to Germany, staying for a time in Hamburg, where he
worked on his translation. Unable to find a printer there, he
moved to Cologne in June, 1525. Such an enterprise was now,
of course, closely identified with Protestantism, and could
therefore be counted upon to arouse the bitter hostility of
those who sided with Rome. The work of printing had to be
kept secret, since Roman sympathizers would do all they
could to stop it. The secret was kept for long enough to permit of considerable progress; but the printers indiscreetly
boasted that what they were doing would throw England into
revolution. John Cochlaeus, a fussy little man and an ardent
enemy of the Reformation, heard of the boast and invited
some of the printers to his house. Plying his guests with generous helpings of liquor, he was able to discover from them
that three thousand copies were being printed and about ten
sheets had already been struck off. There was at that time
strongly pro-Roman sentiment at Cologne; so much so that it
is somewhat odd that Tyndale chose it. Perhaps he had little
choice in the matter; or perhaps it was its very improbability
that made him choose it to avoid suspicion. At Cologne in
1479 had been printed the first two books to bear the imprimatur that is now a familiar feature of the book-censorship
system of the Roman Church. One of these books was a
Latin Bible. It is said that reactionary feeling ran so high
at Cologne that a Roman priest hung a portrait of Erasmus
near his desk so that he might vent his spleen by spitting at
it when he felt inclined. So when Cochlaeus set himself to
wreck Tyndale's venture he was assured of support. Tyndale
was nevertheless successful in making off with the quarto
sheets already printed. By taking a ship up the Rhine he was
able to land at Worms, a city already famous as the scene, four
years earlier, of Luther's celebrated defense. At Worms, where

Reformation sympathies had been aroused, the printing of Tyndale's work went on without hindrance.

Knowing that Cochlaeus had published a description of the quarto edition that was in the press, so that its importation into England might be prevented, Tyndale got the printer, Peter Schoeffer, to do an octavo edition as well. This edition, being without notes, was quickly printed and probably about three thousand copies of it published in 1525, to be followed by a similar number of copies of the larger edition. Early in 1526 the first copies of the first printed English New Testament had reached England. Perhaps Spalatin, a friend of Luther's, exaggerated when he said the demand was so great that the English would have paid a hundred thousand pieces of money for a single copy; but copies were very eagerly bought. The printing had been financed by English merchants, and it was these who got copies secretly imported into the country. The market price was half a crown a copy. It will be recalled that in Wyclif's day the charge for borrowing a manuscript copy of the Bible over a certain period for an hour a day was a load of hay, which in Tyndale's time would have been valued at about five shillings—double the price of a printed New Testament. On the other hand, in terms of wages and food prices, it was still an expensive book. It would have cost a mason, for instance, five full days' wages. Nor was a mason so badly off with his sixpence a day, for that daily wage represented the price of twelve pounds of beef or pork, or eight pounds of mutton or veal. Dutch booksellers were soon undercutting the English price: they were offering the New Testament for thirteen pence. This was surely, in the circumstances, a low figure for what the Lord Bishop of London was calling a "pestiferous and most pernicious poison."

The first printed edition of the New Testament in English met with ferocious opposition from the bishops. Cuthbert Tunstall, Bishop of London, claimed he could find three thousand errors in it, and Sir Thomas More charged that many of the errors were wilful and for the promotion of heresy. The claim was a gross exaggeration and a piece of bluff, for in fact the number of errors was, in the circumstances, remarkably small. The charge was likewise unfair: Tyndale's integrity is incontestable. "I call God to record," he wrote to his friend Fryth, "against the day we shall appear before the Lord Jesus to give a reckoning of our doings, that I never altered one syllable of God's word against my conscience; nor would do, this day, if all that is in the earth, whether it be honour, pleasure, or riches, might be given me." The book was solemnly burned at St Paul's Cross, London. The bishops even subscribed money to buy up all available copies. An old chronicler relates that Tyndale was delighted by this step, since it served the double purpose of immediately providing funds for the continuation of his work on the Bible and of discrediting the bishops as destroyers of God's Word. As the same chronicler puts it, the Bishop of London thought he "had God by the toe, when indeed he had the devil by the fist." Meanwhile, reprint after reprint of Tyndale's New Testament poured into England almost as fast as they could be bought or burned. That the authorities were thorough in their policy of destruction is indicated by the fact that of the many thousands of copies of Tyndale's printings of the New Testament to fall from the press between 1525 and 1534, all that survives is one solitary fragment of the first quarto edition—this fragment is in the British Museum—and two copies of the octavo edition, one now at the Baptist College, Bristol, and the other, an imperfect one, at St Paul's Cathedral, London.

Tyndale was now at work on the Old Testament. In 1530 came the first part of it, the Pentateuch, translated from the Hebrew with marginal notes. It seems that the five books of the Pentateuch were printed at Marburg separately, for

Genesis and Numbers are done in black letter, while the other three books are in what is the now more ordinary type. In 1531 came the Book of Jonah. Only one copy of this, and one copy of the Pentateuch survive: they are both in the British Museum.

Unauthorized by Tyndale, a revised edition of his New Testament was made by a man called George Joye and published in 1534. To this act of piracy Tyndale replied by publishing, at Antwerp, in the fall of the same year, a diligent revision of his own. This edition contained introductions to each chapter and a much-improved marginal commentary as well as a corrected text. At the end were printed lessons from the Old Testament for use in public worship. Its appearance was timely, for it was in November of that year that the jurisdiction of the Pope in England—long resented by many—was officially repudiated by the Act of Supremacy. The malice against Tyndale himself was unabated; but the climate of opinion changed in favor of an English Bible. The Queen, Anne Boleyn, was among those who wanted it, and Tyndale was able to present her with a sumptuous copy which is preserved in the British Museum.

Tyndale was now living in the free city of Antwerp, as a resident of the "English house" that some English merchants had established there. For a victim of Roman spite it was probably as safe a place as any. But Tyndale's enemies had not forgotten him. In 1535 a man called Henry Philips gained his confidence and even borrowed money from him. Philips, who was in the pay of Tyndale's enemies, borrowed forty shillings from his victim just before kidnapping him and handing him over to officers of the Emperor Charles V, who was pledged to destroy the enemies of the Pope. It was then that Tyndale was taken to Vilvorde for a tedious imprisonment to be terminated by a martyr's death. By this time Henry VIII was supposedly a supporter of the Reformation; but he was interested in what he could get out of the Reformation rather than in what he could contribute to it. So he did nothing to use his influence to obtain Tyndale's release. Wolsey was now dead; but Henry's selfish indifference was as bad for Tyndale as would have been Wolsey's angry pride.

It is worthy of note at this point that Tyndale and others who contributed to the dissemination of the Bible at this time are often reproached for the asperity of their language. But in the forthrightness of his speech Tyndale was but a child of his age. It was not the fashion to be polite in controversy, which was conducted more in the manner of a cockfight than, as now, a game of bridge. For instance, Tyndale believed that Thomas More was an opportunist ready to sell his pen for political advancement. Tyndale was probably mistaken in this. Thomas More had succeeded Wolsey as Lord Chancellor of England; but he had certainly no political advantage in the long run, for his opposition to Henry's divorce eventually cost him his head. Canonized in 1935 by Pope Pius XI, Thomas More is now an official saint of the Roman Church. His language towards his opponents was more colorful than Tyndale's. He called them "apes that dance for the pleasure of Lucifer," and "hell hounds that the devil hath in his kennel." When Tyndale had spoken disrespectfully of Thomas Aquinas, whom Rome had by then exalted to pre-eminence among the medieval doctors of the Church, More retaliated by calling Tyndale a "devilish drunken soul" and affirmed that "this drowsy drudge hath drunken so deep in the devil's dregs that but if he wake and repent himself the sooner he may hap to fall into the mashing fat and turn himself into draff [1] that the hogs of hell shall feed upon." Though Tyndale's own language was often not ladylike, it was never as coarse as that.

[1] *hogwash*

Tyndale's translation of the New Testament was in many ways an enormous improvement on Wyclif's. In the first place, it was from the original tongue. In the second place, it was in the free, idiomatic English of the day and had an immense influence on the King James Version. It is true that some of Wyclif's phrases are, as we have seen, the ancestors of much-loved phrases in the King James Version. But Tyndale's influence was greater still. He paid much attention to English style. Here is an example from a familiar chapter of the New Testament: "Though I spake with the tonges of men and angels, and yet had no love, I were even as soundinge brasse: or as a tynklynge Cymball. And though I coulde prophesy, and vnderstode all secretes, and all knowledge: yee, yf I had all fayth so that I coulde move mountayns oute of ther places, and yet had no love, I were nothynge. . . . Love suffreth longe, and is corteous. Love envieth not. Love doth nott frowardly, swelleth not dealeth not dishonestly, seketh not her awne, is not provoked to anger, thynketh not evyll, reioyseth not in iniquite. . . . When I was a chylde, I spake as a chylde, I vnderstode as a childe, I ymagened as a chylde: but assone as I was a man I put awaye childesshnes. Now we se in a glasse even in a darke speakynge: but then shall we se face to face. . . . Now abideth fayth, hope, and love, even these thre: but the chefe of these is love." [2]

Tyndale's martyrdom prevented his completion of the Bible. But meanwhile, another English scholar had been at work. As early as 1526, just after the publication of Tyndale's first New Testament, a group of scholars were meeting at a house in Cambridge. One of these was Miles Coverdale, also a North countryman. A priest and Austin friar who had joined the Reformation cause, Coverdale was a man of whom one of his contemporaries says that he was "very sober in diet,

[2] *The New Testament*, translated by William Tyndale, 1534 (ed. N. Hardy Wallis, for the Royal Society of Literature), Cambridge University Press, 1938.

godlie in life, friendlie to the godlie, liberal to the poor, and
courteous to all men, void of pride, full of humilitie, abhor-
ring covetousness, and an enemy to all wickedness and wicked
men." The full details of how Coverdale went about his work
are not known; but the result was that in the fall of 1535,
while Tyndale was in prison, Coverdale's translation of the
Bible into English had been completed and was published in
October of that year, almost exactly a year before Tyndale's
death. Even the place of printing is not certain, though it
was probably Marburg, Germany. A dedication to Henry
VIII, apparently printed at Southwark, England, was included, having perhaps been inserted with the unbound
sheets imported from the continent. Tyndale had been able
to claim that he "had no man to counterfeit, neither was
holpe with englysshe of any that had interpreted the same, or
soche lyke thinge in the scripture beforetyme." Coverdale's
undertaking was more modest. He did not pretend to Tyndale's knowledge of the ancient tongues, and being an honest
man he did not disguise the fact but freely admitted his shortcomings. He did the best he could by using Tyndale's translation, in the case of the books for which it was available,
and referring to German and Latin versions for the rest. He
followed Luther's example in segregating from the rest of
the Old Testament the books that had not been included in
the Hebrew canon, and inserting these "apocryphal books"
at the end. Coverdale's practice here influenced later English
translators who either followed his example or else, as we
shall see, omitted the Apocrypha altogether.

The temper of England had undergone considerable modi-
fication from the days when Tyndale's New Testaments had
caused such a commotion. In 1534, the Upper House of Convocation of Cambridge [3] petitioned the Crown to authorize a

---

[3] There are, in England, two ecclesiastical provinces, Canterbury and York.
Each has its own Convocation. In earlier times, bishops and other clergy sat

translation of the Bible into English. It seems that Cranmer devised a project for the translation of the Bible by about ten bishops and scholars; but nothing came of this scheme. Coverdale's work, though it constituted the first complete printed English Bible, was scarcely of sufficient merit to be so authorized, and it would have been impolitic to authorize the work of Tyndale, while allowing him to be imprisoned, then strangled and burned on foreign soil, when all this could have been prevented.

A revision of the work of Tyndale and Coverdale was made, however, by John Rogers, a friend of Tyndale's and an ardent worker for the Reform. It is not surprising, in view of the hazards attending such activities, to find that he apparently adopted a pseudonym, Thomas Matthew. It was this Bible, the work of Rogers, though commonly known as Matthew's Bible which, having been printed abroad (probably at Antwerp) and published in 1537 at the expense of two London merchants, was welcomed by the authorities. At the request of Cranmer, it was presented by Thomas Cromwell, Archbishop of Canterbury, to Henry, who gave it the royal licence that was desired. This meant that it could be owned and read, bought and sold, without interference from the authorities. The Bible that Rogers published was in fact a very light revision of Tyndale's work, with as much of Coverdale as was needed for completeness. That Henry VIII, having allowed Tyndale to be martyred in 1536, should within a year give his licence to what included, for all practical purposes, the very work for which Tyndale had been so bitterly persecuted, accords entirely with the character of that monarch. It also reflects, however, the lukewarm support of the Reformation in England on the part of others in places of high authority. The battle for Reform was in fact only beginning, and

---

together. Since the fifteenth century they have been divided into "Houses," the Upper House (bishops) and the Lower House (other clergy).

Rogers, though his Bible was the first to obtain official approval in England, was destined to be the first of the three hundred Protestant martyrs to be put to death during the brief and unforgettable reign of Mary Tudor. That Bloody Mary, as she was called, was childless, has indeed been accounted the chief manifestation of divine mercy during her terrible reign.

IX

COMPETITIVE VERSIONS

"WHAT A COUNTRY is this!" exclaimed a foreign visitor to England about the year 1540. "On the one side they are hanging the Pope's friends; on the other they are burning his enemies." Families were divided in their allegiance, some leaning to the old ways, others favoring the new. For those—and there were many—who cared little one way or another, it no doubt seemed difficult at times to know which flag to fly. In 1540, the year of Thomas Cromwell's execution, Protestant and Papist were about equally represented under the axe. But for all that, the English Bible had come to stay. It was a question of getting a definitive version, and many versions were to appear before 1611, when one was produced under the patronage of King James that was to remain practically the undisputed victor for two and a half centuries, exercising an incomparable influence on both English and American literature and life.

The so-called Matthew's Bible had received, in 1537, the royal licence; but while this gave, as we have seen, an immunity to persons engaged in the private use of it, it did not confer upon it any authorization for use in public worship. It was plain to the authorities that face could not be saved unless a version were produced that would not be so blatantly indebted to Tyndale as had been both Coverdale's version and Matthew's Bible. Coverdale, a man of peaceable disposition, seemed right for the task, and he was duly commissioned to undertake the preparation of yet another version of the Bible that would replace both his own and Matthew's Bible. Coverdale acquiesced. The work he was set to do was eventually to be known as the Great Bible. The project was so ambitiously conceived that it was felt England had neither good enough paper nor sufficiently skilled printers to produce the sumptuous edition that was desired. So Coverdale was sent to Paris, where a better quality of paper and a greater elegance of printing could be expected. Coverdale had now also more ample materials for the work of translation itself, including the Complutensian Polyglot to which we referred in a previous chapter, a work containing original texts. He was also provided with the necessary grammars and dictionaries and the help of an assistant, Richard Grafton. The licence of the French King Francis I was obtained, and in 1538 printing was begun at Paris. While the work was in the press, however, relations between France and England became more than usually strained, and the Inquisition, encouraged by the French ambassador in London, ordered confiscation. Four "great dry vats" of sheets were actually sold as waste paper. The printer was arrested. Coverdale had already, however, sent some of the sheets to England, and with the aid of English agents he succeeded not only in rescuing some more but even in secretly conveying type, presses and labor to London, where the work was resumed. In 1539 the first edition of the Great Bible duly appeared.

It was a magnificent achievement, well deserving the name Great Bible. Splendidly printed on paper measuring 11 by 16½ inches, it bore a frontispiece,[1] depicting a singularly ascetic Henry VIII handing a Bible to Archbishop Cranmer

---

[1] This was formerly believed by some to have been the work of Holbein— an opinion now generally repudiated.

on one side and Thomas Cromwell, Secretary of State, on the other. Lower down in the picture, on one side Cranmer is presenting a copy to a kneeling priest, while on the other side is to be seen Cromwell giving one to a group of noblemen. At the bottom is a more crowded scene, in which a priest is preaching to a congregation of common people, out of whose mouths flow ribbons containing the words VIVAT REX: Long live the King! Behind this devoted congregation rises the sinister outline of Newgate Prison, from the bars of which those not currently in the royal favor enjoy a view of the proceedings impeded by prison bars. In the clouds immediately above Henry's royal head nestles God, unmistakably accorded a slight precedence over the monarch. But it is a very "spiritual" precedence, for God is not very easily disentangled from the clouds, below which there is no difficulty in discerning the clear figure of Henry. The artist must surely have enjoyed himself, while fulfilling his task of designing a frontispiece that would win the King's favor.

This first edition of the Great Bible, the first English Bible to be authorized for public use in churches, is sometimes known as Cromwell's Bible. Cromwell's personal copy of it, beautifully illuminated on vellum, is now in the possession of St John's College, Cambridge. It was quickly followed by a second edition, sometimes called Cranmer's Bible, because of the preface by him that adorns it. This second edition contained further considerable revisions. Published in April, 1540, it was followed by two further editions the same year, and yet another three in the year following. The parish clergy were instructed to obtain a copy of the Great Bible and to have it chained in some place in church. It evidently excited much interest, for we find Bishop Bonner complaining that "divers wilful and unlearned persons inconsiderately and indiscreetly read the same, especially and chiefly at the time of divine service, yea in the time of the sermon and declaration of the word of God."

The Great Bible took hold of the imagination of the English people. Not only was it read in churches. It was purchased by many who could muster enough money to buy it. A copy could be obtained for about twelve shillings bound or ten shillings unbound. Around those who possessed a copy and could read it, crowds gathered to listen. It enchanted the hearts and minds of the English people as no other literature had done. Indeed the popularity of all other forms of literature, including even the lascivious alehouse tales, seems to have waned rapidly in competition with the rich diversity of its texture and the robust vivacity of its style. There was no doubt an attraction, too, in the *completeness* of the great tome that had become a familiar sight to many. For centuries men had heard allusions to the Holy Scriptures. They had for long listened to bits of it—part of a chapter of an "Epistle of Holy Paul," or of this or that one of the "Holy Gospels." More recently they had perhaps furtively seen or at any rate heard of New Testaments or even of Bibles. But here, right within the parish church itself, was the *whole* Bible. The common man who could not himself read it would ask a literate friend what was written on the title page. What a thrill he must have felt as his friend slowly enunciated the exciting words: "The Byble in Englyshe, that is to saye the content of ALL the holy scrypture. . . ."

Here was an incitement to learn to read, if ever there was one. For once you mastered the art you could hope, given time and patience, to read the entire Bible. So it is at this time that there is to be noticed a marked awakening of interest among ordinary people in the art of reading itself. A program for universal literacy was still three centuries away, yet the impetus to learn how to read was already there. Having the much-discussed book lying in your parish church and not being able to read it must have been for many almost like being at the seashore and not knowing how to swim.

What did the Great Bible sound like, compared with the later versions with which we are more familiar? There is no need to give examples. You have only to look at the Psalms in the Book of Common Prayer, which has preserved them in the form in which they appeared in the Great Bible, except for modernization of the spelling. Though less accurate a translation than was provided in later versions, the Psalter as it appeared in the Great Bible had a peculiar charm, a melodious phrasing, that endeared it to English hearts. Even when the later version was provided and authorized, the English Church went on using the version men had grown to love so much that they could not bear to replace it by any other, however technically superior as a translation of the original Hebrew. It was the nearest approach one can well imagine in English to the inimitable beauty of the Latin Psalter that had for a thousand years been chanted in the cloister.

About the time of the publication of the Great Bible, another version appeared that might have received greater acclaim had it not been overshadowed by so formidable a competitor. This was a version by Richard Taverner, who had got into trouble in his youth at Christ Church, Oxford, for reading Tyndale's New Testament. Taverner was a lawyer by profession, though in later years, under the reign of Edward VI, when preachers were scarce, he received a licence as a lay preacher. He evidently knew Greek well, but not Hebrew. A few of his renderings in the New Testament were adopted in later versions. Perhaps the most notable of these is his use of the word "parable" for "similitude," a very familiar feature in most of the versions that are nowadays read. Though the sale of Taverner's Bible was, as we should expect, very adversely affected by the appearance of the Great Bible at almost the same time, there was sufficient demand to call forth a second edition.

The triumph of the Great Bible could not have been achieved without widespread interest in and sympathy with the Reformation that was sweeping Europe. But we have seen that the country was divided. Above all, the Reformation in England had a great weakness: it lacked powerful leadership. Had England been under a less wicked king, the absence of such leadership for the reform of the Church might have mattered little, since the popular sympathy for it might have grown strong enough in time. But in Henry's England, where the Reformation itself was at the mercy of a monarch's fickleness, so also was the English Bible. Henry had promoted the reading of the Bible so long as it suited him, as he had promoted other salutary reforms. The time came when it did not suit him. It was easy, of course, to point to evils attending the widespread dissemination of the Bible. For one thing, it was causing people to argue about religion, and religious controversy ill suited Henry's absolutist aims. Moreover, among those who were now reading the Bible for themselves were some very foolish men and women, and their reading did not make them any the less foolish. In giving people freedom or responsibility you give them also the power to abuse it, and you can hardly expect that none of them will. So there were wild men and women who, ignorantly contending that there was now no need for judges or magistrates or clergy, preached a seditious anarchy. The preaching of others would have inculcated anarchy of another sort: members of the "Family of Love," for instance, whose sexual morals were accounted fit for the barnyard.[2] It had always been recognized that the Devil could quote Scripture in his own interest. But now it was hardly in Henry's interest to have the Bible quoted at all,

---

2 Modern research indicates, however, that such reports are gross exaggerations, sometimes wilful calumnies.

and in the closing years of his reign much of the liberty in reading the Bible was withdrawn from the common people. Nor was it a difficult policy to pursue, for there lingered in England much popular sentiment for the old ways. So in 1543 it was enacted that "no manner of persons, after the first of October, should take upon them to read openly to others in any church or open assembly, within any of the King's dominions, the Bible or any part of the Scripture in English, unless he was so appointed thereunto by the King . . . on pain of suffering one hundred months' imprisonment." Women not of noble or gentle birth were forbidden to read the Bible even privately. Private Bible reading was also, on pain of a month's imprisonment, forbidden to certain classes of men; but reading of the Bible in the houses, orchards or gardens of the well-to-do was permitted. Henry had indeed repudiated the jurisdiction of the Pope in England; but it can hardly be said that the Reformation movement was in his debt.

In the brief reign of the precocious boy-king, Edward VI, prospects seemed brighter; but with Bloody Mary's accession in 1553 the situation had so changed that shiploads of Protestant refugees from England were landing at continental ports. Some of these fugitives in quest of havens of safety from the Marian terror were attracted to Geneva, the Swiss city where a community was being molded by Calvin into the cosmopolis that John Knox was to describe admiringly as "the most perfect school of Christ since the days of the Apostles." It was here that yet another important and extremely influential translation of the Bible into English was made. Geneva was a natural place for the work to be done, for on that Swiss lakeside was a unique climate of freedom. At Geneva were many learned men, including Theodore Beza, the greatest living Biblical scholar. French scholars at Geneva were already working on the French Bible that was to become the official version for the Reformed Church in France. So it is not surprising that the English scholars at Geneva should have devoted their exile as they did to the task of producing a revision of the Great Bible. They worked, it is said, "for the space of two years and more day and night." Among them was William Whittingham, Calvin's brother-in-law, who first of all produced a New Testament which was printed, in 1557, in a convenient small octavo form. The crowning glory of the labors of these English exiles was the publication, in April, 1560, of the version to be known as the Geneva Bible. By this time (1558) the death of Mary Tudor, and the accession of Elizabeth to the English throne had made it possible for the exiles to return to England; but some, including Whittingham, remained in Geneva to attend to the final stages of the work.

The Geneva Bible was in several respects an improvement on previous English versions. Four points should be noted at the outset. First, in the Old Testament it followed the Hebrew more closely than its predecessors had done. Secondly, though it followed the customary practice of the day in providing notes to the text, its notes were comparatively free of the controversial violence that was the fashion of the age. Thirdly, the use of a smaller (quarto) page than had hitherto been employed made it an easier book to handle, while the plain Roman type made it more legible than Bibles printed in Gothic letter. This last point was of considerable importance, for though the invention of printing had greatly fostered the demand for spectacles and promoted a flourishing trade in them, not least in Germany where they could be obtained very cheaply, the optical profession was still in its infancy and optical prescriptions fairly simple. Fourthly—and perhaps the most striking feature of all—the plan of division into verses with which we are now familiar was used for the first time for the whole English Bible. In previous translations, paragraphs had been customary. The verse division used for the Old Testament was one that had been devised by Rabbi Nathan in 1448 and used in a Venice edition printed in 1524. It had then been adopted in a Latin Bible printed in 1528, which also employed a similar method for dividing up the New Testament. In 1555 another Bible was issued by Robert Estienne of Paris in which the same verse division was used for the Old Testament, but a different one provided for the New. The Geneva Bible followed the arrangement adopted by Estienne.

The publication of the Geneva Bible was timely. Papal jurisdiction in Scotland was soon afterwards abolished, marking the final triumph of the Reformation in that country. An Act of the Scottish Parliament made it compulsory for every householder whose income was above a specified sum to buy a copy, and the first generation of Scotsmen to enjoy the benefits of the Reformation were nurtured exclusively on this Bible. Though in England it was never authorized for use in churches, it was imported in large quantities from Geneva for household use. In Elizabeth's reign alone there were sixty editions of it, though it never had her official approval, and by the middle of the seventeenth century more than double that number. It was the Bible of Shakespeare and of the Pilgrim Fathers.

Because of its rendering of Genesis iii.7, which relates that Adam and Eve "sewed fig tree leaves together and made themselves breeches," it is often called the Breeches Bible. This was not, however, as novel a rendering as it may sound, or as it is sometimes imagined to be. It had been used in the Wyclif Bible and also in Caxton's *Golden Legend*. The use of the word "breeches" was, of course, intentional, not an error. Among the many editions of the Geneva Bible, however, some contained errors that have since provided collectors with a convenient designation for the particular edition in which they occur. The second edition, for instance, published in

1562, printed "placemaker" for "peacemaker" in Matthew v.9, and is therefore known as the Placemaker's Bible. An edition of the Geneva Bible, in which an Old Testament dated 1598 is bound with a 1597 New Testament, printed "Jesus Church" for "Jesus Christ," at I John v.20, and so is referred to as the Jesus Church Bible. An edition published in 1610 had a more serious misprint: "Judas" instead of "Jesus" at John vi.67. That there were comparatively few such misprints is a testimony to the care of the printers in those still comparatively early years of their craft.

The great popularity of the Geneva Bible as well as the superiority of the scholarship behind it made it from the first a formidable rival to the Great Bible, which could not in competition with it maintain the unique position which, in England, it had formerly enjoyed. But there was opposition to, if not prejudice against, the adoption of the Geneva Bible in the English Church. To meet the situation, the Archbishop of Canterbury, Matthew Parker, who happened to be a Biblical scholar, promoted a scheme in 1563 for a further revision of the Bible by a team of scholars to each of whom was assigned a portion, or "parcel," as it was called, with the Archbishop as editor-in-chief. Because of the predominance of bishops in the team, the resulting work was commonly known as the Bishops' Bible. Published in 1568, it immediately superseded the Great Bible as the authorized version for the English Church. But in spite of its official prestige it could not compete with the Geneva Bible, which went into five times as many editions and remained the favorite Bible of the English household, as it continued also to be the only Bible of the Scots. On the whole, the comparative failure of the Bishops' Bible was not undeserved. It was not, even in the circumstances, a very distinguished piece of work. Parker was an able scholar and editor; but the translators were for the most part undistinguished. Moreover, they had worked too hastily and, despite the supervision of the archiepiscopal editor, very independently, so that the result, especially in the Old Testament, was uneven. Both Cranmer's preface to the Great Bible and a new preface by Parker were included, together with a portrait of Elizabeth on the title page.

The illustrations were of mediocre quality; some of them curiously pagan. The second edition, for example, published in 1572, was enlivened with drawings illustrative of Ovid's *Metamorphoses*. The Book of Hebrews was adorned by one such illustration depicting the legend of Leda and the Swan, on which account this edition is known to collectors as the Leda Bible. Leda, in Greek mythology, was the daughter of Thestios, King of Aetolia, and the wife of Tyndareus, King of Sparta. Zeus, Father of the gods, fell in love with her and used his divine power to accomplish her seduction, transforming himself into a beautiful swan so that he might prove irresistible to the lady of his desire. The ruse worked, and the children of this remarkable union, the Dioscuri, half gods, half mortals, are supposed to have appeared in storms in the form of the electrical phenomenon later known as St Elmo's fire. Picturesque, no doubt; but hardly suitable for the adornment of a Bible intended to replace, with the aid of the royal might of Elizabeth, the Geneva Bible for which there was really much more to be said from every point of view. Nor was it only in woodcut and drawing that the fancy of the compilers ran free; it was by no means inhibited in the notes. For example, in the note to Psalm xlv.9 we learn that "Ophir is thought to be the Ilande in the west coast, of late found by Christopher Colombo; fro whence at this day is brought most fine golde."

Being intended for church use, the Bishops' Bible was originally designed as a tall and massive tome. However, even when smaller copies of it became available, as they soon did, it could not hold its own. The Geneva Bible continued to be read. The last edition of the Bishops' Bible appeared in 1606; but many editions of the Geneva Bible, we shall see, were issued between then and 1644.

Meanwhile, Roman Church authorities had been much alarmed by the influence of the English Bible; most of all by its influence on the decreasing minority of the Pope's adherents in the English-speaking world. Some of the conservative English families had remained loyal to the papacy throughout the vicissitudes of the Reformation in England. The fact that they possessed no English Bible approved by Rome and yet were surrounded by Bible readers frightened their ecclesiastical leaders, who feared the influence of the Geneva Bible would in time alienate them from their allegiance. In principle, Rome was against the indiscriminate accessibility of the Bible to the common people. The Pope claimed to be in possession of an ecclesiastical dominion giving him the means of directing the consciences of all men with infallible certainty. But in the circumstances there was nothing for the Roman Church to do but produce a translation that would have its approval, being furnished with such notes as would help its English-speaking adherents to hold their own in the course of that theological controversy with their neighbors that was the popular and ferocious pastime of the late sixteenth century.

In 1568 a college had been founded at Douai, in France, for the purpose of educating sons of the Roman Church of English extraction. Its founder, Cardinal Allen, believing that the English people were still Romanist at heart, and that the Reformation would have only a superficial and temporary success in that country, devoted his attention to the training of missionary priests who, he hoped, would one day bring back England to the heel of the Pope. In fact, through his political support of the unsuccessful

Spanish attempt to invade and conquer England in 1588, he ended by provoking the hostility of many of even those who had hitherto kept their allegiance to Rome. Meanwhile, however, he began, with some other English-speaking scholars at Douai, a new version of the Bible. The college at Douai migrated to Rheims in 1578 and there, in 1582, a version of the New Testament was completed and published. The college later returned to Douai where, in 1609-10, the version afterwards known as the Douai Bible was published in its entirety. We shall see in a later chapter that this version was often revised, notably by Bishop Challoner. For long the traditional Bible of English-speaking Roman Catholics, the Rheims-Douai-Challoner Version has now been largely replaced by other versions more recently approved by the Roman Church.

All previous English Bibles since the invention of printing had been intended as translations from the Hebrew and Greek. The compilers of the Douai Version, ignoring the work of both Ximenes and the Reformers, did their translation from the Vulgate only. For this reason it cannot be compared with the other versions, for it is not even on the same footing. Even within its own great limitations, however, the Douai Version was open to grave criticism. Ostensibly a translation from the Latin, it was sometimes at best half a translation. Probably the most famous example to illustrate this is the use of the phrase "he exinanited himself." This purported to translate a phrase[3] in which the Latin has the verb *"exinanivit."* But "he exinanited himself" was no better English in the days of the Douai translators than it is today. The phrase has been elsewhere translated "he humbled himself" or "he emptied himself." The tendency to retain the technical terms and phrases of the Latin Vulgate rather than to put them into a plainer

[3] Philippians ii.7.

English form had some effect even on the King James Version, as we shall see. In the Douai Bible it was so characteristic that the general effect is to mystify rather than enlighten even the more intelligent reader. More serious still, however, were the attempts of the translators to perpetuate the misconceptions the Latin Vulgate had helped to instill. More must be said about this when we come to consider the story of Roman Catholic translations of the Bible into English, to which two later chapters will be devoted.

X

THE MOST HIGH
AND MIGHTY PRINCE

BEFORE WE TURN to an examination of the methods used in constructing the most influential version of the most influential book in human history, the King James Version of the Bible, it will be well to look for a moment at the character of the man who had most to do with its promotion, to whom also it was dedicated, and after whom it is named.

In the front of a modern copy of this version you will find a dedication beginning as follows: "To the Most High and Mighty Prince, James, by the Grace of God, King of Great Britain, France, and Ireland, Defender of the Faith, &c. The Translators of the Bible wish Grace, Mercy, and Peace, through JESUS CHRIST our Lord. Great and manifold were the blessings, most dread Sovereign, which Almighty God, the Father of all mercies, bestowed upon us the people of England, when first he sent Your Majesty's Royal Person to rule and reign over us. . . ." The recipient had, however, very human qualities, mostly bad ones, and eccentricities more exasperating than endearing, that are undisclosed in the exceedingly formal and hyperbolic language of this "epistle dedicatory." He had also a remarkable parentage and education. Before he began, in 1603, "to rule and reign over" the people of England, he had been King of Scotland for thirty-six years.

His mother, the beautiful, famous and unhappy Mary Queen of Scots, having become heiress to the Scottish throne a few days after her birth in 1542, had been brought up at the court of France where she married, at the age of sixteen, the fourteen-year-old Dauphin Francis, a precocious and sickly half-wit who died two years later. The following year, 1561, the nineteen-year-old Mary came to Scotland as the Queen whose presence had long been awaited. Four years later, in July, 1565, with the approval of the Pope —for she was a devout adherent of Rome—she married her cousin Henry Stuart, Lord Darnley. Meanwhile, David Riccio, an Italian *valet de chambre* at the Scottish court, had been advanced with very noticeable rapidity to the position of secretary and personal adviser to Mary. One evening in March, 1566, when she, being six months pregnant, was sitting at supper in a room in the Palace of Holyrood House, Edinburgh, with Riccio and one of the court ladies, a band of armed men burst in upon them and demanded that Riccio accompany them to an adjoining bedroom. Riccio, screaming hysterically and clutching Mary's skirt, was dragged off. It is said that fifty dagger wounds were later found on his dead body. Darnley, mad with jealousy, had instigated the murder with the willing aid of nobles whom Mary had alienated. In February of the following year, Darnley was murdered by the Earl of Bothwell. A few weeks after the murder, Mary married the murderer, and when, a few weeks later still, she was seized and taken prisoner by some of her nobles, the angry bystanders roared after her in the streets of Edinburgh: "Burn the whore!"

The child that Mary carried in her womb that evening

when supper with Riccio had been stormily interrupted
—her only child by her second marriage—was none other
than the Most High and Mighty Prince, James.

So much for his parentage. What of his education? The
"epistle dedicatory" describes him as having been enriched
by God's heavenly hand "with many singular and extraordinary graces." It was indeed no ordinary prince who had,
before the age of twenty, written, besides sonnets and other
works, a "Paraphrase on the Revelation of St John." As
a child, his principal tutor had been George Buchanan,
the greatest of the Scottish humanists and a supporter of
the Reformation of the Scottish Church. Buchanan's own
earlier career was of a pattern colorful enough to provide
a fitting background to the task with which he was entrusted, the education of the astonishing progeny of Mary
Queen of Scots. An excellent Latinist, Buchanan had in
his youth studied at the Sorbonne; he had served with
French troops in Scotland; he had, by royal command of the
King of Scots, his future pupil's grandfather, satirized
the Franciscans and then suffered imprisonment for it at
the instigation of the odious Cardinal Beaton. Afterwards
he had escaped to Bordeaux and taught Latin there for
several years, with Montaigne as one of his pupils; he had
written amatory verses; he had been head of the college at
Coimbra, Portugal; he had been jailed in a monastery there
when news leaked out of his youthful attack on the Franciscans; he had spent his imprisonment writing a metrical
Latin version of the Psalms; he had, on his release, associated himself with the Reformation cause in France. Returning eventually to Scotland he had been in 1562 appointed
tutor to the young Mary Queen of Scots; four years later
he had become head of St Leonard's College in the University of St Andrews; and in the year of James's birth
he was Moderator of the General Assembly of the Church

of Scotland. After sitting with the English commissioners at York in judgment on the now disgraced Mary, he played a notable part in her condemnation. He was then, in 1570, against Mary's wishes, appointed tutor to her son, James, when the latter was three years old. Buchanan's later writings, which include a history of Scotland that purports to dispose of both "English lies and Scottish vanity," reveal much interest in the principles of constitutional monarchy. Such principles Buchanan had endeavored to inculcate into his royal pupil, to whom he also imparted a taste, then unusual in princes, for languages, literature and theology.

James was a willing and able pupil. Never manly or robust, he had been officially King James VI of Scotland since his mother's abdication when he was a year old, and his curious but genuine taste for literary pursuits and theological disquisitions made him seem odd and pedantic. His policy (or, as he would have put it, his "king-craft") was often unpopular and sometimes disastrous; nevertheless he displayed also much wisdom and even accomplished some good, not least in his native land. Scotland had never had a strong monarchy: the king was generally at the mercy of a band of turbulent nobles—a great weakness in the government of a country in those days. James seemed the last man to be able by moral strength or personal drive to succeed in establishing a central power in the Scottish Crown where his predecessors had failed; yet, by whatever means, he did it. He attributed his success in this and all such matters to the superior education he had enjoyed, not to say to his native intellectual power. Others regarded it as a triumph of the trickery and double-dealing that are the characteristic refuge of weak men called to high office.

James was in fact proud of his virtuosity in guile, an attitude that surely betokens abnormality rather than malice.

But the sixteenth century was disinclined for making such allowances, and there is no doubt that James's curious temperament greatly contributed to his unpopularity in the long run. When Mary Queen of Scots was beheaded at the order of her jealous cousin Elizabeth, James, though he had by then reached manhood, made no serious protest. A man does not make it very easy for even his friends to admire his best qualities when these are found in a nature so habituated to guile and wedded to intrigue that he lets his mother have her head chopped off rather than risk offending her enemy whom he happens at the time to deem it expedient to flatter.

Though he was by no means popular in Scotland, James knew how to handle the Scots. Up to a point, at any rate. They did not, on the whole, think well of him; but at least they understood him in a way, and perhaps better than they knew. In 1603, at the Union of the Crowns, he became "James Sixt and First"; that is, of course, James VI of Scotland and I of England. The English, who thus became subject to him who for so long had been King of Scots, had been by no means unprepared to welcome him. Indeed, they had been at that time so apprehensive about what might happen in the train of Elizabeth's death that they would almost have been ready to welcome James even if he had had two heads, let alone two crowns. The flattering welcome they did give him is echoed in the "epistle dedicatory" to the version of the Bible published eight years after that event. The flattery titillated James's vanity, making him seem surer than ever of himself and more confident that his claim to be a master of "king-craft" had been plainly vindicated.

English historians have generally complained that he never understood the English. But perhaps this is too much to expect. The English are not easy to understand. If James, coming as a middle-aged foreigner to the English throne, had really understood the English, he would have been a god rather than a man. He certainly was not a god. Perhaps he was not even very much of a man. Even his bookishness was as effeminate as his other vices. There was much significance in the aphorism of the day that King Elizabeth had been succeeded by Queen James. If some, thankful for small mercies, had rejoiced that at any rate the Lord had not made Elizabeth a man, fervent must have been their gratitude that he had not made James a woman.

On the other hand, it may be that James did not misunderstand the English quite as much as some great historians have held. Their institutions, it is true, were new to him. The Scotland of his day had no exact counterpart of the parliamentary system England was slowly developing. The Scottish Parliament had been run on different lines. Nevertheless James had had plenty of opportunity to see democratic processes at work. He had seen them in the Kirk and understood them very well. Too well. He did not like them. "A Scottish Presbytery," he said, "agreeth with a monarchy as God with the Devil."

But whether James understood the English or not, it is certain they found him beyond comprehension. To them he was both enigmatic and ridiculous. His lack of royal bearing—his appearance was not regal and he was accounted slovenly in his personal habits—might have mattered little in the circumstances. His advent had saved the English from civil war, so that they were not disposed to grumble at his looks. What they could not stomach was his insufferable vanity. He was not merely vain; his vanity was of an exceptionally irritating kind—a woman's vanity without a woman's enchantment. He had a habit of talking endlessly and donnishly on subjects that interested others less than himself; yet his manner betokened less a vision of himself as Solomon

come to unfold his wisdom to a race of barbarian upstarts, than
the Queen of Sheba posing as King of Israel in a foreign
land. To this not very endearing trait James added his
ingrained habit of intrigue that suggested no mere disregard for all ethical principle but a willingness to enlist
ethical principle too in the service of his personal vanity.
It was not that the English were unaccustomed to vain
kings. They had already seen both kingly and queenly
vanity take curious forms. But never this. If James had
been more of a man he would not have taken his new subjects so much by surprise. As things were, the English
did not merely feel their new king was too much of a
Scotch professor; they felt he was a Scotch professor with
the mentality of a French courtesan. Well might people
ask what dead King Elizabeth would have thought of the
new Queen James.

Such was the Most High and Mighty Prince who, on his
way from Edinburgh to London in 1603, was presented with
the Millenary Petition, so called because it contained about
a thousand signatures. The petition set forth the grievances
of the Puritan party in the English Church. If the signa-
tories imagined that because their new king came from
Scotland he would be on their side, they were much mistaken. The Scots had an outlook and tradition that made
the spirit of English Puritanism in many ways foreign to
them. But even had it been otherwise James would not
have been their man. The Puritans had views about kingship that were far from pleasing to such a king. "I will
make them conform," he said, "or I will harry them out
of the land, or yet do worse."

Still, they were a force in his new domain, and James was
much too wise a ruler to ignore them. So in response to
their petition a conference was called at Hampton Court
in January, 1604, for the purpose of hearing and judging

upon "things pretended to be amiss in the Church." By his rudeness to the Puritans at that conference, James horrified many who could not fail to notice the contrast between his attitude to them and his demeanor to the Papists whom all parties in the Church more or less distrusted and disliked. Not all observers perceived that James, who acted on principle from the basest motives, was relatively courteous to the Papists just because they were to be distrusted and feared. He thought that as there was less need to fear the Puritans, so he could more freely allow himself the pleasure of being rude to them when he felt so inclined. To the extent that a man of his character could be said to have sympathies of any kind, James was Protestant at heart and in mind; but his pathological vanity led him to regard himself as not only above all religious parties but above all religious principles. This, in turn, enabled him to indulge in a vision of himself as a great peacemaker. If a king were clever enough, would he not be able to encourage religious toleration, playing off one party against the other? It stands to reason that James did not favor the Puritans, who were disposed to be critical of his absolutism; but he really favored nobody other than himself. There was, indeed, much grumbling because of his numerous favorites at court; but these were favored only because he thought them favorable to his aims, agreeable to his tastes, or otherwise conducive to his personal aggrandizement.

It was at the Hampton Court Conference in 1604 that John Reynolds, President of Corpus Christi College, Oxford, and a distinguished representative of the Puritan party, raised the question of the desirability of having an authorized English Bible that would be acceptable to all parties. The Bishops' Bible had been authorized but was anything other than universally acceptable, while the Geneva Bible was widely accepted, especially among the Puritans, but was

not authorized. Ought not there to be a new translation
that would be both authorized and universally acceptable?

In spite of the Puritan source of this proposal, James in-
stinctively liked it. It appealed to his bookish tastes. He
had a temperamental feeling for the making of books. Editors,
revisers, translators and the like were men who commanded
his respect. To have a hand in a grander-than-ever translation of the Bible was a prospect that fired his imagination.
To him it was what the building of Versailles was to be to
Louis XIV.

Nevertheless, perhaps if he had known the magnitude of
the undertaking that was to develop out of Reynolds's suggestion, he might have thought twice about it. It is fortunate
that he received no encouragement to hesitate. The results
of such hesitation might have deprived posterity forever
of the version that bears his name. It is said that when
Henry III of France conceived the idea of having a French
translation on a similarly elaborate scale he took the precaution of first asking one of his advisers how long it would
take and how much it would cost. The adviser, mentioning
a staggering price, informed the French King that the work
would take thirty years; that thirty learned divines would
be required to do it; and that he could not guarantee that
the result would be entirely free of faults. That French
translation was never made.

We may rejoice that the English Court was less reflective.
The Scot on the English throne was anything other than
canny. He was a notorious spendthrift. When the work
began, the royal treasury, thanks to James's spendthrift policy,
was conveniently empty. He contributed little or nothing
towards the cost of the translation. There was an abortive
attempt to defray the expenses by an appeal for funds to
the bishops and clergy. When nothing came of this, James
advised the bestowal of ecclesiastical preferment for the

encouragement of the translators, and this seems to have worked well. The translators were also entertained free of charge at the universities of Oxford and Cambridge, where they dined in hall. On the whole, therefore, the work must have been done with remarkable and commendable economy.

Not that James would have grudged financial provision for the enterprise. He would have grudged it less than he grudged the principal disbursements that monarchs of his day were expected to make. War, for instance. James was a pacifist by temper and conviction—the only pacifist ever to have wielded England's scepter. It was said that his horror of the sword was due to his mother's fright at the supper party when, carrying in her womb him who was to unite the crowns of England and Scotland, she beheld her lover dragged to his assassination. Be that as it may, James certainly hated war and never doubted the superiority of pen over sword. He took more pride in the Biblical achievement that was dedicated to him than he had taken in England's recent spectacular victory over Spain.

In keeping with his pacific policy, James also attempted to relax the restrictions that had been imposed by Elizabeth upon his Papist subjects. The attempt, because it disclosed that Rome had a more considerable allegiance in England than had commonly been supposed, caused widespread panic and a demand for stricter measures of security against all suspected of loyalty to the Pope. Meanwhile, however, the relaxations briefly introduced had raised the most lively Papist hopes for the reconquest of England. The Papists, when these more liberal provisions were withdrawn and stricter laws than ever reintroduced against them, were furious. Their rage was picturesquely expressed, and in the eyes of the vast majority of Englishmen their intentions were forever revealed, in the Gunpowder Plot in 1605. This was an outstanding enterprise for its day, exhibiting only too clearly the kind of vitality that characterized the perpetrators. The old-fashioned method of rebellion had been to kill the King. Gone were the days when that was enough. Now, if you wanted to seize power, you had to destroy the entire Parliament as well. This was exactly the purpose for which the Gunpowder Plot was designed, and it was almost successful. Since its success would have made it impossible for the King James Version to have been written, it is worth while looking briefly at the circumstances—for long afterwards regarded by many as a miraculous intervention by divine Providence—by which its success was averted.

The conspirators in the Gunpowder Plot were, with only one exception, Roman Catholics of good family. The exception was the trusted servant of one of them. At least two Jesuits were directly involved in the plot. The physical preparations were made with great professional skill by men who had served as officers in the Spanish army in the Netherlands, and they included the placing of more than a ton and a half of gunpowder in thirty-six barrels concealed, in March, 1605, under coal and fagots in a vault that had been hired by one of the conspirators immediately under the House of Lords. The conspirators in this ambitious enterprise then dispersed. For months nothing happened. Then, on October 26, Lord Monteagle received a letter that is believed—though its authorship has never been definitely established—to have come from his brother-in-law, Francis Tresham, one of the conspirators. Monteagle had formerly been engaged in Romanist plots against the government, and the letter was for the purpose of warning him, since he had not been let in on the secret of this one, to avoid his death by absenting himself from Parliament. It appealed to him to "devise some excuse to shift of your attendance of this Parliament, for God and man hath concurred to punish the wickedness of this time. And think not slightly of this advertisement, but retire yourself into your country, where you may expect the event in safety, for though there be no appearance of any stir, yet I say they shall receive a terrible blow, the Parliament, and yet they shall not see who hurts them. This counsel is not to be contemned, because it may do you good and can do you no harm, for the danger is past as soon as you have burnt this letter: and I hope God will give you the grace to make good use of it, to whose holy protection I commend you."

Unfortunately for the author of the kindly thought so piously expressed in this letter of good counsel, and for his fellow conspirators, Lord Monteagle had given up his interest in such murky plots and had become a loyal subject of James. He therefore immediately showed the letter to some of the King's ministers. Apparently no one could at first guess the nature of the plot that had been so calculatingly hatched; but at last, on November 4, the eve of the day for which the dramatic spectacle was scheduled by the conspirators, a search was made. Barrels of gunpowder were discovered in the building where Parliament was to meet. Within a few days the conspirators were rounded up. Some were killed in the process; eight others were executed, while Tresham died in the Tower. One of the Jesuits known to have been implicated was also executed; others escaped. Arrest may have been facilitated by the fanaticism of one of the conspirators who tried, after the failure of the plot was known to him, to incite further trouble—in a desperate bid for last-minute victory— by lying to a fellow conspirator that the King was dead.

These doings bred such distrust of Papists that not only during the rest of the reign of James but for at least two hundred years after his death, the vast majority of Englishmen looked upon the slightest expression of sympathy with Rome in much the same light that Americans today look upon such an expression of sympathy with Moscow. Rome had shown her hand and the English did not like the look of it. The mood is reflected in the "dedicatory epistle" in the King James Version, in which the translators refer to the security they enjoyed in face of being "traduced by Popish persons at home or abroad." For generations afterwards there were Englishmen who would scarcely trust a Papist to boil an egg. Even when toleration came into fashion in England, people were quick to point out that there must be no toleration of that intolerance of which Rome was the symbol, and on the subject of Popery even the most liberal-minded generally had considerable reservations. It was accounted evidence of weak judgment, perhaps even lack of character, to express any sentiment on the subject that was not vividly and solidly against. The feeling is expressed in an adaptation of Psalm cxxiv published [1] a generation after the plot. This adaptation is described as a paraphrase of the psalm "By waye of thanksgiving for our great deliverances from the Papists Powder Plot." It was apparently intended to be sung to a tune now traditional in Scotland, where it is known as The Old 124th, which was taken from a French Psalter of 1551. The tune itself, being well suited to congregational singing, is so impressive in solemn simplicity that it is here reproduced to indicate the effect of this paraphrase of the psalm sung as an expression of England's deliverance from the plot to subjugate her once again to the Pope:

1 By I. Vícars, 1631.

A-men.

Now May England
Confess and say surely;
    If that the Lord
    Had not our cause maintain'd,
If that the Lord
Had not our state sustain'd
    When Antichrist
    Against us furiouslie
Made his proud Brags
And said, we should all die.

Not long ago
They had devoured us all:
    And swallowed quicke
    For ought that we could deeme:
Such was their rage
As we might well esteeme:
    And as proud floods
    With mighty force do fall;
So their mad-rage
Our lives had brought to thrall.

Our King and Queene
The Prince and princely race;
    Their Counsell grave,
    And chief Nobility;

The Judges wise
And prime tribe of Levi;
    With all the prudent
    Statesmen of the Land,
By Pouder fierce
Had perished out of hand.

The raging streames
Of Rome with roaring noise
    Had with great woe
    Ore-whelm'd us in the Deepe:
But, blessèd Lord,
Thou didst us safely keep
    From bloodie teeth
    And their devouring jawes:
Which as a prey
Had griped us in their clawes.

But, as a bird,
Out of the fowler's grin,[2]
    Escapes away:
    Right so it far'd with us;
Broke were their nets
And Wee have scapèd, Thus,
    God that made heaven
    And earth was our Helpe then
His mercy saved us
From these wicked men.

O let us therefore
With all thanks and praise,
    Sing joyfully
    To Christ our heavenly King:
Whose wisedome high
This fact to light did bring:
    Grant then ô Lord
    We doe thee humbly pray

2 gin

We may accord
To praise thy name alway.
                        AMEN.

Such verses expressed the feelings of England in regard to
the Gunpowder Plot and what was believed to be England's
providential deliverance from the revolution it had been so
carefully devised to incite. In view of all this, it is not difficult
to imagine how unpopular James was when, through neglect
of the navy and through other such prestige-losing policies, he
allowed Papist Spain to recover a good deal of the power of
which it had been divested by Elizabeth's England. James,
even apart from his pacifist tendencies, had little notion of
the importance to England of the navy. His Scotland had
never thought in such terms. Perhaps almost any other Scotsman—indeed perhaps almost any other human being—called
at that time to the English throne, would have been quick to
learn. Not only was James too obstinate to learn the importance to England of her navy; he let the navy decline from
its Elizabethan splendor to such an extent that pirates raided
English ships with impunity even in the English Channel,
while Spaniards openly laughed at James's pedantically diplomatic protests against the treatment his subjects were receiving. He even had England's seafaring hero, Sir Walter
Raleigh, beheaded to appease the pride of the Spanish ambassador.

What a monarch to bequeath his name to the most influential version of the Bible! He had united the crowns of
England and Scotland and made himself exceedingly and de-
servedly unpopular on both sides of the Border. Yet the
irony of all this is perhaps more apparent than real. Perhaps
James, who has been called "the wisest fool in Christendom,"
saw beyond his own vanity and folly. He had tried his hand,
in his earlier days, at translating the Psalms into verse, and is

said to have translated about thirty of them. His metrical version, characteristically entitled "The Psalmes of King David Translated by King Iames," was never approved by the Scots, who for nearly a hundred years after the Reformation clung to a metrical version the Reformers had brought from Geneva, and then, in 1650, adopted, with many variations, one by Francis Rous, an English Puritan. James's metrical version of the Psalms was, however, sanctioned by his successor, Charles I, and bound with the so-called "Laud's Liturgy"—the reading of which in 1637 at St Giles's, Edinburgh, was the occasion of a riot. There is no doubt, therefore, of the genuineness of James's interest in Biblical translation. The version of the English Bible that was done under his direction and dedicated to him might have had a worthier monarch's name for posterity to attach to it; yet perhaps in all human history it could not have had the name of any monarch to whom the enterprise of translating the Bible was dearer to his heart. It is indeed no small part of the romance of the story of the Bible that it has been transmitted by weak men and yet, as no other book, has strengthened the hearts and minds of its readers.

XI

THE MAKING OF THE
KING JAMES VERSION

T HE LEADING FEATURES of the scheme for making the great new version of the English Bible were suggested by James himself. The universities of Oxford and Cambridge were to play a prominent part in it. It was intended that the result of the translators' labors should be approved by the bishops and other leading churchmen, by the Privy Council, and—needless to say—by James himself. There is no evidence, however, that the work was ever in fact formally reviewed in this way.

What happened was as follows. The names of proposed translators were submitted to the King, who announced, in July, 1604, that he had appointed certain learned men, fifty-four in number, to translate the Bible into English. Some, at least, of the translators began their work about this time; but it was not until 1607 that it was formally undertaken. The number of men actually engaged upon it was forty-seven, and of these several died before the work was done. The forty-seven translators were divided into six companies, two of which met at Oxford, two at Cambridge, and two at Westminster. To each company was assigned a portion of the work of translation. We shall see in the next chapter how it was actu-

ally parcelled out. Eventually, twelve delegates—two from
each of the six companies—met together daily for nine months
at Stationers' Hall, London, as a revision committee. In
comparison with the main body of translators, for whom no
adequate financial provision was made, this committee was
privileged: each of its members received from the King's
Printer during this period the sum of thirty shillings a week.
Then there was a final revision by a committee of two, consisting of Miles Smith, one of the translators, and Thomas Bilson,
appointed from outside their number.

In 1604, Richard Bancroft had become Archbishop of
Canterbury. Bancroft, who for five years before that date had
been virtually acting as such, on account of the age and in-
capacity of John Whitgift, his archiepiscopal predecessor, had
for long been known as a determined enemy of the Puritans.
Indeed, he had been their vigorous opponent twenty years
earlier, and as a champion of the view that episcopacy is of
divine institution, he had likewise opposed the Scottish Presbyterians. It was almost certainly he who was responsible for
drafting the elaborate instructions with which the translators
were provided.

These regulations, designed chiefly to insure that the new
version should be a Church of England version rather than
one to reflect the opinions of this or that party within the
Church, were fourteen in number. One of the provisions was
that the version to be undertaken should be an elaborate revision of the Bishops' Bible rather than an entirely fresh
translation. Yet this was not to be held as in any way restrict-
ing the freedom of the translators to make corrections. There
was to be complete freedom to amend the older version where
amendment was plainly necessary; but the older version was
to be kept in mind as a basis for the work, and not departed
from without reason. The translators were also enjoined to
see that the names of the prophets and other names in the

Biblical text were kept as near as possible to the original forms.

This last rule sounds a sensible one. Its application, however, was not always attended by happy results. It was the cause of troubling the reader with two names for the same person: for instance, Elijah and Elias, the Hebrew and Greek forms, respectively. The older versions had sometimes mitigated the fearsome aspect of some of the Hebrew names; but the regulations required the new version to grant the reader no such indulgence. In Genesis xxxv.8, for instance, the older versions had said that the oak under which Deborah was buried "was called the oak of lamentation." Now the translators felt obliged to say that the oak "was called Allon-bachuth."

The Geneva Version had used the word "Congregation" in preference to "Church." The issue is an extremely technical one which it is impossible, and in any case unnecessary, to discuss here. It is noteworthy, however, that the instructions to the new translators were that "the old ecclesiastical words" were to be kept, and that when a word had "divers significations" that was to be kept which "had been most commonly used by the most eminent Fathers." It is not surprising that rules of this sort gave rise to questions of interpretation, especially since such rules were really weighted against the Puritans who, it was feared, would throw ecclesiastical tradition to the winds. It seems it was at Cambridge that a question under this head was first raised. Bancroft had no difficulty in dealing with it: it was the King's pleasure, he replied, that three or four of the most eminent divines of the University should supervise the work to see that rules relating to such matters should be obeyed. A similar conservatism lay behind the rule that the traditional division into chapters should be altered as little as possible, and preferably not at all. The only marginal notes to be allowed were such as might be necessary for the explanation of those Hebrew and Greek words whose meaning could not without circumlocution be expressed in the text, and such as might occasionally seem fitting for the purpose of referring from one passage of Scripture to another.

The rule concerning marginal notes was of great significance. Previous versions of the English Bible had been furnished with marginal commentaries, sometimes extensive. It had been determined from the outset that the new version should be presented as far as possible without any such apparatus. The text, it was held, ought to speak for itself. The marginal commentaries of the earlier versions had been much associated with controversy. Their design had been for the most part the defense of this or that position in controversy, so that they had made the Bibles to which they were attached the Bibles of this or that party. The Douai Bible, for instance, still in use among Roman Catholics, carries to this day these polemic notes which in its case are aimed, of course, "at the Protestants." The purpose of the sanction against marginal notes was to eliminate party propaganda within the covers of the Bible. Some have felt that it might have been better to omit also the brief explanatory notes that the regulations permitted.

The retention in the King James Version of the conventional system of chapter division has been much criticized. The convention was not, we have seen, a very ancient one. It went back no earlier than the thirteenth century. Devised at a time when interest in the Bible had been revived among scholars at the recently founded University of Paris, but long before the renaissance of learning and the Reformation had brought a deeper knowledge and fresh understanding of the Bible, it had little to be said for it except that it was customary. In many cases it obscures the sense. This was excusable in the thirteenth century, when the sense was not clearly understood. There was less to be said for it in the seventeenth century, when scholars had learned better. But as the original preface to the King James Version reminded the reader, it is notorious that anything new, especially in religion, "is sure to be misconstrued, and in danger to be condemned." Some modern versions, we shall see, depart from these older methods of division into chapter and verse that were preserved in the King James Version. The value of retaining the old divisions was, however, by no means entirely negligible. At a time when the Bible was becoming at last really known to the people and referred to by many in daily conversation, the division into chapter and verse, arbitrary though it was, provided a handy means of reference. It was of some importance, too, to have, in so external a matter as the "dress" of the Bible, that link with the immediate past that the preservation of such a custom could provide.

It is a pity that the preface to the King James Version is not printed in modern editions. Entitled "The Translators to the Reader," it is attributed to Miles Smith. Though far too lengthy, it provided a useful explanation of the project. This was summed up as follows: "Truly, good Christian reader, we never thought from the beginning that we should need to make a new translation, nor yet to make of a bad one a good one, . . . but to make a good one better, or out of many good ones one principal good one, not justly to be excepted against; that hath been our endeavour, that our work. To that purpose were many chosen, that were greater in other men's eyes than in their own, and that sought the truth rather than their own praise." The number of these men was "not too many, lest one should trouble another; and yet many, lest many things might haply escape them."

The value of translation is described in these terms: "'Translation it is that openeth the window, to let in the light; that breaketh the shell, that we may eat the kernel;

that putteth aside the curtain, that we may look into the most
holy place; that removeth the cover of the well, that we may
come by the water; even as Jacob rolled away the stone from
the mouth of the well, by which means the flocks of Laban
were watered." Without translation of the Bible, it was affirmed, the people are like the children at Jacob's well, with
plenty of water at their feet but thirsty for lack of a bucket.

The Bible itself is extolled as "not only an armour, but also
a whole armoury of weapons, both offensive and defensive;
whereby we may save ourselves and put the enemy to flight.
It is not an herb, but a tree, or rather a whole paradise of
trees of life, which bring forth fruit every month, and the
fruit thereof is for meat, and the leaves for medicine." The
fourth-century Greek Father, St Basil, is recalled as having
likened the Bible to a "physician's shop" containing "preserv-
atives against poisoned heresies."

The plan of action for the translators was that in each of
the six companies every member should first work on a chapter or chapters individually and then meet his colleagues so
that the company might decide together upon variations and
disputed points and eventually agree upon what should stand.
Then, when a company had so completed a whole book of the
Bible, it was to pass on the result to another company, and so
on, for review, for "His Majesty is very careful on this point."
If a company, in reviewing the work of another, should find
cause to question the rendering at any point, it was to notify
the responsible company accordingly, marking the place in
question and submitting reasons for the dissent or doubt. If
the difference could not be so resolved, the question was to
be held in abeyance for the general meeting of the leaders of
each company to be held at the end of the proceedings. Provision was also made for inquiries upon particularly difficult
points to be directed to "outside" scholars known to be spe-
cialists on the subjects in question. Every bishop in the coun-

try, moreover, was to admonish his clergy to direct all persons who might be skilled in the ancient tongues to send their particular observations to the appropriate company. It would require more than human daring to make such an invitation in our own day; but in seventeenth-century England fewer people made pretensions to literacy, and those who did felt a less urgent necessity to prove them. Each company was to be under the direction of a churchman eminent by his official position: the Regius Professors of Hebrew and Greek at Oxford for the two Oxford companies respectively; their counterparts at Cambridge for the Cambridge companies; and the Dean of Westminster and the Dean of Chester for the companies at Westminster. There was also a regulation providing that when an earlier English version—Tyndale's, Coverdale's, Matthew's, the Great Bible, or the Geneva Bible—agreed better than did the Bishops' Bible with the text, that version was to be followed. But in fact, besides these earlier English versions, the translators had before them a great many other versions, including, for instance, Luther's and Zwingli's German translations, Italian and Spanish translations, the Latin Vulgate, and several other Latin versions. And besides the best Hebrew and Greek manuscripts available, which of course provided the basis of the whole undertaking, the translators also used the Syriac New Testament and the Aramaic Targums. In respect of both equipment and method, therefore, the translation was made according to the highest standards of scholarship and the most advanced knowledge of the day.

XII

THE MAKERS OF THE
KING JAMES VERSION

THE FINEST EQUIPMENT and the most up-to-date methods are always worthless in themselves, apart from the caliber of the men who use them. What of the forty-seven men to whom was entrusted the main burden of the work of translation? They were divided, we have seen, into six companies. As it is of paramount importance and interest to know something about them, let us consider the six companies in turn, looking briefly at the men who composed them and paying a little more attention to some who, for one reason or another, are of special interest.[1]

The First Company, which met at Westminster, and to which was assigned that portion of the Old Testament from Genesis to Kings, consisted of ten men. The first of these, who presided, was Lancelot Andrewes, Dean of Westminster, a man who, quite apart from his work on the translation, is accounted one of the foremost figures in the history of the English Church. He stands, indeed, as the very pattern of English churchmanship at its best. Not only was he an ex-

[1] Despite much scholarly research on the subject, the identity of the translators is, in a few cases, in doubt. This question is of so little importance to the general reader that no detailed account of it need be given here.

tremely accurate and painstaking scholar, the master of fifteen languages; he was a preacher of great power and, not least, a man whose high sense of churchmanship was exhibited in a deep and mature personal piety. This piety was expressed in his beautiful *Private Prayers,* a classic of Anglican devotion that witnesses to the profound historical sense that lay behind the lyrical qualities of this great man.

Born in 1555 in the parish of All Hallows, Barking, Andrewes went to Cambridge, where he became a Fellow of Pembroke Hall. His preaching gifts attracted the attention of Queen Elizabeth, who offered him in turn the bishoprics of Salisbury and Ely. These he declined, being unwilling to consent to certain conditions imposed. He became, however, Dean of Westminster in 1601. It is to the great credit of James that he recognized the qualities of Lancelot Andrewes, who, under him, became Bishop of Chichester in 1605, Bishop of Ely in 1609, and in 1619 Bishop of Winchester, then the richest see in England as well as one of the most ancient. His linguistic gifts came out in his sermons, which were enriched with Greek and Latin quotations. It is said that during his vacations he would seek out a master of some language he did not already know and devote the time at his disposal to learning it. One of his contemporaries once declared he might have been "Interpreter General at Babel." He held a high doctrine of the Eucharist and desired the English Church to enjoy, besides the benefits of the Reformation, an impressive and orderly ceremonial, with lights, incense, and all the externals of historic Catholic usage. At the same time he was an indefatigable and effective controversialist against Cardinal Bellarmine, the leading Jesuit theologian of his day. He never married. His hospitality was a byword: "My Lord of Winchester keeps Christmas all the year round," it was said. Yet he knew, too, the practical advantages of fasting, as may be seen from the anecdote about him that reveals also a wry sense of humor. At Cambridge, an alderman could not keep awake during sermon in his parish church and found it embarrassing to be roused from his slumbers and publicly rebuked from the pulpit. He asked Andrewes what he ought to do. Andrewes apparently suspected that the alderman was too well fed: as another English divine once remarked, "it is hard work preaching to two pounds of beef and a pot of porter." So he advised him to dine sparingly. Apparently this still failed to produce the desired state of wakefulness during sermon, and the alderman again appealed to Andrewes for advice. This time the prescription was even more to the point: the alderman was told that fasting in his case was evidently not enough; he had better also take a nap *before* approaching the mysteries of the Word. It is said that the result was very satisfactory.

Such, then, were the qualifications and character of the president of the First Company. The remaining nine members were: John Overall, Hadrian à Saravia, Richard Clarke, John Layfield, Robert Tighe, Francis Burleigh, Geoffrey King, Richard Thompson, and William Bedwell.

Overall, who was born in 1559, became a Fellow of Trinity College, and Regius Professor of Divinity, at Cambridge. At the time of his work on the translation he was Dean of St Paul's. Later, under James, he became, first, Bishop of Lichfield, in 1614, and then, four years later, Bishop of Norwich. But James never approved of him, for Overall, steeped in medieval learning, defended a traditional political theory about the nature of kingship that was at variance with the Tudor conception of the Divine Right of Kings which James wished to uphold. Overall taught that when, after a lawful revolution—and such a revolution he believed to be possible— a new government was firmly established, it could claim the obedience of the people as a duty to God. His teaching on this subject had interesting consequences, for when, after the

English Revolution in 1688, William and Mary were invited to the throne, there were some conservatives who, though at first they felt they could not in conscience take the oath of allegiance, were persuaded by reading Overall that it was their duty to do so.

Saravia was a distinguished foreigner. Born in 1531 of Hispano-Flemish Protestant parentage, he became a pastor at Antwerp. The religious disturbances in the Low Countries drove him eventually to England for a time; but he returned to Holland as Professor of Divinity at the University of Leyden. In 1585 he was again in England, where he became at length a prominent champion of episcopacy. One of his writings was among the first to stress the importance of preaching the Gospel to the heathen in far-off lands, an activity to which, at that time, Protestants had not given the attention they later lavished upon it. When work on the translation began he was Vicar of Lewisham. Since English was not his native tongue, his value to the company of which he was a member lay less in his ability to turn the Bible into English than in his general linguistic skill, for which he was famous.

Of the other members of the First Company, not the least interesting is Bedwell, who was the father of Arabic studies in England. Born in 1561 or 1562, he devoted many years to compiling an Arabic lexicon. He rightly believed that a knowledge of Arabic was of great importance for an understanding of the exact sense of Hebrew words. Not only was he a pioneer of Arabic studies in England; his activities as an orientalist included work on a Persian dictionary. Nor were his interests confined to his special field. Mathematics attracted him also, and he fostered the use of a ruler invented by his uncle for geometrical purposes, which came to be known as "Bedwell's Ruler."

The Second Company, which met at Cambridge, undertook the Old Testament from Chronicles to the Song of Solomon.

It comprised eight members: Edward Lively, John Richard-son, Lawrence Chatterton, Francis Dillingham, Thomas Harrison, Roger Andrewes, Robert Spalding, and Andrew Byng. All were Cambridge men.

Edward Lively, who was Regius Professor of Hebrew, died in 1605, in the midst of the preliminaries of the translation, leaving his eleven children destitute. Chatterton, the first head of Emmanuel College, Cambridge, which was founded in 1584, was one of the four Puritan divines who took part in the Hampton Court Conference. When he adopted Puritan opinions in his student days, his father, who clung to Rome, wrote him to say that if he would renounce them he would receive all the care an indulgent father could bestow; but in case young Lawrence should feel disinclined to alter his opinions, his father enclosed with the letter a shilling for the purpose of buying a beggar's wallet. Far from being intimidated by this, however, the young student not only persevered in his opinions but when, late in life, he feared he might not be succeeded as Master of Emmanuel by someone of Puritan views, he resigned to insure the appointment of a successor after his own heart. Chatterton survived, however, not only the successor to whom he had given place, but two further occupants of the position. He is said to have lived to the age of 103 in such good health that even in his last years he could read his Greek Testament without spectacles and carry on conversation without any sign of the repetitiousness that is associated with the talk of some elderly men.

Dillingham was a great Greek scholar. The English universities are naturally tenacious of long tradition, and it was still the custom for disputations to be conducted in Latin, according to medieval practice. Dillingham, however, is reported to have debated in Greek. Harrison, a known Puritan, was famed for his meekness and charitable attitude towards his adversaries. A story recounted about him illustrates this.

When it was reported to him that one of his students had abused him in a speech, Harrison asked quietly whether the student had actually named him, Thomas Harrison, as the object of his venom. On receiving the reply that the student had not in fact referred to him by name, Harrison quietly observed: "Then I do not believe that he meant me." Roger Andrewes was a brother of Lancelot, and Robert Spalding the successor of Edward Lively.

The Third Company met at Oxford. Consisting of seven members, it was responsible for the remaining books of the Old Testament, that is, Isaiah to Malachi. The members were: John Harding, John Reynolds, Thomas Holland, Richard Killbye, Miles Smith, Richard Brett, and Richard Fairclough.

Reynolds was not only the most notable member of the Third Company; to him may be attributed the inspiration for the whole project. For, it will be remembered, it was he whose remark at the Hampton Court Conference, on the desirability of putting out a new translation of the Bible that should command the approval of all parties, set the wheels in motion. A Devonshire man, born in 1549, Reynolds became a leading English exponent of Calvinistic doctrine. He was also in sympathy with the Puritan cause, of which, at the conference, he was the principal champion. So great, however, was the esteem in which he was held even by his enemies that these had to admit, grudgingly perhaps, both the remarkable sweep of his learning and the striking probity of his character. As for his friends, they had a saying that it was hard to decide whether it was his scholarship or his piety that ought to command the greater admiration. It is not surprising, therefore, that Reynolds, despite James's distaste for his Puritan opinions, was from the first marked out for a prominent part in the making of the new Bible. Besides his role in this work he has many claims to historical distinction, not least, surely, the fact that he numbered among his students Richard Hooker, who is generally admitted to be a classic exponent of the Anglican position. Unfortunately, Reynolds died in 1607, at the age of fifty-eight, while the work of translation was in progress. It was generally believed that his extreme devotion to the task hastened his death. Even during his illness his colleagues met at his lodgings every week to go over their work and compare notes. Some of his friends, seeing his extremely emaciated condition, begged him not to throw away his life for the cause of learning. But he greeted their well-intentioned concern for him only with a few wise words and a smile.

Thomas Holland, who also took a prominent part in the work, died soon after its completion. Richard Kilbye was a friend of the famous Isaac Walton, who has an anecdote about him. A young preacher in Derbyshire once treated his congregation of simple country folk to a sermon that consisted chiefly of criticism of the new translation. No doubt hoping to impress his people with his own learning, the young clergyman gave them three reasons why a certain word should have been translated otherwise. Kilbye sent for the youthful preacher afterwards and told him he might have given them more nourishing food for their souls, adding that as for his three reasons, the translators had carefully taken every one of them into account but had concluded that they did not outweigh thirteen reasons for translating the word as had been done. Miles Smith, an extreme Puritan, is noteworthy as the author of the Translators' Preface.

The Gospels, the Acts of the Apostles, and the Revelation of St John the Divine, were entrusted to the Fourth Company, which also met at Oxford and comprised eight members. These were: Thomas Ravis, who presided, George Abbot, Richard Edes, Giles Thomson, Henry Savile, John Peryn, Ralph Ravens, and John Harmer. It seems that, on account of the impoverishment of this company through the death or resignation of some of its members, it was replenished by the later addition of Leonard Hutton and also of James Montague, who was appointed to assist.

Ravis, noted for his antipathy to the Puritans, succeeded Bancroft as Bishop of London, when the latter became Archbishop of Canterbury. His policy followed closely that of his predecessor. "By the help of Jesus," he affirmed, "I will not leave one preacher in my diocese who doth not subscribe and conform." He felt, as did others who shared his attitude, that the strength of the Reformation in England depended upon unity of practice as well as upon unity of principle, and he regarded the Puritans as threatening that unity. He died in December, 1609, before the work of translation was completed, and was buried in St Paul's. Edes died at a much earlier stage of the proceedings, in November, 1604. As chaplain to Queen Elizabeth and later to James, his suavity had been much admired at court. Giles Thomson, also a royal chaplain, and registrar of England's highest and most ancient order of chivalry, the Most Noble Order of the Garter, is reputed to have been very diligent in the matter of the translation. The two most notable members of this company, however, were Abbot and Savile.

George Abbot, born in 1562, was the son of a cloth-worker. At the beginning of the proceedings he was Dean of Winchester and Master of University College, Oxford. His marked Puritan sympathies made him distasteful to the opposite party in the English Church. In 1606, however, he defended, against Overall, certain political views congenial to James's own opinions on the nature of kingship. He went on a mission to Scotland in 1608 for the purpose of endeavoring to make episcopal government acceptable to the Scots. It ought to be borne in mind that the Scottish Reformers, like the continental theologians who inspired much of their

thought, had not opposed episcopacy in principle. John Knox
and his associates, in planning the government of the Reformed Kirk, had expressly provided for a body of superin-
tendents whose functions were episcopal. Bishops within the
Presbyterian system are not unknown today, and indeed their
absence has been dictated by political circumstances rather
than by any fundamental objection to bishops on the part of
well-informed and historically-minded Presbyterians. The
Scots were, however, not without reason, suspicious of James,
and the bitter prejudice that grew up within the Kirk was
largely the fruit of the policy pursued by him and his immediate successors to the English throne. Yet in itself there was
nothing in episcopacy that the Scots needed to distrust, and
from a man of Abbot's sympathies it could be made to seem
quite wholesome. At any rate, Abbot was successful in his
mission, and the way seemed open for the fulfilment of one of
James's greatest desires—the union of the Church of England
and the Church of Scotland. From this point onwards, pre-
ferments in the Church came in swift succession to Abbot,
culminating in his advancement in 1611 to the archiepiscopal
See of Canterbury. In this high office he proved himself to be
fearless in speaking out against what he disapproved, and
since his Puritan views were becoming less and less fashionable among the upper classes he found himself increasingly
isolated. But he persevered, and his courage in opposing even
the King on a matter of principle won him the respect of
English churchmen of all parties.

A mishap befell him at the age of sixty. One day, while out
hunting, he aimed an arrow at a deer, and the arrow glanced
from a tree and killed a gamekeeper. The latter had been
cautioned to keep out of the way, and his death was a pure
accident. It was, however, a source of great distress to Abbot,
who is said to have imposed upon himself a monthly fast for
the rest of his life besides bestowing a liberal annuity on the

victim's widow. However, according to Canon Law, he had become a "man of blood" and thereby disqualified from the service of the Church. Suspended for a time, he was arraigned before a commission of six bishops and four laymen, whose opinion was divided on the verdict. James, however, cast a decision in his favor, so that he was dispensed from the technical irregularity. Restored to his position, Abbot did not, however, diminish his firmness in resisting royal edicts of which he disapproved. His severity towards clerical delinquents was resented by many of the lower clergy; yet besides being a man of such outstanding integrity he is also said to have had a "very fatherly presence." It was he who, on the death of James, crowned Charles I. He had a great love for Guildford, his native place, whither he was taken on his death in 1633 for burial. All in all, he must have been a singularly impressive man.

Sir Henry Savile was born in 1549. An Oxford man, who became Warden of Merton College and Provost of Eton, he acquired in his youth a great reputation as a scholar. After travelling in Europe, where he collected manuscripts and rare books which he later contributed to the Bodleian Library, he was appointed Greek tutor to Queen Elizabeth. It was, of course, rare in those days for women to have education of this kind. Sir Henry's own wife had none of it, and it is said that when he was working on his monumental edition of the works of St Chrysostom she complained with some bitterness of the enormous devotion he lavished upon his work.

"I wish I were a book," she said. "Then you would a little more respect me."

When her husband took ill, she, thinking Chrysostom was killing him, threatened to burn the work.

"So to do were great pity," suggested a tactful scholar-friend of Sir Henry's.

"Why?" she asked. "Who was Chrysostom?"

"One of the sweetest preachers since the time of the Apostles," explained her husband's friend.

"Then I would not burn him," replied the lady generously.

But perhaps Lady Savile never overcame her jealousy. When the edition of Chrysostom was eventually issued (in eight folio volumes from her husband's private press at Eton, at his own personal expense of about eight thousand pounds, in type especially imported from Holland), she probably welcomed the event only as the death of a rival.

Sir Henry Savile, from his portraits at Eton and Oxford, seems to have been a handsome man. He was also a versatile one, being interested in mathematics and the new sciences as well as in the humanities. He founded at Oxford new professorships in geometry and astronomy. His Chrysostom was the first really grand-scale work of learning, apart from the Bible, to be printed in England. From a commercial point of view it must have been a failure. At nine pounds a copy the cost was prohibitive to most buyers, at a time when you could buy fifty or sixty carcasses of mutton for such a sum of money. Sir Henry received his knighthood from James about the time of his appointment as one of the translators of the Bible; but he is said to have declined further honors. The death of his son about the same time deeply grieved him, and it was this bereavement that stimulated his resolve to devote his fortune as well as his labors to the cause of learning. He died in 1622.

The Fifth Company, which met at Westminster, was entrusted with the rest of the New Testament; that is, all the Epistles. Its seven members were: William Barlow, Ralph Hutchinson, John Spencer, Roger Fenton, Michael Rabbett, Thomas Sanderson, and William Dakins.

Barlow was a member of the Hampton Court Conference and its historian. He became Dean of Chester shortly afterwards and was, at the time of his death in 1613, Bishop of

Lincoln. He had been much admired by Elizabeth, who said of a sermon of his on the plow that, though his text was "taken from the cart," his talk was good instruction for the court. Hutchinson, a Londoner by birth, became President of St John's College, Oxford, in the chapel of which he is buried. He died within two years of his appointment as one of the translators. Spencer became President of Corpus Christi College, Oxford, and represented the party that disliked Puritanism as much as Popery. Fenton, a Lancashire man, born in 1565, was a popular preacher in his day. He became a Fellow of Pembroke Hall, Cambridge. One of his admirers, who writes of the deep grief felt at his death, refers to the "natural majesty of his style, like a master bee without a sting."

In an earlier chapter we considered the varying degrees of esteem in which the Apocrypha has been held. Full provision for it was made, however, in the scheme for translation. The whole of the Sixth Company, consisting of seven members, were charged with this work. These members, who met at Cambridge, were: John Duport, William Branthwaite, Jeremiah Radcliffe, Samuel Ward, Andrew Downes, John Bois, and William Ward (or Warde) who was a Fellow of King's College, Cambridge.

These were all distinguished Cambridge men. Duport, whose family had come to Leicestershire from Caen, Normandy, was four times Vice-Chancellor of the University, where he became Master of Jesus College. Branthwaite was a Fellow of Emmanuel and later Master of Gonville and Caius College. Radcliffe was Vice-Master of Trinity. Samuel Ward became Master of Sidney Sussex College, which acquired a reputation as a breeding-ground of Puritanism. Oliver Cromwell was an undergraduate there.

John Bois, who was born at Nettlestead, Suffolk, in 1560, is reported to have been an extraordinarily precocious child, who could read the Hebrew Bible at the age of six and write the Hebrew alphabet with elegance. The legends of his precocity are matched by those relating to his industry. As an undergraduate at Cambridge he is said to have worked from four o'clock in the morning till eight at night. Having small-pox at the time of his election, in 1580, as a Fellow of St John's College, he was carried thither, it is said, in a blanket. About this time Bois thought of medicine as a career. The modern reader, learning of these public health arrangements, may be inclined to feel that the need for medical studies must have been urgent. Medicine was backward, it is true, and the physician lacked prestige in comparison with other learned professions. It was, however, already an honorable profession and was soon to become much more so, acquiring a dignity that was for long to be retained in England and en-hanced. The opinion held by Bois, which dissuaded him from pursuing a medical career, reflects, no doubt, the feeling of the age: it seemed to him that reading about diseases induces hypochondria. In any case Bois no doubt felt he was better suited to another kind of study, so he pursued that which led eventually to his appointment as one of the translators. Partly on account of his wife's improvidence he encountered some financial difficulties which, however, he overcame by adding still further to his labors. His indefatigability apparently agreed with him, for he lived to be eighty-three. He not only took part in the regular work of the Sixth Company; he as-sisted the Second also and was one of those who shared in the work of the general revision. He and Andrew Downes were the two delegates appointed from the Sixth Company to par-ticipate in the work of that committee that met for nine months at Stationers' Hall, London.

To the forty-seven translators accounted for in the six companies may be added the name of Thomas Bilson who, though not one of the translators, took part with Miles Smith in the work of final revision that was entrusted to these two men. It was Bilson who provided the summary at the head of each chapter, intended to indicate briefly the contents of the chapter. Born at Winchester, Bilson became a Fellow of New College, Oxford, and eventually Bishop of Winchester. He was descended from a German family having connections with the Duke of Bavaria. The interpretation of Christ's descent into hell was in those days a lively subject for theological controversy, and Bilson maintained that, contrary to the opinion of some who connected it with the dereliction on the cross—Christ is recorded as having declared himself on the cross to be forsaken by God—the descent into hell was not in order to suffer but in order to signalize his victory over the powers of evil. As Bilson would have put it, it was "to wrest the Keys of Hell out of the Devil's hands." Elizabeth encouraged him not to desert this doctrine. He also wrote ably in support of episcopacy. In June, 1616, he died, and is buried in Westminster Abbey.

A word may be said here about Hugh Broughton, a Biblical scholar of great eminence who nevertheless was not invited to participate in the proposed work. As early as 1593, Broughton had been trying to obtain support for a translation of the Bible he desired to undertake himself. It seems he had received some encouragement from eminent churchmen in this project; but Whitgift, then Archbishop of Canterbury, actively opposed it. There was no question of Broughton's learning and ability. He had sketched a plan for his projected work and he afterwards published independent translations of some of the books of the Bible, which no doubt the translators of the King James Version had before them together with the other documents at their disposal. But his attacks on the Bishops' Bible, though largely justified, were too outspoken for the liking of many. He is said to have been of the sweetest disposition when among his friends, and he was beloved by his students. But in controversy he was so waspish that his opponents could not stomach him. One of his contemporaries, Thomas Morton, who became Bishop of Durham, is said to have once greeted him with the request that he (Morton) be called at the outset of the conversation a dolt, a dullard, and any other such epithet that Broughton intended to bestow upon him, so that the course of the conversation itself might not be so frequently interrupted. Apparently Broughton took this in good part as a joke. But it did not improve his temper. His translation plan was not at all unpractical. He did not intend to tackle the whole Bible singlehanded: he was to have had five associates. After his plan had fallen through, he made it known that his services were available for the great new translation that was to be done. It seems there was nothing against him but the heat of his temper, and he was himself aware of this shortcoming, expressing on his deathbed his penitence for it. That such a great man should have been on this account excluded from a translation committee of some fifty men is not one of the more creditable of the arrangements. Had the temper of the others been unalterably serene they could have borne with his to the profit of the work. In the end they elicited only his criticism of the finished product, and this was, as might be expected, vitriolic. He counted the number of "idle words" in various passages for which, he said, the translators would have to render account in the Day of Judgment, and he prognosticated that the destination of Richard Bancroft, Archbishop of Canterbury, was hell.

XIII

THE KING JAMES VERSION
IN PRODUCTION

A T LAST, in 1611, the book that had for so long claimed the attention of the great team of scholars who so diligently labored upon its preparation, issued from the press of Robert Barker, Printer to the King's Most Excellent Majesty.

It was a handsome production. In folio, and printed in fine black Gothic letter, its fifteen hundred pages had a thickness of over three inches excluding binding. The type was set in double columns, and each page enclosed in rules measuring 9 inches wide by 14¼ inches long. Copies having sufficient margin to make them acceptable to book collectors as "fine and large" copies will be found to measure 10½ inches by 16½ inches to the page.

The title reads: *The Holy Bible, conteyning the Old Testament and the New: Newly Translated out of the originall Tongues: and with the former Translations diligently compared and revised, by his Majestie's speciall Commandement. Appointed to be read in churches.* This title forms the center of an engraving showing the figures of Moses and Aaron to the right and to the left respectively. At the corners appear the Four Evangelists. At the top is the name of God in Hebrew, below which appears the Sacred Dove, symbol of the Holy Spirit, and again below this the Lamb, symbol of Christ. At the foot of the page is the Pelican which, "vulning" herself, that is, wounding herself with her beak to feed her young with her own blood, is a traditional symbol of Christ's redeeming work, especially in the Eucharist. The New Testament is provided with a separate title within a woodcut border representing along one side the badges of the twelve tribes of Israel, and along the other the Twelve Apostles, with the emblems of the Four Evangelists. These, based on Revelation vi.4-10, are: a man for St Matthew, a lion for St Mark, an ox for St Luke, and an eagle for St John.

This great version of the English Bible dedicated to King James, has come to be universally known in England as the "Authorized Version." However, this designation is perhaps misleading. The work was certainly initiated and planned by the highest authorities in Church and State, with the intention that it should command, by reason of its excellence, univeral acceptance throughout the land. The book went forth accordingly with the highest approval of these authorities. It is indicated in the preliminary matter, however, that these words refer merely to the fact that the Scriptures contained in the book were set forth in a manner approved for reading in public worship.[1] So far as is known there was never any legal instrument conferring authority upon the version, though it was unquestionably intended to supersede all previous versions, whatsoever the measure of authority these had acquired. Its appearance was the subject of no Act of Parliament, no royal Proclamation, no Edict of Convocation, no Privy Council decision. The designation "Authorized Version" does less than justice to the kind of authority this version did in fact eventually

1 The version was described as "Appointed to be read in Churches."

command, which, springing rather from the fact that it gradually made its own way as a book whose excellence was admitted on all sides, was far greater than could have been conferred upon it by any legal instrument or official decree. If it is to be called the Authorized Version, let it be known that it was authorized, not by an edict imposed upon the people, but by popular acclamation. This bestowed upon the new version an authority so powerful and so real that it seems an understatement merely to call it authorized, for this suggests that it attained its position artificially.

It it a common supposition that the text of the King James Version has never varied. This is, however, far from the case. Because of a peculiar circumstance, even the first edition, printed in 1611, was not uniform. The first edition was really a pair of issues produced separately yet apparently at the same time. Twenty thousand copies were required. This was a very large number in those days—so large that probably no printing office in the country could fill the order in the time desired. At any rate, two issues came out, both standard, yet quite distinct in every leaf, and there were between them a great many, mostly minute, discrepancies. One of the more important of these, occurring at Ruth iii.15, gave the pair of issues their respective names. In one the text read: "he measured six *measures* of barley, and laid *it* on her: and hee [Boaz] went into the city." The other read: "and she [Ruth] went into the city." So the issues came to be known as the Great Hee Bible and the Great She Bible respectively. These two issues each came to be used as copy in making later editions of the King James Version, so causing the discrepancies to be repeated. As we are about to see, there were many further departures from the text. Which of the two original issues was the more completely correct is debatable.

In 1612 a beautiful quarto edition in Roman type was published, and also one in octavo whose appearance recalled that of the octavo copies of the Geneva Bible. A duodecimo edition of the King James Version of the New Testament appeared in 1611, and was followed by a quarto edition of this in 1612. As the new version gained favor, editions began to follow in rapid succession. By 1613 an edition had already more than three hundred variations from the two original issues. Revision was called for, and a revised edition appeared in 1629, followed by another revision in 1638.

These revisions did not by any means, however, eliminate error. Among the errors to be found in the 1638 revision (the first Cambridge edition in folio), was one at Acts vi.3, where the twelve apostles, requiring the help of "seven men of honest report, full of the Holy Ghost and wisdom" to help them in the work of the Church, call upon their fellow Christians generally to look out for these. The text should make the apostles say, referring to these candidates for the ministry, "whom we may appoint over this business." In the 1638 edition the text read, instead, "whom ye may appoint." It was alleged that Oliver Cromwell bribed the printers to the tune of one thousand pounds to falsify the text in the interests of his cause, for the error gave the appearance of Biblical support for the appointment of ministers of the Church by the people—a notion abhorrent to Anglicans and Scottish Presbyterians alike, but favored by Oliver Cromwell's party. On the whole, however, the 1638 edition showed evidence of extensive and careful revision, and it remained the standard text of the King James Version for well over a century. Then, in 1762, an edition prepared by Thomas Paris of Trinity College, Cambridge, and issued by the Cambridge Press, showed evidence of such diligent correction of the text, emendation and regularization of spelling and punctuation, and elimination of printers' errors, that it came to be called the Standard Edition. Much of the stock was destroyed in a bookseller's fire at Cambridge. It was followed, in 1769, by folio and quarto editions at Oxford, revised by Benjamin Blayney, Regius Professor of Hebrew in the University of Oxford. The text of these Oxford editions, which included modernization of the spelling, came to be known as the Oxford Standard. It is the text of the King James Version with which we are familiar today.

The number of editions of the King James Version between 1611 and 1800 was enormous. The catalogue of the British and Foreign Bible Society enumerates nearly a thousand editions of that version of the Bible or part of it that saw the light before the close of that period. That errors should have crept into the text in the course of so much printing is not surprising. But that there should have been so many of them calls for explanation. One circumstance greatly aggravated the confusion: the printers seem to have had a habit of binding together sheets from different printings, and the use of these as copy accelerated the spawning of errors.

Meanwhile, certain editions of the King James Version contained mistakes so notorious that they have become bibliographical curiosities. Notable among these is an edition published in 1631, which in the course of setting forth the Ten Commandments rendered the Seventh: "Thou shalt commit adultery." This lively but unwarranted departure from the text cost the printers three hundred pounds in fines and caused the edition to be designated the Wicked Bible. A similar type of error led to the naming of an edition published in 1653 which, having the reading at I Corinthians vi.9, "the unrighteous shall inherit the Kingdom of God," earned the designation the Unrighteous Bible. In 1702, Cotton Mather complained of "Scandalous Errors of the Press-work" through which "The Holy Bible itself . . . hath been affronted," and referred to an edition of the Bible, not identified, which at Psalms cxix.161: "Princes have persecuted me," gave artistic expression to the truth of his complaint by putting "Printers have persecuted me."

An Oxford edition of 1717 had as the heading of the twentieth chapter of Luke, which treats of the parable of the vineyard, "The Parable of the Vinegar." Known accordingly to bibliophiles as the Vinegar Bible, it was sumptuously produced, printed in large type and copiously illustrated with steel engravings. At least three copies were on vellum. Its looks were, however, the best of it. Printed by J. Baskett, it was so full of misprints that it was dubbed a "basketful of printers' errors." In 1804 came an edition known as the Murderer's Bible. At Numbers xxxv.18, for "the murderer shall surely be put to death" it read "the murderer shall surely be put together." There is also an octavo of 1801 in which, at Jude 16, "murmurers" reads "murderers."

An early American edition published by Jesper Harding at Philadelphia is known as the Dagger Bible because the printers had put, instead of the symbol †, the word "dagger" by which the symbol is known, so making the text read, at I Kings i.21, "The King shall dagger sleep." A similar error found its way into a Cambridge Bible of 1805. The proof-reader's marginal instruction "to remain" was incorporated in the text, so that Galatians iv.29 was made to read "him that was born after the Spirit to remain." This error was repeated in later editions published in 1806 and 1819 respectively. In an 1806 edition, for "the fishers shall stand upon it," at Ezekiel xlvii.10, was printed "The fishes shall stand upon it." This error was likewise repeated twice, in 1813 and in 1823. Perhaps it is the Cockney pronunciation of the printer that is reflected in the mistake occurring in an Oxford edition of 1807, at Matthew xiii.43, where there is an injunction to him who has "ears to ear." The same edition, at Hebrews ix.14, has "good works" for "dead works." An Oxford edition of 1810, at Luke xiv.26, enjoined the aspirant to discipleship to hate "his own wife," so winning the designation, the Wife Hater's Bible. The Rebekah Bible is one printed at London in 1823 in which it is written that Rebekah arose with her "camels," not her "damsels."

Errors were not, however, the only source of bibliographical oddities. In 1670, at Aberdeen, for instance, a Bible was produced measuring one inch square by half an inch thick. This diminutive curiosity is known as the Thumb Bible. Mention may also be made here of the edition superintended by Bishop Lloyd at Oxford, which appeared in 1701 and included in the margin Archbishop Ussher's ingenious computation of Biblical chronology according to which the creation of the world took place in the year 4004 B.C. The Irish Archbishop was nevertheless a great scholar in his day.

Nor were all the alterations silently introduced into successive editions of the King James Version due to error. Many of them were plainly intentional, and some of them a definite improvement upon the text of 1611. Here are a few from the Gospels to illustrate how later editions departed from that text: The reading of the 1611 edition, "Thou art Christ" (Matt. xvi.16) became, from 1762, "Thou art the Christ." From the same date "the words of Jesus" (Matt. xxvi.75) became "the word of Jesus." The reading "for press" (Mark ii.4) was altered, from 1743, to "for the press." For "he came and worshipped" (Mark v.6) was substituted, from 1638 onwards, "he ran and worshipped." From the same date we have, instead of *there is* no man good but one" the rendering *"there is* none good but one." From 1629 onwards, "understanding of things" (Luke i.3) became "understanding of all things." "The servant is not greater than the Lord" (John xv.20) was changed in 1762 to "The servant is not greater than his lord."

It is not to be supposed, however, that a reader accustomed to the ordinary modern editions of the King James Version would find the 1611 edition unfamiliar. Apart from spelling, such a reader might go through many chapters of the original edition without detecting any differences at all. This may be illustrated by the familiar Twenty-third Psalm which is here reproduced according to the text of the 1611 edition:

> The LORD *is* my shepheard, I shall not want.
> 2. He maketh me to lie downe in greene pastures: he leadeth mee beside the still waters.
> 3. He restoreth my soule: he leadeth me in the pathes of righteousness, for his names sake.
> 4. Yea, though I walke through the valley of the shadowe of death, I will fear no euill: for thou *art* with me, thy rod and thy staffe, they comfort me.
> 5. Thou preparest a table before me, in the presence of mine enemies: thou anointest my head with oyle, my cuppe runneth ouer.
> 6. Surely goodnes and mercie shall followe me all the daies of my life: and I will dwell in the house of the LORD for euer.

A word may be said here concerning the use of italics in the King James Version. This device was employed to help the reader to distinguish between those English words which actually translated words in the original and those which were added only to make sense in English. The latter words were italicized, and this practice has been perpetuated. In black letter editions "Roman small" type was used for such words.

The Bishops' Bible was immediately superseded in public

worship by the King James Version, on the appearance of the latter. There had been, apart from about half a dozen reprintings of the New Testament, no issue of it after 1606. The Geneva Bible was less quickly vanquished. It did not entirely die out in 1611. Even so, between 1611 and 1614 it went into only six editions, against at least seventeen of the King James. And for the 182 editions of the latter, issued between 1611 and 1644, no more than fifteen of the Geneva Bible appeared. The popularity of the Geneva Bible among the English Puritans persisted, however, and it was this Bible that the Pilgrim Fathers used. A copy actually read on the *Mayflower* is preserved at Harvard.

It was at the height of Puritan influence in England that the King James Version may be said to have achieved final victory, and it must not be supposed that this version went unchallenged. There were vitriolic attacks on it. By some it was denounced as theologically unsound; by others it was charged with unfaithfulness to the Hebrew text and too much dependence on the Septuagintal Greek; by others again it was despised for its alleged deference to the foibles and superstitions of an earthly king. The translators were accused of blasphemy; they were called "damnable corruptors" of God's Word.[2] But in spite of such hostility in some quarters, the King James Version steadily won favor. All parties came to recognize its intrinsic merits. There was strong sentimental attachment to the Geneva Bible which succored a demand for this in Puritan households; but the demand gradually waned. Even in Scotland, where the Geneva Bible had for long been generally accepted, it was fairly soon supplanted. The first Scottish edition of the King James Version was printed in 1633 by Robert Young.

2 In our own times, the Revised Standard Version of the Bible has, despite enormous sales, received a similarly hostile reception in several quarters. See Chapter XVII.

We must note here the volume of selected passages from the Geneva Bible issued for Cromwell's troops in 1643 and entitled: *The Souldiers Pocket Bible: containing the most (if not all) those places contained in holy Scripture, which doe shew the qualifications of his inner man, that is a fit Souldier to fight the Lords Battels, both before the fight, in the fight, and after the fight.* About fifty thousand copies of reissues of this store of Biblical ammunition were circulated as morale-boosters in the American Civil War. But this was only a curious survival of the older version, over which the King James had really been assured of victory from the beginning.

As early as 1688, an American edition of the Bible was proposed by William Bradford of Philadelphia. It was almost a century later, however, before the proposal was followed by any tangible result. Cotton Mather spent fifteen years preparing an American edition; but he could not find a publisher for it either in America or in England. His manuscript has been preserved in the Massachusetts Historical Society. John Fleming, a Boston printer, offered to produce a Bible in fortnightly instalments if he could find three hundred subscribers. He promised that only American paper should be used and that what he proposed to produce should be "as *correct* and *beautiful* an Edition of the Sacred Writings" as any in the world. The desired quota of subscribers was not, however, attained, and the scheme fell through. The War of Independence brought fresh obstacles.[3] A committee of Congress, reporting shortly afterwards on the question of a proposal to produce an American edition of the Bible, declared that the "proper types" were "not to be had in this country, and the paper cannot be procured." The committee was, however, sympathetic to the project and recom-

---

[3] It also, however, removed an important obstacle—formerly it had been necessary to obtain the King's licence.

mended to Congress the importing of twenty thousand Bibles from Holland, Scotland, and elsewhere in Europe. Seven colonies were in favor of the recommendation, six against.

In 1769, a Scottish printer, Robert Aitken, had come to Philadelphia. Encouraged by the Congressional discussion on the subject, this enterprising Scot published the New Testament in 1777. Three other editions followed, in 1778, 1779, and 1781. With an endorsement from Congress, Aitken then published, in 1782, the first American edition of the Bible.[4] It was brought out in two volumes, though a few copies were bound in a single one. Copies are now very rare: only about thirty are known to have survived. It was not a financial success. The Presbyterian Synod of 1783 recommended Aitken's Bible; nevertheless he labored under very great difficulties and lost much money. Congress declined to give him the exclusive right of publication, and in the next decade or so other editions followed.

Interesting terms were offered by Isaiah Thomas to his prospective customers. The price was to be forty-two shillings; but he announced that he was prepared to receive half this sum in wheat, rye, corn, butter, or pork, to be delivered to his stores in Boston or Worcester on or before December 20, 1790. The balance of twenty-one shillings had to be paid to him in cash, and it would fall due as soon as the product was ready for delivery. His first edition appeared in 1791. Thomas was a much-respected citizen and received a commendation from George Washington as well as honorary degrees.

In the same year, 1791, Isaac Collins of New Jersey, who had already published a New Testament in 1788, brought out a Bible notable for the accuracy of the printing. The only errors later found in it were a broken letter and a

---

[4] It is thought, however, that a Bible was printed in America about thirty years earlier, surreptitiously, by forgery of a printer's name.

punctuation mark, which is less surprising when we learn it was claimed that the proofs were read eleven times. At New York the New Testament was published in 1790 by Hugh Gaine, and the Bible in 1792. Before the close of the eighteenth century there were at least three other American Bibles: one issued by Hodge and Campbell, also in 1792; Brown's "Self-Interpreting" Bible, which bore as a frontispiece an engraving by William Dunlap; and in 1794 a Bible published by William Young at Philadelphia. The Cary Bible was, in 1806, also issued at Philadelphia.

Not even Shakespeare has more deeply affected English literature than has the King James Version. The extent of its influence, which it is practically impossible to exaggerate, is well known. Like the man who, taken to see *Hamlet,* remarked later that it was a good play though with too many quotations in it, the most godless adult whose mother tongue is English cannot fail to find in the Bible much that is already exceedingly familiar. The King James Version, having been injected into the stream of the language, invigorated and enriched all subsequent English prose. There is hardly a book today in decent English that echoes no cadence from it or reflects no phrase. Its effect on English literature was immediate as well as permanent: within a generation or so after its appearance it had shown that it could transform an itinerant tinker such as was John Bunyan into an exemplar of English style.

The cause of all this is, however, less well known than are the facts. It was no mere accident that made one book have such a dominant influence on the literature of a whole people. Nor was it only the intrinsic power of the message of the book itself, though the effect of this was immense. It was also the language, the peculiar style. Wherein lay its secret? The answer relates to a fact about style itself. Much

of the excellence of the King James Version was due to a circumstance over which the translators and editors had no
control, and of which many of them would probably have
been glad to have been relieved. They were not free to
write the translation exactly as they pleased. They were
restricted. They had to follow the Bishops' Bible except
where other versions agreed better with the original text.
In any case they had to revise or amend previous translations
rather than create something that would represent the latest
stylistic vogue. Harnessed to this conservative principle,
they went forth on their literary pilgrimage; yet though
they were as eager to write well as every author ought to
be, they could go no more jauntily than their book of rules
and the original Greek and Hebrew would allow. Not only
was their path determined by what the originals required
them to say in their English idiom; their tongues were
bridled by the conservative principle dictated by the Archbishop of Canterbury.

Besides all this, they were writing, of course, at a fortunate
time, when the Renaissance had already enriched and enlivened their language. Yet there is nothing in all the religious prose of the Renaissance that matches the excellence
of their achievement. Their secret lay beyond their own
good literary taste. It lay in the discipline imposed upon
them; in the fact that even where their taste might have
failed them their orders insured that the language of the
King James Version should be delicately flavored with the
past. It was not archaic, for that would have been contrary
to the very purpose of the book. But it was sufficiently
tinged with usages that preserved a continuity with the past.
It was molded upon the best in the literary inheritance of
the day; yet it evinced that vitality that comes from awareness of the ceaseless flow of a living speech. What they did
for the English language was different from that which Dante

did for his native Italian. Yet it was certainly no less a contribution. The King James Version of the Bible is unique among the literary wonders of the world.

But the Bible, though nothing if not a literature, has never been merely a literature. As the norm of faith in the Church, it has been in life and death the guide of a billion hearts and minds. It has taught, consoled, enlightened, civilized and disciplined millions who have read little else. It has puzzled and astonished the learned, and formed the characters of those who have led the English-speaking peoples in the development of such distinctive virtues as they may possess. Political and religious idealisms conceived in pretended independence of its influence have often owed far more to it than their authors have known; more, also, than many of them who knew have dared to acknowledge, lest the lofty theories they have proposed should appear to be parasitic upon a life that is not their own.

The Bible itself belongs to men of all tongues; yet to the English-speaking peoples the King James Version has bestowed a peculiar privilege. Conceived as a revision rather than a translation, it has done far more than even the best translation might have been expected to do. As a translation it was not, we are about to see, without shortcomings; nor can any translation into a living language remain forever what it was. A language grows and fades like a flower: "the flower fadeth: but the word of our God shall stand for ever." It was the genius of the King James Version that it made that "word" speak so directly to those who heard it that though men knew it was a translation—the title page told them so—they could never really think of it as such, for never did a translation speak with such directness and lifegiving power.

It is written that when the apostles spoke on the day of Pentecost, their hearers "were confounded, because that every man heard them speak in his own language. And they were all amazed and marvelled, saying one to another, Behold are not all these which speak Galilæans? And how hear we every man in our own tongue, wherein we were born?" But such was the power of the King James Version that generations of English-speaking men and women have not even asked the question. To them it was as if God had spoken in English. Could the learned men who toiled over the technicalities of their task have foreseen the full fruit of their undertaking, they might well have exclaimed with the Psalmist: "Not unto us, O Lord, not unto us, but unto thy name give glory."

XIV

THE BACKGROUND OF
THE REVISED VERSION

IN THE COURSE of the proceedings that had led to
the publication in 1611 of the King James Version, a
very remarkable man had attained influence in a part
of the world far from England's line of vision. This man,
Cyril Lucar, born in Crete in 1572, was destined to become
the first theologian of any importance in the Greek Orthodox
Church since the fall of Constantinople in 1453. In his youth
he had gone, partly because of his interest in and respectful
affection for the Roman Catholic Church, to study at Venice
and Padua. Such an attitude, it must be noted, is unusual,
not to say eccentric, among the Greek and Russian Orthodox,
who traditionally view Rome with a peculiarly bitter hostility. Apparently as a result of the first-hand observations
and contacts with the Roman Church that his studies in
Italy afforded him, his youthful inclination towards it underwent a marked change, and he became instead more and
more sympathetic towards and interested in the Reformed
Church. In 1602, two years before the Hampton Court
Conference, he became Patriarch of Alexandria. As the
occupant of this ancient patriarchal see, his views were sufficiently well known in the West to make his appointment

in 1620 as Patriarch of Constantinople both gratifying to
the theologians of the Reformed Church and more than
ordinarily distasteful to the Jesuits.

About 1625, Cyril Lucar, as Patriarch of Constantinople,
arranged through the British ambassador, Sir Thomas Roe,
to present to King James a Greek manuscript of the Bible.
The manuscript was sent about that time to George Abbot,
Archbishop of Canterbury and—it will be remembered—
lately a member of the Fourth Company of translators. Its
arrival was, however, delayed. By the time it did reach
England in 1627, sixteen years after the publication of the
King James Version, James was dead and had been succeeded
by Charles. The manuscript, which consisted of the Septuagint Old Testament and the New Testament in Greek,
naturally aroused great interest among Biblical scholars.
Other very old manuscripts had by then been arriving in
France and England from the East. But this one was unique.
Since the Codex Vaticanus was in those days inaccessible to
scholars, the new manuscript, dating from the early fifth
century, was at that time the oldest available manuscript
of the Bible. It was named the Codex Alexandrinus. The
makers of the King James Version, for all their care and
diligence, were now seen to have labored under disadvan-
tages. They had been hampered, scholars perceived, by their
lack of access to Biblical manuscripts of such antiquity and
importance as the Codex Alexandrinus.

The Codex Ephraemi had been in Paris since the sixteenth
century, having been brought thither by Catherine de Mé-
dicis. It is now in the Bibliothèque Nationale. But this
fifth-century manuscript had been converted before 1200
into a palimpsest. The New Testament text over which
other writing had been superimposed was not deciphered
till early in the eighteenth century. At the time at which
the King James translators worked, it was not known that

it even contained a New Testament text at all. Ancient versions such as the Old Syriac and Old Latin, to which allusion was made in an earlier chapter, are valuable tools for the modern scholar; but the King James translators had no access to them.

Within half a century of the first appearance of the King James Version, English scholars had begun to moot the question of further revision in the light of the new knowledge that was already becoming available. In 1653, the Long Parliament actually made an order for bringing in a Bill on the subject of such proposed revision, and a few years later a committee was appointed to consider the matter in detail. The committee met for some time, but the turn of political events put an end to such discussions, and the proposals came to nothing. Editors of new editions of the King James Version did, as we have seen, make discreet alterations and emendations of an unobtrusive sort, modifying spelling and punctuation, and also, here and there, a phrase. Scholars felt the need, however, for much more than such editing could hope to accomplish.

Several private translations, now almost forgotten, appeared in the course of the eighteenth century. Of these, one of the first was by Daniel Mace, a Presbyterian whose ideas on Biblical criticism were in advance of the general standards of his time. In 1729 he published a Greek text of the New Testament [1] which, based on his use of the more recently available manuscripts, was offered as an improvement of

---

[1] A chain of error has caused this work to be erroneously attributed to William Mace, who was a lecturer in Civil Law. Published anonymously, it was so attributed in Cotton's *Editions of the Bible,* a standard source, and even in the British Museum Catalogue. Even the most reliable scholars, e.g., Dean Luther Weigle and Father Hugh Pope, O.P., are among those who reproduce the error, the perpetuation of which illustrates, by the way, how easily errors have been transmitted in the Biblical text itself. See H. McLachlan, "An Almost Forgotten Pioneer in New Testament Criticism" in *Hibbert Journal,* XXXVII (1939), pp. 617-25.

the generally accepted text. With this he published his own translation, couched in English that accorded with the literary fashion of the day. William Whiston, who was Sir Isaac Newton's successor as Professor of Mathematics at Cambridge and is well known to many as the translator of the Jewish historian Josephus, published a translation, directly from the Greek, of three New Testament manuscripts.[1a] Probably more influential, because of the spread of Methodism, was the translation published in 1755 by John Wesley.[2] This, which was really a fairly conservative revision of the King James Version, was entitled, *The New Testament with Notes, for Plain Unlettered Men who know only their Mother Tongue.* In 1768 was published Harwood's *A Liberal Translation of the New Testament,* which was as bold in its departure from the King James as Wesley's had been cautious. Harwood's translation was "liberal" indeed. It was really a lengthy paraphrase in which the Lord's Prayer was several times its ordinary length. A similar spirit lay behind the florid "translation" which a Quaker, Anthony Purver, issued in 1764. He called it a *New and Literal Translation,* and it came to be known as the Quaker Bible.[3] In his version of the Lord's Prayer, "hallowed" becomes "sacredly reverenced," while "The flowers appear on the earth" (Song of Solomon ii.12) is transmogrified as "Earth's lap displays her infant flowers." For non-Quakers, at any rate, this was neither a simplification nor otherwise an improvement. Towards the end of the century such private versions continued to be made. Gilbert Wakefield, a Unitarian, issued one in 1791; Archbishop Newcome another.

A revision of the Douai Bible was issued in the middle of the seventeenth century for English-speaking Roman Cath-

---

1a See Appendix I.
2 There were later, slightly revised editions. See Appendix I.
3 See Appendix I.

olics, by Bishop Challoner, who is also famed as the author of *The Garden of the Soul,* still widely used as a book of popular Roman Catholic devotion. Versions of the Pentateuch were issued; [4] but Jewish scholars, though they shared the feeling that revision was needed, were hampered by lack of any critical edition of the Hebrew text. No such critical edition was ever attempted by Jewish scholars till 1861, when Seligman Baer and Franz Delitzsch published a portion of their cautious and unfinished work on the Hebrew text at Leipzig. To the subject of Roman Catholic and Jewish translations special chapters will be devoted later on.

The French Revolution had for some time an unfortunately retarding effect on intellectual ideas in England. Such was the fear of a repetition in England of the political upheaval that had shaken France, that to express a view not obviously conservative in every way was to be marked down by many as a sympathizer with those dreaded revolutionary principles. The epithet "French atheist" was readily hurled at those whose adherence to Tory tradition seemed to be less than staunch. In such an anti-intellectual climate of opinion, there was little encouragement, in the years immediately following the French Revolution, to talk of revising the Bible which, in the King James Version, had by then for more than a century taken firm root in British life.

In America, Charles Thomson, Secretary to Congress, retired in 1789 to devote himself to the task of translating the whole Bible, the Old Testament from the Septuagint and the New Testament from the original Greek. Thomson had not been trained for this sort of work. He had once picked up at auction a part of the Greek Septuagint, knowing nothing more about it, apparently, than what the auctioneer told him, which was that it contained "outlandish letters." Knocked down to the distinguished buyer for a few cents, it fascinated

4 See Chapter XVIII.

him. As a result, he set himself to learn Greek and, encouraged by a letter from his friend Thomas Jefferson, he attempted a translation of the Bible. The result appeared in 1808. This was the first translation of the Septuagint into English.[5] It was followed in England by Sir Lancelot Brenton's independent translation of the Septuagint in 1844. It is noteworthy that neither of these translators included the Apocrypha, though this is an integral part of the Septuagint Version.

Benjamin Franklin was among those interested in the project of a new translation. Noah Webster, dissatisfied with the King James Version, published a Bible of his own at New Haven in 1833; but his revision is of no importance and would scarcely merit mention but for the fame of the author on another account. Nor was anything useful achieved by the issue in 1828 of a Bible, published through the efforts of the Quakers, in which passages "unsuitable for a mixed audience are printed in italics below the text."

As early as 1810, however, a clear stand was taken by Herbert Marsh, then Lady Margaret Professor of Divinity at Cambridge and later Bishop of Peterborough. "It is probable," he declared, "that our Authorized Version is as faithful a representation of the original Scriptures as *could* have been formed at *that period.* But when we consider the immense accession that has been made, both to our critical and philological apparatus; when we consider that the most important sources of intelligence for the *interpretation* of the original Scriptures were *likewise* opened after that period, we cannot possibly pretend that our Authorized Version does not require *amendment.*" Marsh was thinking particularly of the critical work that was beginning to be done in Germany: he did much to foster attention in England to what the Germans were saying on the subject.

[5] See Appendix I.

By no means the least remarkable of the nineteenth-century private translations is one entitled *The Sacred Writings of the Apostles and Evangelists of Jesus Christ, commonly styled the New Testament,* which appeared in 1826. The translators, Campbell, Macknight and Doddridge, are designated "Doctors of the Church of Scotland." [6] In 1833, *A New and Corrected Version of the New Testament* by Rudolphus Dickinson was published at Boston. It was designed to avoid what the translator called the "quaint monotony and affected solemnity" of the King James Version, with its "frequent rude and occasionally barbarous attire." The claim of the translator is to achieve instead "a splendid and sweetly flowing diction" suited to the use of "accomplished and refined persons." The style is similar to Harwood's though the translation is more literal. "Thou" is replaced by "you." The style, far from having the "splendid and sweetly flowing diction" the translator hoped to provide, is such as to indicate that he could not have recognized good English when he heard it.

A periphrastic document came from the pen of Edward Barlee, Rector of Worlingworth, Suffolk, England, who in 1837 published *A free and explanatory version of the Epistles.* This consisted substantially of the King James Version with explanatory phrases in brackets. More characteristic of nineteenth-century translations, however, is the aspiration to produce a more literalistic rendering than the King James Version gave. *A literal translation of the Apostolical Epistles and Revelation, with a concurrent commentary,* is an early example of these nineteenth-century endeavors. Its author was William Heberden, physician-in-ordinary to King George III. After his wife's death in 1812 he went into semi-retirement at Windsor and devoted much of his time to Biblical studies. In 1854 *A literal translation of the last eight books of the New Testament* was published at London under the

6 See Appendix I.

pseudonym of Herman Heinfetter,[7] who also produced *An English Version of the New Testament from the text of the Vatican Manuscript.* He began a translation of the Old Testament but had not got further than Genesis when he died. Perhaps the most literal translation of the Bible ever made is *The Holy Bible . . . translated according to the letter and idiom of the original languages,* first published in 1862. This was the work of Robert Young, the author of a famous concordance of Scripture. Young was a bookseller; but though his scholarship was limited he had indubitably acquired a great knowledge of Hebrew and Greek. He had some curious notions and ingenious theories about the translation of Hebrew. "King James' translators," he wrote in the preface to the first edition of his Bible, "were almost entirely unacquainted with the two distinctive peculiarities of the Hebrew mode of thinking and speaking, admitted by the most profound Hebrew scholars in *theory,* though from undue timidity, never carried out in *practice,* viz., (1) That the Hebrews were in the habit of using the *past* tense to express the *certainty* of an action taking place, even though the action might not really be performed for some time. And (2) That the Hebrews, in referring to events which might be either *past* or *future,* were accustomed to *act on the principle of transferring themselves mentally to* the period and place of the events themselves, and were not content with coldly viewing them as those of a bygone or still coming time; hence the very frequent use of the *present* tense."

Here is an example of his treatment: "And Abram goeth up from Egypt . . . and Abram is exceedingly wealthy in cattle, in silver, and in gold. . . . And also to Lot, who is going with Abram, there hath been sheep and oxen and tents, and the land hath not suffered them to dwell together, for their substance hath been much, and they have not been able to

7 The pseudonym seems to be that of one F. Parker.

dwell together, and there is strife between those feeding Abram's cattle and those feeding Lot's cattle, and the Canaanite and the Perizzite *are* then dwelling in the land." [8]

The very literalness of Young's version draws attention to and confronts us with the poetic form of those books whose poetic character is almost lost in most translations. For instance:

> Jehovah *is* my Shepherd, I do not lack.
> In pastures of tender grass he causeth me to lie down,
> By quiet waters he doth lead me.
> My soul he refresheth,
> He leadeth me in paths of righteousness,
> For His name's sake,
> Also—when I walk in a valley of death-shade,
> I fear no evil, for Thou *art* with me,
> Thy rod and Thy staff—they comfort me.
> Thou arrangest before me a table,
> Over—against my adversaries,
> Thou hast anointed with oil my head,
> My cup is full!
> Only—goodness and kindness pursue me,
> All the days of my life,
> And my dwelling *is* in the house of Jehovah,
> For a length of days!

In spite of its oddities, Young's version was, for its day, a very remarkable achievement.

Several other private translations of the New Testament or of parts of it appeared before the end of the century. An English vicar, G. W. Brameld, claimed for his translation of the Gospels, published in 1870, that "the spurious passages are expunged; the doubtful bracketed; and the whole revised after the texts of Griesbach, Lachmann, Tischendorf, Alford

8 Genesis xiii.1-7. See also Appendix I.

and Tregelles." The claim reflects the new awareness that the work of such critical scholars of the Greek text had important consequences for the Biblical translator. John Bowes, an independent minister at Dundee, Scotland, produced a translation of the New Testament "from the purest Greek," published in 1870. In 1875, a notable Presbyterian scholar whose views on the Old Testament text had got him into trouble, published *The New Testament translated from the critical text of Von Tischendorf.* The intention behind *The Greek Testament Englished,* which was the work of an English curate, William Burton Crickmer, was that of providing, in an English version, indications of the exact disposition of the words and phrases in the Greek original. The nature of this work exhibits the characteristic quest, in the England of the period, for a more literal version of the Bible. We shall see that it was to be fulfilled.

Meanwhile, two little-known American versions of the same period were made that merit notice. One is *The Gospels, a new translation,* published at Boston in 1855. This version, by Andrew Norton, was unlike the sort of translation that was being done in England at the time. It was, rather, a precursor of the modern translations into everyday speech. Norton's aim was to avoid archaic language and write ordinary nineteenth-century English. "You" replaced "thou." Similar in style was *The New Testament, translated from the original Greek with chronological arrangement of books,* by Leicester Ambrose Sawyer. Sawyer also used "you" for "thou"; but in the case of prayer addressed to God he retained the "thou" and other conventional usages.

There were also several private attempts in the nineteenth century to produce, not fresh translations, but revisions of the King James Version. A modest attempt of this kind, with limited revisions, was made by T. J. Hussey, Rector of Hayes, Kent, England, in an edition of the Bible published in 1844-

45. The King James Version was printed with a revised version in parallel columns. H. Highton's *A Revised Translation of the New Testament,* published in 1862, must also be classed with revisions rather than translations. Baptist revisions have been published in which the word "baptize" is replaced by "immerse."

An important work is that of Henry Alford, who in 1869 published *The New Testament, newly compared with the original Greek, and revised.* Dean Alford was an eminent scholar, and his work was a very definite preparation for the grand-scale revision that was to be undertaken in the course of the next decades, resulting in the Revised Version, whose story remains to be told. Dean Alford himself took part in that great enterprise.

XV

THE REVISED VERSION

THE DESIRE for a full revision of the King James Version was widespread among Protestant scholars from the middle of the nineteenth century onwards. The progress in Biblical scholarship that marked the period between 1850 and 1870 transformed the wish into an insistent demand. Many ancient manuscripts and other fresh evidences had been coming to light for many decades. The Codex Alexandrinus was now one of the treasures of the British Museum. The Codex Vaticanus was now at last more accessible to scholars and was recognized to be of first-rate importance in establishing the original Greek text. It is true that the Codex Vaticanus had been listed in a catalogue of the Vatican Library as early as 1475. Its *existence* must have been widely known to scholars by at least 1587, in which year had been published at Rome, under the authority of Pope Sixtus V, an edition of the Septuagint Old Testament based upon it. But the manuscript itself was closely guarded by the Popes, who did not choose to make available to scholars the precious text, including a large part of the New Testament, that it contains. Napoleon carried the manuscript to Paris, however, as a prize of war, and it was studied there before being returned to Rome in 1815. It was owing to its having been removed to

Paris that its importance was recognized by the scholarly world. The dramatic circumstances of the discovery in 1859 of the Codex Sinaiticus by Constantin Tischendorf have already been described, in our opening chapter. This event was of crucial importance in the movement for revision of the King James Version, and may be said to have been the means of clinching the decision that was eventually made in the Convocation of Canterbury in 1870, which took up the whole question and appointed a committee of revisers with instructions to introduce as few alterations as possible into the text of the King James Version, "consistently with faithfulness," and "to limit, as far as possible, the expression of such alterations to the language" of the King James and earlier English versions. A two-thirds majority was to be required for any change in the text; but changes recommended by a simple majority might be noted in the margin.

The preliminary procedure was as follows. On February 10, 1870, the first step was taken in the form of a resolution moved in the Upper House of Convocation by Samuel Wilberforce, Bishop of Winchester, and seconded by Charles John Ellicott, Bishop of Gloucester and Bristol, that a committee of both Houses of Convocation be appointed to report on the desirability of a revision of the King James Version of the New Testament. On the motion of Bishop Ollivant, seconded by Bishop Thirlwall, it was agreed to enlarge this resolution to include the Old Testament as well. The resolution so amended was eventually adopted and its adoption notified to the Lower House of Convocation the following day, where it was accepted without a division. The committee that was appointed consisted of seven bishops and fourteen members of the Lower House. On March 24 they met and agreed to report that revision was desirable and ought to be undertaken. They recommended that it should comprise both marginal readings and such emendations in the text of the King James

Version as might be found necessary, and that there should be no new translation or alteration of the language except when such change was, in the judgment of the most competent scholars, required. They also recommended that it was desirable that convocation should nominate a body consisting of its own members to undertake the work; nevertheless, these should be free to invite the co-operation of eminent scholars from other countries and from outside the Church of England. This report was presented to the Upper House on May 3. It was carried unanimously and a committee was appointed to put it into effect. There was, indeed, an attempt in the Lower House to confine the work of revision to scholars within the Anglican Communion; but this was unsuccessful, and in the end the committee's report was approved with only two dissenting voices. The joint committee held its first meeting on May 25, when it was decided to separate into two companies, one for the Old Testament and the other for the New. A list of scholars was drawn up who should be invited to join one or other of the two companies. Rules, the general nature of which has already been briefly described, were drafted for the guidance of the revisers.

It was originally planned that the two companies should each consist of twenty-four members. In the course of the ten years of their labors there were, as might be expected, changes in their composition, and eventually there were sixty-five British participants in the work. Forty-one of these were from the Church of England, five from the Church of Scotland, two from the Episcopal Church of Ireland, one from the Episcopal Church in Scotland, five from the Scottish Free Church, four representing the Baptists, two the Methodists, three the Congregationalists, one the United Presbyterians, and one the Unitarians.

American co-operation was invited and obtained. An American Committee of Revisers was, after some delay, organized under the leadership of Philip Schaff, a distinguished American scholar, and from 1872 this committee exchanged readings with the English revisers and exercised a limited influence upon the work.

Let us look first at the work of the New Testament Company. Their assignment may appear the less onerous, and it did in fact take less time; yet it was fraught with peculiar difficulties. The great advances that had been made in Biblical scholarship had particularly affected the New Testament, so that it was here the thorniest questions were likely to arise. The New Testament Company met for the first time on Wednesday, June 22, 1870, in the Chapel of Henry VII in Westminster Abbey. After they had participated in the Eucharist they formally entered upon their assignment. The place of meeting set aside for their work by the Dean of Westminster (Arthur Penrhyn Stanley), was the Jerusalem Chamber. It was an apposite choice. This room in the Abbey is one of special historical interest. It was originally the parlor of the Abbot's palace. Here, too, had sat the Assembly of Divines who prepared the Westminster Confession of Faith and the Westminster Catechisms that have played a prominent role in the history of Presbyterianism. The Westminster Divines had met originally, on July 1, 1643, in the Chapel of Henry VII in the Abbey; but this was too cold when the fall came, and they moved, on October 2, to the Jerusalem Chamber where they continued to meet till their closing Session on February 22, 1649. It was in the Jerusalem Chamber also that a Prayer Book Commission had met half a century later, in the days of William III.

The meetings of the New Testament Company were held on four consecutive days each month, August and September excepted. The procedure was as follows. They assembled at 11 A.M. Prayer was offered and any matters of business correspondence were then dealt with. These preliminaries over, the chairman read a short passage from the King James Version and invited textual changes. When these had been given, he then asked for proposals concerning the manner in which the revision should be rendered in the place in question. After discussion, the vote of the company was taken. The day's work continued till 6 P.M. with only an interval of half an hour. After nine days of this regime, it was found that they had been working at the rate of only seventeen verses a day. The pace quickened later on; yet it seems never to have risen above about thirty-five verses a day. The first revision of Matthew was completed on May 24, 1871, the thirty-sixth day of meeting. The first revision of the whole of the New Testament was not finished till April 20, 1877, the two hundred and seventy-third day of meeting. A second revision was made, which took ninety-six further meetings, over the course of about two and a half years. It was completed on December 13, 1878. Suggestions from the American Committee, and other questions, occupied the attention of the New Testament Company till November 11, 1880, when, at five o'clock in the afternoon, the work of this company was ended. That evening, the Feast of St Martin, the company assembled in the Church of St Martin's-in-the-Fields, where they offered thanksgiving for the happy completion of their work in a spirit of brotherly affection and prayer that God might deign to use the fruit of their labor for the good of man and the honor of God's name. The New Testament in the Revised Version thus prepared was published on May 17, 1881, and a special copy presented to Queen Victoria.

Included in the New Testament Company were the following: F. J. A. Hort, J. B. Lightfoot, W. Milligan, W. F. Moulton, F. H. A. Scrivener, and B. F. Westcott. Hort and Scrivener were at the time probably the two most learned textual critics in the world, and the result of the researches done by Hort in collaboration with Westcott on the text of the Greek New Testament greatly influenced the work of the company, though the later famous edition of the text of the Greek New Testament by Westcott and Hort was not published till a few days after the Revised Version of the English New Testament had appeared. Their Greek text varied from the "received text" in nearly six thousand instances. This text was of great importance to the revisers. The King James translators had had nothing better than Beza's Greek text, which had been printed in 1598 and, being largely based on the text of Erasmus, was fairly good in its way, yet dependent on late and corrupt medieval manuscripts. The first edition of what came to be regarded as the "received text" was not published till 1624.

The Old Testament Company, which included E. H. Browne, A. B. Davidson, F. Field, C. D. Ginsburg, J. J. S. Perowne, E. H. Plumptre, N. C. Thirlwall, and C. Wordsworth, worked according to a similar regime; but most of their meetings were for six hours a day, and they sat for a session of ten days at a time. Beginning on June 30, 1870, they completed their labors on June 20, 1884, having sat for seven hundred and ninety-two days. They likewise concluded their proceedings with prayer and thanksgiving.

The actual work of revision was governed by five canons. Words might be changed, (1) if the best texts positively required the change; (2) when the old version was plainly incorrect; (3) when the meaning was ambiguous or obscure; (4) when the meaning was inconsistent with the rendering in other places; and (5) when a change was necessary in order to make the whole work consistent. In regard to this last question, the revisers were much more strict than had been their seventeenth-century predecessors, and their rigor in this matter was the occasion of many small changes.

The King James Version reads (I Cor. xi.29): "For he that eateth and drinketh unworthily, eateth and drinketh damnation to himself, not discerning the Lord's body." But the word "damn" had acquired by the nineteenth century a specific vigor that it did not have in the seventeenth, when it was a fitting translation of a Greek word that means no more than "judge." So for "damnation" the revisers put "judgement." Many such accommodations to changing language were made. "The secret of the Lord," for instance, was changed to "the friendship of the Lord," and "to ear" became "to plough." Some of the changes were less happy, notably the seeming preference for Latin and Greek derivatives rather than plain English words—"finished" for "ended," "epistle" for "letter," and the like. These examples will indicate the character of the revision.

In setting forth the Psalms and other books of the Old Testament that were originally written as poetry, the revisers adopted the original structure. The rest of the text was arranged in paragraphs instead of verses, though apparatus was provided so that the verses might be distinguished for reference purposes.

The question of revising the King James Version of the Apocrypha had not been forgotten; but it was decided not to undertake it until the rest of the work should have been done. On March 21, 1879, arrangements were made that when the rest of the work should be terminated, the task of revising the Apocrypha should be entrusted to three committees. The revision of the Apocrypha was completed in 1895.

About three million copies of the Revised New Testament were sold within a year of its appearance—two million within the first few days. The book arrived from England in New York on May 20, 1881. On May 22, the entire New Testament was reprinted in both the Chicago *Tribune* and the Chicago *Times*. For this Herculean achievement, ninety-two compositors and five correctors were employed by the

Tribune, which is said to have completed its setting-up of the New Testament in twelve hours.

The Revised Version was and is of great scholarly value. But as a version for ordinary use or for public reading in church its merits were questioned from the first. It was severely criticized in responsible quarters in both Britain and America as being stilted in language and pedantic in style. Few parish churches in England adopted it for regular use, and its use for ordinary private purposes was, despite its huge initial sale, more and more confined to those engaged in serious study rather than ordinary reading or private devotion. Within its own limits, however, it was an impressive achievement.

The sharpest criticism, indeed, came not from merely conservative circles but from those, rather, where interest in and sympathy for the project were warmest. In July, 1881, for instance, the *Edinburgh Review,* a very important journal, devoted an article to it that was, generally speaking, very favorable. But its conclusion was to the effect that the revisers had been appointed to do something more than provide a schoolboy's crib to the Greek New Testament. The complaint was, like that behind practically all the responsible criticism, not that it was a bad translation from the Greek, but that it was, rather, so faithful to the Greek that it was insufficiently englished. Spurgeon, the most renowned popular preacher of his day, called the new version "strong in Greek, weak in English."

This complaint was not confined to popular preachers. It was voiced in the highest places in the English Church. Samuel Lloyd, a Governor of the British and Foreign Bible Society, published in 1905, as a memorial of the society's centenary, *The Corrected English New Testament,*[1] which purported to be an independent revision of the King James

[1] An example of a passage from this version is included in Appendix I.

Version. In his introduction, he observed that the revisers had been "undoubtedly strong in Greek" but that nevertheless their work "cannot be accepted as conformed to the standards of the purest English." Lloyd's version bore a preface by the Bishop of Durham who pointed out that in view of his position in the Church it was "not altogether easy" for him to speak out critically on the subject of the Revised Version, since his "two eminently great immediate predecessors" in the See of Durham had played a leading part in the work. Nevertheless, the Bishop went on with commendable candor as follows: "But they would have been the first to wish every student to express an opinion absolutely free. . . . And I feel compelled, after years of use of the Revised Version of the New Testament, to own to the conviction that while it is beyond all praise as an aid to study, it seriously lacks that ENGLISH FELICITY, if I may use the phrase, which should entitle it to take the place of the Authorized Version in our national heart."

Some of the suggestions of the American Committee were adopted in the text of the Revised Version. Others were only noted in an appendix. For example, it seemed to the American Committee that "spirit" should be substituted for "ghost." The word "ghost" had undergone much change of meaning since the days of the earlier versions of the English Bible. It did not originally have the "spooky" connotation it was to acquire. "Ghostly counsel" meant "spiritual advice," and the phrase the "Holy Ghost" did not evoke the puzzlement it does in the minds of many people today. The English revisers recognized all this, of course; but they felt a change of this kind was not warranted by the conservative rules to which they were committed. Their reluctance to make such changes ought not to be too lightly dismissed as a mere perverse attachment to bygone usage.

In any case, bygone usage itself is not always unfamiliar to the modern ear: sometimes it is much more understandable than are the formal literary phrases of more recent times. The eighteenth-century Quaker's rendering of "hallowed" in the Lord's Prayer as "sacredly reverenced" is not only tastelessly florid: it now sounds more antiquated than does "hallowed." On the other hand, there are phrases in Tyndale, written as early as about 1530, that sound more modern today than do their counterparts in even the more recent translations of the Bible. For instance, where the King James Version called Joseph (Gen. xxxix.2) "a prosperous man," Tyndale just called him "a luckie felowe"—a phrase which, though belonging to a more archaic version, is as familiar to a modern ear as the most relaxed everyday conversation. Again, the King James and other versions tell us that when Eve reflected upon God's warning that if she and Adam ate the fruit they should die, the Devil, tempting her, said (Gen. iii.4): "Ye shall not surely die." The translation is correct; but the dialogue is pedantic for a devil. Once again, Tyndale's rendering makes the Devil sound much more realistic and convincing to our ears: "Tush, ye shall not dye." That is how we should expect the Devil to talk to Eve!

The American Committee wanted, at any rate, a more extensive elimination of archaic words and phrases than the English revisers felt inclined to allow. They also naturally wanted a version that would take account of American usage. For this reason, but also because some unauthorized editions of the New Testament were published in America, incorporating in the text the American suggestions that had been relegated to the appendix, it was decided by the American Committee to publish a separate American edition of the Revised Version. This was published on August 26, 1901, and came to be known as the American Standard Version, though strictly speaking it was more an American *edition* than a separate version. One feature of the American Standard Version that has been widely criticized is its use of the term "Jehovah" where the English revisers kept "Lord" or "God." There is, indeed, much to be said from several points of view against the use of "Jehovah." But in many other respects the American Standard had a great deal to be said for it.

Be its merits what they may, the American Standard Version certainly found more widespread acceptance in America than ever the Revised Version obtained in Britain. It has been and still is in regular use in a great many Protestant churches in America, while the use of the Revised Version in British churches has always been rare. The influence of the American Standard is reflected in the form of the opening words of the Lord's Prayer as this is recited in America: "Our Father, who art in heaven." This form is unknown in England, except among Roman Catholics, who inherit it from their own English version. In England the influence of the older versions persists: "Our Father, which art in heaven."

It is generally admitted that the Revised Version, both in its original English form and in that of the American Standard Version, was a premature undertaking. So much was, as we shall see, about to be discovered. In retrospect, this seems true enough. But at the time the enterprise, far from seeming premature, seemed to many long overdue. And after all, had it never been undertaken, the task of replacing the King James Version by any other designed to have the authority of the Church behind it would have been far more difficult. For all its shortcomings, the Revised Version was not only a noble achievement in itself, but one that will be found to have played a vital part in the movement to keep the Bible in a language "understanded of the people." This movement is essential to the genius of the Christian Church itself, which claims to be ever new, yet ever the same; ever whole, yet ever standing in need of reform.

XVI

INDEPENDENT MODERN
ENGLISH VERSIONS

THE SPATE of modern English translations of the Bible from the beginning of the present century onwards received much of its first impetus from the prevailing dissatisfaction with the work of the revisers. The scholarly but stilted version these had produced stimulated one private individual after another to try his hand at a translation that would convey the original into a more lively modern English prose. Those who aspired to make such a translation generally felt that what was needed was a Bible that would read more like an ordinary book: not only should it be divided into paragraphs; quotation marks should be used to indicate dialogue as in a biography or novel; coins and measures should be given in their modern equivalents, as far as possible; and above all the style, while avoiding vulgarisms and slang, should be sufficiently like colloquial speech to attract the reader and hold his attention.

There were various stimuli to such an undertaking. It has already been noted that the appearance of the Revised Version was in some ways premature. Almost immediately after the revisers had given out the result of their labors, a stream of fresh discoveries of ancient manuscripts and other important evidence began to confront scholars with materials that, to say the least, it would have been better for the revisers to have known. The Washington Codex, dating from perhaps as early as the late fourth century, and the Chester Beatty papyri,[1] which date from the early third century, are examples of such manuscripts. It is doubtful, however, whether an acquaintance with them would have affected the work of the revisers as much as might at first sight be supposed. Some passages would certainly have been rendered differently; but the general pattern of the Revised Version would not have been greatly altered.

A much more radical discovery was made about this time, however, that may be said to have put the whole of the Revised Version of the New Testament out of date at one swoop. This discovery was far more exciting than the mere unearthing of Biblical papyri. It had been supposed by the revisers, as by their predecessors, that the Greek of the New Testament was a special, "Biblical" Greek. That it was different from the Greek of Pindar and Plato was, of course, obvious and known to all. But in 1895 a great German scholar, Adolf Deissmann, drew attention to samples of a huge quantity of Greek papyri that were coming to light—not Biblical papyri, but commonplace things such as bills, receipts, jottings, letters and other very ordinary writings and scribblings. The significance of these for Biblical scholars lay in the fact that

[1] The Washington manuscripts of the New Testament are part of a collection purchased in 1906 from a Cairo dealer. The volume of the Gospels consists of 374 pages, thirty lines to the page, written in a small sloping uncial on vellum. The Chester Beatty papyri were purchased from dealers in Egypt by Mr Chester Beatty, an Englishman, in 1931. They constitute a very valuable collection consisting of twelve distinct manuscripts. Eight books of the Old Testament are represented in the collection: Genesis, Numbers, Deuteronomy, Isaiah, Jeremiah, Ezekiel, Daniel and Esther. Some of the manuscripts, which are in different hands, are very beautifully written. Three of the manuscripts contain New Testament books—ten of them, mostly incomplete but of great value to New Testament scholars.

they showed over and over again that there was nothing at all special or "sacred" about the Greek used in the New Testament. It was the international commercial tongue of the day that the New Testament writers had naturally chosen as their medium for communicating what they had to say about the Good News of Christ. This kind of Greek, now known to scholars as *Koinē* [2] was the cosmopolitan vernacular of the first century A.D. throughout the Mediterranean area. It was anything other than a pedantic or academic language. It was the racy, fluid, living speech of the market-place. The revolutionary importance of this discovery must not be overlooked. It is disastrous for a translator to treat an ordinary living language as though it were a special idiom.

Suppose one were to try to translate a piece of modern slang such as: "This guy sure knows how to make a fast buck but he got it coming to him" into a pedantic classical Latin, with a scrupulous care to preserve as far as humanly possible every word of the original. The result would be comical. Now, the men who wrote the New Testament did not use slang; but they used a very ordinary sort of Greek. It was the kind of Greek that is to be found in letters of the period written by mothers to their sons in the army, for instance— letters full of gossip and chatter. New Testament Greek is never vulgar or cheap; but it is essentially colloquial, even chatty.

Everyone now saw that the way to go about translating the New Testament was radically different from that which the revisers had considered it to be. The prospect of seeing the everyday Greek of a bygone age turned into the equally commonplace English of the present day was one that naturally captured the imagination of many people, whether they had personal ambitions to undertake the exciting work or not.

The case of the Old Testament was different; yet here too

2 Pronounced *koynay*.

was seen the need for making a less pedantic translation. It had become a Bible translator's tradition to tamper with the Hebrew as little as possible. So the idiomatic Hebrew phrase "And it came to pass" was so rendered, though it was not an English way of expressing the idea at all. The phrase reflected, indeed, a habit of speech among the Hebrews rather than an idea. It said little if anything more than "It was like this, you see" or "Now here's what happened." It was a Semitic *cliché*. Of course, once translated into English, it had become familiar and associated with the Bible, the book that generations of English-speaking peoples have so deeply loved. To many people, phrases of this kind were so closely associated with Bible reading that a Bible that did not have them would be to them like an expatriate Londoner's return to a London that had given up changing the Guard. The Hebrew phrase "in the day that" meant simply "when"; but to translate it "when" seemed not only to be "playing fast and loose" with the Hebrew text but to deprive the Bible of that mysterious, far-off quality that had come to be associated with its style.

Many now saw, however, that the presence of that mysterious, far-off quality was an important factor in causing the Bible to be in many ways radically misunderstood. There is, indeed, a place for mystery and remoteness in religion, for a religion that can be entirely understood is no religion at all. There is indeed nothing so derelict on the face of the earth as a religion with the sense of wonder taken out of it. It is no more a religion than a eunuch is a ma... But through the influence of certain kinds of Puritanism in the English-speaking world, the Bible had become for many almost the only place where that sense of wonder and mystery remained. It was the last surviving stronghold of it. If the mysterious beauty and wonder of its phrases and cadences were taken away, what was there left?

Many who saw all this knew also, however, that there was another side to the question. To have the Bible become a mere treasure house of antique phrases and haunting cadences was to turn it into a magical incantation. In the Middle Ages the Bible had become exceedingly remote to most people, as we have abundantly seen; yet we have also seen that it was highly venerated. Was not this happening all over again? If people were to be lulled into a tranquil ecstasy as they sat in their pews listening to the voice of a clergyman entrancing them with his mellifluous diction or stupefying them with his monotonous attempts to seem unmonotonous, while they really did not understand a tenth of anything he read them, nor would understand it much better even after he had gone on, in his sermon, to half an hour's explanation of the passage he had been reading, were they any better off than a medieval congregation? Might they not almost just as well be hearing the Bible chanted in Latin? Perhaps better, since then they would not have to pretend they understood when they did not.

It is obvious that there were many controversial issues involved here. Of one thing, however, all responsible and scholarly churchmen were certain: whatever was done with the Bible publicly in church, there ought to be a Bible that people could read at home or use privately in their pews in church—a Bible that everybody could read and understand. Had not quite simple people understood Paul in his day? For them it had been no problem to understand his language. Thanks to the international medium of Greek, Gentiles could feel they had even learned to understand Moses. The Bible would never come alive for the modern American or Englishman till it was so translated into his everyday speech that he had that same feeling about it. It had been written neither as an incantation nor as a model of literary style, but as very plain speech proclaiming truth that was meant to go straight to a man's heart and did. Now, at the dawn of the twentieth century, a translator's aim must be to make the words of the Bible leap at his modern English-speaking readers as they had leapt at those who heard them two thousand years ago.

The first noteworthy attempt to provide what was felt to be needed came from the pens of a company of about twenty scholars who anonymously brought out *The Twentieth Century New Testament*.[3] The first edition of this was issued in three parts and published between 1898 and 1901. There was a revised edition in 1904. The preface declared the purpose of the new translation: it was to provide Englishmen of the twentieth century with the New Testament in as lively a form as that in which it had been presented to its original readers long ago. The order of the books did not follow the traditional pattern but was changed to what was now regarded as the chronological order. For example, the Gospels were placed in the order in which they are now believed to have been written: Mark, Matthew, Luke, John. The work was arranged in paragraphs, with dialogue in quotation marks as in an ordinary modern book. Measures of time and space were rendered as nearly as possible into the English equivalents of the day.

Ferrar Fenton, an English businessman, published, in 1895, *The New Testament in Modern English,* and this was followed in 1903 by *The Bible in Modern English.* It is a curious work in several ways, containing oddities such as the use of "Ever-living" for "the Lord." It has not any very conspicuous merits; but though its influence has been but slight it should be noted as one of the pioneer modern translations.

More impressive and also more popular was the translation made by Richard F. Weymouth and published in 1903 under

---

[3] For an example of a passage from this and other versions mentioned in this chapter, see Appendix I.

the title, *The New Testament in Modern Speech.*[4] Weymouth, a Londoner, used an up-to-date critical Greek text,
upon which he based what he announced as "an idiomatic
translation into everyday English." It was not Weymouth's
intention to provide a translation that would take the place
of the "standard" or "authorized" versions. He aimed, rather,
at providing one that would supplement these. Nor was he
addicted to the use of daring colloquialisms. On the contrary, his usage was attractively conservative, for he sought
to keep as much dignity of style as was compatible with
idiomatic modern English. He recognised that idiomatic
modern English is not necessarily vulgar. An American
edition was published in 1943.

Though less a modern translation than a modern aid to
Bible study, the work of Richard G. Moulton, a professor
in the University of Chicago, should be mentioned. After
parts of it had appeared in a series of twenty-one separate
publications, it was issued in 1907 under the title, *The
Modern Reader's Bible.*[5] Based on the English Revised Version, it set forth marginal readings for discretionary use but
made only very slight changes by way of adaptation to modern
literary practice. The most characteristic features of Moulton's work consisted in the considerable explanations, introductions, and even suggestions for methodical study, that
he provided. Moulton's principal aim was apparently to
simplify the Bible for the modern reader by breaking down
the impediment of antiquated structure rather than by re-
casting the language into the idiom of the twentieth century.

One of the most important and influential of all modern
translations has been that of James Moffatt, a Scotsman who,
having taught in Scotland, came to Union Theological Seminary, New York. After publishing in 1901 a scholarly intro-

4 See Appendix I.
5 See Appendix I.

duction to the New Testament that incorporated a fresh translation based on a critical Greek text, he issued at Edinburgh in 1913 *The New Testament, a New Translation,*[6] whose preface announced that it had been the author's aim to translate the New Testament as one would translate any other piece of Greek literature of the same period; that is, he had regarded it, not as a sacrosanct book or "special case" but as what it was now more fully recognized to be, the testimony of men filled with joyful excitement at the Good News of which they were writing in the ordinary language of their day. In 1924 Moffatt issued his translation of the Old Testament, and the complete Bible in 1926. After many printings, the Moffatt Bible was issued in what was described as a "revised and final edition," in 1935. Moffatt did not hesitate to use words and phrases that startled many readers. Noah's ark, for example, becomes a barge.[7] Sentences are sometimes introduced with a "Well then." [8] Solomon calls together the Sheiks of Israel and the chiefs of the clans.[9] Titus is enjoined by Paul to give "a hearty send-off to Zenas the jurist." [10] The high priests "made fun of" Jesus on the cross.[11] Not all tastes will be pleased all the time in this or any other translation of the kind; but Moffatt's is a remarkable achievement. He was a very able scholar and translator.

In 1923, a translation appeared under the title, *The Riverside New Testament,* which was the work of William G. Ballantine, a former President of Oberlin College. Acknowledging a debt to other pioneers—Weymouth, Moffatt, and *The Twentieth Century New Testament,* Ballantine pro-

6 See Appendix I.
7 Genesis vi.14.
8 Hebrews iv.1.
9 II Chronicles v.2.
10 Titus iii.13.
11 Matthew xxvii.41.

duced a translation in a very readable form without verse numbers and with an index such as one would expect in a good modern historical or biographical work.

Very different and much more eccentric was the aim of Arthur E. Overbury, of Monrovia, California, who in 1925 published *The People's New Covenant (New Testament) Scriptural Writings,* which claimed to interpret the Scriptures from a "meta-physical standpoint, and recognizes *healing* as well as *teaching* as a component part of true Christianity." Overbury claimed also that his version was "a revision unhampered by so-called ecclesiastical authority." It is noteworthy, however, as an example of a version avowedly designed in the interests of a special and highly dogmatic religious theory.[12]

A translation that claims to be "safe, sane, and scientific" is not above suspicion. Such was the claim of the *Concordant Version of the Sacred Scripture, "New Testament," An Idiomatic, Consistent, Emphasized Version,* which also claimed to conform "to the basic laws of language, in that, as far as feasible, each expression selected constantly represents its closest Greek equivalent, and each Greek word is given one, exclusive English rendering." A considerable and remarkable apparatus accompanies the translation, including even a "Revision of the Greek Grammar" and copious notes such as one to the effect that punctuation does not form part of the inspired Word of God. It was published by the Concordant Publishing Concern, Los Angeles.[13]

Edgar J. Goodspeed, a prominent Biblical scholar, issued in 1923 a translation motivated by an intention similar to that of Moffatt, but in American rather than the latter's British English. It was accordingly entitled, *The New Testa-*

12 A specimen of his work is given in Appendix I.
13 See Appendix I.

ment, an American Translation.[14] Other twentieth-century translators, though they had modernized the forms "thou," "thee," "thy," in ordinary conversation in the Bible, had retained them in cases in which God was being addressed. Goodspeed modernized this usage even in the latter case. It has been a very popular translation in the United States. The University of Chicago Press, at whose invitation Goodspeed had undertaken the work of translating the New Testament, published in 1927 a companion volume, *The Old Testament, An American Translation.* This was the work of four scholars, T. J. Meek of the University of Toronto, Leroy Waterman of the University of Michigan, A. R. Gordon of McGill University, and J. M. P. Smith of the University of Chicago. The first edition reflected the variety of the translators, being uneven in style. This defect was mitigated by subsequent editing. In 1931 this Old Testament translation was published along with the Goodspeed New Testament as *The Bible, An American Translation.* This work, though exhibiting some "advanced" features such as the use of "you" in addressing the Deity, is on the whole considerably more traditional and less free than the Moffatt Bible. *The Complete Bible, An American Translation,* appearing in 1939, included a translation of the Apocrypha by Goodspeed.

In commemoration of the centenary of the American Baptist Church, *The Centenary Translation of the New Testament* [15] was published in 1924 by the American Baptist Publication Society. The translator, Mrs Helen Barrett Montgomery, of Rochester, New York, was a graduate of Wellesley College. It shared the now common aim of trying to make the Biblical language relive in everyday English. This was likewise the aim of the *Berkeley Version of the*

14 See Appendix I.
15 See Appendix I.

New Testament [16] prepared by Gerrit Verkuyl and published at Berkeley, California, in 1945. Verkuyl's translation of the whole Bible has since been published.

There is even a translation into "Basic English." This is a language invented on the principle of simplifying English by limiting the vocabulary. In general, only 850 words are used, but since it was apparently found impracticable to produce an English version within the compass of such a limited vocabulary, this was extended to a thousand words for the special case of the Bible. Under the direction of S. H. Hooke, Professor Emeritus of Old Testament in the University of London, a committee undertook the work of rendering the Bible into Basic English. The results of their labors were reviewed by a committee formed by the Syndics of the Cambridge University Press, which published *The New Testament in Basic English* [17] in 1941 and *The Basic Bible* in 1950.

In 1940 George Lamsa's translation "from original Aramaic sources" appeared under the title, *The New Testament according to the Eastern Text*. This was followed, in 1957, by his version of the whole Bible. While Lamsa's work is not without merit, the claims he makes are generally questioned. Contrary to scholarly opinion, and working on a superficially fascinating but entirely unproven, not to say untenable, theory of his own, he maintains that the Peshitta (Aramaic-Syriac) Version represents the "original Eastern text of both the New and Old Testaments." Lamsa, who was born in Kurdistan, can claim an Aramaic dialect as his mother tongue, and it is well known that Christ spoke Palestinian Aramaic which, though different from the Aramaic-Syriac of the Peshitta is nevertheless akin to it. There are, however, complicated reasons which have for long con-

16 See Appendix I.
17 See Appendix I.

vinced scholars that the Peshitta is a comparatively late translation of the Bible and by no means an original text itself.

Lamsa's renderings are often not without interest. He has been much influenced by the King James Version. Here are some passages to illustrate how he departs from it: [18]

(a) *John xx.22*

King James: And when he had said this, he breathed on *them*. . . .

Lamsa: And when he had said these things, he gave them courage. . . .

(b) *I Corinthians vii.5*

King James: Defraud ye not one the other, except *it be* with consent for a time, that ye may give yourselves to fasting and prayer; and come together again, that Satan tempt you not for your incontinency.

Lamsa: Therefore do not deprive one another except when both of you consent to do so, especially at the time when you devote yourselves to fasting and prayer; and then come together again, so that Satan may not tempt you because of your physical passion.

(c) *I Corinthians ix.27*

King James: But I keep under my body, and bring *it* into subjection: lest that by any means, when I have preached to others, I myself should be a castaway.

Lamsa: But I conquer and subdue my body so that, by no chance, when I have preached to others, will I despise myself.

That public interest is easily aroused may be seen from the widespread attention recently given to the Yonan Codex, a manuscript of the New Testament in Aramaic-Syriac which was exhibited in the Great Hall of the Library of Congress,

[18] Reproduced by kind permission of A. J. Holman Company, Philadelphia. See also Appendix I.

at an "unveiling" ceremony on April 5, 1955. According to the report of an art historian, Professor John Shapley of the Catholic University of America, it is a vellum manuscript consisting of 227 leaves (folios) measuring about 7 by 9 inches. The writing is in black ink, now somewhat brownish in part, and is in one column of twenty-eight to thirty-one lines to the page. The handwriting, uniform and very skillful, seems to be the work of one scribe, who, Professor Shapley says, "probably took serious account of his materials, for he gives a wide berth on folio 207 to a hole in the vellum—perhaps from the slaughter of the animal." The binding, though not contemporary with the manuscript, is old. Professor Shapley estimates the date of the manuscript itself (from paleographical evidence) to be in or about the fifth century. On March 28, 1955, the *Christian Science Monitor* published a picture of President Eisenhower scanning the pages of the codex as it was held out to him by the owner, Mr Norman Yonan. For its brief journey from a bank vault to the White House and thence to the Library of Congress, the manuscript was insured for $1,500,000 and later permanently insured for that sum. A resolution adopted by the Society of Biblical Literature on December 30, 1955, at its annual meeting in New York City, however, as a result of careful study of the manuscript by a company of experts who devoted part of the Christmas vacation to the task, was to the effect of deploring the publicity attending efforts "to raise by popular subscription $1,500,000 for the purchase of the so-called Yonan Codex." The society's report continues as follows:

"According to members of our Society who have examined the manuscript, the Yonan Codex is a copy of the Syriac Peshitta, a version which was made from the Greek New Testament at about the beginning of the fifth century and which contains twenty-two of the twenty-seven books of the

New Testament. Edessene Syriac, the language of this version, differs considerably from the Palestinian Aramaic used by Jesus more than four centuries earlier. About three hundred manuscripts of the Peshitta version are known to exist in the libraries of this country and Europe. Several of these are older than the Yonan Codex, which some of our members who are expert in Syriac paleography date in the seventh or eighth century. According to certain members of the Society who have frequently arranged for the purchase of Biblical manuscripts, a fair estimate of the value of a manuscript like the Yonan Codex is about $5,000." [19]

Translations continue to appear. *The New Testament, A New Translation in Plain English,* by Charles Kingsley Williams, which was published in 1952, is an interesting example. In 1958, J. B. Phillips, whose *Letters to Young Churches* had for long enjoyed a deserved popularity, brought out a complete translation of the New Testament.[20]

By far the greatest achievement in Bible translation in the present century that has so far been published is unquestionably that which has come to be known as the Revised Standard Version. Of this the New Testament appeared in 1946; the Bible followed in 1952.[21] So important is this work of twentieth-century American scholarship that instead of making further comment upon it at this point, a special

[19] The Society of Biblical Literature reports only the scholarly opinion of those of its members who conducted the investigation. Every scholar must be free to express the views to which his scholarly research leads him. It is to be clearly understood that no reflection is cast either by the society or by the present writer on the integrity of the motives of Mr Yonan, who has expressly disclaimed the intention of making personal profit out of the codex, and whose foundation has proclaimed its resolve to devote the proceeds, when expenses shall have been met, to the establishment of chairs in Aramaic in the theological seminaries.

[20] Specimens of both these translations are provided in Appendix I.

[21] The Apocrypha is also available in the Revised Standard Version, separately bound.

chapter will be devoted to giving an account of its construction and general character.

Meanwhile, stimulated by the appearance of the Revised Standard Version of the New Testament in 1946, the General Assembly of the Church of Scotland appointed, in 1947, a committee, of which the present writer was a member, to consider the question of a new translation of the Bible into colloquial English—a translation that would be no mere addition to the spate of modern versions of the Bible but would have the backing of the ecclesiastical authorities of all the larger denominations in Britain. The Roman Church was excluded only because it is its present policy to refuse to co-operate in any such enterprise, or in the ecumenical movement whose aim is the visible unity of the Christian Church. The authorities of the Church of England, the Baptists, the Methodists, the Congregationalists, and other bodies were approached and, when they had agreed to co-operate in the project, a joint committee was formed. The joint committee appointed one of the most eminent Biblical scholars in Britain, Professor C. H. Dodd, to suggest and preside over a panel to translate the New Testament, and the distinguished Hebrew scholar, Professor Theodore H. Robinson, to do the same in respect of the Old Testament. A panel of literary advisers was set up under Dr Williams, who was at that time Bishop of Durham (now Bishop of Winchester) with a view to ensuring that the English of the proposed version should be as good as possible. A fourth panel was appointed to attend to the Apocrypha. The work has for long been in progress and it is hoped that the New Testament will be issued early in 1961.[22] It will be published by the university presses of Oxford and Cambridge.

Dr Robinson, addressing the English Baptist Assembly

[22] For this information I am indebted to Professor J. K. S. Reid of the University of Leeds, Secretary of the Joint Committee.

in 1957,[23] gave an admirable account of the translators'
difficulties and described the method that he and his colleagues have adopted. He said: "Our method is as follows.
A draft is prepared by a single scholar, who need not be a
member of the relevant panel. Old Testament drafts are
first submitted to a scholar who is, perhaps, the greatest
Semitic philologist living, to whom I handed over the con-
venership of the panel at the beginning of this year. His
suggestions often include meanings which are as yet to be
found in no dictionary or lexicon. Then the panel as a whole
discusses and modifies the draft, and it is sent to the literary
advisers. Their recommendations are most valuable, and
are always accepted unless, in the judgment of the translating panel, they fail to give the real sense of the original.
When agreement has been reached between the two panels,
the result is presented to the Joint Committee in the form
of a Pink Book, and filed till the whole work is completed
when it will be subjected to final revision.

"We may now look at various kinds of problem which
the translator has to face. Some of these, of course, are common to all translators, whatever be the languages with which
they are concerned. In the first place we have to decide
what we are to translate. It is not enough to have any
one text before us; the writer's original words have been
copied again and again, and it may safely be said that there
are few cases . . . in which changes have not been made by
accident or design.

"For the New Testament we have a very large number
of ancient MSS, and the translator has to decide for himself
which of them is to be followed, in practically every verse.
With the Old Testament the problem is different. The
newly-discovered Jordan scrolls show that from the begin-

---

23 Reported in the English *Baptist Times* (May 16 and 23, 1957), vol. ciii,
5326-7.

ning of the Christian era the utmost care has been taken
by copyists to secure accuracy, and differences between MSS
are rare and commonly quite unimportant. But we know
that the Jewish community settled in Egypt by Alexander
the Great in the fourth century B.C. had copies of the books
included in our Hebrew Bibles. No Hebrew examples have
survived, and this form of text is known to us only through
the famous Greek translation which we call the Septuagint.
. . . This was, as a matter of fact, the Bible of the New Testament writers and the early Christian Church; it was not until
the fourth century that it was superseded in the Western
Church by the Palestinian form of text.

"But even when we have got all the help we can from
the Septuagint and other ancient versions, there remain a
great many places where the common Hebrew text is unintelligible. Sometimes our failure to find a meaning may
be due to ignorance, but in a large proportion the Hebrew
words are simply nonsense. This cannot have been original,
and we are forced to guess what the writer actually set down.
All translators have done this, generally without saying anything about it, but the modern conscience requires that we
should state the facts in a marginal note.

"Then begins the real work of translation. For this task
I, personally, can claim only one qualification, though that
is absolutely indispensable: I know that the task is impossible. This is true of every translation from one language
into another. The best known sentence in all Latin literature
is quite untranslatable: Julius Caesar never thought or said
that all Gaul was divided into three parts. We know what
he did say and mean, and we can explain and paraphrase
it, but explanation and paraphrase are not translation. It is
only rarely that a word in one language exactly covers a single
word in another. There are nearly always overtones and
undertones, delicate shades of meaning which cannot be

expressly rendered in any other language by a single word. We are dealing with minds which do not think in our ways, with languages whose very structure is different from that of English, with writers whose political, social and moral background is often startlingly different from ours. . . .

"Then again how are we to avoid one of the serious defects of the familiar versions and show how different are the styles of the various Biblical writers? . . . No one with any sense of style could possibly confuse the poetry of Ezekiel with that of Isaiah. Prose styles, too, vary considerably in both parts of the Bible. Each evangelist has his own, and all are widely different from that of St Paul. In the Old Testament we have simple stories such as might be told to small children, formal accounts of historical events, biography, legal codes, vivid and powerful rhetoric, even little scientific and philosophical treatises. Any conscious and deliberate attempt to reproduce these styles would be fatal; it could result only in stiff and artificial English. The translator must be so steeped in the original that he unconsciously reproduces for his readers the kind of impression made on him by the Hebrew and Greek—if he can."

Dr Robinson concluded by indicating the translators' policy in regard to the difficult task of steering between excessively traditional and excessively colloquial English. Idioms such as "casting in our lot" (with other people) have become part of normal speech and therefore admissible. Caution is being exercised in the use of technical terms. For instance, there are certain regulations in Leviticus which direct that, when a person is suffering from one of certain diseases and is on that account ceremonially "unclean," he is to observe certain ceremonial customs designed to prevent his contact with other people for a prescribed period of time. One *could* say: "The patient must be placed in quarantine for eight days." But the translators are apparently to resist this temptation. We may find, nevertheless, that the new version will tell us that Jonah, coming aboard his ship, "went down into the hold" or "went below." On the other hand, in the passage in which Jesus, in anger against the money-changers in the Temple, drives them out and quotes an Old Testament passage in allusion to their having made the Lord's house into a "den of thieves," the question arises: How should this last phrase be rendered? Some versions have "den of robbers"; but neither this nor "den of thieves" conveys the sense of the original as well as would the expression "gangsters' hide-out." It seems, however, that such language, being accounted too undignified, will not be used in the forthcoming British version.

That is as much as one dare say of a version that is not yet published. What has been said may, however, convey some notion of the general character of the work that has been for so many years in progress and part of the result of which is soon to appear.

XVII

THE REVISED
STANDARD VERSION

T HE Revised Standard Version of the New Testament was first published in 1946, followed by the whole Bible in 1952. Though it has had to face bitter opposition in some quarters, it has, on the whole, been given a far more cordial reception, both by scholars and by the general public, than was ever accorded to the earlier revisions, now known as the Revised Version and the American Standard. Within the first five years, five million copies were sold. It is true that sales figures do not give any clear indication of the extent to which the Bible has actually been read, for it has acquired a talismanic quality. It is "a book one should have." But there is no doubt that the Revised Standard Version has with spectacular success filled an immense need, and evidence is not lacking that its influence has already been incalculably great.

No translation, of course, is or could be beyond criticism. But the merits of the Revised Standard Version are unparalleled since the appearance of the King James Version itself. They are due chiefly to two qualities. In the first place, the revisers, being charged to make their work "in the direction of the simple, classic English style of the King James Version," had no freedom to indulge in the exciting venture of producing an entirely new idiom such as that of Moffatt or Goodspeed or Phillips. They could not, with Moffatt, call Noah's ark a barge; nor could they, with Good-speed, say of the Virgin Mary that she was "about to become a mother under the influence of the holy Spirit"; [1] still less could they change "Stachys my beloved," as does Phillips, to "dear old Stachys," [2] or render, as does the same translator, "Salute one another with an holy kiss" by the injunction "Give each other a hearty handshake all round for my sake." [3] So, as we shall see in a moment, the Revised Standard Version preserves the familiar cadences of the King James Version although it brings it up to date in terms both of modern scholarship and of modern speech. In the second place, the revisers succeeded in avoiding pedantry, which their predecessors did not, when the Revised Version was made half a century earlier. The style of the Revised Standard Version, dignified and conservative, is eminently readable English. How closely it follows that of the King James Version while modernizing the language may be seen from the following passage: [4]

King James:

Jesus saw Nathanael coming to him, and saith of him, Behold an Israelite indeed, in whom is no guile! Nathanael saith unto him, Whence knowest thou me? Jesus answered and said unto him, Before that Philip called thee, when thou wast under the fig tree, I saw thee. Nathanael answered and saith unto him, Rabbi, thou art the Son of God; thou art the King of Israel. Jesus answered and said unto him, Be-

1 Matthew i.18.
2 Romans xvi.9.
3 Romans xvi.16.
4 John i.47-50.

cause I said unto thee, I saw thee under the fig tree, believest thou? thou shalt see greater things than these.

Revised Standard:

Jesus saw Nathanael coming to him, and said of him, "Behold, an Israelite indeed, in whom is no guile!" Nathanael said to him, "How do you know me?" Jesus answered him, "Before Philip called you, when you were under the fig tree, I saw you." Nathanael answered him, "Rabbi, you are the Son of God! You are the King of Israel!" Jesus answered him, "Because I said to you, I saw you under the fig tree, do you believe? You shall see greater things than these."

Not all passages exhibit quite such a close adherence to the King James Version, of course; but the spirit of the revision is on such lines. So, unlike the arresting modern translation by private individuals, the Revised Standard Version may be read in public worship without any irritating sense of revolutionary change, even in the presence of a congregation accustomed to and familiar with only the King James Version.

Let us turn back for a moment to the events that had led up to the appearance in 1901 of the American Standard Version. It will be recalled that the American Committee had proposed certain emendations that were unacceptable to the English revisers, and that these emendations had been relegated to an appendix. The matter might have rested there, but for the appearance of at least three unauthorized editions of the English Revised Version with these emendations incorporated. The unauthorized editions were unacceptable to the American Committee for various reasons, not least because the list of emendations in the appendix represented only a minimum upon which they had agreed by way of compromise. The American Committee were not content with an edition purporting to be theirs which, published without their authority, included only these minimal emendations. The American Standard Version, incorporating in the body of the text *all* the preferences of the American Committee, was therefore prepared and, "to insure purity of text," copyrighted by the publishers, Thomas Nelson and Sons.

Even this did not eliminate all misunderstandings. Dean Weigle relates that the editor of a Sunday-school publication told him that when his board adopted the American Standard Version for use in Sunday-school textbooks, he received a protest from one parent: "Who is this Tom Nelson who has written a new Bible? I don't want Tom Nelson's Bible. I want the Bible the way the Apostle James wrote it." [5]

In 1928 the copyright was transferred to an organization representative of forty American and Canadian denominations and known at that time as the International Council of Religious Education. This body established the American Standard Bible Committee, now known as the Standard Bible Committee, to which was entrusted the custodianship of the text of the American Standard Version. Their task was not confined, however, to watching over the purity of the text; they had authority to consider a further revision when this should seem warranted and expedient. The committee did meet several times in the early thirties; but it was in 1937 that, acting under the authority of the International Council of Religious Education, they actually began the work of producing the Revised Standard Version. The council set forth the translators' task as follows: they were to produce a "revision of the present American Standard Edition of the Bible in the light of the results of modern scholarship, this revision to be designed for use in public and private worship, and to be in the direction of the simple, classic English

[5] Luther A. Weigle, *The English New Testament* (Abingdon-Cokesbury, 1949), p. 99.

style of the King James Version." Regarding the more technical question of the "original" text from which the translation was to be made, the principles laid down by the revisers for themselves were these: "(1) No one type of text is infallible, or to be preferred by virtue of its generally superior authority. (2) Each reading must be examined on its merits, and preference must be given to those readings which are demonstrably in the style of the author under consideration. (3) Readings which explain other variants, but are not contrariwise themselves to be explained by the others, merit our preference. . . . Each variant reading must be studied on its merits and cannot be adopted or rejected by some rule of thumb, or by adherence to such a theory as that of the 'Neutral Text.' It is this eclectic principle that has guided us in the present Revision. The Greek text of this Revision is not that of Westcott-Hort, Nestle, or Souter; though the readings we have adopted will, as a rule, be found either in the text or the margin of the new (17th) edition of Nestle (Stuttgart, 1941)." [6]

This meant that the men responsible for the making of the Revised Standard Version not only were better equipped for their task than had been their predecessors in the late nineteenth century; they had much better rules. Provision had also been made for the inclusion of some members of the committee chosen for their competence in English rather than in Biblical scholarship. Not fewer than three nor more than five of the committee of fifteen members were to be chosen for their qualifications in English literature and their experience in the conduct of worship and in religious education. Not fewer than ten nor more than twelve were to be chosen on the ground of their Biblical scholarship. The

[6] Frederick C. Grant in *An Introduction to the Revised Standard Version of the New Testament* (International Council of Religious Education, 1946), p. 41.

committee was, however, subsequently extended.[7] Associated with the committee members was an advisory board representing the denominations connected with the International Council of Religious Education, and some members of the panel of British scholars engaged upon the still unpublished version to which reference was made in the preceding chapter also co-operated.

As in earlier undertakings of this kind, the committee was divided into an Old Testament and a New Testament Section. Within these sections, voting on questions of detail in the translation work was to be by a simple majority, and in case of a tie the rendering in the American Standard Version was to be retained. For acceptance of the completed translation, however, a two-thirds vote of the whole committee was to be required.

There was at first some experimentation. Eventually, the procedure adopted was as follows: One book of the Bible would be entrusted, in the first instance, to an individual member of the appropriate section of the committee, who would thereupon make his own translation according to the rules laid down. When this translation had been completed, copies of it were sent to all members of the Old Testament or New Testament Section as the case might be, for use as a basis for the first draft of the revised text. The section then met and considered it phrase by phrase. Since every member was entitled to make suggestions at every point, the text as revised by the section making the first draft generally differed considerably from that which had originally been submitted. Decisions to adopt any variant reading were always made by vote.

When the section had thus reached the first draft of the revised text of a book, the draft was mimeographed with a view to further study along with the other books. Sugges-

7 For a list of names, see Appendix VI.

tions were meanwhile invited. It was in helping to make these suggestions on the first draft that members of the advisory board and certain British scholars principally contributed to the work of the committee. Eventually were amassed nearly a thousand quarto pages of single-spaced typewritten suggestions for the emendation of the first draft of the Old Testament. The Old Testament Section considered all major questions relating to the final revision, relegating to a sub-committee only those minor questions that could be dealt with on general principles laid down by the section as a whole. The procedure in the case of the New Testament differed slightly, and here the draft of each book was revised twice before the final revision was made. In the case of the New Testament, work upon which was done mainly in the war years, the co-operation of the British scholars could not well be obtained.

Most of the work was done at Yale Divinity School (in the "Speech Room," adorned by the original of Edwin White's picture, "The Signing of the Compact on the *Mayflower*"), at Union Theological Seminary, New York, and at the Hotel Northfield, East Northfield, Massachusetts. The inclinations of the members of the committee regarding the kind of translation to be done varied from an extreme conservatism to the radicalism of Goodspeed who wanted a thoroughly colloquialized version. According to Dean Weigle, Moffatt represented the middle-of-the-road position on this question. Of Moffatt it is related that once when he had opposed a suggested rendering, the proposer observed that he had got it from Moffatt's own translation of the Bible. Unhesitatingly, Moffatt replied that it was all right there but would not do here, because now they were engaged, not on a version that was intended only for private use, but on one which was destined also for public worship.

It will be recalled that the King James Version was itself a

revision and that it was one of its greatest merits that it was
not couched in the latest style of the day but was fairly conservative. That quality had helped to make it the extremely
influential book it became. The English Revised Version and
the American Standard Version had been, however, far more
conservative. They had invented archaisms. For instance,
where the King James Version had simply said, "This is the
will of God in Christ Jesus concerning you," [8] the nineteenth-
century revisers had needlessly turned this into, "This is the
will of God in Christ Jesus to you-ward." The Revised Standard Version has, "This is the will of God in Christ Jesus for
you." The nineteenth-century revisers had also greatly increased the use of antique words and phrases such as "must
needs," "howbeit," and "would fain," and in many cases in
which the King James Version reads "lest" they put—for no
good reason—"lest haply." All these archaisms—wholly inde-
fensible on any ground since they are really only "reproduction antiques"—are removed from the Revised Standard.
Excellent as was the style of the King James Version, it was
not perfect even in its day, and though perhaps even at its
worst it might serve as a model of purity for many modern
writers, it is not always as good as is modern English at its
best, which has regained something of Tyndale's simplicity
while retaining enrichments from intervening centuries. So
the Revised Standard often simplifies the King James Version.
For example, "for that" becomes "for"; "because that" is
rendered "because"; for "compass around" we have "surround." Where the King James Version had, "Notwithstanding ye have well done, that ye did communicate with my
affliction," [9] and the American Standard Version, "Howbeit
ye did well that ye had fellowship with my affliction," the
Revised Standard surely did best with "Yet it was kind of you

8 I Thessalonians v.18.
9 Philippians iv.14.

to share my trouble." The improvement in the rendering of Paul's injunction to married couples on the subject of their mutual responsibilities in the sexual relation is striking. The English revisers had followed the King James Version in writing, "Defraud ye not one the other." [10] For this the Revised Standard Version has "Do not refuse one another." The mainspring of all such improvements is, of course, the recognition of the everyday character of New Testament Greek. Since Paul has to be represented as writing English, the English he writes must be simple, unaffected and robust. There ought to be no literary flourishes, and the last thing wanted is a deliberate attempt at reproducing antique style.

Even the titles of the books of the Bible have also been in some cases improved. The word "epistle" is now not merely antiquated; it has in it, for us, both a flavor of the grandiose, like "encyclical," and even a tinge of the ridiculous, since the word "epistle" has come to be occasionally used for "letter" in order to achieve a vaguely comic effect. It is only when we are making a feeble attempt to be funny that we speak nowadays of having received an epistle from a friend. It is letters that we write and receive. So the Revised Standard calls Paul's communications to the Churches letters. This is what they would be called today in circumstances similar to those he knew. "The Acts of the Apostles" becomes, more correctly, "Acts of the Apostles," so eliminating the implication —which is not in the Greek—that a complete list is provided. One of the most inexcusable manifestations of conservatism in the English Revised Version had been the retention of Paul's name in the title of Hebrews. By the time of that revision there was widespread recognition of what is now universally acknowledged, namely, that whoever wrote that letter, it was not Paul. It is as unlike his style as any writ-

10 I Corinthians vii.5.

ing could be. The Revised Standard Version accordingly omits his name from the title.

By the summer of 1943, mimeographed copies of the final manuscript of the New Testament had been sent to the Old Testament Section to secure the approval of the required two-thirds majority of the whole committee. A final meeting of the New Testament Section met at Northfield, Massachusetts, which confided the manuscript to a small editorial committee whose duty it was to prepare it for the press. Then at an impressive ceremony in Columbus, Ohio, on February 11, 1946, the Revised Standard Version of the New Testament was officially published. Dean Weigle presented the first copy to the International Council of Religious Education. A member of the New Testament Section, Professor Clarence T. Craig, was granted leave of absence from Oberlin Graduate School of Theology to devote himself to interpreting the significance of the project to congregations throughout the country.[11]

The manuscript of the Old Testament, submitted likewise to the New Testament Section, was completed by the early summer of 1951, and the Old Testament Section held its last meeting during June 12-26 of that year. An editorial subcommittee of four worked through July and August on the last stages of preparing the Old Testament for the printers, and on September 30, 1952, the Revised Standard Version of the Bible was at last published. The work had taken more than fourteen years. The first printing consisted of about a million copies. It has been estimated that in the first run were used a thousand tons of paper, two thousand gallons of ink, over seventy miles of cloth, and almost enough thread to go halfway round the world. By this time enough thread must surely have been used for editions of this Bible to go nearly halfway to the moon. More importantly, the new ver-

[11] Craig was later, at the time of his death, at Drew Theological Seminary.

sion, by its widespread and increasing popularity among the English-speaking peoples, has burnished and strengthened the bond, so long forged by the English Bible, that binds these peoples together in a very troubled world.

It must not be supposed, however, that the Revised Standard Version of the Bible has evoked no hostility. Its rapid and extensive recognition does not mean that it has not been attacked. Clarence Craig's work in interpreting the New Testament to congregations throughout the United States was followed by efforts on a grander scale when the whole Bible was published in 1952. The publication was accompanied by more than three thousand "observances" in congregations, to introduce it and explain its significance. A Committee on the Use and Understanding of the Bible was appointed for a period of five years, to engage in work similar to that of Craig but on a scale such as no single individual could have attempted. These efforts have indubitably helped much to break down prejudice. Nevertheless, bitter attacks on the Revised Standard Version have been made in several quarters, reminiscent of the hostility that had been elicited by the appearance of the King James Version more than three centuries ago. In spite of the widespread recognition of its merits and the extensive acceptance of it for public as well as private use, it cannot by any means be said to have already universally supplanted the King James Version. However, it is hoped that the more obscurantist forms of prejudice, at any rate, will break down in time. Certainly the intrinsic merits of the Revised Standard Version have already assured it, at the least, a destiny of the greatest importance in the history of the English Bible.

XVIII

EARLY ROMAN CATHOLIC
VERSIONS IN ENGLISH

THAT ROMAN CATHOLICS are forbidden to read
the Bible is a notion which, once prevalent in some
Protestant circles, has for long been discredited. It
originated in a simple-minded misunderstanding. The Roman Church regards Scripture as basic; more so than do many
modern sects that claim a Protestant heritage. A Roman
Catholic theologian feels he is in a strong position when he
can invoke the authority of one of the early Christian Fathers
—Cyprian or Augustine, for instance—but he feels in a
stronger position still when he can invoke the authority of
Scripture itself. For to the Roman Catholic no less than to the
orthodox Protestant, Scripture carries a weight of authority
over all other written documents.

There is, nevertheless, an essential difference between the
Roman and the Reformed attitude towards the Bible. The
Reformed Church, though it recognizes that, as we have seen,
the Bible is, in part at least, the product of the Christian
Church, looks upon it as having an authority that is set over
the Church itself: the Bible is, on this view, the bearer of
God's own voice speaking to the Church. The Roman
Church regards the Bible as, rather, the most important and

basic of the documents committed to her care by God. The difference of outlook is far-reaching. It is not that the Roman Catholic can ever be discouraged from holding the Bible in greater reverence than any other book; it is, rather, that he must always look upon it as a treasure over which the Church has that same custodianship that she exercises over all other things entrusted to her care.[1]

The effect of this is that for the Roman Catholic it is more important that a translation of the Bible should have the approval of the Church than that it should be a good translation. Of course it is better that it should be both. It is better that the letter of your mother's that you cherish should be clearly legible; but if your mother is alive the all-important question is not whether it is clearly legible but whether it is really your mother's, for she is always there to tell you what it says. Moreover, the average Roman Catholic, unless his Church encourages him to read the Bible, will certainly see no reason why he should read it. There is accordingly among Roman Catholics, clerical or lay, no marked sense of duty on the subject of Bible reading. This attitude towards the Bible, which dates from the Middle Ages, made it fairly easy for the medieval Roman Church to *control* Bible reading. As we have seen there were translations of the Bible into various languages before the Reformation; but the resultant versions did not mean to those who read them what the Bible meant to the heirs of the Reformation. In any case, so far as English is concerned, nothing of the Bible was translated with the authority of the Roman Church but the seven "penitential" psalms.[2]

Yet the preoccupation of the Reformed Church with the Scriptures quickly made it impossible for Rome to maintain this attitude. It was plain that since there was no Bible in

[1] See Appendix XII.
[2] Psalms vi, xxxii, xxxviii, li, cii, cxxx, cxliii.

English that had the approval of the Roman Church, many Roman Catholics would read the versions that were not so approved. Not only did the earlier versions available have marginal comments derogatory to Rome; the Roman Church authorities felt, no doubt with good reason, that if the faithful were to read even a translation not provided with these inconvenient marginal observations they would still be puzzled and perplexed by many things in the text itself.

The feeling of the Roman hierarchy was well expressed at the time by Cardinal Allen in a letter written to a professor at Douai College four years before the appearance in 1582 of the Rhemish New Testament of which some notice has been taken in a previous chapter. "Catholics [3] educated in the academies and schools have hardly any knowledge of the Scriptures," he wrote, "except in Latin. When they are preaching to the unlearned and are obliged on the spur of the moment to translate some passage into the vernacular, they often do it inaccurately and with unpleasant hesitation because either there is no vernacular version of the words, or it does not occur to them at the moment. Our adversaries, however, have at their finger tips from some heretical version all those passages of Scripture which seem to make for them, and by a certain deceptive adaptation and alteration of the sacred words produce the effect of appearing to say nothing but what comes from the Bible. This evil might be remedied if we too had some Catholic version of the Bible, for all the English

[3] The Roman Church designates itself the "Catholic Church" in order to advance, repeat, and make continuous the assertion of its claim to be the only and one True Church outside which there is no salvation except by "invincible" ignorance, that is, ignorance which it is not in one's power to avoid. For a Christian who is a non-member of the Roman Church to accord this designation "Catholic" to members of the Roman Church without even a qualifying adjective is to acquiesce in that claim. For such a person to accept the corresponding negative designation "non-Catholic" is to assert that he acquiesces in the view that he is either ignorant or damned. Such expressions ought therefore to be avoided unless the admission is intended.

versions are most corrupt. . . . If his Holiness shall judge it expedient, we ourselves will endeavour to have the Bible faithfully, purely and genuinely translated according to the edition approved by the Church, for we already have men most fitted for the work." [4]

The men chiefly responsible for the Rheims-Douai translation were all Oxford men. They were: (1) William Allen (1532-94), whose letter has just been quoted. Allen had gone to Oxford in 1546 and had become, in 1550, a Fellow of Oriel College; in 1556 he was appointed Principal of St Mary's Hall and a Canon of York. His Romanism led to his flight to Louvain, and eventually, in 1568, he opened the English College at Douai. In 1578 this was removed to Rheims, where the New Testament was issued. Called later to Rome, he founded another English College there and was made a cardinal. He was one of the members of the Roman Church's commission for the revision of the Latin Vulgate. (2) Gregory Martin (d.1582) was a scholar of St John's College. In spite of his delicate health he engaged in scholarly works, of which the most notable was the translation of the Bible. (3) Richard Bristow (1538-81) was a Fellow of Exeter College. Converted to Rome, he joined Allen at Douai. He helped to revise Gregory Martin's translation. (4) William Reynolds (1544-94) was a Wykhamist. Converted to Rome while at New College, Oxford, he went to Rheims, where he lectured on the Pauline epistles. The exact extent of his contribution to the Douai translation is not quite clear: one writer ascribes the New Testament chiefly to him, but it is more probable that his part in the work was less important than that.

The New Testament that was published in 1582 at Rheims was specifically designed as an antidote to the existing English versions. It is now recognized even by Roman Catholics

[4] *Letters and Memorials of Cardinal Allen,* with Introduction by T. F. Knox (London, 1882), pp. 64 f.

themselves to have had very serious defects. It is said that one reader, pointing to the phrase on the title page, "faithfully translated into English," exclaimed: "It is a lie, for it is not English." We have already in an earlier chapter noted a famous example of its shortcomings in this respect, and as early as the eighteenth century Dr Nary, himself a Roman Catholic translator of the New Testament, complained of the English of "the Doway Bible and the Rhemish New Testament." Far worse than the bad English was the fact that it was a translation from the Latin, and thus a translation of a translation. The Rhemish translators were not unacquainted with a Greek text and used this to some extent; but the work was essentially conceived as a translation of the Latin Vulgate. An example will indicate the kind of effect that this has on the work. Greek does not translate well into Latin. For the injunction "repent," the Vulgate reads *"poenitentiam agite,"* which means literally "do penance." The Rhemish translators accordingly translated it "do penance," which of course also accorded well with their partisan preoccupations, for to most Englishmen the distorted emphasis on doing penance (wearing hairshirts, making barefoot pilgrimages, and the like) that had characterized much medieval piety had been one of the worst misrepresentations of the Christian life that the Reformation had been called upon to remedy. The Rhemish New Testament, though not entirely without merits, was vitiated by the limitations of the avowedly polemic element in its purpose. This element in its purpose was very blatantly declared in the notes, which were not merely controversial in the highest degree but were often calculated to indoctrinate the reader with exceedingly fanciful interpretations of the passages that were the objects of controversy.

The Old Testament that eventually appeared in 1609-10 in the Douai Bible, had actually been translated before the

New Testament which, first issued at Rheims in 1582, had gone into a second edition before the Douai Bible came to light. Delay in the publication of the complete Bible had been due principally to lack of funds; but a contributory factor was no doubt the fact that between 1582 and 1609 new editions of the Latin Vulgate itself had appeared and the Douai revisers were bound, of course, to take these into account. For reasons that have been already stated, the Latin Vulgate had always included the Old Testament Apocrypha, which was therefore of course included in the Douai translation.

It is well known to scholars that the Vulgate Psalms, beautiful though they sound in their way, are a far cry from the original Hebrew. One writer calls the Douai Psalms a "positively unintelligible English version of the unintelligible Latin version of a very uncertain Greek translation." [5] The Douai Old Testament generally exhibits the literalistic features of the Rhemish New Testament, not infrequently in a very marked way. We may make sense of "Noemi came from the land of her peregrinations," [6] though we do not acclaim it as a masterpiece of English prose. But "hearing I heard Ephraim going into transmigration" [7] is at the best puzzling, and we are ready to give up when we come to "The ram he shal immolate for a pacifique hoste to the Lord, offering withal the baskette of azymes, and the libamentes that by custom are dew." [8] On the other hand, the notes on the Old Testament are generally less polemic than are their New Testament counterparts. A second edition of the Douai Old Testament was published at Rouen in 1635. Apart from variations of spelling it exhibits no noteworthy change.

The extreme disrepute of Rome in the English-speaking

[5] J. Mombert, *English Versions of the Bible* (ed. 1907), p. 313.
[6] Ruth i.21.
[7] Jeremiah xxxi.18.
[8] Numbers vi.17.

world of the seventeenth century, with the resulting disabilities of the Roman Church in England, put the production of a revised edition of the Douai Bible practically out of the question. The disabilities of Roman Catholics were not notably diminished till late in the eighteenth century and it was not till 1829 that they were virtually removed. There is no doubt that dissatisfaction with the Douai Bible was felt by the more serious-minded of literate Roman Catholics almost as soon as it came into use. But since the Bible played no important part in ordinary Roman Catholic piety, the situation was of little general concern.

The people for whom the Douai Bible was intended were spiritually unprepared to desire an English Bible. The Old Testament was reprinted once in 1635. There were several editions of the New Testament. The circulation was, however, comparatively meager. Ironically, yet not surprisingly, the larger part of the circulation of the Rhemish New Testament appears to have been through the medium of the pages of a Protestant controversialist called William Fulke. This writer printed the Rhemish New Testament together with the Bishops' Bible in order to exhibit the shortcomings of the former! It is likely that Fulke, whose work was very popular in its day, did more to make the Douai Version known than did any of those whom he was concerned to refute.

One of the marginal notes in the Douai Bible characteristically declared that "the holy Scriptures to carnal men and Heretickes are as pearls to swine"; but those who alone were excluded from this condemnation made the scantiest use of them. They were for the most part content to be as Bible-less as had been their forefathers for more than a thousand years. Only where the Reformation had touched men did they seek the Bible. Many made foolish use of it. Do not many do so still? But for countless thousands it emancipated the mind while also hallowing the heart.

Of this great Bible-reading tradition modern Roman Catholic scholars are well aware. The encyclical of the late Pope Pius XII *(Divino afflante spiritu)* on the subject of the study of Scripture was not written without such awareness. The hierarchy of the Roman Church is now hoping to profit from the example of that tradition in the Reformed Church in order to put sufficient backbone into the laity to encourage a more robust form of piety without endangering the traditional docility of the Roman Catholic faithful. It cannot, of course, according to its present pretensions, officially acknowledge so great a debt to the Reformation, though many of its most distinguished scholars privately do so. But while, as a consequence of the impact of the Bible on the English-speaking world that was so largely the result of the excellence in its day of the King James Version, modern English-speaking Roman Catholics are at any rate certainly aware of the importance of the Bible, their seventeenth- and eighteenth-century predecessors were not.

This was not their fault. In those penal days, Roman Catholics suffered great hardships in England. They certainly had more pressing concerns than the improvement of a translation of a book they did not account it necessary to read. That English-speaking Roman Catholic scholars were dissatisfied with the Douai Bible is shown, however, by the appearance of a series of attempts to revise that version. The names chiefly associated with this work are those of Cornelius Nary, Robert Witham, Richard Challoner, and Bernard Mac-Mahon.

Nary's version of the New Testament appeared in 1718. According to an obituary notice at the time of his death in Dublin in 1737, Nary, a doctor of the Faculty of Theology of Paris, was "a gentleman of great Charity, Piety and Learning, and very much esteemed by Protestants, as well as by those of his Religion." His version, like that of Rheims, was a translation from the Latin Vulgate, and in his preface he excused himself for not having translated from the Greek, on the ground that his purpose was the practical one of providing the faithful with a means of understanding "the Scripture as it is read in the Catholick Church, and as they hear it in the publick service, and at their private Devotion." He also expressed the prevalent opinion on the Douai Bible: the language was so obsolete, the spelling so bad, and the translation so literal, that "in a number of Places it is uninteligible, and all over so grating to the Ears" that "most People will not be at the Pains of reading them. Besides, they are so bulky, that they cannot conveniently be carried about for publick Devotion; and so scarce and so dear that the Generality of the People neither have, nor can procure them for their private use."

But though it was only a translation from the Latin Vulgate that Nary purported to provide, he not only knew and constantly referred to the Greek but had a very high ideal of the translator's task and was probably far ahead of his time in his understanding of it. He appended few notes, and these were partly to exhibit the sense of the Greek, where this was badly rendered in the Latin, and partly to try to reconcile seeming contradictions in the New Testament itself. His sense of English rhythm was excellent, as may be seen from the following passage: [9]

1. And it came to pass that *as* the multitudes pressed upon him to hear the word of God, he stood by the Lake of Genesareth. 2. And saw two ships standing by the Lake; but the fishermen were gone *down,* and were washing their nets. 3. And *having gone aboard* one of *them, which* was Simon's, he *prayed* him to *put* back a little from the land, and *he sat*

[9] Luke v.1-11. The words italicized are those which are rendered differently in Challoner's (*infra,* p. 257) 1749 version.

down and taught the *people from aboard* the ship. And when he had *done* speaking, he said *unto* Simon: Launch out into the deep, and let *loose* your nets for a draught.

Robert Witham, whose version appeared in 1730, thought Nary too ready to follow the lead of the Protestant versions. His attitude was more reactionary than that of Nary, and he had far less sense of the importance of the Greek. Indeed, in his defense of the Roman Catholic practice of translating from the Vulgate, he took a position on much shakier ground than did Nary, for his excuse was not, like the latter's, a practical one. It sprang, rather, from a despair of the possibility of finding a perfectly pure Greek text. Of course the fact that such a perfectly pure text may be unobtainable is no reason for not doing all one can to find and use the purest one can get. There is no doubt of the inferiority of Witham's work or of its highly polemic character.

No edition of the Rheims New Testament appeared between that of 1633 and one, known as the fifth edition, which came out in 1738. The latter was a remarkably elegant production, a handsome folio edition with woodcuts and well printed, probably in London, on fine paper. The frontispiece consists of the crucifix, with the Virgin Mary on the right, representing the Roman Church, while on the left, representing the Synagogue, is Aaron. There were a good many modernizations of the text of the earlier editions. For example, the young man who followed Jesus when He was arrested had been described by the Rhemish translators as "clothed with sindon upon the bare"; the change to "cloathed with linnen cloath over his naked body," is a helpful improvement.

It is not known with certainty who edited this revised edition of the Rhemish New Testament, but it is likely to have been the work of Richard Challoner and Francis Blyth. The latter was Vicar-Provincial of the Carmelite Order in England and was for some years attached to the Portuguese embassy in London. Challoner, born in 1691, became Vice-President of Douai College and then Vicar Apostolic of the London district. He was also raised to the Roman episcopate, though only as a bishop *in partibus infidelium*. It should be explained that until 1850 it was the practice of the Roman Church authorities to signalize their claim on England, and their hope of resubjugating it to Rome as soon as opportunity might arise, by appointing vicars apostolic. These ecclesiastics were charged with the oversight of districts, not dioceses, because—such was the theory—England, being for the present an "infidel region," could not have bishops but only ecclesiastical agents of inferior status. In 1850, Pope Pius IX, in pursuance of the same policy of "claiming" England, "restored" it to non-infidel status.[9a]

Challoner, a very practical ecclesiastic, saw how beneficial it would be for English-speaking Roman Catholics to have a simpler and more readable version of the Bible. He was not a great scholar; yet he produced a version of his own that was, for its day and in the circumstances, a fairly good revision of the Rheims-Douai Version. At any rate, in various guises, Challoner's Bible was, till comparatively recently, widely used among English-speaking Roman Catholics throughout the world. Of course it never had among them the place that the King James Version enjoyed throughout the English-speaking world generally; but then no version of the Bible could have such a place within a Church whose attitude towards the use of the Bible is radically different from that which it has enjoyed among the heirs of the Reformation.

An important revision of the Rhemish New Testament, by Challoner, was published in 1749. Notes were few. In the changes he made, Challoner was often very strikingly in-

[9a] Steps were taken, however, to prevent the Roman bishops in England from assuming the names of the historic English sees.

EARLY ROMAN CATHOLIC VERSIONS IN ENGLISH 257

debted to the King James Version. For instance, instead of the Rhemish "But when I was made a man, I did away the things that belonged to a little one," Challoner wrote, "But when I became a man, I put away the things of a child." [10]

The following year the complete Bible appeared. Numerous errors and defects necessitated further revisions. A revised text of the 1749 New Testament was actually included with the 1750 Old Testament in the Challoner Bible as published in the latter year. A third revision of the New Testament was published in 1752, with more than two thousand changes and an attempt at much more drastic modernization of the English. Again the influence of the King James Version is enormous. A second revision of the Old Testament appeared in 1763 and the following year saw a fourth revision of the New Testament. In 1772 came a fifth edition which still contained many misprints besides those included in an appended list.

After Challoner's death in 1781 there was yet another edition of the Rhemish New Testament, with slight emendation of the text of the fifth edition of 1738. This sixth edition of the Rhemish New Testament, which appeared in 1788, was printed at Liverpool, apparently with an eye on the Dublin market, since Rome was now taking increasing hold upon Ireland. In Dublin, two years after Challoner's death, a version of the New Testament had been issued at the suggestion of the Roman Catholic Archbishop of Dublin, Dr Carpenter. This version was the work of Bernard MacMahon, a priest who was apparently unqualified for the task. This edition of the New Testament was provided with an interesting episcopal admonition on the necessity for reading the Bible only under the guidance of the Roman Church.

By this time Bishop Challoner had become the acknowledged Bible translator among English-speaking Roman Cath-

[10] I Corinthians xiii.11.

olics. The appearance, with episcopal approval (to say the least), of MacMahon's version, incorporating numerous ill-advised alterations and corruptions, is surprising. Worse is the fact that it was followed by a version of the whole Bible in 1791 that only exhibited the corrupt features on a grander scale. Assured, by reason of its high ecclesiastical approval, of as wide a circulation among the Roman Catholic faithful as any English Bible could have, it went into numerous editions.

Because of the considerable number of French Roman Catholic refugees who sought and obtained political asylum in England at the time of the French Revolution, an act was passed by the British Parliament in 1791 relieving Roman Catholics in England of some of the disabilities which they had hitherto suffered. Hope was in the air, and the Roman Catholic bishops in Ireland seem to have encouraged the distribution of the Irish Bibles that were certainly no improvement on the work that Challoner had accomplished, which, for all its shortcomings, had been highly creditable. The success of MacMahon's Bibles reflects, on the other hand, no credit on anyone. It was a triumph for the policy of the less desirable elements in the Irish Roman Catholic hierarchy of the period.

The first Roman Catholic Bible to be published in the United States was a large quarto edition of the Douai Version published by Carey, Stewart and Company of Philadelphia in 1790. This was also, by the way, the first *quarto* Bible of any kind *in English* to be published in the United States. It included an approbation purporting to refer to this edition; but it is in fact the approbation that had been given, in 1748, to Challoner's 1749 revision. The text seems to be a mixture of several of Challoner's revisions; but in general the New Testament follows his third (1752) revision. There is little influence from MacMahon. It had first started to make an appearance in a series of pamphlets begun in December, 1789. Because of a decision to publish in book form instead, however, the issue of this series seems to have been abandoned before a hundred pages saw the light.

More remarkable is a now exceedingly rare duodecimo edition of the New Testament that was published in 1792, probably at Edinburgh. Though the text is based mainly on the 1752 Challoner edition, it exhibits the marked influence of an anonymous and very independent editorial hand. Many interesting changes are introduced. For example, the shepherds are said to be "guarding the fields." [11] The creditor, meeting the debtor, "laid hold of him by the throat." [12] The lamps of the foolish virgins "were going out." [13] Sometimes the text goes back to earlier Challoner editions; sometimes there are odd archaisms, such as, "Peter sat without in the Cove." [14] The notes frequently differ from those in Challoner. Some of the more offensively polemic notes are omitted; yet new ones are introduced that are hardly less so. What is perhaps most striking of all, the pernicious influence of MacMahon is lacking. It is a pity for the fortunes of the English Roman Catholic Bible that this anonymous edition had not a wider circulation. Its rarity would indicate that it had little popularity and there is no doubt that its influence was negligible. The spectacularly inferior work of MacMahon, having the support of the Irish hierarchy, had captured the market.

The name of the remarkable eighteenth-century Scottish Roman Catholic priest and scholar, Alexander Geddes, calls for attention here. Geddes, who was born in 1737, produced his work on the Bible in the latter years of his life and died in 1802 under ecclesiastical censure. He was incontestably a

11 Luke ii.8.
12 Matthew xviii.28.
13 Matthew xxv.8.
14 Matthew xxvi.69.

man of great learning and independence of mind, and his work as a pioneer of modern Biblical scholarship is of the greatest historical importance. He was also the author of an unfinished translation of the Bible from the original sources. From his early days his friendships with Protestant scholars and clergy attracted the attention of his ecclesiastical superiors and incurred their disapproval. His fame rests on his critical work on the Biblical text itself rather than upon the merit of his translation; yet the latter has considerable merits in its way. That his ecclesiastical superiors hardly greeted it with an unprejudiced mind is indicated by the observation of Bishop Milner in the *Gentleman's Magazine* of October, 1779. Milner, after formally undertaking to "enter upon the Doctor's translation without any prepossessions," once he had the opportunity of examining it, expressed his suspicion that Geddes would treat the text of Holy Writ "with as little ceremony" as he would that of Homer or Shakespeare, and goes on to say that such considerations made it impossible for him "to trust the translator farther than I can see him."

The first volume of Geddes' Bible, consisting of the Pentateuch or first five books of the Hebrew Scriptures, was published in 1792. The second volume (Judges to Chronicles) appeared in 1797 and was followed in 1800 by *Critical Remarks* in which he dealt very boldly and critically with then currently accepted assumptions about the Bible. For instance, he repudiated the common notion that the Red Sea story was miraculous, and he suggested instead that the event might have been due to the use by the fleeing Israelites of "shallows fordable at low water." In support of this he pointed to certain geographical facts observable in his own day in the region of Suez. He declared both the Garden of Eden and the Flood story to belong to mythological lore. The story of the Flood he recognized to have had probably some historical foundation; but it had been greatly "exaggerated and improved upon by a credulous posterity." (That opinion on the extent of the Flood still varies is attested by a conversation recently overheard by the present writer outside a well-known church in downtown Los Angeles where a man about thirty years old and of apparently normal intelligence and decent education was explaining with much earnestness to a not wholly satisfied group of fellow worshippers how the configuration of the Santa Monica hills could be accounted for by the subsidence of the Flood.) "I believe the narrative of Genesis," wrote Geddes, "to be a most beautiful mythos, or philosophical fiction, contrived with great wisdom, dressed up in the garb of real history." [15] Such views were by no means original by the year 1800. Expressed long before—for instance by the Jewish Benedict Spinoza and the French Roman Catholic Jean Astruc—they were familiar to scholarly divines. But though they did not touch the essence of the Christian faith they were repugnant to the masses, and to the ecclesiastical superiors of Father Geddes they were singularly alarming. On his death his bishop refused a Requiem Mass.

Geddes was a Biblical scholar rather than a theologian, and his theological notions were in fact rather simple-minded. He minimized the difference between Roman Catholic and Protestant. He said that the "vulgar Papist" rested his faith on "the supposed infallibility of his Church; although he knows not where that infallibility is lodged, nor in what it properly consists." But he went on to say that the "case of the vulgar Protestant is even worse" since he grounded it in what "he believes to be the infallible word of God." It was a protest against what, very much later, came to be known in America as "fundamentalism." But though Geddes professed to dislike it in both its Papist and Protestant forms, he considered himself a "Catholic." "I am," he declared, "a Cath-

---

[15] Alexander Geddes, *Critical Remarks on the Hebrew Scriptures corresponding with a New Translation of the Bible* (1800), p. 37.

olic *absolute,* Roman Catholic *secundum quid* . . . neither
Papist nor Protestant: but both between, like good Erasmus,
in an honest mean, a genuine Catholic." Over his tombstone
in the churchyard at Paddington, London, stand his own
words:

Reverend Alexander Geddes, LL.D.
Translator of the Historical Books
Of the Old Testament,
Died Feb. 26th, 1802
Aged 65

Christian is my name, and Catholic my surname.[16]
I grant, that you are a Christian, as well as I,
And embrace you as my fellow disciple in Jesus,
And if you are not a disciple of Jesus,
Still I would embrace you as my fellow Man.

(Extracted from his Works)
Requiescat in Pace

[16] The surname Geddes is that of an old Roman Catholic family in Scotland.

XIX

MODERN ROMAN CATHOLIC
VERSIONS IN ENGLISH

W HEN THE British and Foreign Bible Society was
founded in 1804, Roman Catholics stood aloof from
its declared purpose of disseminating the Bible
throughout the world. If there was at that time any doubt
of the official attitude of the Roman Church towards such
Bible societies, there could be none sixty years later. For in
1864 Pope Pius IX, in his famous *Syllabus of Errors*—a document for long afterwards accounted by many Roman theologians an infallible utterance of the Pope speaking *ex
cathedra* as Head of the Church, though nowadays commonly
no longer so regarded by Roman theologians—condemned
such Bible societies together with communism and other
"pests."

The foundation of the British and Foreign Bible Society
was attended, however, by a curious result. Feeling against
Roman Catholics still ran high in those days, on the eve of
their final political emancipation in England, and their attitude towards the Bible Society reinforced public opinion that
they were enemies of the Bible itself. Because of this, a group
of zealous churchmen, mostly not Roman Catholic but having
a few lay Roman Catholics among its members, launched a

fund whose sole purpose was declared to be, in a prospectus issued on January 12, 1812, "printing the Rhemish version of the New Testament, and dispersing it gratuitously, or at a low price, among the Roman Catholics in the United Kingdom." There were to be no notes, comments or additions, "excepting that the Letter of Pope Pius VI to the Archbishop of Florence, and the Approbation of the English Colleges of Rheims and Douai, always prefixed to this version, will also be reprinted." The intention was, of course, to provide Roman Catholics with their own New Testament, the New Testament that their own Church had approved, since they could not be expected to be willing to read any other. It was a way of bringing to Roman Catholics the benefit of the work of the Bible societies while at the same time respecting their conscience on the subject of the authority of their Church. The feeling was that even a bad translation of the Bible was better than none at all, and if Roman Catholics would read no other, they could at least be provided (free of charge if need be) with a copy of their own. The purpose of this apparent subsidy of the small Roman Catholic community in England, which still labored under great political disabilities, was declared to be "to reflect some rays of light among their brethren, who are still sitting in darkness and the shadow of death." It should be undertaken, as far as possible, by the Roman Catholics themselves. In March, 1813, with this in view, "The Roman Catholic Bible Society" was founded.

This enterprise immediately evoked the ire of Milner, the Roman Catholic bishop who had denounced, in the *Gentleman's Magazine,* the work of Geddes before reading it. Milner contended that the notes (whose extremely anti-Protestant character was notorious) were vital. They were, he said, "precisely the part that is wanted at the present day, to render an English translation of the sacred text *safe* and profitable in the hands of the laity." He also objected to the paragraph form in which the new version was to be printed, even though the conventional verse numbers were being retained in the margin. This attitude seems to have surprised the Roman Catholic laymen participating in the enterprise. It had not occurred to them that the approbation of their Church was given to the publication of the text only when this was accompanied by the notes. After discussion, it was agreed to resort to a compromise. Not all the notes were equally offensive. Only the most offensive should be omitted. The result was that of the 240 notes in Challoner's 1749 revision, only 226 were included. There was also some difficulty about the text of the Rhemish New Testament that should be used. Eventually, though the 1752 Challoner edition, with its two thousand variations from the first Challoner revision of 1749, had become the generally accepted text among Roman Catholics, the comparatively rare 1749 edition was used instead.

Despite the fulminations of Dr Milner, who called the Roman Catholic Bible Society "in its very title a departure from the Catholic Rule of Faith," [1] another Roman Catholic bishop, William Poynter, accepted the presidency of the society, perhaps on the principle attributed to Ignatius Loyola that it is sometimes necessary to enter another man's door in order that he should come out through yours. At any rate, at last the Roman Catholic Bible Society's efforts resulted in the issue at London, in 1815, of two editions, one an octavo and the other a duodecimo. Not only did the text avoid the Mac-Mahon corruptions; it was an improvement on the 1752 Challoner edition commonly used. Based on the 1749 Challoner text, it introduced some pleasing modernizations, such as the substitution of "said" for "saith," "my" for "mine," and the like. The 1752 Challoner edition was followed in one place,

[1] *Supra,* p. 248 n.

however—the famous "exaninivit" phrase, which was rendered "he debased himself," instead of "he emptied himself." Generally speaking, then, it was a good piece of work of its kind, and it had great influence on later Roman Catholic versions of the Bible in the English-speaking world. It was reproduced almost exactly by Sidney and Horrabin in 1818 and, with a few changes, also in that year by Keating and Brown. Bagster reproduced it in 1823 with a few corrections.

Meanwhile, a host of editions for the use of Roman Catholics came out. These included Coyne's Bible (1811), Haydock's Bible (1811-14), the Newcastle New Testament (1812), Syers' Bible (1813), Wogan's Bible (1814), MacNamara's Bible (1813-14), Bregan's New Testament (1816), Gibson's Bible (1816-17). For those Roman Catholics who, listening to the Epistle and Gospel for the day in one version in one parish and another version in another parish, gave any thought to the matter, the situation must have seemed confusing. The predilection of the Roman Church authorities today for uniformity is more understandable in the light of the fact that Roman Catholic practice, when not strictly controlled by the ecclesiastical authorities, has always quickly degenerated into a state of confusion of baffling complexity. Roman Catholic beliefs, too, would run just as wild were they not even more rigidly controlled by Rome. Even as late as 1859, the future Cardinal Newman, trying to sum up the situation he then found, had to say: "The text of the Old Testament as we now have it is practically as it left Challoner's hands, coming down to us through Dr Troy's editions perpetuated by Drs Murray and Denvir, who followed Haydock's text, which again was taken over in Cardinal Wiseman's edition of 1847. In the New Testament the editions of Drs Murray and Denvir may be said to give the text presented in Challoner's earlier editions, while Haydock and Wiseman follow Challoner's later editions and those of Dr Troy." [2]

The editions mentioned by Newman are but a few of the more influential of the nineteenth-century editions in actual use in Roman Catholic churches in the course of the century. After the political emancipation of Roman Catholics in 1829, the output is so prolific and the variety of renderings so staggering that it would require immense research and several volumes to give a full bibliographical account of the astonishing story. So labyrinthine is the maze that it would be often impossible for even the most learned Roman Catholic scholar to discover what edition would be used by a particular priest, at a particular church, on a particular Sunday, in the course of the century after, say, Roman Catholic emancipation in England. Since the editions varied so much in small but sometimes important points, no prudent historian or even novelist would dare without very careful research to reconstruct the Epistle or Gospel as it was actually read in public on any such occasion. The great English Dominican authority on the subject has well written: "In Manchester the Epistle and Gospel might be read from Syers' Bible, adhering mostly to Challoner's earlier revisions, unless that huge folio proved too unwieldy in the pulpit. In Liverpool, Dr Gibson's magnificent folio editions, 1817 and 1822, following Challoner's later revisions, might have been used, if any pulpit could accommodate them. Owing to their condemnation by Dr Troy, Ireland probably never heard Coyne's edition, 1816, nor MacNamara's, 1818, though if they ever were used in the pulpit, people would have had the privilege of listening to the Epistle and Gospel as originally translated in 1582. Nor is it likely that the

2 John Henry Newman, *Tracts Theological and Ecclesiastical* (1891), p. 405. Reprinted from an article in the *Rambler* (July, 1859): "History of the Text of the Rheims and Douay Version of the Holy Scripture."

Dublin clergy would have tolerated Coyne's New Testament, 1820, in their pulpits, despite the prefixed Approbation by Dr Troy; for it was published by the Protestants' Fund for the 'conversion' of the presumed ignorant Irish Catholics." [3]

In the early part of the nineteenth century, Roman Catholics were still a very small and obscure minority in England. They had been for the greater part so long deprived of access to higher education that the ecclesiastical authorities knew, or thought they knew, the names of practically every Roman Catholic in England capable of even the most modest work of scholarship. Eyebrows were therefore raised when an anonymous version of the Gospels translated *from the Greek* was published in London in 1836, with critical notes and purporting to be "by a Catholic." What Catholic in England, the authorities wondered, could be the translator? Their suspicion was aroused. Might not someone be poking fun? Might it not be, even, a hoax by a waggish Protestant playfully recalling that in Reformation times men had been arrested for reading the Greek New Testament? At any rate, in reviewing the work,[4] the future Cardinal Wiseman took the precaution of damning it with faint praise. The translator turned out to be, however, an eminent scholar of the day, John Lingard, who, though a Roman Catholic, had not sought the "approbation" of the authorities before publishing his work.

It was a lively translation. Of the seed that fell on "rocky ground," Lingard says that it "sprouted quickly, because it had no depth of soil." [5] "The children of this world are more provident in their pursuits than the children of light," [6]

---

[3] Hugh Pope, O.P., *English Versions of the Bible* (B. Herder Book Co., 1952), pp. 393 f. (Quoted by kind permission of B. Herder Book Company.)
[4] In "Catholic Versions of the Scriptures" in the *Dublin Review*, ii (1837), pp. 475-492.
[5] Matthew xiii.5.
[6] Luke xvi.8.

is periphrastic but striking. "Repent" was used throughout, rather than "do penance."

The Roman Catholic Church in England grew much more confident after the "restoration of the hierarchy" by Pius IX in 1850. This "restoration," which meant that the Roman Church was now governed in England by regular bishops instead of vicars apostolic, was made possible largely through the new hopes aroused in Rome by the defection of large numbers of Anglican clergy who followed Newman into the Roman fold. There now seemed to be a greater need than ever for remedying the state of affairs arising out of the chaos of Biblical versions. With this in mind, the Synod of Westminster, in 1855, decreed that a new and accurate translation of the Bible should be made by competent scholars chosen by the Cardinal Archbishop of Westminster. In 1857, Newman himself, indubitably the greatest scholar the Roman Church had in England, expressed his willingness to make the required English version. Nothing, however, came of this.

Meanwhile, in the United States, Francis Patrick Kenrick,[7] a Roman Catholic scholar of pioneering days in this country, had begun a translation of the Bible. The first volume, consisting of the four Gospels, appeared in 1849 and was followed in 1851 by the Acts of the Apostles. Between 1849 and 1860, Kenrick published a translation of the entire Bible. It was "translated from the Latin Vulgate, diligently compared with the Hebrew and Greek." Though described also as "a revised and corrected edition of the Douay Version" it exhibited some very independent features. Not all are commendable. Kenrick had recourse to a curious device in translating *"poenitentiam agite,"* the phrase whose controversial overtones made it, we have seen,

[7] Brother of Peter Kenrick, prominent prelate in the Opposition party at the Vatican Council, 1869-70.

a delicate point for a conscientious Roman Catholic translator. He rendered it "repent" and "do penance" alternately. One of his more pleasing phrases is, "Wary as serpents, guileless as doves." [8]

Other editions continued to pour forth on both sides of the Atlantic. Most of them contained peculiarities of a not particularly interesting sort, and all of them either introduced new errors or at least perpetuated old ones. In 1901, however, a remarkable version of the Gospels, translated "from the Greek text direct, with reference to the Vulgate and ancient Syriac Version," made its appearance in New York. It was the work of Francis Spencer, a Dominican Father who in his youth had renounced his Anglican heritage in order to be received into the Roman Church. For some time a Paulist, he had, after ordination, joined the Dominicans. Before his death in 1913 he had completed the New Testament, and this was eventually published by The Macmillan Company, New York, in 1937. Not undeservedly popular, it has been several times reprinted. The presentation is modern: the text is set forth in paragraphs, each under a heading. The words of Christ are printed in italics—a bold idea, since it is not always by any means clear whether the evangelist is attributing words to Christ or is making a comment of his own.

A very different sort of book was *The Layman's New Testament,* first published in London in 1928. Designed for the field work of the Catholic Evidence Guild, a society of zealous English laymen whose mission includes polemics in the out-of-doors, it simply set forth, on the left, a Challoner text and, on the right, provided ammunition for the use of the Church Militant in dealing with Hyde Park hecklers and the like. The stock of ammunition was extended in a second edition published in 1934. Both editions

[8] Matthew x.16.

are said to have been destroyed in a less ecclesiastical Battle of Britain. A third was issued.

The Westminster Version is a much more scholarly enterprise. Edited by a Jesuit, Cuthbert Lattey, it was begun before the War of 1914-18. Both American and British scholars contributed. To each translator was entrusted a particular book or number of books, with full personal responsibility for the assignment. Fascicles were issued until the New Testament was at last completed in 1935. By this time work on the Old Testament had been begun: its first fruit was the issue of the book of the prophet Malachi. Publication was planned in two recensions, a long one in large octavo and a short one in a pocket edition. By 1936 the longer recension of the New Testament was completed in four handsome and finely printed volumes. The pocket edition appeared in 1948. The Old Testament, though parts of it have been issued, is so far uncompleted. In view of the personal responsibility given to the various contributors in terms of the scheme for the work, it was hardly to be expected that there should be uniformity in the character and style of the translation as a whole; yet the result is very pleasantly readable and reveals much scholarly care and skill.

In the United States, the fully americanized edition of the New Testament, edited by scholars under the patronage of the Bishops' Committee of the Confraternity of Christian Doctrine, published in 1941 and widely known as the Confraternity Edition,[9] has superseded previous versions to a very great extent. Because of its use among the armed forces in the War of 1939-45, it also became well known to English-speaking Roman Catholics elsewhere. Despite the now-customary arrangement in paragraph form, the American spelling, the use of quotation marks, the mod-

9 See Appendix I.

ernization of many turns of speech, e.g., "Do not be afraid" for "Fear not," it retains many curiously antique phrases, such as "And it came to pass." The notes are very restrained in comparison with those of the earlier Roman Catholic versions. When the text seems to demand explanation in terms of modern Roman Catholic practice, a brief explanation is given. For instance, where we read that a bishop must be "married but once," [10] a footnote explains that "priestly celibacy as a law is of later ecclesiastical institution." The use of the term "immorality" [11] as a substitute for "fornication" occurs in both this edition and the Revised Standard. It enhances neither. "Immorality" as a synonymn for "fornication" is not only an ignorant "genteelism" of the present day; it is highly misleading, for of course murder, bribery, theft, and all other unethical behavior are immoral, as well as sexual misconduct. On the other hand, "we carry this treasure in vessels of clay," [12] is an example of the Confraternity translation at its best.

Unlike the Westminster Version, the Confraternity Edition was conceived as a revision of the Challoner-Rheims Version and a translation from the Latin Vulgate. The Old Testament, however, has been undertaken as a translation "from the original languages, with the critical use of all the ancient sources," into a thoroughly twentieth-century American English. So we have, for instance, the phrase, "whether or not the LORD had made his trip successful." [13]

In 1939 the Roman Catholic hierarchy in England asked Ronald Knox to undertake a translation of the New Testament from the Latin Vulgate. It was rightly expected that this would be a highly independent translation, for Knox, an Oxford don and convert to Rome, was well known for

[10] I Timothy iii.2.
[11] Matthew xix.9; I Thessalonians iv.3.
[12] II Corinthians iv.7.
[13] Genesis xxiv.21.

his vivacious literary wit. A draft edition, printed by subscription and for private circulation only, was issued in London in 1944 and was followed in 1945 by a final edition having the official approval of the Roman Catholic hierarchy in England. In fact few changes were made: an example is the alteration of "lads" to "friends" in one place.[14] A larger edition was published in 1948, and in 1949 the Old Testament was issued in two volumes of the same format, so completing the Bible in three volumes.

The American edition of Knox's translation of the New Testament followed the draft rather than the final British edition. Published in New York in 1944, it bore the imprimatur of Francis (now Cardinal) Spellman, which, however, is omitted from subsequent impressions. These impressions have continued, moreover, to be printed even since the issue in this country in 1946 of an illustrated edition which follows the final British edition, not the draft.

An interesting example of an independent modern American Roman Catholic translation is provided by James A. Kleist, S.J., and Joseph L. Lilly, C.M., in *The New Testament Rendered from the Original Greek with Explanatory Notes,* published by the Bruce Publishing Company, Milwaukee in 1956. The *Hail Mary* verse [15] is rendered: "Greetings! child of grace! The Lord is your helper! You are blessed beyond all women!"

[14] John xxi.5. See also Appendix I.
[15] Luke i.28.

XX

JEWISH TRANSLATIONS

THE JEWS are called the "People of the Book." We have seen why. From the time of the Exile they learned to depend much upon the Scriptures for inspiration and nourishment. After the destruction of the Temple at Jerusalem in A.D. 70, the Scriptures acquired an even greater significance for Jewry. In their wanderings in many lands, the dispersed Jews found in their sacred literature a common bond. The rabbis were often deeply learned in it.

The medieval Jew in Europe lived more often than not in extremely unnatural conditions. In the daytime, he might move in the "ordinary" world outside the ghetto to which he had to return every night at curfew, and within which he was cut off from the main currents of the civilization of his time and forced to find intellectual nourishment within his own highly inbred society. Within the ghetto he was sheltered from the Gentile world. Hence the development among these ghettoed Jews of certain specialized interests—their preoccupation with intellectual and artistic quests. But even when the medieval Jew left this atmosphere in the daytime, he was by no means any better off. For then he felt acutely conscious of the difference between himself and the Gentile world, which in turn threw him more than ever back upon his Jewish traditions. The keystone of these traditions was, of course, the Scriptures. Though often he read them through a mist of Talmud [1] and Midrash,[2] they remained the symbol, par excellence, of all his Jewishness meant to him.

When at last, in 1789, the French Revolution brought the Jew in Europe a greater measure of emancipation from such conditions than he had been for centuries accustomed even to hope for, he emerged deeply conscious that throughout the centuries of persecution it had been the Scriptures that had guided his fathers in their sufferings. Nor could he be expected quickly to identify himself with the Gentile world that was now open to him. It was a world that had set his fathers apart. He still felt apart. For long ostracized from Gentile society, he could not but continue to look with love and pride upon the pages of those writings that had meant so much to every Jew worthy of the name.

The Jewish ghetto in the Middle Ages was an institution fully recognized by the medieval state. It was a segregated society, and theoretically it was an elective representative democracy, though it was seldom if ever this in practice. Prominent among the officials of the ghetto were the rabbi, the cantor, the beadles, and the ritual slaughterer. The rabbi had a pre-eminent role. The ghetto was governed by a small council which, through various committees, administered synagogues and schools, organized charities, and assessed and collected the taxes that had to be raised both for the Gentile state and for the ghetto itself. The decisions of the council were nevertheless subject to review by the rabbi, who exercised judicial functions in civil matters. He was rarely if ever allowed by the Gentile authorities to

[1] A compilation embodying Jewish oral traditions and discussions of these.
[2] A Jewish method of interpretation of Scripture intended to unfold a meaning beyond the literal one.

exercise criminal jurisdiction. The larger ghettos often employed a liaison man to negotiate with the Gentile authorities.

Conditions varied, of course, from time to time and from place to place, especially in regard to the extent to which the Jew was cut off from the rest of society. But even where they permitted him to absorb a good deal of the "secular" influences of "ordinary" society, he was usually disinclined for the enjoyment of such culture, and the more this culture reflected the influence of the Christian Church, which it inevitably did, the less he liked it. Moreover, the more the Jew was desegregated, the unhappier was his lot in the long run. His condition in Spain, for instance, compared very favorably with his lot in other countries. But it was in Spain that he eventually had to face the bitterest persecution that Jewry ever suffered before the rise of Hitler in modern times. In 1391 and in 1411 Jews throughout the Iberian Peninsula were cruelly massacred, with the result that many who escaped that fate lost heart and sought physical safety by resorting to an external submission to Christian Baptism. This only created a new problem, the problem of the crypto-Jew, and it was chiefly to deal with this that the notorious Inquisition was instituted in 1478. At last, in 1492, the Jews were expelled from Spain where they had for long enjoyed greater liberty than had ever been their lot in northern Europe. Worse was to follow. Within a century they had been expelled from every country in western Europe with the exception of a few regions in Germany and northern Italy, and certain papal possessions in France. From the ashes of these fiery persecutions eventually sprang the Jewish communities founded in England, Holland and America.

The cultural life of the ghetto was lively but inevitably narrow. Every Jewish boy learned to read; but in the elementary school his reading was confined to religious matters. For instruction in other subjects he had to find private teachers. There was ample encouragement for promising boys to pursue their religious studies at schools designed to train them for the rabbinate. These rabbinical academies were, of course, the fountainhead of Jewish culture. In them Hebrew lore was preserved and Hebrew studies diligently fostered.

Classical Hebrew, the language of the Old Testament, was already out of everyday use by the time of Christ, when, in the synagogues of Palestine, the Torah or Law would be expounded in Aramaic. In later times it was possible to distinguish between the Hebrew of the Old Testament, on the one hand, and, on the other, the Hebrew used by the scholars who wrote the learned commentaries on them. The latter Hebrew was a sort of outgrowth of the classical kind. The two sorts of Hebrew are not sharply different: indeed, the later books of the Bible are already moving into a style that is not quite classical and yet is not quite the later Hebrew. Classical Hebrew did not suddenly go out of use. Old and beloved words and phrases continued, and the Bible was quoted in the original long after its language had become archaic for ordinary purposes.

Nevertheless, there was a tendency for the Bible to be lost under the vast bulk of the enormous literature written upon it by the rabbinic scholars. Gradually there was a revolt against this, a desire to get behind the weight of the Talmud to the relative simplicity of the Bible. The Talmudic scholars themselves were not unaware of the dangers. Gaon Saadya, in the ninth century A.D., perceived more than did many of his contemporaries that the Scriptures must be the cornerstone of Jewish thought and learning, and that their premier place must not be jeopardized by excessive preoccupation with other literature, however important or useful this might be in its own way. Saadya was a great scholar who, in order to improve the knowledge of classical Hebrew in the Jewry of his day, compiled a Hebrew dictionary and grammar. But he also made a translation of the Hebrew Scriptures into Arabic.[3] Neither too literal nor too periphrastic, Saadya's Arabic translation, with the commentaries he appended to certain books, was designed, of course, for the Jews in the Arab world. It is still read by the Yemenite Jews. But it also served generations of Jewish scholars in many parts of the world.

The first complete Hebrew dictionary was devised and completed by Menahem ben Saruk in Tortosa, Spain, about the middle of the tenth century A.D. Its shortcomings were pointed out by Dunash, a pupil of Saadya's, and the disputes which arose as a consequence stimulated interest among Jewish scholars far beyond the original area of controversy. In the next century, Solomon ben Isaac, better known as Rashi, wrote commentaries on the Bible and the Talmud that have ever since had a great influence on Jewish learning. Rashi's exposition of the Pentateuch became a standard work, the reading of which was expected of every educated Jew. Its appeal lay, apparently, in its moderation: it was neither too extreme in its conservatism nor too bold in its concessions to the rationalism of the day. Rashi was of such immense repute as a scholar that he was sought out even by Christian priests. His commentary was in part translated into Latin by Nicholas de Lyra in the early fourteenth century. The latter's *Postillae Perpetuae,* printed in 1471-72, exerted some influence on Luther's German translation of the Bible.

By this time Jewish scholarship had greatly extended. But the conditions under which Jews lived in the Middle Ages imposed great limitations upon them. In Provence

3 The books of the Hebrew Bible are set forth in Appendix XIV.

were three pioneers, Joseph Kimhi and his two sons, Moses and David. David Kimhi (1160-1235) was the compiler of a Hebrew grammar and dictionary that were for long influential—so influential that when Johann Reuchlin (1455-1522), the first non-Jewish scholar to attempt a Hebrew grammar and dictionary, sought the help of learned Jews for his task, it was to David Kimhi's work that they chiefly directed him. Kimhi's influence on the King James Version, though indirect, is not inconsiderable. His influence was also exerted on a Persian translation made by a Jew about the year 1400.

Translations of the Hebrew Bible into various languages, begin to appear about that time. In 1422 Rabbi Moses Arragel translated the Scriptures from the Hebrew into Spanish, for the Christian Church and with the assistance of Franciscan scholars, and it is upon that version that the Ferrara Bible, printed in 1553, was based. This famous Spanish Bible was intended to serve the needs of both Jews and Christians. Certain deviations were made in the copies intended for Christian readers. For example, where the copies destined for Jews read "young woman," [4] the copies set aside for Christian use put "virgin." Of about the same date as Arragel's Spanish translation is a manuscript of part of the Hebrew Scriptures translated into the Yiddish of the period—a German dialect with an admixture of Hebrew. At Constance, in 1543-44, a translation of the Pentateuch by Michael Adam, a baptized Jew, was printed, and in 1545 was published, at Venice, a translation of the Psalms by Elias Levita. The Teutch-Homesh or Yiddish Pentateuch, said to be in use to this day in eastern Europe, was first printed in Amsterdam in 1649. In that city also, in 1676-78, appeared the first complete translation of the Hebrew Scriptures into Yiddish. It was the work of Jekuthiel Blitz. There

[4] Isaiah vii.14. But cf. R.S.V.

was a later version by Joseph Witzenhausen, published in 1679, likewise at Amsterdam.

There were also numerous Jewish translations of the Hebrew Scriptures into Latin. Jewish scholars were highly critical of the official version approved by the medieval Christian Church. Among these translations into Latin may be mentioned one by Sanctes Pagninus, published in 1541; one by Sebastian Münster, which appeared in 1534-55; one by Leo Juda and several collaborators, published in 1543; one by Chateillon, published in 1551; and one by Immanuel Tremellius, a baptized Jew, which appeared in 1579. Münster's translation exerted some indirect influence on the King James Version. Chateillon also made a translation into French.

While the renaissance of learning in Europe greatly stimulated oriental studies, which made great progress in the seventeenth century both in England and on the continent, the progress of Biblical studies in Jewry was much hindered by the long and widespread sufferings that came in the train of the Inquisition. The Jewish scholar in Spain had profited by his contact with the Moors. It had brought Islamic culture close to him, and it had familiarized him with the Arabic language, the study of which was now pursued increasingly by Christian orientalists. In Italy and Holland there were indeed some Jewish scholars who took advantage of the fact that "secular" thought was comparatively accessible to the Jew in those environments. But these scholars were exceptional men. In Germany and Poland the Jew relapsed more than ever into the maze of Talmudic lore that once again smothered his Bible.

It was, however, out of that unlikely atmosphere of early eighteenth-century German Jewry that Moses Mendelssohn (1729-1786) emerged. Mendelssohn is so famous in the annals of Jewry that he has been called the "third Moses." [5] Born in Dessau, he was the son of a poor scribe. A delicate boy —he suffered from curvature of the spine—he was educated by his father and the local rabbi. In his youth he bought, out of his meager earnings, a Latin copy of Locke's *Essay concerning the Human Understanding*, which, with the aid of a Latin dictionary, he succeeded in comprehending. No doubt it exerted a liberalizing influence upon his youthful mind. At any rate, after attaining considerable literary successes, he was granted by the King of Prussia (Frederick the Great) the title of *Schutz-Jude* (Protected Jew), affording him unmolested residence in Berlin. Now devoting himself to the task of securing emancipation for the Jews, he translated the Pentateuch, issued in 1783, and some other parts of the Hebrew Bible, into High German. The effect of this on German Jews was incalculable. It opened up to them the treasures of the German language and inspired in them a taste for the culture from which they had hitherto been barred. Moreover, Mendelssohn, in accord with the mood of his century, whose intellectual temper we have already seen manifested in the opinions of Alexander Geddes, was inclined to look upon all religions as but relatively true, or, perhaps, as facets of a religion that would one day be common to mankind. The effect of his teaching was, therefore, to minimize the importance of adhering to the traditional Jewish faith, with the result that many Jews, notably Mendelssohn's own descendants, exchanged the synagogue for the church, bringing to the latter the "rationalistic" attitudes that were not welcome to those Christians who cared for their own faith. Mendelssohn's progeny was a distinguished one that included his eldest son, founder of

[5] The "second Moses" had been Moses Maimonides (1135-1204), the greatest Jewish philosopher of the Middle Ages, whose thought influenced the greatest medieval Christian thinker, Thomas Aquinas (1225-1274).

the famous Mendelssohn banking house, and his grandson Felix, the composer.

David Friedländer (1750-1834) completed the work of translating the Hebrew Bible into High German, with the help of other friends and disciples of Mendelssohn. A new school of Jewish interpreters of the Bible arose, known as the Biurists,[6] whose scholarship was in the best Jewish tradition but whose theology lacked critical insight into the history of Hebrew thought. In their train came an enormous wealth of scholarly researches among German-speaking Jews. There was, inevitably, a reaction towards Jewish orthodoxy. Here one of the foremost names is that of Samson Raphael Hirsch (1808-1888), whose German translation of the Pentateuch was published in 1867.

Meanwhile, an Italian Jew, Isaac Samuel Reggio (1784-1855), had published at Vienna an Italian translation of the Pentateuch in 1821. The influence of this work led to the foundation of a rabbinical school at Padua, whose head, Samuel David Luzzato (1800-1865), became one of the greatest Jewish scholars of modern times. Luzzato's fame as a translator and commentator is matched by the immense repute in which he came to be held as a pioneer in the effort to raise Jewish Biblical scholarship to a higher level in which it could take its place alongside the most reputable scholarly disciplines of the academic world.

A very erudite edition of the Bible in French appeared between 1831 and 1851. This, the work of S. Cahen, to which also Solomon Munk and Leopold Dukes contributed, came to be widely known as Cahen's Bible. A French translation of the Pentateuch by Lazare Wogue, which appeared between 1860 and 1869, was the basis of a more popular French version made by the French rabbinate under the direction of Zadoc Kahn. This was published between 1899 and 1906.

6 *Biur* means "interpretation."

An incomplete Dutch translation was made by S. Mulder and published between 1826 and 1838. The Pentateuch and Psalter were rendered into Russian by L. Mandelstamm and printed in 1862 and 1864 respectively. The Italian version of the Bible begun by Luzzato was completed by his pupils and published between 1868 and 1875. Hungarian-speaking rabbis prepared a Hungarian version which was published between 1898 and 1907.

There have been many Jewish translations of the Hebrew Scriptures into English. As early as 1789, the year of the French Revolution, a version of the Pentateuch in English appeared, purporting to be an emendation of the King James Version wherever this "deviates from the genuine sense of the Hebrew expressions, or where it renders obscure the meaning of the text, or, lastly, when it occasions a seeming contradiction." This work was dedicated to the Bishop of Salisbury, Dr Barrington. In 1839, Selig Newman published a similarly conceived work. A complete edition of the Hebrew Bible for English-speaking Jewry was produced by Benisch and made its appearance between 1851 and 1856. Yet another Jewish attempt at the revision of the King James Version was made by Michael Friedländer and issued in 1884.

Isaac Leeser's version of the Hebrew Bible in English, published at Philadelphia in 1853, remained for long the version most widely accepted for use in synagogues in America and Britain. Based upon the King James Version, though often departing from this, it was not a work of great scholarship. It leant heavily on the German versions. While it served its purpose for many decades, its inadequacy was increasingly felt as Jewry in the United States expanded. At length, in 1892, at the second biennial convention of the Jewish Publication Society of America, a project for the thorough revision of Leeser's Bible was considered. A committee to undertake the work was duly appointed, and to each member of this committee was assigned a portion.

The plan was that the result of their labors would be eventually presented to an editorial committee under the presidency of Marcus Jastrow, for final review; but as the work proceeded it was felt that this plan should be reconsidered, since it seemed that the work being done would result in an entirely new translation rather than a revision. In 1903, the Psalms, which had been the portion assigned to K. Kohler, was published. Dr Jastrow died shortly afterwards and was succeeded in the presidency by S. Schlechter, head of the Jewish Theological Seminary of America. In order to expedite the work, the editorial committee was reconstituted in 1908, under an agreement that provided for seven members, S. Schlechter, Cyrus Adler, and Joseph Jacobs, representing the Jewish Publication Society, and K. Kohler, David Philipson, and Samuel Schulman, representing the Central Conference of American Rabbis, with Max L. Margolis as editor-in-chief. In December, 1908, the latter reported upon his progress and described the principles by which he had been guided in preparing a draft of the translation of the Pentateuch, a copy of which draft had been by this time submitted to the members of the editorial committee. The principles were slightly modified, and the scholars, now under the chairmanship of Cyrus Adler, proceeded with the work according to the revised program. This provided that propositions embodied in the manuscript draft remained unless challenged, in which case the suggested amendment, if seconded, was discussed, put to the vote and, if carried by a simple majority, adopted. After the first proofs of the manuscript so amended had been seen by the seven members of the editorial committee, a great number of corrections were made and further improvements devised. By this time the scholars had sat for sixteen sessions of at least ten days each over a period of more than six years. At a seventeenth session, held in the fall of 1915, some queried points—between two and three hundred—that called for further discussion were considered and voted upon.

The Jewish Publication Society's version of the Hebrew Bible in English was at last published in 1917. Jewish in conception and sentiment, it nevertheless echoes the King James Version whose great merits the Jewish scholars were wise enough to recognize. The Jewish Publication Society is presently engaged in the production of a new version.[7]

[7] For a sample of a draft of this, see Appendix X.

XXI

THE BIBLE TODAY

THE BIBLE has for long been a favorite of book collectors. It is not difficult to see why. Even before the invention of printing by movable type, five hundred years ago, some Bibles had become the highly prized treasures of the great abbeys and other ecclesiastical foundations that owned them. Richly decorated manuscripts, sumptuously bound, they were part of the glory and beauty of the institution that housed them, and they were handed down as gold and silver plate and other heirlooms are handed down in an old family.[1]

When printed books became available, this tradition did not die. On the contrary, it was extended, for now it became possible for many people in comparatively modest circumstances to be the proud possessors of a family Bible. What in earlier times only the richest, such as princes and nobles, could hope to possess, might now be owned by ordinary burgesses. As the availability of printed books increased, book collecting naturally developed. Bible collecting was a particularly obvious and attractive form of the art, for

[1] This does not mean that the Bible was not studied in the Middle Ages. We have seen that it was. The evidence amassed by Beryl Smalley and others indicates that it was probably the most studied book.

Louis Braille first published his plan in 1829 and five years later improved upon it; but it did not receive official recognition in Paris till after his death in 1852. It was adapted for use in many languages: a Scottish missionary in China, Dr Murray, even adapted it to Chinese. Many blind people, however, especially those upon whom the misfortune has fallen late in life, are unable to develop the high tactual sensitivity necessary for reading the special Braille alphabet. These often find another system, invented in England in 1847 and known as Moon, much better suited to their needs. This system, in which a simplified form of the ordinary visual alphabet is employed, has retained considerable popularity, therefore, as an alternative to Braille.

For a century and a quarter the American Bible Society has brought this Bible to the blind by means of various systems of embossed printing. Many thousands of volumes of Scriptures for the blind are now distributed annually by this society alone. Bibles for the blind are expensive to produce; but both in America and England they are distributed at nominal prices. The British Society, whose edition of the Bible for the blind is in thirty-nine volumes, subsidizes them to the extent of selling at about a sixth of the manufacturing cost. Towards this subsidy the British Government contributes a grant which in itself, though less than a quarter of the total subsidy, is more than the blind person has to pay. Moreover, any blind person who cannot afford even the nominal price of one of the volumes may, on the recommendation of his pastor, obtain one free of charge. Similar arrangements are made in the United States.

Modern scientific progress has now also brought within the reach of the blind another invention, the "Talking Book." To those who cannot read by touch this is, of course, a priceless boon. Since 1944 the entire Bible has become available in Talking Book records. These are double-sided discs which run for about fifteen minutes on each side. The Bible in this form consists of a library of 169 of these discs—129 for the Old Testament and 40 for the New. The American Foundation for the Blind will supply such a library to a blind person in this country at cost; but even that is at least $150, so that few blind people are in a position to purchase one. The American Bible Society, however, distributes individual discs at the nominal price of twenty-five cents each. The Talking Book Machine on which these records are played is a phonograph made under special patents for use only by the blind. It may be either purchased at cost from the American Foundation for the Blind or borrowed indefinitely from the American Government through the Library of Congress.

A modest but clever little device on the lines of the Talking Bible but much more limited in scope is also made available at a very low price by the American Bible Society. This "finger phonograph" consists of a manually-operated record and "arm" that enable their owner to play, without any mechanical aid other than his own finger, a short portion of Scripture. Records are available in many languages. The whole apparatus, in plastic, is hardly more bulky than an average-sized book and very much lighter.

Even the Talking Bible has by no means, however, entirely replaced the older system of reading the Bible by touch. Nor is this system limited to the English language. Though of course the production of a "tactual" Bible is immensely more difficult than that of a "visual" one, the Bible in Braille is already available in Arabic, German, and Japanese, and parts of it may be had in other languages, including Norwegian, Swedish, Spanish, Portuguese, Italian, and Mandarin Chinese.

The efficiency and ingenuity of the Bible societies in the fulfilment of their more general task is too little known. For example, a few weeks before VE Day, the American Bible

Society received from the headquarters of the European Theatre of Operations the largest single call for New Testaments
ever made upon it: 350,000 copies. Though faced at the same
time by mounting demands from the Pacific Theatre, limitations in paper supply, and other special difficulties, half the
order was shipped at once and the remainder within a few
weeks.

The exciting story of the Turkish Bible no less dramatically
illustrates the resourcefulness of those engaged in the distribution of the Scriptures throughout the world. Turkey has
for long been a land in which the dissemination of the Bible
has met with opposition by the very predominantly Muslim
population. Nevertheless, before the founding of the present
Turkish Republic under Mustapha Kemal Ataturk in 1928,
the Bible had been provided in Turkish. It was available in
three scripts, Arabic, Armenian and Greek, for the Turks had
no script of their own and so used others, mainly Arabic, in
writing their language. In 1928, however, Ataturk decreed
that the Roman alphabet should henceforth be universal in
Turkey. The nationalistic dictator also issued a long list of
the words and phrases of foreign origin, which alone should
henceforth be accounted legal. This seemed to spell the destruction of the old Turkish Bible. Missionaries in Turkey
met the situation, however, by producing the old Turkish
version of the Book of Proverbs with a transliteration of the
same into Roman characters, on the pretext of providing an
introductory reader for Turks who had to learn to read their
language in the new Roman alphabet now prescribed by law.
It was popular. By 1937 the whole Bible had become available in the new script, and according to the new legal re-
quirements.

Abnormal requests are often made to colporteurs in the
course of their duties, and the provision made by the Bible

societies to help them meet these requests is impressive. It also sometimes leads to amusing situations. Francis Carr Stifler of the American Bible Society relates the following story. A deck officer in the port of Alexandria, Egypt, was trying to fend off a persistent colporteur who wanted to sell him a Bible. He decided to chaff the colporteur. He was interested, he said, only in a copy in Irish. The laugh was on him when the colporteur immediately delved into his kit and drew forth a copy of the Bible in that language.

Selling Bibles in new territories demands a knowledge of many techniques of salesmanship and evokes from the successful practitioner of that art all the resourcefulness that is demonstrated by those engaged in selling other products in Los Angeles or New York. These have certainly no cause to envy the financial rewards of the man who sells Bibles in remote parts of the world, for his recompense is meager indeed. But usually they may well envy his exceptional possession of the psychological factor most calculated to insure success—an unshakable belief in the product. A Canadian colporteur called upon a Ukrainian family that had recently settled in Saskatchewan. He had with him, of course, a Bible in the Ukrainian language. The husband declined to buy it, saying that he had no time, no interest, and in any case no money. The colporteur persisted till at last the man agreed to accept a Bible on approval.

"Perhaps my wife will pay you with chickens when she comes home," said the reluctant customer, "or else she will give you back the book."

A few weeks later the colporteur returned for payment. This time neither of the parents were at home, but a seventeen-year-old son and a fifteen-year-old daughter were, and they provided glowing accounts of the delight their parents were taking in reading the Bible, and the immense value that was now placed upon it in the family, where it was being read every evening.[5]

In Japan a team of Bible distributors go out on bicycles with large packages of Bibles strapped to their backs. They have also, however, another allurement for their customers. They are able to promise that there will be a showing that evening of a movie in the village—a movie about the book being sold. Admission will be free, subject to presentation at the door of a complimentary ticket, which will consist simply of any Bible or part of the Bible purchased that day. The movie, which usually consists of scenes from the life of Christ, is shown after dark to a crowded audience.[6] Not only is this a less expensive form of enticement than the gin and lobster with which salesmen in other fields must sometimes stuff their customers; it is also (except perhaps in the case of the sale of gin or lobster) more relevant to the product.

The extraordinary spread of interest in the Bible in Latin America has been to some extent due to remarkably trivial beginnings. Many Protestant congregations there trace their origin to the sale of a Bible. A well-organized and active congregation in the Coffee Mountain area of Brazil, for instance, claims as its origin the sale of a few Bibles by an illiterate Negro thirty-five years ago. Though he could not read himself he had heard Bible stories, and so moving was his testimony that a few literate farmers were persuaded to buy copies. Such was the birth of a community of some hundred and fifty Bible readers.[7] During 1933-42 the average annual distribution of Scriptures in Brazil was a little under a quarter of a million copies. In 1944 it was over a million. In 1954 it

[5] Recounted by Mildred Cable and Francesca French in *The Spark and the Flame*, p. 85.

[6] Recounted by Arthur Mitchell Chirgwin in *The Bible in World Evangelism*, a study sponsored by the United Bible Societies (New York, Friendship Press, 1954), p. 97 f.

[7] J. A. Mackay, *That Other America*, p. 151.

was about 1,500,000, half from the United States and the other half from the British and Foreign Bible Society in London.

Another typical story, coming from Guatemala, illustrates the Bible-reading potentialities of that republic of Central America in which two-thirds of the population consists of pure-blooded Indians. A Bible distributor in Guatemala lost his Bible while riding horseback over a rough trail. Several months later he happened to be covering the same ground and inquired at several villages whether his Bible had been found. Eventually, at a poor village, Sabana Grande, he discovered that it had been picked up by an illiterate Indian farmer, who had taken it back to the village and handed it to the only man there who could read. A few of the villagers gathered round this man to hear, out of curiosity, what he read aloud out of the book. They enjoyed the reading and came back every evening to hear more. By the time of the Bible distributor's return they were ready to be organized into a congregation. A year later they built themselves a small chapel. Later still, two young Indians from the village went to Chichimula to be trained for missionary work.[8]

The acceptance by Pan American World Airways of "Gideon" Bibles for the use of passengers who may desire them for reading during their plane trip provides yet another illustration of how vast may be the development of a movement seemingly trivial in origin. The Gideons took their beginning in the chance encounter of two men, strangers to each other, in a Wisconsin hotel in 1898. The men, discovering that they were both ardent Bible lovers, were impressed by what they took to be a providential meeting. They discussed their longing to see copies of the Bible in every hotel and other place where travellers lodge. The following summer, they and a third traveller organized themselves as the

[8] Francis Carr Stifler, *The Bible Speaks* (New York, Duell, Sloan and Pearce, 1946), pp. 104 f.

Gideons, taking the name, of course, from the Old Testament hero who had been divinely guided to devise a screening test for the selection of soldiers fit for a commando operation against the Midianites.[9] Soon they developed into an important organization for the distribution of the Bible. By now they have placed several million copies of the Bible in hotels, hospitals, ships, railroad cars, schools and prisons in the United States. During the War of 1939-45 they distributed over nine million copies of the New Testament and Psalms among the men and women of the armed forces. The Canadian Gideons alone have distributed half a million Bibles. The organization, world-wide in scope, now holds international conventions.

Such chance developments are by no means rare; but of course it is by carefully planned organization that the most systematic work has been done in spreading copies of the Bible to millions of people in remote parts of the world. We have seen that illiteracy has been the most serious obstacle; but the need for translating the Bible into all the languages of the world has presented a Herculean task. A glance at a list of the languages into which any one of the large Bible societies has translated the Bible or parts of it [10] will indicate something of the extent of the present achievement and the perseverance of the translators in pursuing their work during the past century and a half. Yet this work of translation is by no means nearing completion. According to figures published by the French Academy, there are 2,378 languages spoken in the world today. Into half of these not a single sentence of the Bible has been translated. And though parts—often very considerable parts—have been translated into the other half of the world's languages, the entire Bible has so far been trans-

[9] Judges vii.
[10] The formidable list of languages into which parts at least of the Bible have been translated through the efforts of the British and Foreign Bible Society is set forth in Appendix III.

lated into comparatively few tongues—about two hundred only. While the achievements of the Bible societies are, therefore, astounding, the challenge to Bible lovers is hardly less today than it was when the British and Foreign Bible Society was founded in 1804, since when not only has the population of the world increased but literacy has been enormously extended and is, as we have seen, extending at the rate of about fifty million persons a year.

We are reminded by Arnold Toynbee that had the New Testament been written in Aramaic, the language of Christ and the disciples, it would have reached only as far as the Nile, while in fact, by its having been written in the Greek of the market-place, it could and did travel through distant Mediterranean lands, reaching Rome. Such was the importance of a widely used language two thousand years ago. Changing conditions in our own day present us with parallel situations. In Asia and Central Africa local village tongues remain; but rapidly developing highways and other means of communication are fostering the use of new trade languages whose function may be compared to that of the market-place Greek in which the New Testament was written. Swahili, for instance, coined in Arab slavery, is now a trade language that can reach some twenty million people. In the Belgian Congo what was once the local tongue of the Bangala people has been transformed into Lingala, a trade language intelligible to people along a thousand miles of navigable river. These developments do not, however, diminish the need for translation into local languages and dialects. The story of the distribution of the Bible throughout the centuries abundantly shows that it has never dominated the minds of men or touched their hearts till it has been rendered into their own everyday tongue. Surely few are converted through Esperanto!

It is possible within the compass of this book to glance at

the story behind only a few of the vast number of Bible translations mentioned in Appendix III. Modern Yugoslavia is an
interesting case. Proclaimed a republic on November 29,
1945, this country, with a total population of about seventeen
million people, comprises the "People's Republics" of Serbia,
Croatia, Bosnia and Herzegovina, Slovenia, Macedonia, and
Montenegro. Half the total population is traditionally Orthodox. The remaining half is predominantly Roman Catholic;
but there is a Muslim minority of about $12\frac{1}{2}$ per cent, leaving another minority of about $1\frac{1}{4}$ per cent represented by
various groups such as Protestants and Jews. Many people
would imagine this country to be a very unpropitious market
for the Bible. The Yugoslav Government is, however, better
informed: in recent years the import duties on Bibles have
been made almost prohibitive. In 1955, however, when these
duties were temporarily mitigated, the British and Foreign
Bible Society distributed 64,697 volumes of the Scriptures in
that land. The society began this work in 1818 when a grant
of £500 was made for a Bible translation into Serbian.

In Kenya, in recent years, there has been a considerable
demand for Bibles even in prison camps containing members
of the notorious Mau Mau gangs. New Testaments in Kikuyu
have been distributed in a country in which over a million
Kikuyu have recently been resettled in new villages, having to
make a not always easy adjustment from their old way of living in isolated homesteads. The growth of cities such as Nai-
robi has also produced changes of importance in Bible
distribution, while at the same time the growth of the Asiatic
population in East Africa has been so great that it is estimated
that, apart from further immigration, it should reach 425,000
by 1970. It consists at present of over three hundred thousand
persons scarcely touched by Bible work. The annual distribution by the British and Foreign Bible Society in East Africa
is about twenty thousand Bibles and a further fifty or sixty

thousand portions of Scripture in the various languages. Its work in East Africa began in 1869 with the publication of Scriptures in Swahili.

Bible Society work in Ceylon dates from 1812, in which year an auxiliary Bible society was founded at Colombo and a translation of the New Testament into Pali (the traditional Buddhist language) was begun. Today Ceylon has a population of over eight million, of whom about sixty per cent are literate. The principal languages are Sinhalese and Tamil. Hinayana Buddhism, introduced from India in the third century B.C., predominates, with over five million professing that faith. Most of the non-Buddhists are Hindus, Christians and Muslims. The number of Christians is estimated at about 750,000. The Bible Society of India and Ceylon, which took over from the British and Foreign Bible Society in November, 1944, distributed 3,464 Bibles in Ceylon in 1955, of which 3,246 were purchased and only 218 delivered free. The total distribution of volumes of Scriptures in Ceylon that year was 40,387; the previous year it had been 35,493.

These random examples provide only the most slender indications of the work that is going on. A careful study of the statistics set forth in Appendix III will give the reader a fuller notion of the magnitude of the work of this great British society, whose policy has always been to distribute the Bible "without note or comment," letting it be its own interpreter. Between fifteen hundred and two thousand persons are believed to be working on translations of the Bible into the world's many languages at the present time. Apart even from the Bible societies, much translation work has been and is being done by Christian missionaries. Groups such as the Wycliffe Translators also contribute substantially to the work.

So vast and varied is the work connected with the distribution of the Bible and the promotion of Bible study among the peoples of the earth, and so often is it pursued unpretentiously in quiet corners without fuss or stir, that even if an international commission were set up with unlimited funds to investigate the work, a complete inventory of it would be impossible. In the United States alone there are many facets to it. Extensive work is being done among illiterates, especially migrant crop-workers, and among the Indians. The Roman Church approves an annual Bible reading week for its members. Schemes for systematic Bible reading are numerous. Noteworthy among them is the World-wide Bible Reading Program under which passages for Bible reading are distributed between Thanksgiving and Christmas. The weight of evidence of the extensive use of this material is very impressive. The Bible is indeed more widely read and studied than any other literature. Much remains to be done, for we have already abundantly seen that it is by no means an easy book. The greatest obstacles to understanding it are, however, the least obvious, and to these the concluding chapter of this book will be devoted.

XXII

BIBLICAL THINKING: THE
BARRIER BEYOND WORDS

I F THE AVERAGE modern reader, lacking a knowledge
of Hebrew and Greek, were to look at a copy of the
Bible in the original tongues, it would seem obvious to
him that the most serious obstacle to his understanding of
the documents before him was his ignorance of the languages
in which they were written. He would be wrong. If ignorance of Hebrew and Greek were the only or even the principal barrier to an understanding of the Bible, it might be
claimed that the translator's skill had for all practical purposes put the Bible fully within the reach of all. Indeed, since
even the original text is by no means always beyond dispute,
the scholar who has these languages at his command might be
said to be only a little better off than is he who must depend
on a good English translation.

The advantage that a scholar may possess over the ordinary
reader of the English Bible arises, rather, from the insight he
may have into the way in which the writer of the words was
thinking when he wrote them. Our distance from the thought
of the Biblical writers is a more formidable obstacle than the
barrier of language. Yet it is an obstacle that the average
reader, though he lacks acquaintance with the original languages, can do much to surmount.

Language grows out of the living stream of human experience. It expresses the thoughts and emotions of a people in the context of a common experience peculiar to them. Learning a language is more than learning a vocabulary and a grammar. In itself a vocabulary is a language-cemetery, not a living tongue. When you look at a dictionary you are looking at a language in a petrified state—one might almost say an advanced state of petrifaction. But even when you take a single word out of the living stream of language and isolate it, you have laid it to rest in its coffin. When you then begin to translate the word into other languages, what you are really doing is to try to find, say, the French or German equivalent of that which is, linguistically speaking, an American corpse. The more vitality your word had in its animated state, the more startlingly lifeless will be the corpse that results from the process of finding the "dictionary equivalent." This is so not only in regard to notoriously difficult cases such as the French word *"spirituel"* for which not even the boldest lexicographer would pretend to find an English counterpart. Even simple words such as *"pain"* and *"vin"* are ill rendered "bread" and "wine," since the role of both *pain* and *vin* in France is very different from the role of both bread and wine in England or America. *"Métro"* may be taken as the French equivalent of the English "tube" or the American "subway"; but the New York subway hardly plays the role of the Paris *métro*. Even within the same language a word may have very different connotations in different environments or situations. To desert-dwellers, for instance, "water" connotes more than H_2O. Even a preposition in the wrong context may have striking results, as the American discovered who innocently remarked to an Englishman that he had seen the latter's wife on the street.[1]

---

[1] In England the preposition "in" would be used, except in respect of harlots actually engaged in the pursuit of their profession.

The culture, customs and attitudes of a people so affect their use of language that even if Greek, not English, had been the linguistic heritage of America, it would not make so much difference to our understanding of St Paul as might be supposed. More fundamental barriers would remain, arising out of the profound disparity between St Paul's thinking and ours, and between the thought of his world and the thought of ours. Of course it is true that if we spoke in Greek we should think in Greek, and we should be to that extent nearer the thought of any writer, however ancient, whose thought had to be put into a Greek mold. Language affects thought; thought affects language. The fact that Chaucer wrote in English gives a running start to the modern English schoolboy who is for the first time confronted by him. Dante, though close to Chaucer in point of time, is to such a boy hidden, even in translation, behind an Italian cast of thought. Yet when all that is said, it remains true that it is not the fact that St Paul's words are to be found in a Greek dictionary while ours are to be found in an English one that constitutes the most serious barrier to our understanding of him. Much more important is the absence of a counterpart anywhere in our experience, or even our possible experience, of the situation in which he found himself. It is, of course, possible to make some interesting analogies—they crop up in many a sermon on St Paul—but there is no exact parallel.

For instance, in Paul's world it was quite common for intelligent and thoughtful people to think and talk habitually in terms of demons—evil powers bent on mischief. They so talked because "gods" and "devils" were as much part of the vocabulary of the Mediterranean world in the first century as "ideologies" and "neuroses" and "complexes" are part of the vocabulary of twentieth-century Americans. Such talk about "gods" and "devils" is, however, very misleading to us, because in the world we live in it is associated with very ignorant and primitive people—the sort of people who, when they need medical attention, consult the local witch-doctor. But this was not necessarily the case in the first century, when such a "gods-and-devils" vocabulary was used by "intellectuals" as well as by peasants. But then again, as soon as we talk of the "intellectuals" of the first century we are once more in confusion, because the men we are so designating were very different from the men whom we should call "intellectuals" today. Their minds were no less lively; but the scientific notions that are commonplaces today even among school children were unknown to them. They knew nothing, for instance, about magnetic fields; they had never, of course, seen even a camera or a telephone; they were ignorant of many of the now most elementary facts about hygiene and the internal workings of the human body. There are a great many people today in various parts of the world who are as ignorant of such matters as were they; but we should be fundamentally wrong if we were to class thoughtful people of the first century with the backward peoples of the twentieth century whose views seem similar to theirs.

It is the *orientation* of Biblical thought that makes it so difficult for the average modern American to avoid misunderstanding it. We all know that differences of orientation are to be found all around us today. The English newspaper report, "Fog on Channel—Continent isolated," strikes both Europeans and Americans as funny. The American convention of writing and talking of "Paris, France," "Venice, Italy," and "Athens, Greece," as though there were any danger of confusing these ancient vortices of human civilization and culture with their less celebrated namesakes in Ohio, Nebraska and Tennessee, seems odd to Europeans. Our *use* of language reveals, indeed, our attitudes and presuppositions, our orientation, better than if we tried to explain in detail what this orientation is. So, for example, when anyone al-

ludes to the Pope as the "Holy Father" or *"Summus Ponti-*
fex," it is usually safe to conclude he is not a Protestant or a
Jew. He has not actually said so; but his use of language has
made clear his special attitude. Notice, however, that the
awareness of all this on the part of a Protestant or Jew depends upon some previous acquaintance with Roman Catholic usages. Suppose we had none. Then an expression such
as the "Holy Father" would either puzzle us, or else—worse
still—we might even perhaps conclude that our friend was
talking about some family's male parent noted for his sanctity. The individual words used are familiar enough—so familiar that a person entirely ignorant of Roman Catholic
custom might conceivably so jump to an erroneous conclusion.

This is very often the case in our reading of the Bible. It is
not that the words are unfamiliar. Most of the vocabulary of
the Bible is fairly commonplace in our ordinary speech. Nor
is it even that there is any *exceptional* translation difficulty.
Certain passages, and even certain books, such as Job, are
more difficult than others; but on the whole the Bible does
not confront a translator with worse problems than he would
encounter in tackling other comparable literatures. But in
translating any literature into the language of a people whose
thoughts and ways are far removed from that of the culture in
which the literature emerged, there are always tantalizing
problems. This may be strikingly seen in considering the
problems that arise in translating a book of the Bible into
the language of a primitive African tribe. A missionary in
the Sudan has described the difficulties.[2] For instance, the
translator has to render the phrase "as it is written in the book
of the prophet"; but the people for whom his translation is
intended are an illiterate tribe who have no word for "write"

2 J. Lowry Maxwell, quoted in a pamphlet, *Each in His Own Language*
(Edinburgh: National Bible Society of Scotland, 1950), pp. 23 ff.

because they do not write. Moreover, the word "prophet" is troublesome, for all equivalents the translator can think of would conjure up a special image that would mislead them. So he has to write down tentatively, "as has been marked by the man-who-spoke-for-God." Then he has to say "preached" but there is no equivalent, and "talked" will hardly do. What about "repentance" and "sin"? Such ideas are not in the vocabulary of the tribe. But even when it comes to commonplace words the translator runs into difficulties. Having sent his manuscript to a colleague, he receives a reply that runs like this: "Your word for 'lake' means a lake with a hill beside it and no outlet. Won't do for the Sea of Galilee. 'Palsy' is not correctly translated by your word; that would mean paralysis produced by a drug. The word you use for 'bed' refers only to beds that are fixtures in the huts. Portable beds demand a different word. Your word for 'garment' won't do—it's too specifically applied to a garment embroidered in a particular way. You need a more general term. Your word for 'basket' means a basket with a cover, the sort they use for keeping kola-nuts in." And so on.

It is easy enough for us to appreciate all that. We do not so readily see, however, that in our reading of the Bible we are often ourselves in a similar case. It is not merely that when we read the word "street" a picture is conjured up to us that is almost certain to be very remote from what the Biblical writer had in mind. This probably does not matter very much for an understanding of the essential meaning of the Bible. There is more perplexity when we have to deal with, say, the Hebrew way of making various organs of the body stand for various kinds of feeling and emotion. We are accustomed to the use of the word "heart" not only to signify the physical organ that is the concern of cardiologists, but also to designate those romantic impulses and preoccupations to which we refer when we speak of a brokenhearted lover or when we say of a girl that she has lost her heart to a man. But we are un-accustomed to the Hebrew notion of so locating the passions in the kidneys, and even if, to avoid anything so ridiculous as "Examine, O Lord, my kidneys," we say instead, "my reins," we are still far from getting over the difficulty. That God should be invited to examine my heart does not necessarily make him sound like a cardiologist; but that he should be invited to examine my kidneys does make him sound like a urologist. To ask God, as does the Hebrew, to create a right wind within my bowels sounds indelicate to modern English or American ears. The Hebrew took the phrase as naturally as we should accept the statement that a man had stolen a girl's heart. In a culture in which the heart had ceased to be associated with romantic love, a person who heard that a man had stolen a girl's heart might laughingly ask: "How can she look so healthy, lacking that organ?" Or perhaps even: "Has someone notified the police?"

More difficult still for us are Biblical notions such as "sin." When the average American reads of "sin" he usually vis-ualizes a particular act of wrongdoing, such as embezzling $100. But by "sin" the Bible does not intend anything so simple. In the Bible the word has various meanings; for ex-ample, an unhealthy state of mind, a wrong direction or out-look that poisons or distorts a person at the most radical level, such as we might perhaps call a "moral cancer." To know what the Bible means when it uses such words in a sense that is not conveyed by any word in use today, in ordinary speech, you have to try to understand how the minds of the Biblical writers worked.[3] No translator, however clever, can really help

[3] A helpful book for this purpose is Alan Richardson's *Theological Word Book of the Bible* (New York: The Macmillan Company, 1950). An especially valuable, though more advanced and technical, study of the subject is to be found in *Bible Key Words from Gerhard Kittel's Theologisches Woerterbuch zum Neuen Testament,* translated and edited by J. R. Coates (New York, Harper, 1951).

you here. What a good translator can do is to make it possible for you, if you do not know Greek or Hebrew, to *begin* to try understanding how the Biblical writers handled ideas. Any good popular commentary on the Bible should help its readers to do this. Most important of all is a deep longing and firm determination to get behind the words into the thought of the writers. Those who have deeply loved the Bible have often misunderstood passages and gone far astray in their interpretation; but their insight into the general intention and thought of the Biblical writers has usually been far beyond what their very limited knowledge of the more technical aspects of the Bible would lead one to expect. The reason is simple. No one, however odd or foreign his speech, is really hard to understand when you are in love with him. For love helps you to transcend the limitations of language and think *with* the beloved person. At the same time, however, no true lover will neglect any opportunity to learn how he may better understand the mind of the person he loves. Love, reverence, piety, are not substitutes for a patient study of the Bible and the use of all the helps that modern scholarship provides. They ought to be, rather, stimuli to greater effort.

A word should be said here on the subject of what is still called, in America—very misleadingly—"fundamentalism." By this is usually meant literalism in the reading of the Bible; that is, the practice of attempting or claiming to attempt to read the Bible as though it contained no figurative language. Since the language of religion is in the nature of the case even more figurative than are most other kinds of language, though all language is figurative to some extent at least, such a claim is absurd. It also betokens a peculiarly non-religious frame of mind. It is true that some people are more literalistic in their thinking than are others: imagination and intelligence are not universal endowments. But to say that a person's thinking is literalistic is really to imply that he has a block against religious thought, a barrier, indeed, against even the beginnings of a religious attitude. The so-called "fundamentalist" is therefore the most irreligious of men. Not only is the "fundamentalist's" arrogance stupid; it is fundamentally opposed to the indispensable condition required for beginning to understand what religion is about. All religious men in every age have been in some sense poets, though they have been also much else besides. To undertake to read the Bible literalistically is to make certain of wasting one's time. To read the Bible one need not be learned, so long as one is humble enough and earnest enough to make use of the helps the learned have so abundantly provided, often out of a profound love of the Scriptures they have studied with unremitting care. But one must bring to it all the imaginative wonder of a poet, even more than the critical sense of the historian. The Biblical way of saying this—characteristically figurative— is that we must become as little children. People who read the Bible in such a spirit of humility and wonder do not necessarily all come to the same conclusion about it. But at least they are using their imaginations sufficiently to make it possible to say they are reading the Bible with some understanding.

Such people have come to the Bible in various frames of mind, and have brought many different attitudes to bear upon the reading of it. Some come with determined skepticism; others bring to it the more open mind of the scholar; others, again, approach it with undying faith and the conviction that the voice of God bursts through every cadence and his finger writes between every line. But whether to the adoring eye of faith, the raised eyebrow of unbelief, or the scholar's lowered eyelash, the Bible remains to the imaginative the most astonishing book in the world. It is certainly

the most influential, and there is much reason to prognosti-
cate that its influence is likely to wane only to the extent that
humanity declines into an era of mass slavery and unreflecting
barbarism.

APPENDIX I:

A COMPARISON OF PASSAGES IN VARIOUS ENGLISH VERSIONS

Hebrews i.1-4

WYCLIF VERSION (EARLY) 1382

Manyfold and many maners sum tyme God spekinge to fadris in prophetis, at the laste in thes daies spak to us in the sone: whom he ordeynede eyr of alle thingis, by whom he made and the worldis. The which whanne he is the schynynge of glorie and figure of his substaunce, and berynge alle thingis bi word of his vertu, makyng purgacioun of synnes, sittith on the righthalf of mageste in high thingis; so moche maad betere than aungelis, by how moche he hath inherited a more different, [*excellent*] name bifore hem.

WYCLIF VERSION (LATER) 1395-1408

God, that spak sum tyme bi prophetis in many maneres to oure fadris, at the laste in these daies he hath spoke to us bi the sone; whom he hath ordeyned eir of alle thingis, and bi whom he made the worldis. Which whanne also he is the brightnesse of glorie, and figure of his substaunce and berith all thingis bi word of his vertu, he makyth pur-gacioun of synnes and syttith on the righthalf of the maieste in heuenes; and so much is maad betere than aungels, bi hou myche he hath enerited a more dyuerse name bifor hem.

WYCLIF VERSION IN SCOTS (NISBET), *c.*1520

God, that spak sum tyme be prophetis in mony maneris to our fadris, at the last 2 In thir dayis he has spokin to vs be the sonn; quham

he has ordanit aire of all thingis, and be quham he made the warldis.
3 Quhilk quhen alsa he is the brichtnes of glorie, and figure of his substance, and beris althingis be word of his virtue, he makis purgatioun
of synnis, and sittis on the richthalf of his maiestee in huenis; 4 And
sa mekile is made bettir than angelis, be how mekil he has inheritit a
mare dyuerse name before thame.

TYNDALE VERSION, 1525

God in tyme past diversly and many wayes, spake vnto the fathers
by prophets: but in these last dayes he hath spoken vnto vs by hys
sonne, whom he hath made heyre of all thyngs: by whom also he made
the worlde. Which sonne beynge the brightnes of his glory, and very
ymage off his substance, bearynge vppe all thyngs with the worde of his
power, hath in his awne person pourged oure synnes, and is sytten on
the right honde of the maiestie an hye, and is more excellent then the
angels in as moche as he hath by inheritaunce obteyned an excellenter
name then have they.

COVERDALE VERSION, 1535

God in tyme past dyuersly and many wayes, spake vnto ye fathers
by prophetes, but in these last dayes he hath spoken vnto vs by his
sonne, whom he hath made heyre of all thinges, by whom also he made
the worlde. Which (sonne) beynge the brightnes of his glory, and the
very ymage of his substaunce, bearinge vp all thinges with the worde of
his power, hath in his owne personne pourged oure synnes, and is set
on the righte hande of the maiestie on hye: beynge even as moch more
excellent then ye angels, as he hath obtayned a more excellent name
then they.

MATTHEW VERSION, 1537

God in tyme past dyuersly and many wayes, spake vnto the fathers
by ye Prophetes but in these last dayes he hath spoken vnto vs by hys
sonne, whom he hath made heyre of all thinges: by whom also he made
ye worlde. Which sonne beynge the brightnes of his glory, and very
ymage of hys substance, bearynge vp all thynges wyth the worde of hys
power, hath in hys awne person purged oure synnes, and is sytten on the
righte hande of the maiestye on hye, and is more excellent then the
angels, in as moche as he hath by inherytaunce obteyned an excellenter
name then haue they.

GREAT BIBLE, 1539

God in tyme past diuersly and many ways, spake vnto the fathers by Prophetes: but in these last dayes he hath spoken vnto vs by hys awne sonne, whom he hath made heyre of all thinges, by whom also he made the worlde. Whych (sonne) beinge the brightnes of hys glory, and the very ymage of hys substance rulynge all thynges wyth the worde of hys power, hath by hys awne person pourged oure synnes, and sytteth on the righte hande of the maiestye on hye: beynge so moch more excellent then the angels, as he hath by inherytaunce obteyned a more excellent name then they.

GENEVA BIBLE, 1560
1. At sondri times and in diuers maners God spake in ye olde time to *our* fathers by the Prophetes: 2. In these last dayes he hathe spoken vnto us by his Sonne, whome he hathe made heir of all things, by whome also he made the worldes, 3. Who being the brightnes of the glorie, and the ingraued forme of his persone, and bearing vp all things by his mightie worde, hath by him self purged our sinnes, and sitteth at the right hand of the maiestie in the highest places, 4. And is made so much more excellent then the Angels in as muche as he hath obteined a more excellent name then thei.

BISHOPS' BIBLE, 1568
1. God which in tyme past, at sundrie tymes, and in diuers maners, spake vnto the fathers in the prophetes: 2. Hath in these last dayes, spoken vnto vs in the sonne, whom he hath appoynted heyre of all thynges, by whom also he made the worldes. 3. Who beyng the bryghtnesse of the glorie, and the very image of his substaunce, vpholdyng all thynges with the worde of his power, hauing by himselfe pourged our sinnes hath syt on the ryght hande of the maiestie on hye: 4. Beyng so much more excellent then the Angels, as he hath by inheritaunce obtayned a more excellent name then they.

RHEMISH NEW TESTAMENT, 1582
1 Diversely and many vvaies in times past God speaking to the fathers
2 in the prophets: last of al in these daies hath spoken to vs in his Sonne, vvhome he hath appointed heire of al, by vvhome he made also the vvorldes.
3 VVho being the brightnesse of his glorie, and the figure of his sub-staunce, and carying al things by the vvord of his povver, making
4 purgation of sinnes, sitteth on the right hand of the Maiestie in the high places: being made so much better then Angels, as he hath inherited a more excellent name aboue them.

KING JAMES VERSION, 1611

1 God who at sundry times, and in diuers manners, spake in time past vnto the Fathers by the Prophets,

2 Hath in these last dayes spoken vnto vs by *his* Sonne, whom he hath appointed heire of all things, by whom also he made the worlds,

3 Who being the brightnesse of his glory, and the expresse image of his person, and vpholding all things by the word of his power, when hee had by himselfe purged our sinnes, sate down on yᵉ right hand of the Maiestie on high,

4 Being made so much better then the Angels, as hee hath by inheritance obtained a more excellent Name then they.

KING JAMES VERSION (PRESENT-DAY WORDING)

God, who at sundry times and in divers manners spake in time past unto the fathers by the prophets,

2 Hath in these last days spoken unto us by *his* Son, whom he hath appointed heir of all things, by whom also he made the worlds;

3 Who being the brightness of *his* glory, and the express image of his person, and upholding all things by the word of his power, when he had by himself purged our sins, sat down on the right hand of the Majesty on high;

4 Being made so much better than the angels, as he hath by inheritance obtained a more excellent name than they.

MR. WHISTON'S PRIMITIVE NEW TESTAMENT, 1745 [1]

God, who at sundry times, and in divers manners, spake in time past unto the fathers by the prophets, 2 Hath in these last days spoken unto us by *his* Son, whom he hath appointed heir of all things, by whom also he made the ages. 3 Who being a beam of his glory, and the express image of his substance, and upholding all things by the word of his power, when he had by himself purged sins, sat down on the right hand of the Majesty on high: 4 Being made so much better than the angels, as he hath by inheritance obtained a more excellent name than they.

A NEW AND LITERAL TRANSLATION OF ALL THE BOOKS OF THE OLD AND NEW TESTAMENTS (ANTHONY PURVER, "QUAKER BIBLE"), 1764

GOD having spoken many times and many ways of old, to the Forefathers by the Prophets;

---

[1] At least seventy "private" versions, not counting Roman Catholic ones, appeared between 1611 and 1881. Of these only a few are represented here.

2. In these last Days has spoken to us by the Son, whom he put the Heir of all things, by whom also he made the Worlds.
3. Who being the Brightness of the Glory, the Mark of his Substance, and supporting all things with his powerful Word; when he had made a Cleansing of our Sins by himself, sate down at the right Hand of the Majesty on high:
4. And became so much better than the Angels, as he inherited a more excellent Name than they.

THE NEW TESTAMENT WITH AN ANALYSIS (JOHN WESLEY), 1790

God, who at sundry times, and in divers manners, spake of old to the fathers by the prophets, hath in these last days spoken to us by his Son; Whom he hath appointed heir of all things, by whom he also made the worlds: Who being the brightness of his glory, and the express image of his person, and sustaining all things by the word of his power, when he had by himself purged our sins, sat down on the right hand of the Majesty on high, Being so much higher than the angels, as he hath by inheritance a more excellent name than they.

THE HOLY BIBLE . . . TRANSLATED FROM THE GREEK (CHARLES THOM-SON, LATE SECRETARY TO THE CONGRESS OF THE UNITED STATES), 1808

GOD, who in sundry parcels and in divers manners spake in time
2 past to the fathers by the prophets, hath in these last days, spoken to us by a son whom he hath constituted heir of all things, by
3 whom also he made the ages; who being an effulgence of the glory, and an impress of his substance, and upholding all things by the word of his power, having by himself made a purification
4 of our sins, sat down on the right hand of the majesty on high, being made as much superior to the heavenly messengers as the name he hath inherited is more excellent than theirs.

THE SACRED WRITINGS OF THE APOSTLES AND EVANGELISTS OF JESUS CHRIST, COMMONLY STYLED THE NEW TESTAMENT (CAMPBELL, MACKNIGHT AND DODDRIDGE), 1826

God, who in sundry parcels and in divers manners, anciently spake to the fathers by the prophets,—hath in these last days spoken to us by a Son, whom he constituted heir of all things; (through whom also he made the worlds,) who, (being an effulgence of his glory, and an exact image of his substance, and upholding all things by the word of his power,) when he had made purification of our sins by himself, sat down at the right hand of the majesty in high places. He is by so much better than the heavenly messengers, by how much he hath inherited a more excellent name than they.

THE HOLY BIBLE . . . TRANSLATED ACCORDING TO THE LETTER AND IDIOM OF THE ORIGINAL LANGUAGES (ROBERT YOUNG), 1862
1 In many parts and many ways, God of old having spoken to the fathers in the prophets, 2 in these last days did speak to us in a Son, whom He appointed heir of all things, through whom also He did make the ages; 3 who being the brightness of the glory, and the impress of His subsistence, bearing up also the all things by the saying of his might —through himself having made a cleansing of our sins, sat down at the right hand of the greatness in the highest, 4 having become so much better than the messengers, as he did inherit a more excellent name than they.

REVISED VERSION, 1881
1 God, having of old time spoken unto the fathers in the prophets by
2 divers portions and in divers manners, hath at the end of these days spoken unto us in *his* Son, whom he appointed heir of all things,
3 through whom also he made the worlds; who being the effulgence of his glory, and the very image of his substance, and upholding all
4 things by the word of his power, when he had made purification of sins, sat down on the right hand of the Majesty on high; having become by so much better than the angels, as he hath inherited a more excellent name than they.

THE TWENTIETH CENTURY NEW TESTAMENT (FIRST EDITION), 1898-1901
God, who in the old days spoke to our ancestors, through the Prophets, at many different times and in many different ways, has in these latter days spoken to us through the Son, whom he had appointed heir to everything, and through whom he had made the universe. He is the reflection of God's Glory and the embodiment of the divine nature, and upholds all creation by the power of his word. He made an expiation for the sins of men, and then *took his seat at the right hand* of God's Majesty on high, having shown himself as much greater than the angels as the Name that he has inherited surpasses theirs.

American Standard Version, 1901

The Revised Version and the American Standard Version differ only slightly. It happens that in the case of the passage quoted, Hebrews i.1-4, the text of the two editions is identical. The following comparison of Mark xiv.1-5 is therefore provided to illustrate the kind of differences to be found between these two versions.

[Revised Version, 1881]

1 Now after two days was *the feast of* the passover and the unleavened bread: and the chief priests and the scribes sought how they might take him with subtilty, and kill him: 2 for they said, Not during the feast lest haply there shall be a tumult of the people.

3 And while he was in Bethany in the house of Simon the leper, as he sat at meat, there came a woman having an alabaster cruse of ointment of spikenard very costly; *and* she brake the cruse, and poured it over his head. 4 But there were some that had indignation among themselves, *saying,* To what purpose hath this waste of the ointment been made? 5 For this ointment might have been sold for above three hundred pence, and given to the poor. And they murmured against her. (*Mark xiv.1-5.*)

[American Standard Version, 1901]

Now after two days was *the feast of* the passover and the unleavened bread: and the chief priests and the scribes sought how they might take him with subtlety, and kill him: 2 for they said, Not during the feast, lest haply there shall be a tumult of the people.

3 And while he was in Bethany in the house of Simon the leper, as he sat at meat, there came a woman having an alabaster cruse of ointment of pure nard [1] very costly; *and* she brake

---

1 This attempted improvement is unfortunate: there were several ingredients in the ointment besides nard and a liquid base.

the cruse, and poured it over his head. 4 But there were some
that had indignation among themselves, *saying,* To what purpose hath this waste of the ointment been made? 5 For this
ointment might have been sold for above three hundred shillings, and given to the poor. And they murmured against her.
(Mark xiv.1-5.)

THE NEW TESTAMENT IN MODERN SPEECH (WEYMOUTH), 1903

God, who of old spoke to our forefathers in many fragments and
by various methods through the Prophets, has at the end of these days
spoken to us through a Son, who is the predestined Lord of the universe, and through whom He made the world. He brightly reflects God's
glory and is the exact representation of His being, and upholds the
universe by His all-powerful word. After securing man's purification
from sin He took His seat at the right hand of the Majesty on high,
having become as far superior to the angels as the Name He possesses
by inheritance is more excellent than theirs.

THE TWENTIETH CENTURY NEW TESTAMENT (REVISED EDITION), 1904

God, who, of old, at many times and in many ways, spoke to our
ancestors, by the Prophets, has in these latter days spoken to us by the
Son, whom he appointed the heir of all things, and through whom he
made the universe. For he is the radiance of the Glory of God and the
very expression of his Being, upholding all creation by the power of his
word; and when he had made an expiation for the sins of men, he
'took his seat at the right hand' of God's Majesty on high, having shown
himself as much greater than the angels as the Name that he has inherited surpasses theirs.

THE CORRECTED ENGLISH NEW TESTAMENT (LLOYD), 1905

God, having spoken in the prophets in time past, in many portions
and in many ways, to the fathers, hath at the end of these days spoken
to us by a Son, whom He appointed heir of all things; through whom
also He made the world; who, being the effulgence of His glory, and the

very image of His Being, and upholding all things by the word of his [1] power, when he had made purification of sins, sat down at the right hand of the Majesty on high; being exalted so much above the angels, as he hath inherited a more excellent name than they.

THE MODERN READER'S BIBLE (MOULTON), 1907

God, having of old time spoken unto the fathers in the prophets by divers portions and in divers manners, hath at the end of these days spoken unto us in a Son, whom he appointed heir of all things, through whom also he made the worlds; who, being the effulgence of his glory, and the very image of his substance, and upholding all things by the word of his power, when he had made purification of sins, sat down on the right hand of the Majesty on high; having become by so much bet-ter than the angels, as he hath inherited a more excellent name than they.

THE NEW TESTAMENT, AN AMERICAN TRANSLATION (GOODSPEED), 1923

It was little by little and in different ways that God spoke in old times to our forefathers through the prophets, but in these latter days he has spoken to us in a Son, whom he had destined to possess every-thing, and through whom he had made the world. He is the reflection of God's glory, and the representation of his being, and bears up the universe by his mighty word. He has effected man's purification from sin, and has taken his seat on high at the right hand of God's Majesty, showing himself to be as much greater than the angels as his title is superior to theirs.

THE CENTENARY TRANSLATION OF THE NEW TESTAMENT (HELEN MONT-GOMERY), 1924

1. *The Son, God's Word to Man*

God, who in ancient days spoke to our ancestors in the prophets, at many different times and by various methods, has at the end of these days spoken to us in a Son whom he appointed heir of all things; through whom also he made the universe. He, being an emanation of God's glory and stamp of his substance, and upholding the universe by the utterances of his power, after by himself making purification of our sins, has taken his seat on the right hand of the Majesty on High.

---

[1] Note the use of upper case for pronouns referring to the Deity and of lower case for those referring to Christ.

2. *The Son Superior to Angels*

He is as much superior to the angels as the name that he has inherited surpasses theirs.

THE PEOPLE'S NEW COVENANT (NEW TESTAMENT) SCRIPTURAL WRITINGS (OVERBURY), 1925

God, who at sundry times and divers manners, spake in times past unto our forefathers through the prophets, 2 hath in these latter days spoken unto us through a Son, whom He appointed an heir of all things; and for whom also He created the universe; 3 who, being a radiant reflection of His glory, and a complete expression of His being, and upholding all spiritual creation by the power of his word, having exemplified the possible demonstration of the nullification of evil on our behalf, sat down on the right hand of the majesty of God on high, 4 having proved himself superior to the angels, inasmuch as he hath inherited a more excellent name than they.

CONCORDANT VERSION OF THE SACRED SCRIPTURES, "NEW TESTAMENT," AN IDIOMATIC, CONSISTENT, EMPHASIZED VERSION (CONCORDANT PUBLISHING CONCERN, LOS ANGELES), 1926 [3]

By many portions and many modes, of old, God, speaking to the fathers in the prophets, in the last of these days speaks to us in a Son, Whom He appoints enjoyer of the allotment of all, through Whom He also makes the eons; Who, being the Effulgence of His glory and Emblem of His assumption, besides carrying on all by His powerful declaration, making a cleansing of sins, is seated at the right hand of the Majesty in the heights; becoming so much better than the messengers as He enjoys the allotment of a more excellent name than they.

A NEW TRANSLATION OF THE BIBLE (MOFFATT, FINAL EDITION), 1935

Many were the forms and fashions in which God spoke of old to our fathers by the prophets, but in these days at the end he has spoken to us by a Son—a Son whom he has appointed heir of the universe, as it was by him that he created the world. He, reflecting God's bright glory and stamped with God's own character, sustains the universe with his word of power; when he had secured our purification from sins, he sat down at the right hand of the Majesty on high; and thus he is superior to the angels, as he has inherited a Name superior to theirs.

[3] Reproduced by kind permission of Mr. A. E. Knoch.

The New Testament According to the Eastern Text Translated
from Original Aramaic Sources (George M. Lamsa), 1940 [4]

From of old God spoke to our fathers by the prophets in every manner
and in all ways; and in these latter days, he has spoken to us by his Son;
2 Whom he has appointed heir of all things, and by whom also he
made the worlds;
3 For he is the brightness of his glory and the express image of his
being, upholding all things by the power of his word; and when he had
through his person, cleansed our sins, then he sat down on the right
hand of the Majesty on high;
4 And he is altogether greater than the angels, just as the name he has
inherited is a more excellent name than theirs.

The New Testament in Basic English, 1941

In times past the word of God came to our fathers through the
prophets, in different parts and in different ways; but now, at the end
of these days, it has come to us through his Son, to whom he has given
all things for a heritage, and through whom he made the order of the
generations; who, being the outshining of his glory, the true image of
his substance, supporting all things by the word of his power, having
given himself as an offering making clean from sins, took his seat at the
right hand of God in heaven; having become by so much better than
the angels, as the name which is his heritage is more noble than theirs.

The New Testament . . . Translated from the Latin Vulgate (Confraternity Revision of the Challoner-Rheims Version), 1941 [5]

God, who at sundry times and in divers manners spoke in times
past to the fathers by the prophets, last of all in these days has spoken
to us by his Son, whom he appointed heir of all things, by whom also
he made the world; who, being the brightness of his glory and the image
of his substance, and upholding all things by the word of his power, has
effected man's purgation from sin and taken his seat at the right hand
of the Majesty on high, having become so much superior to the angels
as he has inherited a more excellent name than they.

The Holy Scriptures Containing the Old and New Testaments. An

4 Reproduced by kind permission of A. J. Holman Company, Philadelphia.
5 Reproduced by kind permission of The Confraternity of Christian Doctrine.

INSPIRED REVISION OF THE AUTHORIZED VERSION (BY JOSEPH SMITH, JUNIOR) A NEW CORRECTED EDITION, 1944 [6]

God, who at sundry times and in divers manners spake in time past unto the fathers by the prophets,

2 Hath in these last days spoken unto us by his Son, whom he hath appointed heir of all things, by whom also he made the worlds;

3 Who being the brightness of his glory, and the express image of his person, and upholding all things by the word of his power, when he had by himself purged our sins, sat down on the right hand of the Majesty on high;

4 Being made so much better than the angels, as he hath by inheritance obtained a more excellent name than they.

[6] Mormons claim that the wording of this version of the English Bible is directly inspired by God. No more than a whimsical rearrangement of the present-day wording of the King James Version with fanciful additions, it has plainly been designed to eliminate some of the difficulties that an uncritical reading of the Bible presented to even the nineteenth-century Mormons. It will be noted that the passage cited happens to be identical with the King James Version *(supra)*, except for the elimination of italics.

An earlier version, it is claimed, was begun in June, 1830, and finished on July 2, 1833, when Joseph Smith was twenty-eight. After his death in 1844, the Mormons say, the manuscript remained in the hands of his widow. It was, however, delivered in 1866 to a Mormon committee for publication. Many curious and novel additions to the King James Version were made. These are supposed to represent passages that had been excised from Holy Scripture at one time or another. The Book of Mormon which Joseph Smith claimed to have had delivered to him on gold plates from the hands of an angel, and which required special spectacles for deciphering by mortals, alludes to this. "For behold," it says, "they have *taken away*, from the gospel of the Lamb, *many parts* which are *plain and most precious*." It need hardly be said that the Mormon claim is entirely without historical foundation. It is also, by the way, noteworthy that the verse, 1 John v.7, well known to modern scholars as a very late interpolation which does not appear in any known manuscript in any language till far into the Middle Ages, is retained in the nineteenth-century Bible for which direct divine inspiration is claimed.

The "new corrected edition" of 1944, quoted above, bears a preface explaining that the Board of Publication of the Reorganized Church of Jesus Christ of Latter Day Saints (Mormons) had found "some words and phrases transposed or improperly placed" in the nineteenth-century edition of the "Inspired Version." Perhaps even heavenly grammar is not always all it might be.

The passage quoted is reproduced by kind permission of the Reorganized Church of Jesus Christ of Latter Day Saints.

THE NEW TESTAMENT IN THE TRANSLATION OF MONSIGNOR RONALD KNOX, 1944 [7]

In old days, God spoke to our fathers in many ways and by many means, through the prophets; now at last in these times he has spoken to us, with a Son to speak for him; a Son, whom he has appointed to inherit all things, just as it was through him that he created this world of time; a Son, who is the radiance of his Father's splendour, and the full expression of his being; all creation depends, for its support, on his enabling word. Now, making atonement for our sins, he has taken his place on high, at the right hand of God's majesty, superior to the angels in that measure in which the name he has inherited is more excellent than theirs.

BERKELEY VERSION OF THE NEW TESTAMENT FROM THE ORIGINAL GREEK WITH BRIEF FOOTNOTES (GERRIT VERKUYL), 1945

After God had of old spoken to our fathers at various times and in many ways by means of the prophets, He has at the end of these days spoken to us in his Son, whom He has appointed Heir to all things and through whom He made the worlds. As the reflection of God's glory and the true expression of His being, He sustains the universe by His almighty word. And when He had effected our cleansing from sin, He took His seat at the right hand of the Majesty on high.

He became as much mightier than the angels as the name He inherited was superior to theirs.

REVISED STANDARD VERSION, 1946

In many and various ways God spoke of old to our fathers by the prophets; [2] but in these last days he has spoken to us by a Son, whom he appointed the heir of all things, through whom also he created the world. [3] He reflects the glory of God and bears the very stamp of his nature, upholding the universe by his word of power. When he had made purification for sins, he sat down at the right hand of the Majesty on high, [4] having become as much superior to angels as the name he has obtained is more excellent than theirs.

NEW WORLD TRANSLATION OF THE CHRISTIAN GREEK SCRIPTURES, RENDERED FROM THE ORIGINAL LANGUAGE BY THE NEW WORLD BIBLE

[7] From the *New Testament* in the translation of Monsignor Ronald Knox, Copyright 1944, Sheed and Ward, Inc., New York.

TRANSLATION COMMITTEE, A.D. 1950 (WATCHTOWER BIBLE AND
TRACT SOCIETY [8]), 1950

1 God, who long ago spoke on many occasions and in many ways to
our forefathers by means of the prophets, 2 has at the end of these days
spoken to us by means of a Son, whom he appointed heir of all things,
and through whom he made the systems of things. 3 He is the reflection
of his glory and the exact representation of his very being, and he sustains all things by the word of his power, and after he had made a purification for our sins he sat down in the right hand of the majesty in
lofty places. 4 So he has become better than the angels to the extent
that he has inherited a name more excellent than theirs.

THE NEW TESTAMENT. A TRANSLATION IN THE LANGUAGE OF THE PEO-
PLE (CHARLES B. WILLIAMS), 1950 [9]

It was bit by bit and in many different ways that God in olden
times spoke to our forefathers through the prophets, but in these last
days He has spoken to us through a Son, whom He had appointed lawful owner of everything, and through whom He had made the worlds.
He is the reflection of God's glory and the perfect representation of His
being, and continues to uphold the universe by His mighty word. After
He had procured man's purification from sins, He took His seat at the
right hand of God's majesty, thus proving Himself to be as much superior to angels as the title He has inherited is superior to theirs.

THE NEW TESTAMENT, A NEW TRANSLATION IN PLAIN ENGLISH (C. K.
WILLIAMS), 1952

1 In old times God spoke to our fathers by the prophets in many different ways; 2 in these last days he has spoken to us by a Son; he appointed him the heir of all the world; he created the world through
him; 3 he is the reflection of God's glory and the living image of his
being; he holds up the world by his word of power; when he had made
purification from sin, he took his seat at the right hand of the majesty
on high; 4 and so is seen to be as much better than the angels, as the
name which he has come to possess is a better name than theirs.

[8] "Jehovah's Witnesses." Reproduced by kind permission of the Watchtower Bible and Tract Society of Pennsylvania.
[9] Reproduced by kind permission of the Moody Press, Moody Bible Institute, Chicago.

THE NEW TESTAMENT IN MODERN ENGLISH (J. B. PHILLIPS), 1958 [10]

God, Who gave to our forefathers many different glimpses of the truth in the words of the prophets, has now, at the end of the present age, given us the Truth in the Son. Through the Son God made the whole universe, and to the Son He has ordained that all creation shall ultimately belong. This Son, Radiance of the glory of God, flawless Expression of the nature of God, Himself the Upholding Principle of all that is, effected in person the reconciliation between God and Man and then took His seat at the right hand of the Majesty on high—thus proving Himself, by the more glorious Name that He has won, far greater than all the angels of God.

[10] The text is from *Letters to Young Churches,* now incorporated in the completed New Testament with slight revision. Copyright 1947 by The Macmillan Company, New York, and reproduced by their kind permission.

APPENDIX II:

LIST OF THE PRINCIPAL BIBLICAL MANUSCRIPTS

Name	Symbol [1]	Location
Alexandrinus	A	British Museum
Ambrosianus	F	Milan, Bibl. Ambrosiana
Angelicus	L	Rome, Bibl. Angelica
Augiensis	E	Cambridge, Trin. Coll.
Basiliensis	F_2	Basle, University Library
Basiliano-Vaticanus	$\aleph$	Vatican; St. Mark's, Venice
Beratinus	Φ	Berat, Albania
Bezae	D	Cambridge Univ. Library
Bodleian Genesis	E	Bodleian, British Museum; University Library, Cambridge; Leningrad
Boernerianus	G_3	Dresden
Boreeli	F	Utrecht
Borgianus	T	Rome, Coll. Propaganda (Vatican)
Campianus	M	Paris, Bibl. Nat.
Chisianus	87	Rome, Chigi Library
Claromontanus	D_2	Paris, Bibl. Nat.
Coislinianus	M	Paris, Bibl. Nat.
Coislinianus	H_3	Paris; Turin; Leningrad; Mt. Athos; Moscow; Kiev
Cotton Genesis	D	British Museum
Cryptoferratensis	$\overline{\Gamma}$	Grotto Ferrata, Italy
Cyprius	$\overline{K}$	Paris, Bibl. Nat.

[1] Scholars use these symbols as a convenient means of identifying and referring to the MSS.

Name	Symbol	Location
Dublinensis	Z	Dublin, Trin. Coll.
Dublinensis rescriptus	O	Dublin, Trin. Coll.
Ephraemi	C	Paris, Bibl. Nat.
Friderico-Augustanus	$\aleph$	Leipzig
Guelpherbytanus A	P	Wolfenbüttel
Guelpherbytanus B	Q	Wolfenbüttel
Koridethianus	Θ	Tiflis
Laudianus	E_2	Bodleian
Laurensis	Ψ	Mt. Athos, Monastery of the Laura
Marchalianus	Q	Vatican
Moscuensis	K	Moscow
Moscuensis	V	Moscow
Nanianus	U	Venice
Nitriensis	R	British Museum
Petropolitanus	H	Leningrad
Petropolitanus	Π	Leningrad
Porphyrianus	P_2	Leningrad
Purpureus Petropolitanus	N	British Museum; Leningrad; Vatican; Lerma, Italy; Vienna; Patmos
Regius	L	Paris, Bibl. Nat.
Rossanensis	Σ	Rossano, Calabria
Sangallensis	Δ	St. Gall
Sangermanensis	E_3	Leningrad
Sarravianus	G	Leyden; Paris; Leningrad
Sinaiticus	$\aleph$	British Museum; Leipzig; Leningrad
Sinopensis	O	Paris, Bibl. Nat.
Taurinensis	Υ	Turin, Bibl. Naz. Univ.
Tischendorfianus III	Λ	Bodleian
Tischendorfianus IV	Γ	Bodleian and Leningrad
Vaticanus	B	Vatican
Vaticanus	S	Vatican
Venetus ($=\aleph$)	V	Venice, St. Mark's
Verona Psalter	R	Verona, Chapter Library
Vienna Genesis	L	Vienna
Washingtonianus I	Θ	Smithsonian, Freer Gallery
Washingtonianus II	$\overline{1219}$	Smithsonian, Freer Gallery

Name	Symbol	Location
Washingtonianus I	W	Smithsonian, Freer Gallery
Washingtonianus II	I	Smithsonian, Freer Gallery
Zacynthius	Ξ	London, Brit. & For. Bible Soc.
Zurich Psalter	T	Zurich, Stadtbibliothek
	I	Bodleian
	K	Leipzig
	P	Emmanuel Coll., Cambridge
	W	Paris, Bibl. Nat.
	X	Vatican
	Δ	Bodleian
	Π	Leningrad

APPENDIX III:

MODERN LANGUAGES INTO WHICH THE BIBLE HAS BEEN TRANSLATED

It was noted at the outset that the Bible has been translated into over two hundred—parts of it into over a thousand—languages. By far the largest share of the enormous task of translation and distribution has fallen to the British and Foreign Bible Society, by whose kind permission the following tables are reproduced in facsimile from their official report.[1]

TABLE I: LANGUAGES

This Table contains a list of languages and dialects in which the translation or distribution of the Scriptures has been *at any time* promoted by The British and Foreign Bible Society.

Certain of the languages here recorded represent versions which have never been published directly by the Society, but have to some extent been purchased by it from other agencies for re-sale at its depots, or for circulation by its colporteurs. Such languages are designated by

---

[1] The following abbreviations used in Table I, column 3, should be noted:

B.	Bible
Goss.	The four Gospels
N.T.	New Testament

Other abbreviations in this column refer to names of books of the Bible, e.g., Ps. (Psalms), Lk. (Luke), Jn. (John).

the mark §. In not a few of these the Society has assisted the publication of editions by grants of money or paper.

The mark † indicates those versions in which, so far as can be ascertained, no active circulation of the Scriptures is now carried on by the Society.

The languages are arranged in geographical order under five main headings—Europe, Africa, Asia, America, and Oceania—with numerous sub-headings.

1. The first column contains the number assigned *in this recent year's list* to each language for convenient reference.

2. The second column contains the name of the language. Occasionally the names of translators, etc., are given—but only where it is necessary to distinguish between two or more versions in the same language. Similarly, reference is sometimes made to the character—but only in the case of those languages in which editions have been issued in more than one character.

3. The third column records those books of the Bible in each language which have been published, or circulated, by the Society. At the end of each main division a summary states how many of the languages in the section are represented respectively (*a*) by complete Bibles, (*b*) by complete New Testaments, and (*c*) only by some smaller complete portion of Scripture.

4. The fourth column indicates *approximately* where the editions in each language are circulated, or for whom they are designed.

5. The fifth column gives the date when for the first time any version—often of a single book of the Bible, or part of a book—in the language appeared in print.

6. The sixth column gives the date—as far as can be ascertained—when the Society first published, or assisted in publishing, or began to circulate, a version in the language.

Ref. No.	Language	What printed, or known to have been circulated, at any time, by the B.F.B.S.	Where circulated, or for whom designed	Date of first published translation of any part of Scripture	Date of first circulation by the B.F.B.S.
	EUROPE				
	British Isles				
1	English, Authorized Version .	B.	British Empire, etc.	1525	1804
	Revised Version . .	B.			
2	Welsh	B.	Wales	1546	1804
3	Gaelic	B.	Highlands of Scotland, etc.	1767	1807
4	Irish: roman char.	B.	Ireland	1602	1810
	„ Erse char.	B.			
5	Manx	B.	Isle of Man	1748	1810
	France				
6	French, De Sacy	B.	France, etc.	1474?	1805
	Martin	B.			
	Ostervald	B.			
	Segond	B.			
	Version Synodale . .	B.			
7	Breton: Léon	Gen., Ps., N.T.	Brittany, N.W. France	1807	1827
8	Provençal (Languedoc) of La Salle St. Pierre	Mk.	Gard, S. France	1888	1888
9	French Basque: Labourdin .	N.T.	Departments of the Pyrenees, S. France	1571	1825
10	„ Souletin . .	Ru., S. of S., Jon., Jn., 1 & 2 Pet.			
	Spain and Portugal				
11	Spanish, Valera	B.	Spain, S. America, etc.	1490	1806
	Scio	B.			
	Hispano-American .	N.T.			
	[For Judæo-Spanish see No. 62]				
12	Catalan	N.T.	Catalonia, N.E. Spain	1478	1832
13	Spanish Basque: Guipuzcoan .	Lk., Jn.	Basque Provinces, N. Spain	1838	1838
14	Spanish Romany (Gitano)†	Lk.	Gipsies in Spain	1837	1837
15	Portuguese, D'Almeida . .	B.	Portugal, Brazil, etc.	1495	1809
	De Figueiredo .	B.			
	Brazilian version .	B.			
	[For Indo-Portuguese see No. 549]				
	Scandinavia, etc.				
16	Icelandic: gothic char. . .	B.	Iceland, etc.	1540	1807
	„ roman char. . .	B.			
17	Swedish: gothic char. . . .	B.	Sweden, etc.	1526	1810
	„ roman char. . . .	B.			
18	Swedish Lapp†	B.	N. Sweden	1648	1811
19	Norwegian Lapp†	Gen., Ps., Is., N.T.	N. Norway	1838	1838
20	Norwegian: gothic char. . .	B.	Norway, etc.	1819	1823
	„ roman char. . .	B.			
21	Danish: gothic char. . . .	B.	Denmark, etc.	1524	1809
	„ roman char. . . .	B.			

Ref. No.	Language	What printed, or known to have been circulated, at any time, by the B.F.B.S.	Where circulated, or for whom designed	Date of first published translation of any part of Scripture	Date of first circulation by the B.F.B.S.
	Central Europe, etc.				
22	Dutch, States-General version	B.	Holland, S. Africa, etc.	1477	1809
	Visscher	B.			
	Van der Schuur . .	N.T.			
23	Flemish, Louvain version . .	O.T.	Belgium	1477	1825
	Verhulst	N.T.			
	De Jonge	N.T.			
24	Frisian, Western	Mt.	Friesland	1668	1884
25	German, Luther: gothic char..	B.	Germany, Austria, etc.	1466	1805
	. „ roman char..	B.			
	Van Ess	B.			
	Allioli	B.			
	Gossner	N.T.			
	Kistemaker . . .	N.T.			
	Schlatter	N.T.			
26	German: Modern Low . . .	N.T.	Mecklenburg and Holstein	1926	1927
27	Yiddish, or Judæo-German: Hebrew char.	B.	Jews in Europe and America	1540	1821
	„ Rabbinic char.	N.T.			
28	German Romany: South . .	Mk.	Gipsies in S. Germany, etc.	1912	1912
29	„ „ North . .	Jn.	Gipsies in N. Germany	1930	1930
30	Polish, Wujek	B.	Poland, etc.	1522	1810
	Dantzig version: gothic char.	B.			
	„ roman char.	B.			
31	Bohemian, or Czech: gothic char.	B.	Bohemia, etc.	1475	1807
	„ roman char.	B.			
32	Wend, or Sorbian: Upper Wend†	B.	Prussia and Saxony	1597	1818
33	„ Lower Wend†	B.	Prussia	1709	1816
34	Hungarian, or Magyar . .	B.	Hungary, etc.	1533	1814
35	Slovak: gothic char. . . .	N.T.	Czechoslovakia	1832	1884
	„ roman char. . .	B.			
36	Romany: Moravian . . .	Ac.	Gipsies in Czechoslovakia, Moravia, etc.	1936	1936
37	Slovenian	B.	Yugoslavia	1555	1869
38	Hungaro-Slovenian . . .	Ps., N.T.	Slovenians in N.W. Yugoslavia	1771	1817
39	Romany: Yugoslav. . . .	Lk.	N. Yugoslavia	1938	1938
	Italy, Switzerland, etc.				
40	Latin, Vulgate	B.	Students, etc.	1456	1821
	Beza	N.T.			
41	Italian, Diodati	B.	Italy, etc.	1471	1808
	Martini	B.			
42	Piedmontese†	Ps., N.T.	Piedmont, N.W. Italy	1834	1834
43	Vaudois†	Lk., Jn.	Piedmont, N.W. Italy	1830	1830
44	Corsican.	Lk.	N. Corsica	1861	1923
45	Sardinian: Cagliaritan . . .	Lk.	S. Sardinia	1854	1900
46	Romansch: Upper Engadine .	N.T.	Upper Engadine Valley, Grisons, Switzerland	1560	1883
47	„ Lower Engadine .	B.	Lower Engadine Valley, Grisons	1562	1812

Ref. No.	Language	What printed, or known to have been circulated, at any time, by the B.F.B.S.	Where circulated, or for whom designed	Date of first published translation of any part of Scripture	Date of first circulation by the B.F.B.S.
48	Romansch: Oberland . . .	B.	Oberland, Grisons	1648	1818
49	Arabic: Maltese	Ps., Mt., Mk., Jn., Ac.	Malta	1822	1870
	Greece, Balkan States, and Turkey				
50	Greek: Ancient, Septuagint Version	O.T.	Greek Church, Students, etc.	1481	1810
	Textus Receptus . .	N.T.			
	Nestle's text . . .	N.T.			
51	Greek: Modern: Greek char. .	B. Lk., Ac.	Greece, etc.	1547	1810
	„ „ roman char.				
52	Albanian: Gheg	Ps., N.T.	N. Albania	1866	1866
53	„ Tosk: Greek char. .	Gen., Ex., Dt., Job-Eccl., Is., N.T.	S. Albania	1824	1824
	„ „ roman char.	Gen., Ps., Pr., N.T.	Albania, etc.		
54	Rumanian: Cyrillic char. . .	B.	Rumania, Transylvania, etc.	1561	1817
	„ roman char. . .	B.			
55	„ Macedonian . .	Mt.	Macedonia, Albania, and Thessaly	1881	1889
56	Serbian: Cyrillic char. . . .	B.	Serbia, Croatia, etc.	1495	1824
	„ roman char. (Croatian)	B.			
57	Bulgarian: Slavonic char. .	B.	Bulgaria, etc.	1823	1823
	„ Russian char. . .	B.			
58	Bulgarian Romany: South-East	Lk.	Gipsies in S.E. Bulgaria, etc.	1912	1912
59	„ „ Central .	Mt., Jn.	Gipsies in C. Bulgaria, etc.	1932	1932
60	Turkish: Gagauzi	Jn.	W. Shores of Black Sea	1810	1927
61	Turkish Osmanli: Arabic char.	B.	Turkey, etc.	1782	1819
	„ Armenian char. .	B.			
	„ Greek char. . .	B.			
	„ roman char. .	Gen., Prov. N.T.			
62	Judæo-Spanish	B.	Spanish Jews in Turkey, etc.	1547	1829
	North-East Europe and Soviet Republics				
63	Slavonic (Ecclesiastical) . .	B.	Russian Church	1491	1813
64	Russian	B.	Russia, etc.	1815?	1819
65	„ : White Russian . .	Ps., N.T.	W. Russia, Poland, and Lithuania	1517	1927
66	Ukrainian or Ruthenian . .	B.	S. Russia, Galicia, Buko-wina, etc.	1869	1874
	Russian char. . .				
	„ Slavonic char. .	Ps., N.T.			
	„ roman char. . .	Lk.			
67	Russian Lapp†	Mt.	Kola Peninsula, N.Russia	1878	1878
68	Finnish: gothic char. . . .	B.	Finland, etc.	1548	1808
	„ roman char. . . .	B.			

Ref. No.	Language	What printed, or known to have been circulated, at any time, by the B.F.B.S.	Where circulated, or for whom designed	Date of first published translation of any part of Scripture	Date of first circulation by the B.F.B.S.
69	Finnish: Karel	Mt., Jn.	N.E. Finland and frontiers of Russia	1820	1820
70	Estonian: Dorpat	Ps., N.T.	Dorpat,Fellin,and Pernau	1632	1815
71	„ Reval	B.	Coasts of G. of Finland, etc.	1715	1816
72	„ Setu§	Goss.	S. of Lake Peipus	1926	1927
73	Livonian (Eastern)	Mt.	Latvia	1863	1880
74	Latvian: gothic char. . . .	B.	Latvia	1586	1816
	„ roman char. . . .	Ps., N.T.			
75	„ Romany	Jn.	Gipsies in Latvia	1933	1933
76	Latgalian	Goss.	S.E. Latvia	1924	1924
77	Lithuanian: gothic char. . .	B.	Lithuania	1579	1816
	„ roman char. . .	B.			
78	Samogit	N.T.	Lithuania	1816	1816
79	Ziryent: Slavonic char. . .	Mt.	Vologda, Central Russia	1823	1823
	„ Russian char. . .	Mt.			
80	Permt	Mt.	Perm and Vyatka, Central Russia	1866	1882
81	Votiak	Goss.	Vyatka, etc.	1847	1882
82	Chuvash Turkish	Ps., N.T.	Volga valley near Kazan, etc.	1820	1820
83	Cheremiss	Ps., N.T.	Kazan, Simbirsk, Nijni-Novgorod, etc.	1821	1821
84	Kazan Turkish: Arabic char. .	Mt., Mk.	Kazan	1864	1884
	Russian char.	Ps., Goss.			
85	Mordoff, or Mordvin: Ersa .	N.T.	Nijni-Novgorod and Simbirsk	1821	1821
86	„ Moksha	Jn.	Penza, Tamboff, and Saratoff	1879	1893
87	Bashkir Turkish	Goss.	Orenburg, Ufa, Perm, and Vyatka	1899	1902
88	Nogai Turkish	Gen.-Josh. Ps., N.T.	S. Russia	1659	1813
89	Karaite Turkisht	Gen.	Karaite Jews in the Crimea, Turkey, Lithuania, etc.	1819	1819
90	Kumuk Turkish	Mt., Mk.	N.W. shore of the Caspian and N.E. Daghestan	1888	1888
91	Ossete	Ps., Dan., Goss., Jas.-Jude	Central Caucasus	1848	1848
92	Georgian: ecclesiastical char. .	N.T.	Georgia, Transcaucasia	1709?	1816
	„ civil char. . . .	Pent., Ps., N.T.			
93	Transcaucasian, or Azerbaijani Turkish	B.	Transcaucasia, and Azerbaijan, Persia	1842	1842
	International				
94	Esperanto	B.	All countries	1893?	1912
	In European languages {	—	Bibles 44 ⎫ New Tests. 18 ⎬ 94 Portions 32 ⎭		

Ref. No.	Language	What printed, or known to have been circulated, at any time, by the B.F.B.S.	Where circulated, or for whom designed	Date of first published translation of any part of Scripture	Date of first circulation by the B.F.B.S.
	AFRICA				
	North Africa				
95	Shilha: Southern, or Susi . .	Jn.	S. Morocco	1906	1906
96	„ Central, or Berberi .	Lk.		1919	1919
97	„ Northern, or Rifi . .	Mt., Jn.		1885	1885
98	Moorish Colloquial Arabic, or Mogrebi •	Gen., Exod., Ps., N.T.	Morocco	1902	1902
	„ Hebrew char. . .	Mt.			
99	Kabyle: Little* (pubd. locally)	Lk. 1–12	Petite-Kabylie, Algeria	1833	1833
100	„ Great: roman char. .	Gen., Ps., Pr., Is., N.T.	Grande-Kabylie, Algeria	1869	1885
	„ „ Arabic char.	Lk.			
101	Algerian Colloquial Arabic .	Goss.– Phil. 1, 2, 3 Jn., Jude	Algeria	1862?	1908
102	Tunisian Colloquial Arabic .	Lk.	Tunis	1911	1911
103	Judæo-Arabic of North Africa, or Judæo-Tunisian	Dan., Hos., Jon., Hab., Mal., Goss.; Ac., Heb.	Jews of Tunis, Algeria, etc.	1897	1897
104	Tamashek: Tamahaq . . .	Ruth	Sahara	1934	1949
105	„ Timbuktu . . .	Mt.	„	1953	1953
	North-East Africa				
106	Coptic: Bohairic†	Ps., Goss.	Coptic Church	1663	1826
107	Nubian: Fiadidja: italic char. .	Mk.	Between Derr and Kerma, Nile basin	1860	1885
	„ „ Arabic char.	Mk.			
108	„ Kunuzi	Goss.	Between Assouan and Seyaleh	1912	1912
109	Arabic: Egyptian Colloquial · .	Gen., Ex., Ps., Mt., Lk.–Rom., Gal.	Egypt	1905	1905
110	Nuba: Heiban	Mt.– Ac.	Nuba Mts., near Heiban	1925	1931
111	„ Ŋirere, or Abri . .	Mk.	Kordofan Prov., A.E. Sudan	1937	1937
112	„ Moro	Mk.	„	1951	1951
113	Krongo	Mk.	Kordofan Prov. „	1934	1942
114	Nyimang	Mk.	„	1951	1951
115	Arabic: Sudan Colloquial . .	Mk.	Round Omdurman	1927	1927
116	Jieng, or Dinka: Kyec . .	Lk.	White Nile, above R.Sobat	1866	1905
117	„ Bor	N.T.	Round Malek	1915	1915
118	„ Chich	Mk.	N.W. of Melak	1916	1916
119	„ White Nile or Padang .	N.T.	Round Melut	1926	1926
120	Shilluk	Goss., Ac.	„ „	1911	1951
121	Nuer: Western	Lk.	Sudan, border of Abyssinia	1935	1935
122	„ Eastern (Jikany) . .	Jn.		1938	1938
123	Maban	Mk.	Sudan, border of Abyssinia	1946	1946
124	Moru	N.T.	Lado Enclave	1928	1928
125	Bari	N.T.	S. of Rejaf	1927	1927
126	Bari: Kakua	Lk.	Mongalla Province	1930	1930
127	Kunama	N.T.	Eritrea	1906	1927
128	Tigré	Ps., Is., N.T.	Eritrea	1889	1889

Ref. No.	Language	What printed, or known to have been circulated, at any time, by the B.F.B.S.	Where circulated, or for whom designed	Date of first published translation of any part of Scripture	Date of first circulation by the B.F.B.S.
129	Tigrinya	Ps., Is., N.T.	Eritrea and N. Abyssinia	1866	1866?
130	Ethiopic	Ps., N.T.	Abyssinian Church	1513	1815
131	Amharic	B.	Abyssinia	1824	1824
132	Falasha Kara†	Mk.	Jews in the Kara district, Abyssinia	1885	1885
133	Bogos†	Mk.	Bilin tribe, N. Abyssinia	1882	1882
134	Galla: Northern	B.	East and south borders of	1893	1893
135	„ Central	Gen., Ex., Ps., N.T.	Abyssinia and Kenya Colony	1870	1870
136	„ Eastern Shoa, or Ittu† .	Mt.		1886	1886
137	„ Southern, or Bararetta.	Mt., Jn.		1878	1889
138	Sidamo	Mk.	Sidamo Prov., Abyssinia	1933	1933
139	Gofa	Mk.	Gofa Province, Abyssinia	1934	1934
140	Walamo	Jn.	Walamo Prov., Abyssinia	1943	1943
141	Gudeilla	Mt.	Kambata Province, Abyssinia	1935	1935
142	Boran	Lk., Jn., Ac.	Boran Prov., Abyssinia, and Kenya Colony	1934	1934
143	Somali: Ogaden-Harti . . .	Mk., Jn.	Italian Somaliland and Kenya Colony	1915	1915

Eastern Equatorial Africa

Ref. No.	Language	What printed, or known to have been circulated, at any time, by the B.F.B.S.	Where circulated, or for whom designed	Date of first published translation of any part of Scripture	Date of first circulation by the B.F.B.S.
144	Swahili: Central, or Mombasa: roman char.	B.	Mombasa, etc.	1847	1892
	„ „ Arabic char.	Lk., Jn.			
145	Swahili Southern, or Zanzibar: roman char.	B.	Zanzibar, etc.	1868	1869
	„ „ Arabic char.	Mt., Jn.			
	„ Standard	B.			
146	Ganda (Luganda)	B.	Uganda Protectorate	1886	1888
147	Madi	Ru., Mk., Jn.	Uganda and Mongalla Province	1935	1935
148	Karamojong	Gen., Mk., Lk.-Ac.	W. of Lake Rudolf	1930	1932
149	Nyoro (Lunyoro), or Toro .	B.	N.&W.Provinces, Uganda	1900	1900
150	Gang, or Acholi	N.T.	Nile Province, Uganda	1905	1905
151	Lugbara	N.T.	N.E. frontier, Belgian Congo, and West Nile District, Uganda	1922	1922
152	Konjo (Lukonjo)	Mk.	Near Kabarole, Toro, and Belgian Congo	1914	1914
153	Nkole (Lunyankore) . . .	Goss.	Ankole, Uganda	1907	1907
154	Teso (Ateso)	N.T.	E. Province, Uganda	1910	1910
155	Soga (Lusoga)	Jn.	Busoga, Uganda	1896	1899
156	Suk	Mk.	Mt. Elgon, Kenya Colony	1936	1936
157	Shamba	Mk.	Near Mt. Elgon	1931	1931
158	Gisu (Lugisu), or Masaba .	Goss., Ac.	Near Mt. Elgon, Kenya and Uganda	1904	1904
159	Hanga (Luhanga) or Luyia .	Gen. N.T.	W. of Nyanza Province	1914	1914
160	Luo (Dholuo)	B.	N.E. of Victoria Nyanza	1911	1911
161	Kipsigis	N.T.	E. of Victoria Nyanza	1912	1912
162	Nandi	B.	E. of Victoria Nyanza	1926	1935
163	Kisii, or Gusii	N.T.	S. Kavirondo Gulf	1923	1929

Ref. No.	Language	What printed, or known to have been circulated, at any time, by the B.F.B.S.	Where circulated, or for whom designed	Date of first published translation of any part of Scripture	Date of first circulation by the B.F.B.S.
164	Kikuyu	B.	S. of Mt. Kenya, Kenya Colony	1903	1903
165	Masai	N.T.	Kenya Colony	1905	1905
166	Meru	N.T., Ps.	N. & N.E. of Mt. Kenya	1921	1921
167	Tharaka	Jn.	N. & N.E. of Mt. Kenya	1934	1934
168	Pokomo	Ps., N.T.	Witu, Kenya Colony	1894	1894
169	Giryama	B.	N. of Mombasa	1892	1892
170	Kamba (Kikamba): Eastern .	Gen., Dan., N.T.	N.W. of Mombasa	1850	1904
171	Nyika(Kinyika)of Kenya Rabai†	Lk.	Inland from Mombasa	1848	1848
172	„ Ribé†	Mt.		1878	1882
173	Taita: Dabida	Gen., N.T.	Taita Hills, Kenya Colony	1904	1911
174	„ Sagalla	Goss.		1892	1892
175	Rundi	N.T., Ps.	Between Victoria Nyanza and Lake Tanganyika	1920	1935
176	Ruanda (Urunyarwanda) . .	B.	„ „	1914	1914
177	Hangaza	Mk.	N.W. Tanganyika	1938	1938
178	Haya (Luhaya)	N.T.	Bukoba, W. of Victoria Nyanza	1913	1920
179	Zanaki	Mt.	S.E. Victoria Nyanza	1948	1948
180	Jita (Kijita)	N.T.	S.E. Victoria Nyanza	1934	1942
181	Sukuma (Kisukuma) . . .	N.T.	Nassa, Tanganyika Territory	1895	1895
182	Ilamba	Mk., Jn.	N. Central Tanganyika	1939	1939
183	Nyamwezi	N.T.	Unyamwezi, Tanganyika Territory	1897	1897
184	Asu (Chasu)	N.T.	Paré Mts., „	1910	1922
185	Taveta (Kitaveta)	N.T.	S.E. of Kilima-Njaro „	1892	1892
186	Chaga: Mochi	Mt.	S.W. of Kilima-Njaro „	1892	1892
187	„ Machame	Goss.	Near Mt. Elgon „ „	1932	1932
188	Shambala	N.T.	Usambara, Tanganyika Territory	1894	1903
189	Bondei	Mt.	Usambara „	1887	1890
190	Kaguru	Mt., Lk., Jn.	Mamboia „	1885	1885
191	Zigula	Mt.	Ziguland „	1906	1906
192	Gogo (Chigogo) . . .	Gen., Ex., Num., Ru., 1 & 2 Sam., Jon., N.T.	Ugogo „	1886	1887
193	Bena	N.T.	N.E. of Lake Nyasa „	1920	1920
194	Manda	N.T.	E. of Lake Nyasa	1912	1928
195	Mpoto	Mk.	E. of Lake Nyasa	1913	1914
	Nyasaland, Northern Rhodesia, etc.				
196	Nyanja: Eastern	B.	E. of Lake Nyasa	1891	1894
	Union Nyanja	B.	E., S., & W. of Lake Nyasa	1901	1901
197	Nyika of Lake Nyasa, or Nyasa Nyika	N.T.	N.W. of Lake Nyasa	1904	1904
198	Tonga (Chitonga) of Lake Nyasa, or Nyasa Tonga	Jn.	W. of Lake Nyasa	1890	1899
199	Tumbuka§	N.T.	W. of Lake Nyasa	1904	1931
200	Mambwe (Kimambwe) . .	N.T.	S. of Lake Tanganyika	1893	1893
	Mambwe-Lungu, Union Version	N.T.			

Ref. No.	Language	What printed, or known to have been circulated, at any time, by the B.F.B.S.	Where circulated, or for whom designed	Date of first published translation of any part of Scripture	Date of first circulation by the B.F.B.S.
201	Bemba (Chibemba), or Wemba	B.	N. Rhodesia, etc.	1904	1906
202	Namwanga (Chinamwanga) .	Lk.	N.W. of Lake Nyasa	1903	1903
203	Konde (Nyakusa)	N.T., Ps.	N. of Lake Nyasa	1895	1899
204	Nsenga (Chinsenga) . . .	N.T., Ps.	N. Rhodesia, etc.	1916	1919
205	Lamba	Gen.–Lev., Josh., Ru., 1 & 2 Sam., Ps., Pr., S. of S., Dan., Obad., Jn. Ps., N.T.	N. Rhodesia and Belgian Congo	1914	1928
206	Luba: Kaonde	N.T.	S.E. Belgian Congo and N. Rhodesia	1923	1923
207	Mbunda	Mk. – Jn.	N. Barotseland	1919	1926
208	Lozi (Kololo)	B.	Barotseland, N. Rhodesia	1922	1922
209	Nkoya	N.T., Ps.	R. Luampa, N. Rhodesia	1926	1929
210	Mukuni or Lenje	Mk.,Lk.–Ac.	Upper Kafue, N.Rhodesia	1920	1927
211	Ila	Exod., N.T., Ps.	N. Rhodesia	1906	1907
212	Tonga (Zambezi)	Gen., Mt., Mk.	Bet. the Zambezi and Kafue Rivers	1911	1922
	Tonga (Rhodesia or Union) .	1 & 2 Sam. N.T.			
213	Shona	Gen., 1 and 2 Sam., Ps., Is., N.T.	Mashonaland, S. Rhodesia	1898	1898
214	„ Swina Manyika . .	N.T.		1903	1919
	Union Shona	B.			
215	Karanga	N.T.	Mashonaland	1904	1904
216	Tabele	Ps., N.T.	Matabeleland, S. Rhodesia	1884	1901
217	Kalaña	Goss., Ac.	W. of Matabeleland	1904	1904
218	Ndau	Gen., Ex., 1 & 2 Sam., Ps., Is., N.T.	Near Melsetter, S. Rhodesia	1903	1910
	Mozambique, etc.				
219	Yao	B.	E. and S. of Lake Nyasa	1880	1880
220	Makua	Mk., Jn.	S. of Cape Delgado	1881	1927
221	Sena	Mk.	Lower Zambezi	1897	1897
222	Ronga	B.	Lourenço Marques, etc.	1896	1896
223	Tswa (Sheetswa)§	B.	Sofala to Lourenço Marques	1888	1903?
224	Tonga of Inhambane District§	N.T.	Inhambane, etc.	1888	1905?
225	Thonga, or Gwamba, or Shangaan	B.	Valleys of Limpopo and Komati Rivers	1883	1892
226	Chopi	Mt.	Near Inhambane	1902	1932
	Islands off East Africa				
227	Malagasy	B.	Madagascar	1827	1828
228	Malagasy Tsimihety . . .	Lk.	N.W. Madagascar	1924	1924
229	Mauritius Creole	Goss., Ac.	Creoles in Mauritius, etc.	1885	1885

Ref. No.	Language	What printed, or known to have been circulated, at any time, by the B.F.B.S.	Where circulated, or for whom designed	Date of first published translation of any part of Scripture	Date of first circulation by the B.F.B.S.
	South-West, South, and South-East Africa				
230	Afrikaans, or Cape Dutch	B.	S. Africa	1873	1920
231	Venda (Sevenda)	B.	N. Transvaal	1920	1920
232	Pedi (Sepedi)	B.	N. Transvaal	1890	1890
233	Zulu	B.	Zululand and Natal	1846	1865
234	Suto (Sesuto)	B.	Basutoland, etc.	1829	1855
235	Xhosa, or Kafir	B.	Amaxosa, etc., Kaffraria	1833	1836
236	Chuana (Tswana): Tlapi (Setlapi)	B.	Bechuanaland	1826	1830
237	Chuana (Tswana): Central	Mt.	C. Bechuanaland	1941	1941
238	Nama, or Khoi-Khoi	Ps., N.T.	Namaqualand	1831	1831
239	Herero	Ps., N.T.	Damaraland	1849	1875
240	Ndonga	B.	Ovamboland	1878	1891
241	Kuanyama	Ps., N.T.	N. Ovamboland	1894	1894
	Angola and Belgian Congo				
242	Mbundu (Umbundu) of Benguella	Pent.. Ps., N.T.	Central Angola	1889	1923
243	Nyemba	Jn.	,, ,,	1955	1955
244	Luimbi	Mk.	Central Angola	1935	1935
245	Luchazi	N.T.	S.E. Angola	1935	1935
246	Lunda of Kalunda	Gen., Ex., Josh., Jud., Ru., Ps., N.T.	Borders of Angola, Belgian Congo and N. Rhodesia	1914	1916
247	Chokwe	Gen., Ex., Ps., Prov., N.T.	N.E. Angola	1916	1920
248	Mbundu (Kimbundu) of Loanda	Ps., N.T.	Loanda, N. Angola	1888	1888
249	Gimbunda	Mt., Jn.	S.W. Belgian Congo	1934	1934
250	Pende	N.T.	S.W. Belgian Congo	1926	1926
251	Kiyaka	Jn.	S.W. Belgian Congo	1939	1939
252	Kwese	Jn.	S.W. Belgian Congo	1929	1929
253	Kuba: Inkongo (Luna-Inkongo)	B.	Between Sankuru and Lulua, Belgian Congo	1905	1911
254	Kwango or Kongo: Commercial (Kituba)	N.T.	S.W. Belgian Congo	1938	1938
255	Salampasu	Mk.	S. Belgian Congo	1938	1938
256	Wongo	Lk., Jn.	S. Belgian Congo	1938	1938
257	Luba: Lulua	B.	S. Belgian Congo	1903	1913
258	Luba: Songi or Kalebwe, Western	N.T.	S. Belgian Congo	1920	1920
259	,, Kalebwe, Eastern	N.T.	S. Belgian Congo	1937	1937
260	,, Kalanga	Mk.	S. Belgian Congo	1948	1948
261	,, Katanga	B.	Katanga, Belgian Congo	1921	1921
262	Luunda of Mwante Yamvo	N.T. Ps.	Katanga, Belgian Congo	1914	1914
263	Ibembe	Gen.	N.W. Lake Tanganyika	1936	1937
264	Fuliro	Mk.	N. of Lake Tanganyika	1929	1929
265	Mashi	Jn.	S. of Lake Kivu	1917	1953
266	Lega (Kilega)	Mk., Jn., Ac.	E. of Lake Kivu	1934	1934
267	Hunde	Mk.	N. of Lake Kivu	1929	1930

Ref. No.	Language	What printed, or known to have been circulated, at any time, by the B.F.B.S.	Where circulated, or for whom designed	Date of first published translation of any part of Scripture	Date of first circulation by the B.F.B.S.
268	Pere	Jn.	N.W. of Lake Edward	1938	1938
269	Ndandi	Mt., Jn., Ac., Gal.-Col.	W. of Lake Edward	1932	1932
270	Kingwana: Lualaba . . .	N.T.	Belgian Congo	1937	1937
271	„ Ituri	Ps. Prov., N.T.	N. Belgian Congo	1921	1921
	Congo Swahili .	N.T. Ps.		1952	1952
272	Lendu (Batha)	N.T.	W. of Albert Nyanza	1926	1926
273	Lur	B.	W. of Albert Nyanza	1922	1922
274	Logo	Mt., Mk.	N.E. Belgian Congo	1924	1924
275	Bira	Jn.	W. of Albert Nyanza	1930	1930
276	Kele Congo	N.T.	Aruwini R.to Stanley Falls	1900	1927
277	Kakwa of Congo	Mk.	Belgian Congo and borders of Anglo-Egyptian Sudan	1930	1930
278	Momvu	Mk.	N. Belgian Congo	1931	1931
279	Zande	N.T., Ps.	Borders of Belgian Congo, Anglo-Egyptian Sudan, and French Eq. Africa	1918	1918
280	Ngbaka	Jn.	Between Ubangi and Congo Rivers	1935	1935
281	Mongwande	Mk.	Between Ubangi and Congo Rivers	1935	1935
282	Ngala (Bangala): Uele (Welle)	B.	N. Belgian Congo	1916	1916
283	Ngala (Lingala)	N.T.	N.W. Belgian Congo	1942	1942
	Union Ngala	Mk.			
284	Bua (Libua)	Mk.	N. Belgian Congo	1938	1938
285	Ngandu	N.T.	Equatorial Belgian Congo	1920	1921
286	Mongo, or Lolo	Gen., Ex., Prov., N.T.	Equatorial Belgian Congo	1893	1893
	Mongo-Nkundu, Union Version	B.			
287	Eleku	Lk., Jn.	About Lolanga, Belgian Congo	1903	1920
288	Ngombe	N.T.	Near Upoto	1903	1930
289	Ntomba	Goss., Ac., Jas. 1, 2, 3 Jn.	Belgian Congo	1896	1937
290	Bobangi	N.T.	Belgian Congo	1893	1946
291	Nkutu (Bankutu)	Jn.	Equatorial Belgian Congo	1937	1941
292	Okela	Mk.	„ „	1941	1941
293	Sakata	Jn., Ac.	Belgian Congo	1937	1937
294	Kongo (Kikongo): San Salvador	B.	Lower Congo up to Stanley Pool	1888	1893
295	„ Buende, or Fioti (Kifioti)	B.	„ „	1885	1905
	Western Equatorial Africa, Cameroon, etc.				
296	Yaka	Lk.	French Equatorial Africa	1933	1933
297	Lumbu	Mk.	„ „ „	1933	1933
298	Bungili	Mt., Lk.	Sango R., French Equ. Africa	1929	1929

Ref. No.	Language	What printed, or known to have been circulated, at any time, by the B.F.B.S.	Where circulated, or for whom designed	Date of first published translation of any part of Scripture	Date of first circulation by the B.F.B.S.
299	Omyènè: Galwa	Pent., Ps., N.T.	Galwa tribe, Gabun	1903	1903
	Union Omyènè	B.	Galway, Mpongwe, etc.		
300	Fang of Gabun	Gen., Mt.	Gabun R.	1894	1894
301	,, Ogowé, or Pahouin .	B.	Ogowé R., Gabun	1902	1902
302	Ikota	Mk.	Ogowé R., Gabun	1938	1938
303	Kele of Gabun§†	Jn.	Gabun	1879	1879?
304	Kele: Ongom	Mt.	Gabun	1910	1910
305	Benga§	Goss., Ac.	Corisco Is. Gabun	1858	1881?
306	Bulu§	B.	S.W. Cameroon	1896	1896?
307	Bassa of Cameroon. . . .	N.T., Ps.	N. of Sanaga River	1922	1925
308	Duala	B.	S.W. Cameroon	1848	1872?
309	Bamum	Goss., Rom., 1 Cor., Phil., 1 & 2 Thess.	Between Old Calabar and Mbam Rivers, Cameroon	1925	1925
310	Mbum	Goss., Ac.	French Equatorial Africa	1936	1936
311	Kim	N.T.	,, ,, ,,	1944	1948
312	Masana	N.T.	,, ,, ,,	1934	1934
313	Mundang	N.T.	,, ,, ,,	1933	1933
314	Nanjeri	N.T.	,, ,, ,,	1947	1947
315	Ngambai	N.T.	,, ,, ,,	1936	1936
316	Goulei	Jn.	,, ,, ,,	1956	1956
317	Sara: Mbai	N.T.	,, ,, ,,	1932	1932
318	,, Kabba-Laka . . .	Mk., Jn.	,, ,, ,,	1948	1948
319	,, Madjingai	Jn.	,, ,, ,,	1950	1950
320	Banu	Gen., Jon., Mt., Mk., Jn., Ac.	,, ,, ,,	1932	1932
321	Baya: Mbere	N.T.	,, ,, ,,	1933	1933
322	Baya (Gbéa)	Mt., Mk., Jn., Ac.	,, ,, ,,	1934	1934
323	Baya: Kalla	Goss., Ac.	,, ,, ,,	1954	1954
324	Sango	N.T.	,, ,, ,,	1933	1933
325	Karre	N.T.	,, ,, ,,	1931	1931
326	Pana	Jn.	,, ,, ,,	1953	1953
	Nigeria				
327	Hausa: italic char.† . . .	Gen., Ex., Ps., Is., N.T.	N. Nigeria, etc.	1853	
	,, Arabic char. . . .	Mk., Jn.			1857
	,, roman char. . . .	B.			
	,, Aljemi char. . . .	Jn.			
328	Kanakura	Mk.	Bornu and Adamawa Provinces	1937	1937
329	Margi	Mt., Mk. Ac.	Bornu and Adamawa	1946	
330	Bura	N.T.	S.W. Bornu Province	1924	1946
331	Waja	Mt., Jn.	S.E. Corner Bauchi Province	1924	1925 1926
332	Tula	Jn.	S.E. Bauchi Province	1929	
333	Tera	Jn.	R. Gongola, Bauchi	1926	1929
334	Tangale	Ru., Jon., N.T.	S.E. Bauchi Province	1920	1930 1920

Ref. No.	Language	What printed, or known to have been circulated, at any time, by the B.F.B.S.	Where circulated, or for whom designed	Date of first published translation of any part of Scripture	Date of first circulation by the B.F.B.S.
335	Iregwe	Mt.–Rom., Phil., Philem., 1 Jn.	W. Bauchi Province	1923	1923
336	Burum	Goss., Ac.	„ „	1916	1916
337	Jarawa	Mk.	„ „	1940	1940
338	Ganawuri	Mk.	„ „	1940	1940
339	Rukuba	Mk.	N.W. Bauchi Province	1924	1924
340	Angas	Mk., Lk., Jn.	S.W. Bauchi Province	1916	1916
341	Sura, or Maghavul . . .	Gen.,Goss., Ac.	S.W. Bauchi Province	1913	1915
342	Chawi	Mk., Jn.	S.E. Zaria Prov., Nigeria	1923	1923
343	Dakkarkari	Mk.	Sokoto Province	1931	1931
344	Kamberri	Mk., Jn.	Niger, Sokoto, and Ilorin Provinces	1933	1933
345	Nupe	B.	Nupe, Ilorin and Kabba Provinces, etc.	1860	1860
346	Gbari: Gyengyen or Matai .	N.T.	S. of Minna, N. Nigeria	1913	1915
347	„ Yamma Gayegi . .	Mk.	„ „	1913	1925
348	„ Yamma Paiko . . .	Jn.	„ „	1926	1926
349	Jaba	Mk., Jn.,Ac.	N.E. Nasarawa Province	1921	1921
350	Eggon	Jn.	Nasarawa Province	1931	1935
351	Arago	Mk.	Nasarawa Province	1919	1929
352	Igbira	Mt.	Junction of Niger and Benue	1891	1891
353	Bassa of Nigeria	Mk.	„ „ „	1946	1946
354	Igala	N.T.	N.W. Munchi Province, N. Nigeria	1924	1925
355	Agatu	Jn.	S. Munchi Province	1951	1951
356	Idoma	Mk., Lk., Ac.	S. Munchi Province	1927	1927
357	Tiv, or Munchi	N.T., Ps.	S.W. Muri Province	1914	1916
358	Jukun: Wukari	Mk.	„ „	1914	1914
359	„ Donga	Lk.	„ „	1915	1918
360	„ Kona	Mk.	N.E. Muri Province	1927	1927
361	Yergum	Mk.	N.W. Muri Province	1915	1917
362	Wurkum	Lk., Ac.	N. Muri Province	1924	1927
363	Bachama	Mk.	Benue Valley, Yola Province	1915	1915
364	Fula: Adamawa (See Nos. 408 and 414)	Gen., Goss.	Adamawa Province	1859	1919
365	Tsamba	Mk.	„ „	1933	1933
366	Ogoni	Goss., Ac.	Opobo District, S. Nigeria	1930	1930
367	Ibo: Isuama†	Mt.–Ac., 1 Cor.–Phil.	Isuama District, Owerri Province	1860	1860
368	„ Lower, or Delta, or Bonny†	Jn., Gal.–Phil.	Niger Delta, Owerri Province	1892	1896
369	„ Upper, or Niger, or Onitsha†	B.	Onitsha District	1893	1893
	Union Ibo	B.	S. Nigeria		
370	Isoko (formerly Igabo) . .	Goss., Ac.	N.E. Warri Province, S. Nigeria	1920	1920

Ref. No.	Language	What printed, or known to have been circulated, at any time, by the B.F.B.S.	Where circulated, or for whom designed	Date of first published translation of any part of Scripture	Date of first circulation by the B.F.B.S.
371	Sobo (Urhobo)	N.T.	N.E. Warri Province	1921	1927
372	Ijo or Ijaw, Upper: Patani or Kolokuma	Goss.	N.E. Warri Province	1912	1912
373	„ Lower: Nimbi or Brass	Gen., N.T.	Brass, Warri Province	1886	1903
374	Addo, or Edo	Ps., Prov., Goss., 1–2 Cor., Gal.	Benin District	1914	1914
375	Ora	Goss.	Benin District, S. Nigeria	1908	1908
376	Yoruba	B.	Hinterland of Lagos, S. Nigeria	1848	1850
	Dahomey, Gold Coast, etc. etc.				
377	Gu (Ogu), or Dahomey: Alada	B.	S. Dahomey	1886	1886
378	Ewe, or Efe	B.	S. Dahomey, etc.	1858	1875
379	Popo	Mk., Jn.	„	1920	1920
380	Bariba	Jn.	N. Dahomey	1953	1953
381	Accra, or Ga	B.	E. Gold Coast	1805	1843
382	Ashanti: Twi (Otwi), or Tshi (Otshi)	B.	Gold Coast Colony	1859	1859
383	„ Fante	B.	Near Cape Coast Castle	1769	1886
384	Dagbane	Mt.-Ac., Eph. & 1 Pet.	Northern Territories of the Gold Coast, etc.	1935	1935
385	Gourma	Mk.	French W. Africa	1954	1954
386	Dyerma	N.T.	„	1934	1934
387	Atche	Mk.	Ivory Coast	1931	1931
388	Agni	Mk.	„ „	1924?	1927
389	Baouli	N.T.	„ „	1946	1946
390	Ebrié	Goss	„ „	1929	1930
391	Adjukru	Mt., Lk., Ac.	„ „	1926	1927
392	Aladian	Mk.	„ „	1937	1937
393	Dida	Mk., Lk., Jn.	„ „	1930	1930
394	Gouro	Mk.	„ „	1951	1951
	Liberia, Sierra Leone, etc.				
395	Grebo§†	Gen., Mt.-1 Cor.	W. of Cape Palmas, Liberia	1838	1838
396	Kroo	Lk.	N. Liberia	1921	1921?
397	Bassa of Liberia	Jn., Ac.	Liberia	1844	1937
398	Gio	Lk., Ac.	Liberia	1943	1943
399	Mano	Lk.	Liberia	1946	1946
400	Kono	Mt., Mk., Gal.	E. Sierra Leone	1919	1919
401	Mende	Ru., N.T.	S.E. Sierra Leone	1867	1871
402	Yalunka, or Yulanka . . .	Mt.	N. Sierra Leone	1901	1901
403	Limba	Lk., Jn.	N. Sierra Leone	1911	1911
404	Kuranko, or Koranko . . .	Lk., Jn.	N. Sierra Leone	1899	1899
405	Temne	Gen.-Esth. Ps., N.T.	W. Sierra Leone	1854	1865
406	Bullom†	Mt.	W. Sierra Leone	1814	1816
407	Meninka (Malinke) . . .	Mt., Jn.	Fr. Guinea & Fr. Sudan	1931	1933
408	Fula: Futa-Jalon (See Nos. 364 and 404)	Mt.	French Guinea	1929	1929
409	Susu	Jn.	French Guinea	1816	1930

Ref. No.	Language	What printed, or known to have been circulated, at any time, by the B.F.B.S.	Where circulated, or for whom designed	Date of first published translation of any part of Scripture	Date of first circulation by the B.F.B.S.
410	Mandingo: Gambia: roman chr.	Mt., Jn. Mk.	Gambia	1837	1837
	„ Arabic char.				
411	Jolof, or Wolof: Gambia . .	Mt., Jn.	„	1882	1882
412	Habbe	Jn.	French Sudan	1933	1933
413	Bobo (Red)	N.T.	„ „	1954	1954
414	Fula: Macina (See Nos. 364 and 408)	Jn.	„ „	1934	1934
415	Bambara: roman char. . .	Ps., N.T.	Upper Senegal	1923	1923
	„ Arabic char. . .	Jn., 1 Jn.			
	In African languages {	—	Bibles 46 New Tests. 93 } 321 Portions 182		
	ASIA				
	Siberia, etc.				
416	Ostiak§† (published locally) .	Mt. 1–10	Tobolsk, W. Siberia	1868	1868?
417	Vogul	Mt., Mk.	Slopes of Ural Mountains	1868	1882
418	Uzbek Turkish, or Sart . .	Goss.	Uzbeks, Sarts, etc., Turkestan	1891	1891
419	Transcaspian, or Jagatai Turkish†	Mt.	Merv, Turkestan	1880	1880
420	Kashgar Turkish	B.	Chinese Turkestan	1898	1898
421	Kirghiz Turkish: Western . . Arabic char.	N.T.	Lower Volga, S.E. Russia, and Russian Central Asia	1818?	1820
422	„ „ Russian char.	Goss.·			
	„ „ Eastern (Altai) or Qazak: Russian char.	Mk.	Altai and Thian Shan Mts., Zungaria, and Chinese Turkestan	1894	1894
	„ „ Arabic char.	Gen., Goss., Ac.			
423	Yakut Turkish	Goss.	N.E. Siberia	1858	1898
	Turkey, Syria, etc.				
424	Armenian: Ancient . . .	B.	Armenian Church	1565	1814
425	„ Modern: Western, or Constantinople	B.	Asia Minor, etc.	1802	1825
426	„ Modern: Eastern, or Ararat	B.	Transcaucasia, Iran, etc.	1831	1831
427	Kurdish: Kurmanji . .	N.T.	N. Kurdistan	1856	1856
428	„ Kermanshahi . .	Goss.	Kurds in Iran territory	1894	1894
429	„ Mukri	Goss.	N. and Central Kurdistan	1909	1909
430	Hebrew, Massoretic text . Delitzsch's version .	O.T. N.T.	Jews, Students, etc.	1477	1817
431	Arabic: Arabic char. . . .	B.	Arabia, Syria, Egypt, etc.	1516	1811
	„ Syriac char. (Carshuni)	N.T.	Syrians who read Arabic in Syriac character		
	„ Hebrew char. (Judæo-Arabic)	Pent., Ps., Mt., Jn., Ac., Heb.	Jews who read Arabic in Hebrew character		

Ref. No.	Language	What printed, or known to have been circulated, at any time, by the B.F.B.S.	Where circulated, or for whom designed	Date of first published translation of any part of Scripture	Date of first circulation by the B.F.B.S.
	Arabic: Tunisian script . .	Lk.	Tunis	1903	1903
	[For other forms of Arabic see Nos. 49, 98, 101–103, 109, 115 & 432]				
432	Arabic: Palestinian . . .	Mt.,Mk.,Jas.	Palestine, etc.	1940	1940
433	Syriac: Ancient, Peshitta text: Jacobite char.	B.	Syrian Churches in Syria, S. India, etc., and Students	1555	1811
	„ „ Nestorian char.	Ps., N.T.			
	„ „ Estrangelo char.	Pent.			
434	Syriac: Modern§	B.	Turko-Iranian border-land between Van, Urumia, and Mosul	1844	1864
435	Persian: Persian char. . . .	B.	Iran, etc.		
	„ . Hebrew char. (Judæo-Persian)	B.	Jews who read in Hebrew character	1546	1809
	N.W. and N. frontiers of India, etc.				
436	Pashto, or Afghani . . .	B.	Afghanistan, etc.	1818	1818
437	Balochi: Persian char.† . .	'3 Gospels'	Baluchistan, etc.	1815?	1815?
	„ roman char. . . .	Gen., Ex., 1 Sam.– 2 Kgs., Ps., Is., N.T.			
	„ Arabic char. . . .	Mk.–Rev.			
438	Brahui: roman char. . . .	Jn.	E. Baluchistan and N. Sind	1905	1905
	Arabic char. . . .	Jn.			
439	Kashmiri: Sarada char.† . .	Gen.–2 Kgs. N.T.	Kashmir	1821	1821
	„ Persian char. . .	B.			
440	Shina: Gurezi	Mk.	Kishenjunga Valley, Kashmir	1929	1929
441	Tibetan	B.	Tibet, and adjoining districts of India and China	1860	1883
442	Zangskari . '.	Jn.	N. Kashmir	1951	1951
443	Balti	Mt., Lk.–Ac.	Baltistan, N.W. Kashmir	1903	1903
444	Ladakhi	Mk.	Ladakh, E. Kashmir	1905	1908
445	Lahuli: Bunan	Mk.	Lahul, etc., borders of W. Tibet	1907	1911
446	„ Manchad . . .	Mk.		1908	1914
447	„ Tinan	Mk.		1914	1914
448	Chambiali	Goss.	Chamba	1882	1882
449	Kulu	Jn.	Kangra District, Panjab	1932	1932
450	Kanauri: Devanagari char. .	Mk.	Kunawar, Bashahr	1909	1909
	„ Tankri char. .	Jn.			
451	Garhwali: Srinagaria . . .	N.T.	Srinagar, Garhwal	1827	1827
452	„· Tehri: rom. char. .	Mt.	Tehri, etc.	1895	1895
	„ „ Devanagari char.	Mt.			
453	Jaunsari: roman char. . . .	Mt.	Jaunsar Bawar, Dehra Dun District	1895	1895
	„ Devanagari char.	Mk.			
454	Kumaoni §†	Mt.–Col.	Kumaon and W. Nepal	1825?	1825?
455	Palpa §†	N.T.	W. Nepal	1827	1827
456	Nepali	B.	Nepal, etc.	1821	1821

Ref. No.	Language	What printed, or known to have been circulated, at any time, by the B.F.B.S.	Where circulated, or for whom designed	Date of first published translation of any part of Scripture	Date of first circulation by the B.F.B.S.
457	Lepcha, or Rong	Gen., Mt., Lk., Jn.	Sikkim, etc.	1845	1872
	N. India, Panjab, etc.				
458	Sanskrit: Devanagari char. .	B.	Sacred language of Brahmans	1808	1808
	„ Bengali char.† . .	Gen., Ps., Pr., Lk.			
	„ Oriya char.† . .	Ps.			
	„ Malayalam char.† .	Jn.			
	„ Grantha char.† . .	Jn.			
	„ Kanarese char.† .	Mt.			
	„ Telugu char.† . .	Lk.			
459	Hindostani, or Urdu: Devanagari char.†	N.T.	Hindostan, etc.; a *lingua franca* over a large part of India	1743	1814
	„ Arabic char. .	B.			
	„ Persian . . .	B.			
	„ roman char. .	B.			
	„ Gujarati char. .	Mt.			
460	Lahnda, or Multani: Landa char.†	N.T.	W. Panjab	1819	1819
	„ Persian char. . . .	Goss.			
461	„ Hindko	Jn.	Peshawar and Hazara	1929	1929
462	Panjabi	Gen.–Lam., Dan., Jon., Mal., N.T.			
463	„ Musalmani-Panjabi: Persian char. .	Gen.	Mohammedans and others in Central Panjab	1884	1884
	roman char. .	N.T. ◆ Goss., Ac.			
	„ Musalmani-Panjabi: Gurmukhi char.	Goss.		1884	1884
464	„ Dogri §†	N T.	N. Panjab	1826	1826
465	Bhatneri §†	N.T.	Bhattiana, S. Panjab	1826	1826
466	Marwari †	N.T.	Marwar-Mallani, etc.	1821	1821
467	Bikaneri §†	N.T.	Bikaner	1820	1820
468	Mewari §†, or Udaipuri . .	Mt.	Mewar	1815?	1815?
469	Jaipuri §†	Mt.	Jaipur	1815?	1815?
470	Harauti §†	N.T.	Bundi, Kota, etc.	1822	1822
471	Malvi §* or Ujjaini . .	N.T.	Malwa, etc.	1826	1826
472	Hindi: Devanagari char. . .	B.	Hindostan	1806	1811
	„ Kaithi char. . . .	Gen., Ex., Ps., Pr., Goss., Ac.			
	„ roman char. . . .	N.T.			
	„ Colloquial . . .	Goss.			
473	Kanauji §†	N.T.	Lower Doab, U.P.	1821	1821
474	Braj Bhasha §†	N.T.	Central Doab, U.P.	1820	1820
475	Awadhi §*, or Kausali . .	Mt., Mk.	Oudh. etc.	1820?	1820
476	Bagheli §* or Baghelkhandi .	N.T.	Baghelkhand, etc.	1821	1821
477	Chhattisgarhi	Mk., Lk., Jn.	Raipur, Bilaspur, etc.	1904	1904
478	Kurku	Mk.	Western Districts of Central Provinces	1900	1900
479	Gondi: Mandla . . .	Lk., Jn.	Mandla, etc., C.P.	1895	1895

Ref. No.	Language	What printed, or known to have been circulated, at any time, by the B.F.B.S.	Where circulated, or for whom designed	Date of first published translation of any part of Scripture	Date of first circulation by the B.F.B.S.
480	Gondi: Chhindwara . . .	Mt., Mk.	Chhindwara, etc., C.P.	1872	1872
481	„ Betul	Jn.	Betul, C.P.	1948	1948
482	Bhili: Central	Mk.	Borders of C.P., Central	1916	1916
483	„ Southern: Dehwali . .	N.T.	India, Rajputana and Bombay Presidency	1918	1918
484	„ „ Valvi . .	N.T.	W.Khandesh and Baroda	1927	1930
	Bengal, etc.				
485	Kurukh, or Uraon	N.T.	Chota Nagpur, etc.	1895	1895
486	Mundari, or Kol: Devanagari char.	B.	Ranchi, etc.	1876	1876
	Oriya char.† .	Mk.			
487	Ho	Lk.	Singbhum, etc.	1915	1915
488	Bihari: Magahi †	N.T.	S. Bihar, and Hazaribagh	1826	1826
489	„ Bhojpuri: Kaithi char.	Jn.	W. Bihar, etc.	1911	1911
	„ „ Devanagari char.	Jn.			
490	„ Nagpuria Kaithi char.	Mt.–2 Cor.	Chota Nagpur	1907	1907
	„ „ Devanagari char.	Mt.,Mk.,Jn.			
491	Santali: roman char. . . .	B.	Santal Parganas, Manbhum, etc.	1868	1886
	„ Bengali char. . . .	Mk., Lk., Jn.			
	„ Oriya char. . . .	Ps., Mk.			
492	Malto	Ps., Goss.	Rajmahal Hills, Bengal	1881	1881
493	Bengali: Bengali char. . . .	B.	Bengal	1800	1806
	„ roman char. . .	N.T.			
	„ Colloquial Bengali .	Lk.			
494	„ Musalmani-Bengali .	Gen.,Ps.,Is., Goss., Ac.	Bengali-speaking Mohammedans	1854	1854
495	Kharia	Jn.	S. Bengal	1951	1951
496	Assamese	B.	Assam	1819	1819
497	Garo: Achik	B.	Garo Hills, etc.	1875	1875?
498	Bodo, or Mechi	Goss.	Dooars, E. Bengal	1906	1906
499	Boroni	N.T.	Dooars, E. Bengal	1934	1934
500	Dimasa	Mk.	Cachar	1905	1908
501	Rabha: Rangdania . . .	Mk.	Goalpara, etc.	1909	1909
502	Khasi: Bengali char.† . . .	N.T.	Khasi and Jaintia Hills	1816	1827
	„ roman char. . .	B.			
503	Biete	Mk.	„	1949	1949
504	Lushai	Gen., Ex., Josh.–1 & 2 Kgs.,Neh., Ps., Is., N.T.	Lushai Hills	1898	1898
505	Hmar, or Mhar	Gen., Exod., Lev., N.T.	N.Lushai Hills and Manipur	1920	1920
506	Gangte	Mt.	Manipur, Burma, etc.		
507	Chin: Northern: Thado-Kuki [See also Nos. 553–561]	N.T.	N. Lushai Hills and Manipur	1921	1924
508	„ Thado: Vaiphei subdial.	Jn.	N. Lushai Hills and Manipur	1917	1917
509	Lakher, or Mara	Ex.–Deut. Jon., Mal., N.T.	E. Lushai Hills	1912	1912
510	Manipuri or Meithei: Devanagari char.	N.T.	Manipur, etc.	1827	1827
	„ Bengali char . . .	N.T.			

Ref. No.	Language	What printed, or known to have been circulated, at any time, by the B.F.B.S.	Where circulated, or for whom designed	Date of first published translation of any part of Scripture	Date of first circulation by the B.F.B.S.
511	Kom	Mt.	Manipur	1954	1954
512	Paite	N.T., Ps.	„		
513	Mikir	B.	Mikir Hills, E. Nowgong District	1904	1918
514	Naga: Angami	Gen., N.T.	Naga Hills	1890	1918
515	„ Ao	Gen., N.T.	N.E. Naga Hills	1883	1914
516	„ Chang	Mk.	„ „	1947	1947
517	„ Konyak	Mt., Mk.	„ „	1951	1951
518	„ Lhota	N.T.	Naga Hills	1931	1932
519	„ Mzieme	Mt.	Naga Hills		
520	„ Rengma	Goss.	Naga Hills	1928	1928
521	„ S. Rengma (Ntenyi) .	Mt.	Naga Hills	1944	1944
522	„ Sangtam	Mt., Mk.	Naga Hills	1944	1944
523	„ Sema	N.T.	N.E. Manipur	1928	1928
524	„ Tangkhul	N.T.	N.E. Manipur	1904	1904
525	„ Mao	Mk., Jn.	N.E. Manipur	1946	1946
526	„ Zeme or Kachcha . .	Mk.	N. Cachar Hills	1928	1928
527	Abor Miri	Mk., Jn.	Borders of Tibet and N. Assam	1932	1932
528	Singpho, or Northern Kachin . [See No. 571]	Lk., Jn., Ac.	N.E. Assam, N. Burma, etc.	1907	1907
529	Oriya, or Uriya	B.	Orissa	1809	1809
	Madras, etc.				
530	Khondi or Kui: Ganjam: roman char.	N.T.	Ganjam, etc.	1893	1893
	Oriya char.	Rom.			
531	„ Kuvi	Lk.	Vizagapatam, etc.	1916	1916
532	Sora	Prov., Jn.	Ganjam, etc.	1940	1940
533	Gondi: Koi: roman char. . .	Lk., 1 Jn.	Godavari, etc.	1882	1882
	„ „ Telugu char. .	Lk.			
534	Telugu	B.	Centre and East of S.India	1812	1812
535	Kanarese	B.	Mysore, etc.	1812	1820
536	„ Badaga: Kanarese char.	Jon., Mk., Lk.	Nilgiri Hills	1852	1890
	„ „ Tamil char.	Jon., Mk.			
537	Toda	Ps., Mk., Jn.	Nilgiri Hills	1873	1897
538	Tulu	Gen., Ex., Ps., Pr., Dan., N.T.	S. Canara, Madras	1842	1885
539	Dakhini, or Southern Hindostani†: Arabic char.	Gen., Ps., N.T.	Mohammedans in S. and W. India	1745	1839
	„ Persian char. . .	Gen.,Ps.,Pr., Goss., Ac.			
540	Tamil: Tamil char. . . .	B.	S. India, and Ceylon	1714	1806
	„ roman char. . . .	Mk.			
	„ Arabic char. . . .	Jn.	Tamil-speaking Moslems		
541	Malayalam: Malayalam char.	B.	Malabar Coast	1811	1811
	„ Arabic char. . .	Lk.	Moplah		
	Bombay, etc.				
542	Sindhi: Arabic char. . . .	B.	Sindh	1825	1825

Ref. No.	Language	What printed, or known to have been circulated, at any time, by the B.F.B.S.	Where circulated, or for whom designed	Date of first published translation of any part of Scripture	Date of first circulation by the B.F.B.S.
	Sindhi: Gurmukhi char. . .	Gen., Mt., Lk., Jn., Ac.			
	„ Devanagari char. . .	Mt.			
	„ Banya char. . . .	Mt.			
543	Kachchhi †	Mt.	Cutch, etc.	1834	1834
544	Gujarati: Gujarati (Kaithi) char.	B.	Gujarat, Baroda, etc.	1809	1809
	„ Devanagari char. .	N.T.			
545	„ Parsi-Gujarati . .	N.T.	Parsees in Bombay Presidency, etc.	1861	1864
546	Marathi: Balbodh (Devanagari) char.	B.	Bombay Presidency, etc.	1805	1806?
	„ Modi char. . . .	Goss., Ac.			
	„ roman char. . . .	Jn.			
547	„ Konkani: Devanagari char.	Pent., N.T.	S. Konkan, etc.	1818	1818
	„ „ Kanarese char.	Mk., Jn.			
	„ „ roman char. .	Mk., Lk., Jn.			
	Ceylon, etc.				
548	Sinhalese	B.	S. Ceylon	1739	1813
549	Indo-Portuguese	Pent., Ps., N.T.	Descendants of Portuguese and Dutch settlers in Ceylon and adjacent coast of India	1819	1819
550	Pali: Burmese char. . . .	N.T.	Sacred language of Buddhism in Ceylon, Burma, Siam, etc.	1827	1827
	„ Sinhalese char. . . .	Mt.			
	Burma, Indo-China, etc.				
551	Burmese	B.	Burma	1811	1815
552	Mro	Mt.	N. Arakan	1934	1934
553	Chin: Khumi: Awa . . .	Jn.	„	1939	1939
554	„ „ Ahraing . .	Mk.,Jn.,Ac. and Jas.	„	1941	1941
555	„ Anal	Mk.	„		
556	„ Kamhau	N.T.	Tiddim Dist.	1915	1915
	[See also Nos. 507, 508]				
557	„ Zotung	Mt.	Haka Sub-Division		
558	„ Lai or Haka . . .	N.T.	Haka Sub-Division	1920	1946
559	„ Laizo	N.T.	Falam, Chin Hills		
560	„ Ngawn	Mk.	Falam, Chin Hills		
561	„ : Asho (Southern) . .	N.T.	Arakan and Irrawaddy Valley	1921	1921
562	Shan : Burmese char. . . .	Goss.	Shan States, Burma, and Yunnan, S.W. China	1871	1902
	„ Yunnanese char. . .	Lk., Ac.			
563	„ Yunnanese	Mk.	Border of Yunnan and Burma	1931	1931
564	„ Hkun	Jn.	Kengtung State	1938	1938
565	Lahu	N.T.	„		
566	Akha	Mk.	„	1939	1955
567	Wa	N.T.	„		
568	Riang-lang	Mk.	Shan States		
569	Taungthu, or Bao	Goss. Ac.	S. Shan State and Thaton district	1912	1912

Ref. No.	Language	What printed, or known to have been circulated, at any time, by the B.F.B.S.	Where circulated, or for whom designed	Date of first published translation of any part of Scripture	Date of first circulation by the B.F.B.S.
570	Mon, formerly Talaing ..	B.	Pegu, Tenasserim, etc.	1837	1847
571	Kachin: Jinghpaw	N.T., Ps.	Burma	1895	1932
	[See No. 528]				
572	Karen: Sgaw	B.	Lower Burma	1843	1867
573	„ Pwo	B.	„ „	1847	1861
574	„ Bghai	Gen., Ps., Jas., 1, 2 and 3 Jn.	„ „	1857	1857
575	Mawken	Mk.	Mergui Archipelago	1913	1913
576	Nicobarese: Nancowry ..	Mt.	Nicobar Islands	1884	1890
577	„ Car ..	Gen., N.T.		1913	1913
578	Siamese, or Tai §	B.	Siam, etc.	1834	1881?
579	„ Eastern Laotian ..	B.	Basin of Mekong River	1906	1906
580	Annamese or Vietnamese ..	B.	Viet-Nam	1872	1890
	„ Chinese char. ..	Mk., Jn.			
581	Radé	Mt.,Mk.,Jn.	„	1934	1942
582	Jorai	Mk., Ac.	„		
583	Bahnar	Mk.	„		
584	Tho or Tonkin	Mk.	„	1938	1938
585	Cambodian	B.	Cambodia	1899	1899
	Malaya, etc.				
586	Malay: High Malay: roman char.	B.	Malaya	1629	1814
	„ „ Arabic char.	B.			
587	„ Low Malay ...	Gen., Ex., N.T.	Java, etc.	1815?	1863?
588	„ Baba Malay ...	N.T.	Babas, i.e. folk of Chinese race or descent, in the Straits Settlements	1891	1891
	„ Union Malay ...	N.T.			
589	Batta, or Batak: Simalungu .	Lk.	N. Sumatra	1939	1939
590	„ „ Toba: rom. char.	B.	Central Sumatra	1853	1877
	„ „ Batta char. ..	N.T.			
591	„ Angkola-Mandailing: roman char.	Ps., N.T.		1873	1878
	„ „ Batta char. ..	Mt., Lk., Jn.			
592	Nias	Goss., Ps.	Nias, etc.	1874	1874
593	Mentawei	Lk., Ac.	Mentawei Islands	1911	1939
594	Sundanese: roman char. ..	B.	W. Java	1854	1866
	„ Arabic char. ..	Lk., Jn., Ac.			
595	Javanese: Javanese char. ..	B.	Java	1829	1829
	„ Arabic char. (Pegon)	Goss., Ac.			
	„ roman char. ..	N.T.			
596	Madurese §: Javanese char. .	Goss., Ac., Phil.	Madura, etc.	1890	1890?
	„ roman char. ..	Lk.			
597	Balinese	Lk., Jn.	Bali	1910	1910
598	Sasaks	Jn.	Lombok		
599	Wajewa	Lk.	Sumba	1948	1948
600	Kambera	Lk.	„		

Ref. No.	Language	What printed, or known to have been circulated, at any time, by the B.F.B.S.	Where circulated, or for whom designed	Date of first published translation of any part of Scripture	Date of first circulation by the B.F.B.S.
601	Rotti §	Lk.	Rotti, etc.	1895	1915
602	Timorese	N.T.	Timor	1930	1941?
603	Balantian	Mk.	W. Dutch Borneo		
604	Dyak: Ngaju §	B.	S.E. Dutch Borneo	1842	1847
605	„ Sea Dyak . . .	N.T.	Sarawak	1864	1912
606	„ Land Dyak, or Beta .	Goss., Ac.		1863	1912
507	„ Manyan	Lk.	„	1950	1950
608	Murut	Mk.	Brunei, Borneo	1947	1947
609	Bisaya	Mk.	Sarawak	1937	1937
610	Sangir: Siaow	Ps., Pr., N.T.	Siaow and Tagulandang, Sangir Islands	1872	1880
611	Macassar §	Goss., Ac.	S. Celebes	1864	1864?
612	Mori	N.T.	C. Celebes	1939	1938
613	Kulawi	Lk.	„ „	1933	1939
614	Kaili	Lk.	„ „	1939	1939
615	Ta'e	Goss.	„ „	1933	1946
616	Bugis §	Goss., Ac.	Celebes	1863	1863?
	Philippines				
617	Ibanag §	N.T.	N. Luzon, etc.	1907	1907?
618	Igorot: Bontoc	Mk., Lk.	N. Luzon	1908	1908
619	Moro: Sulu	Lk.	Sulu Archipelago	1918	1918
620	Ilocano	B.	N.W. Luzon	1899	1899
621	Pangasinan	B.	N.W. Luzon	1887	1887
622	Pampangan §	B.	Pampanga, Luzon	1901	1901?
623	Tagalog	B.	Central Luzon, etc.	1898	1898
624	Bicol	B.	S. Luzon, etc.	1898	1898
625	Visayan: Panayan	B.	Panay	1899	1900
626	„ Cebuan §	B.	Cebu	1902	1902?
627	„ Samareño § . . .	Goss., Ac.	Samar, etc.	1908	1908?
	China, etc.				
628	Mongolian: Literary . . .	B.	Mongolia, Siberia, etc.	1819	1819
629	„ Buriat	Mt.	Irkutsk and Transbaikalia	1909	1909
630	„ Kalmuk . . .	N.T.	W. border of Gobi Desert, and Kansuh; and Kalmuk Steppes, S.E. Russia	1815	1815
631	„ Khalkha . . .	Mt.	Mongolia	1872	1872
632	Manchu	N.T.	N.W. China	1822	1822
633	Chinese: High Wenli . . .	B.	China, etc.	1805	1810
634	„ Easy Wenli . . .	B.	China	1883	1883
	Union Wenli . .	B.			
635	„ Kuoyu (Mandarin): Nanking, or Southern dial.	N.T.	S. China	1854	1864?
636	„ Kuoyu (Mandarin): Peking, or Northern: Chinese char.	B.	N. China	1864	1864
	„ Kuoyu (Mandarin): Peking, or Northern: roman char.	N.T.			
	„ Kuoyu (Union Mandarin): Chinese char.	B.	China		

Ref. No.	Language	What printed, or known to have been circulated, at any time, by the B.F.B.S.	Where circulated, or for whom designed	Date of first published translation of any part of Scripture	Date of first circulation by the B.F.B.S.
	Chinese: Kuoyu (UnionMandarin): phonetic script, Chu Yin system	Gen., Ex., Ps., Jon., N.T.			
	„ Kuoyu (UnionMandarin): phonetic script, Wang Chao system	N.T.			
637	„ Kuoyu (N.Mandarin): Kiaotung or E. Shantung	Mt.	E. Shantung	1918	1920
638	„ Kuoyu (N.Mandarin): Chihli Colloquial	Lk.	Chihli Province	1925	1925
639	„ Shanghai Colloquial.	B.	Shanghai, etc.	1847	1882?
640	„ Ningpo Colloquial .	B.	Ningpo, etc.	1852	1865
641	„ Taichow Colloquial	B.	Taichow, etc.	1880	1893
642	„ Wenchow Colloquial	N.T.	Wenchow, etc.	1892	1892
643	„ Kienyang Colloquial	Mt.	Kienyang, etc.	1898	1900
644	„ Kienning Colloquial	Gen., Ex., Ps., Is., Dan., N.T.	Kienning, etc.	1896	1896
645	„ Foochow Colloquial: Chinese char.	B.	Foochow, etc.	1852	1852
	„ „ roman char.	B.			
	„ „ phonetic script	Mk., Lk., Ac.			
646	„ Tingchow Colloquial	Mt.	Tingchow Prefecture, Fukien	1919	1919
647	„ Amoy Colloquial .	B.	Amoy, etc., and Taiwan (Formosa)	1852	1852
648	„ Swatow Colloquial .	Gen., Ru., 1 & 2 Sam., Hos.–Mal., N.T.	Swatow, etc.	1875	1877
649	„ Hakka Colloquial: italic char.	Lk.	Kwantung	1860	1865
	„ „ roman char. .	N.T.			
	„ „ Chinese char.	B.			
650	„ „ Wukingfu .	N.T.	N. and N.E. Kwantung	1910	1918
651	„ Canton Colloquial: Chinese char.	B.	Canton, etc.	1862	1867
	„ „ roman char.	B.			
652	„ Hainan Colloquial .	Gen., Hag.–Mal., Goss., Ac., Gal.–Philem., Jas.–Jude	Hainan	1891	1891
653	Chungchia	Mt.	S.W. China	1904	1904
654	Na-hsi	Mk.	Yunnan	1932	1932
655	Miao: Hwa	N.T.	S.W. China	1905	1907
656	„ Chuan	Mk.	S.W. China	1922	1922
657	„ Hé or Black . . .	N.T.	S.W. China	1928	1928
658	Nosu	N.T.	S.W. China	1923	1923
659	Laka	Mk., Jn.	S.W. China	1912	1912
660	Lisu: Eastern	N.T.	S.W. China	1912	1912

Ref. No.	Language	What printed, or known to have been circulated, at any time, by the B.F.B.S.	Where circulated, or for whom designed	Date of first published translation of any part of Scripture	Date of first circulation by the B.F.B.S.
661	Lisu: Western or Hwa	N.T.	Border of Yunnan and Burma	1915	1921
662	Atsi	Mk.			
663	Kado	Lk.	S.W. Yunnan „ „	1939	1939
664	Kopu	Mk.	S.W. China	1913	1913
	Japan, etc.				
665	Japanese: Japanese char.	B.	Japan	1837	1873
	„ roman char.	B.			
666	Ainu	Ps., Jon., N.T.	Yezo, N. Japan	1886	1886
667	Luchu †	Lk.-Rom.	Riukiu (Luchu) Islands	1855	1858
668	Korean	B.	Chosen (Korea)	1882	1883
669	Bunnun	Mt.	Formosa		
	In Asiatic languages {	—	Bibles 62 ⎫ New Tests. 72 ⎬ 254 Portions 120 ⎭		
	AMERICA				
	North America				
670	Eskimo: Greenland †	Ps., N.T.	Greenland	1744	1813
671	„ Labrador	B.	Labrador	1810	1810
672	„ Baffin Land	Gen., Ex., Ps., Prov., Is., N.T.	Shores of Baffin Land and Hudson Bay	1878	1881
673	„ Western Arctic	Lk., Jn., Ac.	Mackenzie River Delta	1938	1938
674	„ Mackenzie River (and Copper)	Mk.	Mackenzie River and Coronation Gulf	1907	1920
675	Chinook Jargon	Mk.	From Oregon to Alaska	1912	1912
676	Haida	Mt., Lk., Jn., Ac.	Queen Charlotte Is., etc.	1891	1891
677	Kwagutl	Goss., Ac.	Vancouver Is., etc.	1882	1882
678	Tukudh	B.	Yukon River	1873	1873
679	Slave, or Tinné†: syllabic char.	N.T.	Mackenzie River	1868	1868
	roman char.	N.T.			
680	Beaver †	Mk.	Peace River	1886	1886
681	Chipewyan †	N.T.	South of Lake Athabasca	1878	1878
682	Mohawk	Is., Lk., Jn.	Ontario	1715	1804
683	Iroquois	Goss.	Quebec and Ontario	1880	1880
684	Cherokee §†	N.T.	N. Carolina and Oklahoma	1829	1862?
685	Blackfoot	Mt.	Alberta	1887	1890
686	Cree: Western, or Plain	B.	Alberta, Saskatchewan, etc.	1853	1855
687	„ Eastern, or Swampy	Ps., Mt., Mk., Jn., 1 Jn.	Lower Saskatchewan Valley	1847	1859
688	„ Coastal	Jn.	Near James Bay	1921	1921
689	„ Moose	N.T.	Nr. Moose Ft., Hudson Bay	1854?	1876
690	Chippewa, or Ojibwa †	Gen., Ps., Hos.-Mal., Mt., Jn.	Ontario, Manitoba, Michigan, Wisconsin, etc.	1828	1831
691	Maliseet†	Jn.	New Brunswick, etc.	1863	1870

Ref. No.	Language	What printed or known to have been circulated, at any time, by the B.F.B.S.	Where circulated, or for whom designed	Date of first published translation of any part of Scripture	Date of first circulation by the B.F.B.S.
692	Micmac †: phonetic char. . .	Gen., Ps., Mt., Lk., Jn., Ac.	Nova Scotia, New Brunswick, etc.	1853	1853
	„ roman char. . .	Ex., Goss., Rom.-Rev.			
693	Choctaw §†	Ps., N.T.	Oklahoma, Mississippi, and Louisiana	1827	1850?
694	Dakota §†	B.	Dakota, Montana, etc.	1839	1851?
	Central America and West Indies				
695	Mexican †, or Aztec . . .	Lk.	Mexico, etc.	1833	1833
696	Maya †	Goss.	Yucatan	1862?	1862?
697	Quiché	Mk.	Guatemala	1898	1898
698	Cakchiquel	Mk.	Guatemala	1902	1902
699	Moskito §	N.T.	E. Coast of Nicaragua	1846	1905
700	Bribri	Jn.	Costa Rica	1905	1905
701	Carib	Mk., Jn.	West Indies and shores of Caribbean Sea	1847	1896
702	Dominica, or French Patois of W. Indies	Mk.	Dominica, St. Lucia, Grenada and Trinidad	1894	1894
	South America				
703	Negro English	Ps., N.T.	Dutch Guiana	1811?	1829
704	Arawak §†	Ac.	British Guiana	1799	1913
705	Makuchi	Jn.	Near Rapunini River, British Guiana	1923	1923
706	Shipibo	Mk.	Peru	1954	1954
707	Quechua: Peruvian (Cuzco) .	N.T.	„	1880	1880
708	„ Huanuco . .	Goss.	Huanuco, Peru	1917	1923
709	„ Junin	Lk.	„ „	1954	1954
710	„ Ayacucho . .	Lk.	„ „	1954	1954
711	„ Ancash	Jn.	Ancash, Peru	1946	1946
712	„ Bolivian	N.T., Ps.,	Bolivia	1907	1917
713	„ Ecuadorean . .	N.T.	Ecuador	1917	1917
714	Aymara	N.T.	S. Peru and Bolivia	1829	1829
715	Aguaruna	Lk.	N. Peru	1926	1942
716	Piro	Mk.	C. Peru		
717	Guarani . . . -. . .	N.T. & Ps.	Paraguay, etc.	1888	1888
718	„ Izoceño	Mk., Jn.	S.E. Bolivia	1931	1931
719	Tupi: Guajajara	Mk.,Jn.,Ac.	Maranhão, Brazil	1930	1932
720	Lengua	Goss., Ac.	Paraguayan Chaco	1900	1908
721	Mataco, or Vejoz	Goss., Ac. Epp.	Rio Bermejo, Argentina	1919	1919
722	Toba	Mk.,Lk.,Ac.	N.E. Argentina	1938	1938
723	Mapudungu	Mt., Mk.	S. Chile and Argentina	1901	1926
724	Yahgan	Lk., Jn., Ac.	Tierra del Fuego	1881	1881
	In American languages }	—	Bibles 4 ⎫ New Tests. 14 ⎬55 Portions 37 ⎭		

Ref. No.	Language	What printed, or known to have been circulated, at any time, by the B.F.B.S.	Where circulated, or for whom designed	Date of first published translation of any part of Scripture	Date of first circulation by the B.F.B.S.
	OCEANIA **Australia and New Zealand**				
725	Dieri §†	N.T.	Cooper's District, S. Australia	1880	1897?
726	Narrinyeri † (published locally)	Extracts from O.T. and N.T.	Lower Murray River, etc., S. Australia	1864	1864
727	Aranda	Goss.	C. Australia	1925	1925
728	Pitjantjatjara	Mk.	,,	1949	1949
729	Worrora	Mk., Lk.	N.W. Australia	1930	1930
730	Gunwingu	Mk., 1 Jn.	N. Australia	1942	1942
731	Nunggubuyu	Mk., Jas.	,,	1947	1947
732	Maori	B.	New Zealand	1827	1827
	Torres Straits and New Guinea				
733	Kapauku	Mk.	W. New Guinea	1955	1955
734	Bentuni	Lk.	N.E. New Guinea	1937	1937
735	Kate	Lk., 1 & 2 Thess.	Hinterland of Finschhafen	1910	1926
736	Jabim	Ps., Prov., N.T.	From Bussim to Langemak, N.E. Papua	1908	1924
737	Amele	1 & 2 Thess. 1 & 2 Tim.	Madang District		
738	Ragetta	Lk., Ac., 1 Thess., Philem., Jas.	Round Astrolabe Bay, Papua	1911	1925
739	Mabuiag	Goss.	Mabuiag and Western Islands, Torres Straits	1900	1900
740	,,　Saibai	Mk.	lands, Torres Straits	1884	1884
741	Mer, or Miriam	Goss.	Murray and Eastern Islands, Torres Straits	1879	1879
742	Kiwai	Goss.	Fly River	1895?	1911
743	,,　Goaribari	Goss., Eph., Phil., 1 Jn.	N.E. of Fly River	1926	1926
744	Bamu	Mk.	N. bank of Fly River		
745	Gogodala	Mk. & Jn.	Fly and Aramia Rivers		
746	Namau (Eurika)	N.T.	Purari Delta	1902	1910
747	Orokolo	Goss., Ac.	Between Purari and Bailala Rivers, Papua	1923	1926
748	Toaripi	N.T.	From Purari Delta to Cape Possession	1886	1902
749	Motu	N.T.	Port Moresby	1882	1882
750	Roro	Goss.	N.W. of Port Moresby	1891	1947
751	Keapara	Mt.–Rom., Eph., Phil., Col., 1 Jn.	Hood Lagoon	1878	1892
752	Hula	N.T.	,,		
753	Kunini	Mt.	Fly River, Papua	1933	1933
754	Mailu, or Magi	N.T.	Toulon Island	1907	1907
755	Daui, or Suau	Mt.–Rom., Eph., Phil., 1 & 2 Thess., 1 & 2 Tim.	South Cape, etc.	1885	1885
756	Tavara	Mt., Mk.	Milne Bay	1898	1903

Ref. No.	Language	What printed, or known to have been circulated, at any time, by the B.F.B.S.	Where circulated, or for whom designed	Date of first published translation of any part of Scripture	Date of first circulation by the B.F.B.S.
757	Wedau	Pent., N.T.	Goodenough Bay	1895	1897
758	Ubir	Jn.,1,2,3 Jn.	Collingwood, Papua		
759	Bwaidoga	Mk.	Ferguson and Goodenough Islands	1934	1934
760	Mukawa	B.	Cape Vogel	1904	1904
761	Binandere	Lk.	Mamba River, etc.	1903	1912
762	„ Notu	Mk., Jn.	Oro Bay, etc.	1930	1930
763	Dobu	B.	Normanby Island	1894	1894
764	Tubetube	Lk.	Slade Island	1897	1928
765	Panaieti (Misima)	NT.	Deboyne Island	1894	1894
766	Manus Island	Mk.	N.E. Admiralty Group	1921	1921
767	Kiriwina	Mk.	Trobriand Group	1899	1929
	New Britain Group				
768	New Britain	Gen., Ex., Dt., Josh., Ezra–Est., Ps., Prov., Is.–Lam., Dan.–Mal., N.T.	New Britain	1885	1886
769	Duke of York Island	Mt., Mk.	Duke of York Island	1882	1882
770	Omo	Mk.	New Ireland	1912	1921
771	Patpatar	Jn.	Central New Ireland	1919	1921
	Solomon Islands, etc.				
772	Petats	Mk.	Island of Petats, off Buka	1934	1934
773	Siwai (Motuna)	Mk.	Bougainville Island		
774	Bambatana	Mt. Rom.	Choiseul Island	1915	1927
775	Vella Lavella: Bilua, etc.	Mk., Lk., Ac.	Vella Lavella	1919	1919
776	Roviana	N.T.	New Georgia	1912	1916
777	Marovo	Mk.	East. part of New Georgia	1931	1931
778	Bugotu	Ps., Is., Hag., Zech., N.T.	S.E. Ysabel	1882	1901
779	Mwala: Saa	N.T.	S.E. Mwala (or Malaita)	1898	1905
780	„ Lau	Gen., N.T.	N.E. Mwala	1905	1910
781	„ Malu (Toa Baite)	Gen., Ps., Neh., N.T.	N. Mwala	1914	1914
782	„ Fiu	Mt.	N.W. Mwala	1909	1909
783	„ Kwara'ae	Mt., Jn.	N. Mwala	1929	1930
784	Guadalcanar: Vaturanga	Goss. & Ac.	Guadalcanar	1905	1948
785	Florida Island	N.T.	Florida Island	1882	1923
786	Ulawa	N.T.	Ulawa	1890	1899
787	San Cristoval: Arosi	Goss., Ac.	W. San Cristoval	1921	1921
788	„ „ Tawarafa	Mk.	S.E. San Cristoval	1927	1927
789	„ „ Anganiwei	Lk.	Central San Cristoval	1935	1935
790	Rennel	Goss, Ac.	Rennel & Bellona Islands	1942	1942
791	Mota	B.	Banks Islands	1864	1928
	New Hebrides				
792	Santo: Santo Bay	Jon., Hag., Mal., Mt., Jn.,Ac.,Phil., 1 & 2 Tim.	St. Philip Bay, N.E. Espiritu Santo	1904	1904

Ref. No.	Language	What printed, or known to have been circulated, at any time, by the B.F.B.S.	Where circulated, or for whom designed	Date of first published translation of any part of Scripture	Date of first circulation by the B.F.B.S.
793	Santo: Nogugu	Mk., Lk., Jn., Ac., Eph., Jas.–Jude	Nogugu, N.W. Espiritu Santo	1901	1901
794	„ Tasiriki	Gen., Jon., Jn.	Tasiriki, S.W. Espiritu Santo	1909	1909
795	„ Hog Harbour . . .	Ps.,Mk.,Lk., Jn., Ac., Gal.–Thess. Jas.–3 John Rev.	Hog Harbour, E. Espiritu Santo	1905	1905
796	„ Tangoa	Mt., Jn., Ac., Gal.	Tangoa, S. Espiritu		
797	Opa: Nduindui	1 Thess.	Oba (Opa, or Lepers' Island)	1913	1916
798	Malo	Goss., Ac., Gal.–Phil., Tim.– Philem. Jas., Jn., Jude	St. Bartholomew, etc.	1892	1892
799	Raga: Qatvenua	Lk.	Pentecost Island	1882	1910
800	Malekula: Uripiv	Mk., Lk., Ac.	N.E. Malekula (or Mallicolo)	1893	1893
801	„ Pangkumu . .	Lk., Jn., Ac.	E. Malekula	1892	1897
802	„ Aulua . . .	Jon., Mt., Lk., Ac.	E. Malekula	1894	1894
803	„ Ahamb	Jn.	Maskelyne Islets,Malekula	1906	1934
804	„ Kuliviu	Mk.	Maskelyne Islets,Malekula	1906	1906
805	Fanting, or Lonwolwol . .	Lk., Jn.	Ambrim	1899	1899
806	Paama	N.T.	Paama	1907	1907
807	Epi: Baki	Ps., Mt., Mk., 1 & 2 Cor., Phil., 1 & 2 Thess.	W. Epi	1886	1886
808	„ Bieria	Lk.	S.W. Epi	1898	1898
809	„ Tasiko	Mt.	S.E. Epi	1892	1892
810	„ Lewo	Jn.	E. Epi	1897	1897
	Tasiko-Lewo . . .	Lk.			
811	Nguna, or Nguna-Tongoa .	Gen., Ps., N.T.	Nguna, Tongoa, etc.	1875	1882
812	Nguna: Efate	Gen., N.T.,	Efate	1866	1866
	Nguna-Efate	O.T.	Nguna, Tongoa, Efate, etc.		
813	Eromanga	Gen., Ru., N.T.	Eromanga	1864	1869
814	Aniwa	Gen., Jon., N.T.	Aniwa	1871	1877
815	Tanna: Eastern (Weasisi) . .	N.T.	N.E. Tanna	1868	1888
816	„ Kwamera § . . .	Mt., Ac.	S.E. Tanna	1869	1878?
817	„ Lenakel dial. . . .	Goss., Ac., 1, 2 & 3 Jn., Rev.	S.W. Tanna	1900	1900

Ref. No.	Language	What printed, or known to have been circulated, at any time, by the B.F.B.S.	Where circulated, or for whom designed	Date of first published translation of any part of Scripture	Date of first circulation by the B.F.B.S.
818	Futuna	Ps., Jon., Mk., Ac., Rom.–Rev.	Futuna	1869	1888
819	Aneityum	B.	Aneityum	1853	1857
	Loyalty Islands				
820	Uvea, or Iaian	B.	Uvea (or Iai)	1860	1878
821	Lifu	B.	Lifu	1855?	1873
822	Maré, or Nengone	B.	Maré (or Nengone)	1847	1870
	New Caledonia				
823	Houaïlou (Wailu)	N.T.	E. New Caledonia	1903	1910
824	Ponérihouen	Mk.	E. New Caledonia	1910	1910
	Fiji				
825	Fiji	B.	Fiji	1836	1853
826	Rotuma	N.T.	Rotuma	1857	1870
	Friendly Islands				
827	Tonga	B.	Tonga (or Friendly) Islands	1831	1852
	Navigator Islands				
828	Samoa	B.	Samoan (or Navigator) Islands	1836	1849
	Cook Islands				
829	Rarotonga	B.	Rarotonga, Cook (or Hervey) Islands	1828	1836
830	Niué	B.	Niué (or Savage) Island	1861	1863
	Society Islands				
831	Tahiti	B.	Tahiti, etc.	1817	1838
	Marquesas Islands	Some chapters of Jn.			
832	Marquesas† (published locally)		Marquesas Islands	1836?	1836
	Sandwich Islands				
833	Hawaii §	B.	Hawaii, etc.	1827	1837
	Caroline Islands				
834	Mortlock §	N.T.	Mortlock Island, etc.	1880	1883?
835	Kusaie §	Goss., etc.	Kusaie	1862	1882
	Gilbert Islands				
836	Gilbert Islands §	N.T.	Gilbert Islands, etc.	1860	1867

In languages of Oceania { Bibles 16 / New Tests. 27 / Portions 69 } 112

Grand Total of Languages
Bibles 171 / New Tests. 220 / Portions 441 } 832

The total number of languages in which the British and Foreign Bible Society has, within comparatively recent years, printed or circulated versions of the Scriptures is estimated to be about 782.

Index to The Table of Languages

TABLE II: EDITIONS

Estimated number of Scriptures printed for the British and Foreign Bible Society from 1804 to 31st December, 1955.

Language	Bibles and Old Tests.	New Tests. and N.T. and Psalms	Portions	Total
Abor-Miri	—	—	2,000	2,000
Accra.....................	48,010	18,719	41,119	107,848
Addo	—	—	21,710	21,710
Adjukru	—	—	2,000	2,000
Afrikaans, (or Cape Dutch) .	1,490,744	615,700	633,885	2,740,329
,, with English	—	14,700	—	14,700
Agatu.....................	—	—	2,034	,034
Agni	—	—	1,022	1,022
Aguarana	—	—	1,012	1,012
Ainu......................	—	100	1,029	1,129
Aladian	—	—	505	505
Albanian	—	10,542	62,500	73,042
,, (Tosk) with Mod. Greek	—	6,000	29,000	35,000
Ambrymese................	—	—	3,000	3,000
Amele	—	—	2,000	2,000
Amharic	34,776	31,280	287,456	353,512
,, with Ethiopic	—	—	63,861	63,861
Aneityum	—	4,040	16,590	20,630
Angas	—	—	1,515	1,515
Aniwa	—	1,000	500	1,500
Annamese (see Vietnamese)				
Arabic	342,065	331,430	2,937,052	3,610,547
,, with English	—	75	3,780	3,855
,, with French	—	—	15,095	15,095
,, (in Hebrew character)	—	—	67,667	67,667
,, (in Syriac character) .	—	4,000	—	4,000
,, (Palestinian)	—	—	3,000	3,000
,, Egyptian	—	—	50,000	50,000
,, Sudan	—	—	5,000	5,000
,, Algerian	—	—	136,857	136,857
,, Mogrebi	—	3,150	169,622	172,772
,, Tunisian	—	—	59,398	59,398
Arago	—	—	1,010	1,010
Aranda	—	1,000	2,020	3,020
Arawak	—	—	25	25
Armenian (Ancient)........	2,865	21,306	31,348	55,519
,, (Modern)	25,546	63,093	109,550	198,189
,, ,, with English	—	—	10,070	10,070
,, (Ancient and Mod.)	—	3,000	100	3,100
,, (Ararat)..........	18,560	39,520	137,298	195,378
,, with Ancient in par. cols.	—	12,029	—	12,029
Arosi.....................	—	—	1,000	1,000
Ashanti: Fanti	38,650	36,988	53,899	129,537
,, Twi...............	181,091	101,622	21,648	304,361
Assamese	4,502	12,000	189,300	205,802
Asu	—	970	—	970
Atche	—	—	1,010	1,010

Language	Bibles and Old Tests.	New Tests. and N.T. and Psalms	Portions	Total
Atsi	—	—	2,000	2,000
Aymara with *Spanish*	—	—	6,792	6,792
Bachama	—	—	275	275
Badaga	—	—	5,001	5,001
Balinese.................	—	1	18,014	18,015
Balochi	—	—	21,000	21,000
Balti	—	—	5,000	5,000
Bambara	—	4,014	19,285	23,299
Bambatana	—	—	2,020	2,020
Bamu	—	—	1,000	1,000
Bamum	—	—	9,090	9,090
Bankutu	—	—	1,000	1,000
Bangala (see *Ngala*)				
Banu	—	—	5,564	5,564
Baouli	—	5,000	2,000	7,000
Bari	—	9,508	154,273	163,781
Bariba	—	—	5,000	5,000
Basa (of Cameroon)	—	30,300	30,279	60,579
Bassa (of Liberia)	—	—	7,010	7,010
„ (of Nigeria)	—	—	500	500
Basque (*French* and *Spanish*).	—	2,000	26,279	28,279
Batta: Simalungen	—	—	2,000	2,000
„ Toba	6,000	42,870	105,604	154,474
Baya	—	10,000	26,296	36,296
Beaver	—	—	510	510
Bemba	—	84,620	62,018	146,638
Bena	—	10,560	5,000	15,560
Bengali	97,650	117,742	4,877,638	5,093,030
„ (Roman character) ..	—	3,026	1,000	4,026
„ with *English*	—	2,018	5,000	7,018
„ Musalmani	—	—	355,060	355,060
Bentuni	—	—	1,526	1,526
Bhili (various)	—	1,500	10,000	11,500
Bhojpuri	—	—	10,500	10,500
Bicol	5,000	8,001	75,050	88,051
Bihari: Magahi	—	—	2,000	2,000
„ Nagpuria	—	—	34,000	34,000
Binandere	—	—	6,510	6,510
„ Notu	—	—	6,000	6,000
Bira	—	—	506	506
Bisaya	—	—	514	514
Blackfoot	—	—	504	504
Bobangi	—	8,540	—	8,540
Bodo	—	—	9,000	9,000
Bogos....................	—	—	300	300
Bondei	—	—	505	505
Bontoc Igorot	—	—	506	506
Boran	—	—	1,500	1,500
Boroni	—	—	10,000	10,000
Brahui	—	—	1,000	1,000
Breton	—	41,341	82,125	123,466
Bribri...................	—	—	500	500
Bua (*Libua*).............	—	—	1,010	1,010
Bugis	—	—	7,157	7,157
Bugotu	—	1,012	11,096	12,108
Bulgarian	107,265	316,911	928,761	1,352,937
„ with *English*	—	2,156	18,500	20,656
Bullom with *English*	—	—	1,500	1,500

Language	Bibles and Old Tests.	New Tests. and N. T. and Psalms	Portions	Total
Bunan	—	—	1,250	1,250
Bungili	—	—	2,020	2,020
Bura	—	6,500	8,096	14,596
Burmese	29,883	26,345	2,348,669	2,404,897
Burum	—	—	16,062	16,062
Bwaidoga	—	—	3,000	3,000
Cakchiquel	—	—	2,040	2,040
Cambodian	1,062	5,250	163,220	169,532
Carib	—	—	2,538	2,538
Catalan	—	11,071	161,758	172,829
Cebuan	444	6,138	5,677	12,259
Chaga: Machame	—	—	16,040	16,040
„ Mochi	—	—	506	506
Chambiali	—	—	7,012	7,012
Chawi	—	—	525	525
Cheremiss	—	—	7,000	7,000
Cherokee	—	6	—	6
Chhattisgarhi	—	—	35,000	35,000
Chin	—	1,102	48,086	49,188
Chinese	1,216,549	3,731.398	118,691,084	123,639,031
„ with English	—	14,205	55,077	69,282
Chinook Jargon	—	—	1,015	1,015
Chipewyan	—	1,010	3,273	4,283
Chippewa (or Ojibwa)	—	289	—	289
Chokwe	—	10,532	6,512	17,044
„ with Portuguese	—	13,574	19,594	33,168
Chopi	—	—	2,530	2,530
Chuana	187,426	199,193	68,264	454,883
Coptic with Arabic	—	37	4,014	4,051
Corsican	—	—	10,000	10,000
Cree	12,605	26,001	19,311	57,917
Croatian	12,060	10,070	40,320	62,450
Czech	723,924	973,004	1,066,311	2,763,239
„ with English	—	—	25,021	25,021
Dagbane	—	—	2,400	2,400
Dakhini	—	2,000	172,080	174,080
Dakkarkari	—	—	262	262
Dakota	6	25	—	31
Danish	—	3,500	—	3,500
Daui (or Suau)	—	2,000	9,037	11,037
Dida	—	—	8,032	8,032
Dieri	—	750	—	750
Dimasa	—	—	1,010	1,010
Dinka (or Jieng)	—	—	7,580	7,580
„ Bor	—	7,030	4,042	11,072
„ Padang	—	3,386	—	3,386
Dobu	5,167	9,686	17,628	32,481
Dominica	—	—	506	506
Duala	19,500	49,795	12,000	81,295
Duke of York Island	—	—	3,500	3,500
Dutch	2,249,765	1,466,200	571,302	4,287,267
„ with English	—	35,808	70,657	106,465
Dyak: Ngaju	—	2,512	14,048	16,560
„ Land Dyak, or Beta	—	—	1,012	1,012
„ Sea Dyak	—	2,000	—	2,000
Dyerma	—	3,176	1,010	4,186
Ebrié	—	—	2,020	2,020
Efik	4	—	1	5

Language	Bibles and Old Tests	New Tests. and N.T. and Psalms	Portions	Total
Eggon	—	—	1,000	1,000
Eleku	—	—	504	504
English	58,012,514	52,337,942	37,752,573	148,103,029
Epi, S.E. (Tasiko)	—	—	606	606
„ West (Baki)	—	—	5,077	5,077
„ S.W. (Biera)	—	—	2,000	2,000
Eromanga	—	4,000	7,523	11,523
Eskimo	—	9,519	32,260	41,779
„ with English	—	—	2,024	2,024
„ (Greenland)	—	2,000	1,200	3,200
Esperanto	16,091	41,780	20,250	78,121
Estonian	85,641	261,182	407,943	754,766
„ Setu	—	—	250	250
Ethiopic (see also Amharic)	—	20,052	2,100	22,152
Ewe or Efe	45,849	39,917	12,904	98,670
Falasha Kara	—	—	525	525
Fang of Gabun	—	—	1,615	1,615
Fang of Ogowe (Pahouin)	4,000	4,694	18,808	27,502
Fanting	—	—	1,000	1,000
Fiji	48,275	171,098	5,000	224,373
Finnish	721,133	1,248,153	393,201	2,362,487
„ with English	—	—	36,715	36,715
Flemish	7,625	252,891	749,219	1,009,735
Florida	—	5,050	—	5,050
French	3,163,338	11,231,260	16,544,975	30,939,573
„ with Arabic	—	—	5,000	5,000
„ with Breton	—	5,040	—	5,040
„ with English	—	41,165	40,767	81,932
„ with Flemish	—	—	10,000	10,000
„ with German	20,570	—	—	20,570
Frisian	—	1	2,031	2,032
Fula	—	—	4,600	4,600
„ Macina	—	—	173	173
Fuliro	—	—	1,010	1,010
Futuna	—	—	1,706	1,706
Ga	—	—	5,000	5,000
Gaelic	76,811	85,756	—	162,567
Galla	2,000	—	10,582	12,582
„ (Bararetta)	—	—	505	505
„ (Ittu)	—	—	500	500
Ganawuri	—	—	1,012	1,012
Ganda	261,820	259,741	195,189	716,750
Gang	—	101,064	57,008	158,072
Garhwali (Tehri)	—	—	3,200	3,200
Garo	2,500	2,000	85,000	89,500
Gbari	—	—	4,873	4,873
Georgian	—	17,008	93,736	110,744
German	8,153,740	18,211,479	5,731,997	32,097,216
„ with Bohemian	—	—	10,550	10,550
„ with English	—	77,636	151,308	228,944
„ with Greek	—	13,860	—	13,860
„ with Italian	—	—	3,175	3,175
„ Low	—	12,500	28,081	40,581
Gimbunda	—	—	2,019	2,019
Gio	—	—	2,000	2,000
Giryama	1,013	3,010	16,703	20,726
„ with Swahili	—	—	504	504
Gofa	—	—	750	750

Language	Bibles and Old Tests.	New Tests. and N.T. and Psalms	Portions	Total
Gogo	—	32,855	20,141	52,996
Gogodala	—	—	4,000	4,000
Gondi.....................	—	—	2,501	2,501
Gourma	—	—	1,012	1,012
Gouro	—	—	2,000	2,000
Grebo.....................	—	—	125	125
Greek (Ancient)	208	703,912	455,650	1,159,770
,, ,, with *English*.	13	33,003	—	33,016
,, ,, with *French*..	—	3,000	—	3,000
,, ,, with *German*	—	12,132	—	12,132
,, ,, with *Latin*...	—	6,226	—	6,226
,, ,, with Modern	—	96,952	19,102	116,054
,, ,, with *Urdu* and *Persian*	—	—	1,000	1,000
,, (Modern)	254,951	770,265	2,026,163	3,051,379
,, ,, with *English*.	—	—	23,464	23,464
,, ,, with *French*.	—	—	10,100	10,100
Gu	4,560	3,222	8,602	16,384
Guadalcanar: *Vaturanga*.....	—	—	1,000	1,000
Guarani	—	5,800	—	5,800
,, with *Spanish*	—	—	10,650	10,650
,, (*Izoceno* dialect)	—	—	3,030	3,030
Gudeilla...................	—	—	750	750
Gujarati...................	33,131	72,253	2,808,429	2,913,813
,, with *English*	—	—	13,550	13,550
,, (*Parsi*)	—	1,751	523	2,274
Gunwinggu	—	—	1,000	1,000
Habbe	—	—	218	218
Haida	—	—	2,040	2,040
Hanga....................	—	35,036	63,227	98,263
Hangaza	—	—	1,010	1,010
Hausa	67,274	17,504	52,247	137,025
Hawaii	3	—	—	3
Haya	—	10,000	13,245	23,245
Hebrew	1,009,691	277,271	2,147,593	3,434,555
,, with *Bulgarian*	—	—	1,000	1,000
,, with *English*	52,389	—	332	52,721
,, with *French*	5,035	—	24,446	29,481
,, with *German*	36,844	—	127,014	163,858
,, with *Hungarian*	—	—	7,500	7,500
,, with *Italian*.........	—	—	17,000	17,000
,, with *Polish*	5,000	—	9,000	14,000
,, with *Russian*........	35,449	—	118,239	153,688
,, with *Turkish*	—	—	4,500	4,500
,, with *Yiddish*	2,160	—	—	2,160
Herero....................	—	10,310	3,000	13,310
Hindi	128,042	359,541	8,929,468	9,417,051
Hkun	—	—	2,090	2,090
Hmar.....................	—	—	7,000	7,000
Houailou (*Wailu*)	—	7,030	2,020	9,050
Hula	—	—	5,000	5,000
Hunde	—	—	1,010	1,010
Hungarian	931,202	2,041,287	1,961,600	4,934,089
,, with *English*	—	—	20,647	20,647
Hungaro–*Slovenian*	—	8,000	—	8,000
Ibanag	—	230	150	380
Ibo	434,598	15,334	37,734	487,666
Icelandic	49,123	73,265	14,380	136,768

Language	Bibles and Old Tests.	New Tests. and N.T. and Psalms	Portions	Total
Idoma	—	—	2,826	2,826
Igabo	—	—	20,110	20,110
Igala	—	10,080	3,771	13,851
Igbira.....................	—	—	505	505
Igorot	—	—	1,000	1,000
Ijo	—	2,893	13,146	16,039
Ikota	—	—	1,010	1,010
Ila	—	24,578	14,666	39,244
Ilamba	—	—	2,010	2,010
Ilocano	2,102	9,865	48,445	60,412
„ with English	—	—	100	100
Indo–Portuguese	—	11,000	8,001	19,001
Iregwe.....................	—	—	2,153	2,153
Irish	15,903	86,846	21,222	123,971
Iroquois	—	—	1,010	1,010
Italian	1,173,868	2,034,050	10,600,841	13,808,759
„ with English	—	1,647	69,244	70,891
„ with Latin...........	—	200	2,000	2,200
Jaba	—	—	400	400
Jabim.....................	—	6,040	10,000	16,040
Japanese	222,364	1,676,031	9,666,302	11,564,697
„ with English	—	10,750	42,500	53,250
Jarawa.....................	—	—	1,012	1,012
Jaunsari...................	—	—	1,252	1,252
Javanese	8,008	106,321	1,406,384	1,520,713
Jita (Kijita)	—	1,235	—	1,235
Jolof	—	—	3,031	3,031
Jorai	—	—	4,976	4,976
Judaeo–Arabic	—	—	2,975	2,975
Judaeo–Spanish	1,212	20,300	48,181	69,693
Judaeo with Hebrew	669	—	313	982
Jukun (Donga)..............	—	—	1,012	1,012
Kabyle	—	3,585	—	3,585
„ with French	—	—	5,300	5,300
Kachchhi	—	—	500	500
Kachin	6,129	11,411	76,345	93,885
Kaguru	—	—	1,515	1,515
Kakwa of Congo	—	—	1,010	1,010
Kalaña.....................	—	—	9,590	9,590
Kalanga	—	—	1,000	1,000
Kalmuk	—	—	35,880	35,880
Kamba.....................	—	43,307	3,545	46,852
Kamberri...................	—	—	266	266
Kanakura	—	—	500	500
Kanarese	61,329	66,554	1,608,960	1,736,843
„ with English	—	—	2,500	2,500
„ with Sanskrit	—	—	3,000	3,000
Kanauri	—	—	1,510	1,510
Karamajong	—	—	6,069	6,069
Karanga	—	46,680	39,796	86,476
Karelian	—	—	3,000	3,000
Karen (Bghai)	—	—	11,000	11,000
„ (Pwo)	6,846	4,597	17,755	29,198
„ (Sgau)	72,579	37,390	136,567	246,536
Karre	—	—	5,058	5,058
Kashmiri	—	400	86,900	87,300
Keapara	—	—	11,820	11,820
Kele	—	21,851	25	21,876

Language	Bibles and Old Tests.	New Tests. and N.T. and Psalms	Portions	Total
Kele Ongom	—	—	500	500
Kelega	—	—	2,020	2.020
Khasi	21,651	77,214	119,934	218,799
Khondi	—	—	1,800	1,800
Kikuyu	30,084	193,500	105,115	328,699
Kim	—	1,098	1,000	2,098
Kipsigis	—	10,660	2,512	13,172
Kiriwina	—	—	8,052	8,052
Kisii	—	3,333	6,050	9,383
Kituba	—	—	2,512	2,512
Kiwai	—	—	7,552	7,552
Koho	—	—	3,000	3,000
Koi	—	—	2,526	2,526
Kololo	—	6,070	2,020	8,090
Konde	—	21,105	3,000	24,105
Kongo: Fioti	67,696	74,544	10,000	152.240
„ San Salvador	31,608	40,885	10,100	82,593
„ „ with Portuguese	—	10,000	—	10,000
Konjo	—	—	2,028	2,028
Kono	—	—	1,518	1,518
Kopu	—	—	11,000	11,000
Koranko	—	—	2,521	2,521
Korean	166,390	1,652,961	18,043,541	19,862,892
„ with Chinese	—	—	3,000	3,000
Krongo	—	—	505	505
Kroo	—	—	3,006	3,006
Kuanyama	—	26,668	9,664	36,332
Kuba: Inkongo dialect	2,030	6,549	2,098	10,677
Kulu	—	—	1,500	1,500
Kunama	—	1,070	—	1,070
Kunini	—	—	506	506
Kurdish	—	33	15,923	15,956
Kurku	—	—	1,000	1,000
Kurukh	—	—	7,018	7,018
Kwagutl	—	—	2,539	2,539
Kwese	—	—	2,020	2,020
Ladakhi	—	—	825	825
Lahnda (or Multani)	—	—	3,000	3,000
„ (Hindko)	—	—	2,000	2,000
Lahu	—	—	17,000	17,000
Laka	—	—	5,000	5,000
Lakher	—	1,000	12,712	13,712
Lamba	—	30,390	2,530	32,920
Lapp	—	—	5,000	5,000
Latgalian	—	—	10,000	10,000
Latin	13,150	110,497	20	123,667
Latvian	173,403	559,931	410,900	1,144,234
Lendu (Batha)	—	7,372	14,166	21,538
Lengua	—	—	2,025	2,025
Lenje (or Mukuni)	—	—	16,130	16,130
Lepcha	—	—	4,000	4,000
Lifu	6,627	4,035	4,047	14,709
Limba	—	—	2,010	2,010
Lisu, East	—	—	12,035	12,035
„ West	—	—	11,500	11,500
Lithuanian	54,159	110,990	497,845	662,994
„ with English	—	—	13,587	13,587

Language	Bibles and Old Tests.	New Tests. and N.T. and Psalms	Portions	Total
Livonian	—	—	3,000	3,000
Logo	—	—	1,012	1,012
Lozi	—	20,082	5,000	25,082
Luba: Kalebwe	—	12,500	3,110	15,610
„ *Kaonde*	—	14,620	4,050	18,670
„ *Katanga*	27,066	31,763	56,025	114,854
Luba–Lulua	—	2,030	20,079	22,109
Luba Songi	—	—	3,042	3,042
Luchazi and *Portuguese*	—	8,030	—	8,030
Luchu	—	—	2,000	2,000
Lugbara	—	24,257	27,276	51,533
Luimbi and *Portuguese*	—	—	1,506	1,506
Lumbu	—	—	1,010	1,010
Lunda of Kalunda	—	21,870	46,578	68,448
„ of Mwante Yamvo...	—	9,422	5,000	14,422
Luo	20,179	93,696	78,473	192,348
Lur......................	7,200	8,030	17,170	32,400
Lushai	—	52,100	320,038	372,138
Luyia	—	—	1,000	1,000
Maban....................	—	—	1,000	1,000
Mabuaig	—	—	1,513	1,513
Macassar	—	—	6,165	6,165
Madi	—	—	4,052	4,052
Madurese	—	15	5,110	5,125
Mailu	—	3,000	3,783	6,783
Makua	—	—	2,520	2,520
Makuchi	—	—	506	506
Malagasy	429,666	586,771	797,182	1,813,619
Malay	31,589	134,099	1,315,750	1,481,438
Malayalam	251,056	281,184	2,301,835	2,834,075
„ with *English*	—	—	7,000	7,000
„ with *French*	—	—	500	500
„ with *Sanskrit* ...	—	—	3,000	3,000
Malekula: Aulua	—	—	5,542	5,542
„ *Pangkumu*	—	—	6,060	6,060
„ *Uripiv*	—	—	2,000	2,000
Maliseet	—	—	1,520	1,520
Malo	—	1,500	3,517	5,017
Maltese	—	—	38,338	38,338
Malto	—	—	7,002	7,002
Malu	—	—	5,566	5,566
Mambwe	—	15,565	26,181	41,746
Manchad	—	—	200	200
Manchu	—	2,002	6,000	8,002
Manda....................	—	2,012	2,010	4,022
Mandingo	—	—	3,013	3,013
Manipuri	—	—	30,500	30,500
Mano.....................	—	—	2,500	2,500
Manus Island	—	1,000	1,012	2,012
Manx	5,000	2,250	—	7,250
Maori	18,540	102,018	64,409	184,967
Mapudungu	—	—	1,024	1,024
Marathi	75,781	114,343	4,341,848	4,531,972
„ with *English*	—	—	5,500	5,500
„ *Konkani*	—	—	34,170	34,170
Mare (or *Nengone*)	6,220	4,047	13,030	23,297
Margi	—	—	12,500	12,500
Marovo	—	—	1,010	1,010

Language	Bibles and Old Tests.	New Tests. and N.T. and Psalms	Portions	Total
Marwari	—	—	1,000	1,000
Masaba	—	—	1,520	1,520
Masai	—	5,060	3,528	8,588
Masana	—	—	2,509	2,509
Mashi	—	—	2,000	2,000
Mataco, or *Vejoz*	—	—	4,950	4,950
Mauritius Creole	—	—	11,664	11,664
Mawken	—	—	470	470
Maya..................	—	—	3,552	3,552
Mbai: Maisila	—	7,500	3,020	10,520
Mbundu	—	8,960	19,796	28,756
,, and *Portuguese*	—	70,872	136,780	207,652
Mbum	—	—	505	505
Mende	—	—	40,991	40,991
Meninka	—	—	630	630
Mer	—	—	1,013	1,013
Meru	—	9,000	24,940	33,940
Mexican	—	—	250	250
Miao: Chuan	—	—	3,000	3,000
,, *He* or *Black*	—	—	2,000	2,000
,, *Hwa*..............	—	22,000	34,820	56,820
Micmac	—	—	9,311	9,311
Mikir..................	—	—	15,000	15,000
Mohawk	—	—	2,000	2,000
Momvu	—	—	1,012	1,012
Mon..................	1,015	500	8,000	9,515
Mongo Nkundu	12,400	30,734	—	43,134
,, (or *Lolo*)	—	21,950	13,820	35,770
Mongolian..................	—	5,045	291,530	296,575
Mordoff (or *Mordvin*)	—	—	3,860	3,860
Mori	—	250	34	284
Moru	—	9,314	13,632	22,946
Mota	2,545	1,113	2,000	5,658
Motu	—	24,357	8,088	32,445
Mpoto	—	—	1,012	1,012
Mro	—	—	100	100
Mukawa	1,010	1,012	1,517	3,539
Mundang	—	8,500	3,034	11,534
Murut	—	—	1,000	1,000
Mwala: Fiu	—	—	500	500
,, *Kwara'ae*	—	2,020	10,110	12,130
,, *Lau*...............	—	—	2,530	2,530
,, *Malu*	—	3,000	1,000	4,000
,, *Saa*	—	4,630	505	5,135
Naga (*Ao*)	—	—	30,500	30,500
,, *Angami*	—	—	24,500	24,500
,, *Kabui*..............	—	—	1,000	1,000
,, *Lhota*	—	—	4,000	4,000
,, *Sema*	—	—	7,000	7,000
,, *Tangkhul*	—	1,000	6,315	7,315
Nama	—	4,001	3,000	7,001
,, with *English*	—	—	950	950
Namau	—	1,012	506	1,518
,, *Urika*	—	2,000	—	2,000
Namwanga	—	—	1,010	1,010
Nandi	17,055	2,010	—	19,065
Nanjeri	—	—	3,000	3,000
Ndandi	—	—	13,154	13,154

Language	Bibles and Old Tests.	New Tests. and N.T. and Psalms	Portions	Total
Ndau	—	15,435	63,245	78,680
Ndonga	8,500	59,078	23,713	91,291
Negro–English	—	15,949	—	15,949
Nepali	3	1	365,628	365,632
New Britain		34,274	9,420	43,694
Ngala (Bangala): Uele (Welle)	10,000	82,680	162,548	255,228
„ (Lingala)	—	47,214	30,000	77,214
Ngambai	—	9,700	12,000	21,700
Ngandu	—	6,000	5,060	11,060
Ngbaka	—		3,030	3,030
Ngombe	—	12,080	3,000	15,080
Nguna–Efate..............	5,002	4,510	15,845	25,357
Nguna–Tongoa	—	6,050	2,525	8,575
Ngwana: Ituri { See	—	44,662	17,878	62,540
Lualaba { Swahili (Congo)	—	27,046	10,150	37,196
Nias	—	—	1,010	1,010
Nicobarese	—	3,220	17,028	20,248
Niue.....................	7,699	11,580	15,092	34,371
Nkole	—	—	38,398	38,398
Nkoya	—	7,512	7,012	14,524
Norwegian................	116,075	27,100	—	143,175
„ and Danish......	574,453	1,378,785	665,825	2,619,063
„ with English	—	3,565	72,110	75,675
Nosu	—	—	4,000	4,000
Nsenga	—	8,867	10,080	18,947
Ntomba	—	—	6,502	6,502
Nuba: Heiban	—	—	3,395	3,395
„ Moro	—	—	1,005	1,005
„ Nirere	—	—	1,012	1,012
Nubian	—	—	12,507	12,507
Nuer	—	—	1,012	1,012
„ (Eastern or Jikany)	—	—	2,030	2,030
Nunggubuyu	—	—	1,000	1,000
Nupe	5,000	8,534	11,115	24,649
Nyamwezi	—	8,110	6,575	14,685
Nyanja	44,351	41,935	60,006	146,292
Nyasa Tonga	—	965	5,756	6,721
Nyamba and Portuguese	—	—	2,039	2,039
Nyika of B.E. Africa	—	—	2,026	2,026
„ or Nyasa Nyika	—	4,224	—	4,224
Nyimang..................	—	—	2,020	2,020
Nyoro	70,904	74,014	81,590	226,508
Ogoni....................	—	—	9,725	9,725
Ojibwa...................	—	4	—	4
Okela	—	—	2,022	2,022
Omo	—	—	3,000	3,000
Omyene	1,996	2,539	3,040	7,575
Ora	—	—	2,020	2,020
Oriya (Uriya)	12,917	6,460	481,781	501,158
Orokolo..................	—	—	8,032	8,032
Ossete	—	—	5,670	5,670
Paama	—	2,000	—	2,000
Pali	—	500	6,981	7,481
Pampangan	947	2,397	33,840	37,184
Panaieti	—	2,012	4,002	6,014
Pangasinan	3,000	7,400	122,567	132,967
Panjabi	—	26,060	904,620	930,860

Language	Bibles and Old Tests.	New Tests. and N.T. and Psalms	Portions	Total
Pashto (or *Afghan*)	—	6,012	106,253	112,265
Patpatar	—	—	1,010	1,010
Pedi	31,540	78,759	20,000	130,299
Pende......................	—	8,785	3,030	11,815
Pere	—	—	1,010	1,010
Perm	—	—	5,000	5,000
Persian	57,298	116,417	968.237	1,141,952
„ with *English*	—	—	15,356	15,356
„ with *French*	—	—	5,312	5,312
„ *Judaeo*	—	1,546	44,533	46,079
Petats	—	—	1,012	1,012
Piedmontese	—	1,000	—	1,000
„ with *French*	—	—	2,030	2,030
„ with *Italian*.....	—	—	1,010	1,010
Pitjantjatjara	—	—	500	500
Pokomo	—	3,491	4,046	7,537
Polish	697,227	1,141,243	2,080,174	3,918,644
„ with *English*	—	—	26,000	26,000
Ponerihouen	—	—	1,020	1,020
Popo	—	—	3,000	3,000
Portuguese	1,162,988	1,725,185	6,654,121	9,542,294
„ with *English*	—	107	31,900	32,007
Provençal	—	—	504	504
Quechua	—	—	3,733	3,733
„ with *Spanish*.......	—	2,325	19,070	21,395
Quiché....................	—	—	7,710	7,710
Rabha (*Rangdania*)	—	—	1,000	1,000
Raga	—	—	2,000	2,000
Ragetta	—	—	3,040	3,040
Rarotonga	34,356	10,605	—	44,961
Red Bobo	—	2,087	—	2,087
Rennellese	—	—	2,000	2,000
Riang–Lang................	—	—	1,000	1,000
Romansch	6,025	13,222	300	19,547
Romany...................	—	—	16,585	16,585
Ronga	12,985	20,300	504	33,789
Roro	—	—	2,000	2,000
Rotuma	—	8,040	—	8,040
Roviana	—	4,000	6,040	10,040
Ruanda	10,000	73,942	51,79ᶠ	135,738
Rukuba	—	—	26ᵧ	269
Rumanian	294,551	944,245	943,072	2,181,868
„ with *English*	—	—	10,000	10,000
„ (*Macedonian dialect*)	—	—	5,000	5,000
Rundi....................	—	40,075	18,456	58,531
Russian	344,292	6,898,720	7,755,552	14,998,564
„ with *Slavonic*	—	278,035	3,220,989	3,499,024
„ with *English*	—	—	31,734	31,734
„ White Russian	—	10,000	160	10,160
Sakata....................	—	—	4,030	4,030
Salampasu	—	—	1,515	1,515
Samareno	—	5	316	321
Samoa	144,098	21,923	—	166,021
Samogit	—	5,200	—	5,200
San Cristoval	—	—	1,518	1,518
Sangir	—	8,112	19,530	27,642
Sango	—	201,034	14,151	215,185
Sanskrit	—	3,981	30,218	34,199

Language	Bibles and Old Tests.	New Tests. and N.T. and Psalms	Portions	Total
Santali...................	11,092	24,000	193,066	228,158
Santo Bay (N.E. Santo)	—	—	1,543	1,543
" East (Hog Harbour)	—	—	2,974	2,974
" Nogugu	—	—	5,515	5,515
" Tangoa	—	—	1,000	1,000
" Tasiriki	—	—	3,305	3,305
Sara: Madji-Ngai	—	—	4,040	4,040
Sardinian (Cagliaritan dialect)	—	—	4,000	4,000
Sena	—	—	1,009	1,009
Serbian	59,439	145,000	40,000	244,439
" and Croatian	125,356	502,584	1,305,219	1,933,159
" with English	—	—	15,000	15,000
Shamba	—	—	2,020	2,020
Shambala	—	7,006	1,010	8,016
Shan	1,004	1,017	51,848	53,869
" Yunnanese	—	—	6,008	6,008
Shilha (Southern or Susi)....	—	—	11,662	11,662
" (Northern or Rifi) ...	—	—	2,778	2,778
Shina Gurezi.............	—	—	500	500
Shona	107,691	135,011	31,885	274,587
Siamese	—	93	955	1,048
" Laotian	4,000	—	11,800	15,800
Sidamo	—	—	750	750
Sindhi	—	2,500	205,758	208,258
Singpho	—	—	1,531	1,531
Sinhalese	51,362	77,835	1,447,587	1,576,784
Siwai	—	—	3,000	3,000
Slave (or Tinne)	—	—	4,297	4,297
Slavonic	—	438,183	2,103,645	2,541,828
" with Bulgarian	—	1,000	—	1,000
Slovak	10,000	85,853	223,840	319,693
Slovenian	20,108	75,659	221,400	317,167
Sobo (Urhobo)	—	5,000	8,044	13,044
Soga	—	—	2,516	706
Somali: Ogaden-Harti	—	—	2,516	2,516
Spanish	3,211,542	2,716,241	14,663,611	20,591,394
" with English	—	11,337	48,804	60,141
" with Latin	1,000	—	—	1,000
Suk	—	—	1,010	1,010
Sukuma	—	13,575	23,295	36,870
Sundanese	142	378	16,081	16,601
Sura.....................	—	—	13,602	13,602
Susu and French	—	—	2,020	2,020
Suto	339,204	298,558	50,310	688,072
Swahili (Congo).............	—	15,000	—	15,000
" (Standard)	100,000	98,400	110,154	308,554
" (Mombasa).........	44,520	55,111	50,270	149,901
" (Zanzibar)	16,807	168,345	121,445	306,597
Swedish	672,528	2,392,135	548,505	3,613,168
" with English........	—	6,076	10,100	16,176
Syriac	9,347	44,183	44,759	98,289
" and Carshuni	—	2,000	—	2,000
" (Nestorian character) .	—	—	2,000	2,000
Tabele	—	18,032	12,770	30,802
Tae	—	—	800	800
Tagalog	31,783	59,157	672,371	763,311
Tahiti.................	59,305	18,173	6,050	83,528
Taita: Dabida	—	12,536	6,570	19,106

Language	Bibles and Old Tests.	New Tests. and N.T. and Psalms	Portions	Total
Taita: Sagalla	—	—	2,036	2,036
Talaing	—	—	5,000	5,000
Tamil	496,261	375,131	9,136,238	10,907,630
„ with English	—	—	40,501	40,501
Tangale	—	6,211	1,418	7,629
Tanna (Lenakel dialect)	—	6,000	2,000	8,000
„ (Weasisi dialect)	—	—	1,212	1,212
Taungthu	—	—	32,500	32,500
Tavara	—	—	2,010	2,010
Taveta	—	—	3,541	3,541
Telegu	185,123	165,804	5,353,767	5,704,694
„ with English	—	—	20,001	20,001
„ with Sanskrit	—	—	7,500	7,500
Temne	—	—	15,637	15,637
Tera	—	—	500	500
Teso	—	42,876	96,074	138,950
Thado Kuki...............	—	—	5,500	5,500
Tharaka	—	—	524	524
Thonga	61,446	80,278	21,613	163,337
Tibetan	2	7,033	632,681	639,716
Tigre	—	2,000	6,500	8,500
Tigrinya..................	—	13,146	16,885	30,031
Tivi	—	17,034	5,054	22,088
Tinan	—	—	200	200
Toaripi	—	13,197	10,137	23,334
Toba	—	—	250	250
„ with Spanish	—	—	1,000	1,000
Toda	—	—	1,501	1,501
Tonga	37,213	26,160	11,012	74,385
„ of Inhambane	—	2,360	—	2,360
„ of Zambezi	—	—	2,550	2,550
„ (Union or Rhodesian) .	—	3,000	3,022	6,022
Tsamba...................	—	—	2,524	2,524
Tsimihety	—	—	10,100	10,100
Tswa (Sheetswa)	8,742	19,819	80	28,641
Tubetube	—	—	3,020	3,020
Tukudh	1,010	1,011	6,399	8,420
Tula	—	—	250	250
Tulu	—	5,500	28,201	33,701
Tumbuka	—	282		282
Turkish (Osmanli)	20,739	49,810	352,754	423,303
„ „ with English	—	—	1,000	1,000
„ „ with French	—	—	1,000	1,000
„ „ with Italian	—	—	1,000	1,000
„ (Armenian character)	6,702	23,360	26,675	56,737
„ (Greek character) ...	25,072	48,118	102,012	175,202
„ Bashkir	—	—	1,000	1,000
„ Chuvash	—	20,000	48,600	68,600
„ Gagauzi	—	—	10,000	10,000
„ Jagatai	—	—	3,535	3,535
„ Kashgar	6,000	—	21,605	27,605
„ Kazan	—	—	20,600	20,600
„ Kirghiz	—	8,800	26,390	35,190
„ Kumuk	—	—	1,510	1,510
„ Nogai	—	—	1,000	1,000
„ Transcaucasian	2,516	13,516	43,985	60,017
„ Uzbek	—	—	7,510	7,510
„ Yakut	—	—	4,500	4,500

Language	Bibles and Old Tests.	New Tests. and N.T. and Psalms	Portions	Total
Ukrainian (Ruthenian)	82,630	83,423	353,466	519,519
„ with *English*	—	2,814	21,034	23,848
Ulawa	—	2,830	955	3,785
Urdu	207,673	398,274	6,024,569	6,630,516
„ with *English*	—	24,006	45,150	69,156
„ with *Arabic*	—	—	1,000	1,000
Uvea	4,008	1,000	1,505	6,513
Vaudois with *French*	—	—	3,020	3,020
Vella Lavella	—	—	1,011	1,011
Venda	18,712	4,530	14,340	37,582
Vietnamese (Annamese)	6,000	18,688	1,112,329	1,137,017
Visayan: Panayan	653	3,167	41,889	45,709
Vogul	—	—	3,000	3,000
Votiak	—	—	10,000	10,000
Wa......................	—	3,090	8,000	11,090
Waja	—	—	768	768
Walamo	—	—	1,000	1,000
Wedau	—	—	4,021	4,021
Welsh	109,067	181,506	38,825	329,398
„ with *English*	—	23,974	—	23,974
Wend: Lower	1	5,000	—	5,001
„ Upper	10,006	8,000	—	18,006
Wongo	—	—	2,236	2,236
Worrora	—	—	1,505	1,505
Wurkum	—	—	411	411
Xhosa (Kafir)	471.823	219,154	51,960	742,937
Yahgan	—	—	2,529	2,529
Yaka	—	—	2,030	2,030
Yalunka	—	—	1,019	1,019
Yao.....................	—	7,026	22,752	29,778
Yergum	—	—	506	506
Yiddish (Judaeo-German) ...	10,216	217,009	724,379	951,604
„ with *English*	—	—	21,685	21,685
„ with *Hebrew*	35,600	—	43,651	79,251
Yoruba	837,040	25,014	78,836	940,890
Zande	—	18,180	36,582	54,762
Zigula	—	—	505	505
Ziryen	—	—	5,000	5,000
Zulu	229,667	495,800	72,919	798,386

APPENDIX IV:

THE ENGLISH OF THE REVISED
STANDARD VERSION [1]

The action of the International Council of Religious Education which authorized the preparation of the Revised Standard Version of the Bible, required the revision to be "designed for use in public and private worship, and to be in the direction of the simple, classic English style of the King James Version."

That does not mean that the present revisers were instructed to return to the errors and archaic language of the King James Version, but rather that they were charged to recover its simplicity and directness. These qualities had been lost in the versions of 1881 and 1901, and with them had gone much of the beauty and power of the older version. The major defect of the English Revised Version and of its variant, the American Standard Version, is that these are literal, word-for-word translations, which follow the order of the Greek words wherever possible, rather than the order which is natural to English.

It was unnecessary, for example, to change the third petition of the Lord's Prayer to: "Thy will be done, as in heaven, so on earth." The Revised Standard Version restores the familiar order of the words: "Thy will be done on earth as it is in heaven."

[1] This Appendix consists of an article by Dean Weigle, Chairman of the Revision Committee, and is reproduced here by kind permission of the Division of Christian Education of the National Council of the Churches of Christ in the United States of America, from *An Introduction to the Revised Standard Version of the New Testament* (New York, Nelson, 1952).

Note, in the following passages, how the KJ translation is complicated in the ASV by changes due to following the order of the Greek
words; and contrast with both versions the more direct, terse renderings
of the RSV:

Luke 9.17. KJ: "And they did eat, and were all filled: and there
was taken up of fragments that remained to them twelve baskets."
ASV: "And they ate and were all filled; and there was taken up that
which remained over to them of broken pieces, twelve baskets." RSV:
"And all ate and were satisfied. And they took up what was left over,
twelve baskets of broken pieces."

Luke 20.1-2. KJ: "And it came to pass, *that* on one of those days,
as he taught the people in the temple, and preached the gospel, the
chief priests and the scribes came upon *him* with the elders, And spake
unto him, saying, Tell us, by what authority doest thou these things? or
who is he that gave thee this authority?" ASV: "And it came to pass, on
one of the days, as he was teaching the people in the temple, and
preaching the gospel, there came upon him the chief priests and the
scribes with the elders; and they spake, saying unto him, Tell us: By
what authority doest thou these things? or who is he that gave thee this
authority?" RSV: "One day, as he was teaching the people in the temple
and preaching the gospel, the chief priests and the scribes with the
elders came up and said to him, 'Tell us by what authority you do these
things, or who it is that gave you this authority?' "

Luke 23.8. KJ: "And when Herod saw Jesus, he was exceeding
glad: for he was desirous to see him of a long season, because he had
heard many things of him; and he hoped to have seen some miracle
done by him." (Here is an example, incidentally, of the inaccuracy of
KJ. The Greek reads, and good English demands, "to see" instead of
"to have seen.") ASV: "Now when Herod saw Jesus, he was exceeding
glad; for he was of a long time desirous to see him, because he had
heard concerning him; and he hoped to see some miracle done by him."
RSV: "When Herod saw Jesus, he was very glad, for he had long desired to see him, because he had heard about him, and he was hoping
to see some sign done l / him."

The versions of 1881 and 1901 tend to use the definite article
wherever it is used in the Greek, with almost complete disregard of
the fact that English usage with respect to articles does not permit blind
following of the idiom of another language, be it French or German or
Latin or Hebrew or Greek. So they contain such unnecessary changes
and such awkward English as: "Is not the life more than the food, and

the body than the raiment?" (Matt. 6.25). The RSV has: "Is not life more than food, and the body more than clothing?"

The versions of 1881 and 1901 eliminated some of the archaisms of the King James Version. Notably, they substituted the personal relative pronoun "who" for the neuter "which" where this refers to persons. Paul is no longer made to say, as in KJ, "I am verily a man which am a Jew" (Acts 22.3), but simply, "I am a Jew." In Luke 20.20 the description of the spies in KJ, "which should feign themselves just men," became in ASV, "who feigned themselves to be righteous," and now reads in RSV, "who pretended to be sincere."

ASV got rid of the misleading archaisms "let" for "hinder" (Rom. 1.13), and "prevented" for "spoke first to" (Matt. 17.25); but it kept "provided" where the Greek means "foreseen" (Heb. 11.40), because "provide" once meant "foresee" just as "prevent" once meant "precede." It kept "providence" in the sense of "provision" (Acts 24.2). It retained the word "suffer" in the sense of "let," "allow," or "permit"; and it kept "communicate" in the sense of "share." The RSV makes the necessary changes with respect to these words.

Among the archaisms of the King James which the ASV retained, but which have been changed in the RSV, are the following:

"Of" becomes "by," when the actor or agent is denoted. Jesus was baptized "by John" rather than "of John," and tempted "by Satan" rather than "of Satan." This change of preposition occurs in many passages.

"Because that" and "for that" become "because" and "for." (Luke 9.7; Acts 8.11; 2 Cor. 5.4; etc.)

"Was yet a coming" and "I go a fishing" lose their "a." "The more part" is "the majority." "Nothing bettered" is "no better." "Compass round" is "surround." "Swellings" means "conceit" in 2 Cor. 12.20. The word "magnify" is kept only in the Magnificat, when it is retained for liturgical reasons.

"Is come" means "has come," and in general "is," "are" and other forms of the verb "be" as auxiliaries for the perfect tense of intransitive verbs of motion, are replaced by the corresponding forms of the verb "have."

Where Paul wrote "would that" the King James Version made him say "would to God"; and in fourteen cases where he wrote "be it not so," the King James Version reads "God forbid." The ASV corrected the former of these expressions, but not the latter; the RSV removes the insertion of the name of God.

At some points the revisers of 1881 and 1901 introduced archaisms which were not in the King James Version. They greatly, and unnecessarily, increased the use of such words as "holden," "aforetime," "Sojourn," "must needs," "would fain," and "behooved." They joined the word "haply" to the word "lest" in seventeen cases where the King James did not have it; the Revised Standard Version has eliminated the word "haply" in all cases.

One of the great issues which the present revisers faced was whether or not to retain the second person singular, "thou," with its correlative forms, "thee," "thy," "thine," and the verb endings "-est" and "-edst." After two years of debate and experiment it was decided to abandon these forms and to follow modern usage, except in language addressed to God. The "-eth" and "-th" forms for verb endings in the third person are not used at all. Something is lost, be it granted, by the elimination of the plural nominative "ye"; but this is a loss that has been sustained by the English language.

In general, the Revised Standard Version uses the simpler forms, as "to" for "unto" and "on" for "upon." "Enter into" is "enter." The "so" is omitted from "whosoever," "whatsoever," and the like. "According as" is simply "as." "Insomuch that" is "so that." "They that" and "them that" are "those who." "Exceeding" and "sore" are not used as adverbs. Such phrases as "on this wise" and "set at nought" and such words as "privily," "wherein," "whereby," "thereabout," and "divers" are replaced by modern equivalents.

In the use of "shall" and "will" modern usage is followed. The inverted order of subject and predicate is avoided unless it is necessary to reproduce the meaning and emphasis of the original Greek. In punctuation, and in the use of quotation marks, modern usage prevails.

The printing in italics of English words demanded by the sense but not explicitly represented by a corresponding word in Greek, was a misleading feature of the former versions. How inconsistently it was done will be manifest even to the reader who knows no Greek if he will compare the KJ printing of Matthew 5.3-12 and Luke 6.20-26 with the ASV printing of the same pages. The RSV omits italics altogether, on the principle that only words necessary to convey the meaning in English are used.

We must speak with caution, for there has been no set purpose to reduce the number of words and no sufficient count has been made. But a count of the words in a few chapters, chosen from various books, shows that the style of the Revised Standard Version is terse. It probably contains fewer words than the former authorized versions, and certainly fewer than other modern versions such as those of Weymouth, Moffatt, and Goodspeed. Here are the figures:

	KJ	ASV	RSV
Matthew 5	1,081	1,056	1,002
Mark 1-2	1,654	1,618	1,534
Luke 8	1,431	1,431	1,367
John 4	1,096	1,085	1,038
Acts 10	1,108	1,128	1,022
Romans 8	904	898	898
1 Cor. 15	1,165	1,169	1,151
Ephesians 3	410	418	405
Philippians 1	632	653	639
Colossians 2	503	515	502

Yet we have not hesitated to use more words than the older versions, if that was necessary to convey the meaning. An interesting example is 1 Cor. 7.19, which starts out with more words in the initial clause, but ends with a total of one less. The verse reads in KJ: "Circumcision is nothing, and uncircumcision is nothing, but the keeping of the commandments of God." This is ambiguous, for "but" may be taken to mean "except." In ASV the wording is unchanged, and the meaning is made to depend upon the punctuation, changing the comma after "nothing" to a semicolon. The RSV reads: "For neither circumcision counts for anything nor uncircumcision, but keeping the commandments of God."

A requirement that has constantly been kept in mind by the present Committee is that the Bible should be translated into language that is euphonious, readable, and suited for use in public and private worship. It must sound well, and be easy to read aloud and in public. The choice of words and ordering of phrases must be such as to avoid harsh collocations of sound, and consonantal juxtapositions over which tongues will trip and lisp—that sentence is an example of what must not be in the English Bible!

Much even of the prose of the King James Bible has the beauty, and something of the rhythm, of poetry. But it is a mistake to assume that all of the Bible is poetry, or that, to be readable and suited for use in public worship, the translation must be rhythmic.

For use in public and private worship, it is not necessary that the language of the English Bible be stiff or strange or antique, or that it convey the impression of a self-conscious effort to be reverent. But it must not be irreverent, and it must not be colloquial or trivial. For use in worship the Bible must be cast, not in what is merely the language of today, but in enduring and simple diction which is worthy to stand in the great tradition of Tyndale and the King James Version.

LUTHER A. WEIGLE

APPENDIX V:

SOME MISLEADING WORDS IN THE KING JAMES VERSION AND THEIR CORRECTION[1]

The following is a selected list of words used in the King James Version which have so changed in meaning, or acquired such new meanings, that they no longer convey to the reader the meaning which they had for the King James translators and were intended to express. Most of them were accurate translations in 1611; but they have now become misleading.

The list here given is far from complete; it contains only about one-fourth of the words of this sort in the King James Version. It does not undertake to list all the occurrences of the misleading terms, but gives only one or two references for each, except in a few cases where more are required to show the term in varied contexts. There is no attempt to give the inflection of the word in each case.

The term used in the King James Version is given first, then the Biblical reference; this is followed by the term used in the American Standard Version of 1901; then come the letters RSV, followed by the term used in the Revised Standard Version.

In cases where the American Standard Version retains the reading of the King James Version, the term is not repeated. In cases where

[1] Reproduced from *An Introduction to the Revised Standard Version of the Old Testament* (New York, Nelson, 1952), by kind permission of the Division of Christian Education of the National Council of the Churches of Christ in the United States of America.

the reading of the American Standard Version is retained by the Revised Standard Version, this is indicated by = RSV.

For example, at 1 Samuel 2.17, KJ uses "abhor," ASV uses "despise," and RSV "treat with contempt." In Acts 17.3, both KJ and ASV use "allege," and RSV uses "prove." In Job 31.35, KJ has "book," and ASV and RSV have "indictment."

abhor	1 Samuel 2.17 despise; RSV treat with contempt
abroad	Deuteronomy 24.11 without; RSV outside
	Judges 12.9 RSV outside his clan
advertise	Numbers 24.14 RSV let you know
	Ruth 4.4 disclose it to you; RSV tell you of it
allege	Acts 17.3 RSV prove
amazed	Mark 14.33 RSV distressed
amiable	Psalm 84.1 RSV lovely
ancients	Isaiah 3.14; Jeremiah 19.1; Ezekiel 7.26 elders=RSV
anon	Mark 1.30 straightway; RSV immediately
apparently	Numbers 12.8 manifestly; RSV clearly
artillery	1 Samuel 20.40 weapons=RSV
book	Job 31.35 indictment=RSV
bowels	Genesis 43.30 heart=RSV
	Philippians 1.8 tender mercies; RSV affection
by and by	Mark 6.25 forthwith; RSV at once
careful	Jeremiah 17.8 RSV anxious
	Luke 10.41 anxious=RSV
careless	Judges 18.7 in security=RSV
	Isaiah 32.9, 10, 11 RSV complacent
	Ezekiel 30.9 RSV unsuspecting
carelessly	Isaiah 47.8 securely=RSV
	Zephaniah 2.15 RSV secure
carriage	1 Samuel 17.22 baggage; RSV things . . . baggage
	Judges 18.21 goods=RSV
	Acts 21.15 baggage; RSV made ready
charity	1 Corinthians 13 love=RSV
coast	Exodus 10.4 border; RSV country
	Joshua 1.4 border; RSV territory
	Joshua 17.9 border; RSV boundary
	Matthew 2.16 borders; RSV region
	Acts 19.1 country=RSV
communicate	Galatians 6.6 RSV share
	Hebrews 13.16 RSV share
comprehend	Isaiah 40.12 RSV enclose
	John 1.5 apprehend; RSV overcome

convenient	Proverbs 30.8 needful=RSV
	Ephesians 5.4 befitting; RSV fitting
	Philemon 8 befitting; RSV required
	Jeremiah 40.4, 5 right=RSV
conversant	Joshua 8.35 were; RSV lived
	1 Samuel 25.15 went=RSV
conversation	1 Peter 3.1, 2 behavior=RSV
convince	Job 32.12 RSV confute
	John 8.46 convict=RSV
cunning	Genesis 25.27 skilful=RSV
	1 Samuel 16.16 skilful=RSV
	1 Chronicles 22.15 skilful; RSV skilled
curious	Exodus 28.8 skilfully woven=RSV
	Exodus 35.32 skilful; RSV artistic
	Acts 19.19 magical=RSV
curiously	Psalm 139.15 RSV intricately
delectable	Isaiah 44.9 that they delight in=RSV
denounce	Deuteronomy 30.18 RSV declare
discover	Psalm 29.9 strip bare=RSV
	Isaiah 22.8 take away the covering=RSV
	Micah 1.6 uncover=RSV
dote	Jeremiah 50.36 become fools=RSV
duke	Genesis 36.15 chief=RSV
was entreated	Genesis 25.21 RSV granted his prayer
	2 Samuel 21.14 RSV heeded supplications
	1 Chronicles 5.20 RSV granted their entreaty
feebleminded	1 Thessalonians 5.14 fainthearted=RSV
footmen	Numbers 11.21 RSV on foot
	Jeremiah 12.5 RSV men on foot
forwardness	2 Corinthians 9.2 readiness=RSV
furniture	Genesis 31.34 saddle=RSV
grudge	Psalm 59.15 tarry; RSV growl
	James 5.9 murmur; RSV grumble
halt	Psalm 38.17 fall=RSV
	1 Kings 18.21 go limping=RSV
harness	1 Kings 20.11 armor=RSV
	1 Kings 22.34 armor=RSV
harnessed	Exodus 13.18 armed; RSV equipped for battle
headstone	Zechariah 4.7 top stone=RSV
health	Psalm 42.11 help=RSV
	Psalm 67.2 salvation; RSV saving power
herb	Genesis 1.11 herbs; RSV plants
	Psalm 105.35 RSV vegetation
hitherto	Job 38.11 RSV thus far

imagine	Genesis 11.6 purpose; RSV propose
	Psalm 2.1 meditate; RSV plot
	Psalm 10.2 conceived; RSV devised
leasing	Psalm 4.2 falsehood; RSV lies
	Psalm 5.6 lies=RSV
let	Isaiah 43.13 hinder=RSV
	Romans 1.13 hindered; RSV prevented
Libertines	Acts 6.9 RSV Freedmen
mean	Proverbs 22.29 RSV obscure
meat	Genesis 1.29, 30 food=RSV
	Deuteronomy 20.20 food=RSV
	Matthew 6.25 food=RSV
	John 4.32 RSV food
meat offering	Leviticus 2.1 meal-offering; RSV cereal offering
mortify	Romans 8.13 put to death=RSV
	Colossians 3.5 put to death=RSV
munition	Isaiah 29.7 stronghold=RSV
	Isaiah 33.16 RSV fortress
	Nahum 2.1 fortress; RSV ramparts
naughtiness	1 Samuel 17.28 RSV evil
	Proverbs 11.6 iniquity; RSV lust
	James 1.21 wickedness=RSV
naughty	Proverbs 6.12 worthless=RSV
	Proverbs 17.4 mischievous=RSV
	Jeremiah 24.2 bad=RSV
nephew	Judges 12.14 sons' sons; RSV grandsons
	Job 18.19 son's son; RSV descendant
	1 Timothy 5.4 grandchildren=RSV
occupied	Exodus 38.24 used=RSV
	Judges 16.11 wherewith no work hath been done; RSV used
occupier	Ezekiel 27.27 dealer=RSV
occupy	Ezekiel 27.9 deal; RSV barter
	Luke 19.13 trade=RSV
outlandish	Nehemiah 13.26 foreign=RSV
out of hand	Numbers 11.15 RSV at once
overran	2 Samuel 18.23 outran=RSV
peculiar	Exodus 19.5 mine own possession; RSV my own possession
	Deuteronomy 14.2 for his own possession=RSV
person	Deuteronomy 1.17 RSV be partial
	Proverbs 28.21 RSV show partiality
	Acts 10.34 RSV shows no partiality
persuade	Acts 19.8 RSV pleading
	Acts 28.23 RSV trying to convince

pitiful	Lamentation 4.10 RSV compassionate
prefer	Esther 2.9 remove; RSV advance
	Daniel 6.3 distinguished=RSV
	John 1.15 become; RSV rank
presently	1 Samuel 2.16 first=RSV
	Proverbs 12.16 RSV at once
	Matthew 21.19 immediately; RSV at once
	Matthew 26.53 even now; RSV at once
prevent	Job 3.12 receive=RSV
	Psalm 119.147 anticipate; RSV rise before
	Matthew 17.25 spake first to him; RSV spoke to him first
	1 Thessalonians 4.15 precede=RSV
provoke	2 Corinthians 9.2 stir up=RSV
	Hebrews 10.24 RSV stir up
publish	Deuteronomy 32.3 proclaim=RSV
	1 Samuel 31.9 carry the tidings; RSV carry the good news
purchase	Psalm 78.54 gotten; RSV won
	1 Timothy 3.13 gain=RSV
quarrel	Leviticus 26.25 vengeance=RSV
	Mark 6.19 set herself against; RSV grudge
	Colossians 3.13 complaint=RSV
quick	Numbers 16.30 alive=RSV (Note that KJ has alive for the same Hebrew in Numbers 16.33)
	Psalm 55.15 alive=RSV
	Psalm 124.3 alive=RSV
quicken	Psalm 119.50 RSV give life
	1 Corinthians 15.36 RSV come to life
	Ephesians 2.1 make alive=RSV
record	Job 16.19 witness=RSV
	Philippians 1.8 witness=RSV
recover	2 Kings 5.3, 6, 7, 11 RSV cure
refrain	Job 7.11 RSV restrain
	Psalm 119.101 RSV hold back
	Proverbs 10.19 RSV restrain
reins	Job 16.13 RSV kidneys
	Psalm 7.9 hearts=RSV
repent self	Deuteronomy 32.36 RSV have compassion on
	Judges 21.6, 15 RSV have compassion on
replenish	Genesis 1.28 RSV fill
	Genesis 9.1 RSV fill
require	Ezra 8.22 ask=RSV
reward	Deuteronomy 32.41 recompense; RSV requite
	Psalm 54.5 requite=RSV
	2 Timothy 4.14 render to; RSV requite

rid	Genesis 37.22 deliver; RSV rescue
	Exodus 6.6 RSV deliver
	Leviticus 26.6 cause to cease; RSV remove
riotous	Proverbs 23.20 gluttonous=RSV
	Proverbs 28.7 gluttons=RSV
road	1 Samuel 27.10 raid=RSV
room	2 Samuel 19.13 RSV place
	1 Chronicles 4.41 stead; RSV place
	Psalm 31.8 place=RSV
	Luke 14.7 seat; RSV place
secure	Judges 8.11 RSV off its guard
	Judges 18.7, 10 RSV unsuspecting
securely	Proverbs 3.29 RSV trustingly
slime	Genesis 11.1; 14.10 RSV bitumen
sottish	Jeremiah 4.22 RSV stupid
strait	2 Kings 6.1 RSV small
	Isaiah 49.20 RSV narrow
	Matthew 7.13 narrow=RSV
straitly	Genesis 43.7 RSV carefully
straitness	Deuteronomy 28.53, 55, 57 distress=RSV
	Job 36.16 RSV cramping
	Jeremiah 19.9 distress=RSV
suffer	Genesis 20.6 RSV let
	Matthew 19.14 RSV let
take thought	1 Samuel 9.5 be anxious; RSV become anxious
	Matthew 6.25 be anxious=RSV
tale	Exodus 5.8, 18 number=RSV
	1 Samuel 18.27 number=RSV
	1 Chronicles 9.28 count=RSV
target	1 Samuel 17.6 javelin=RSV
	1 Kings 10.16 buckler; RSV shield
tell	Genesis 15.5 number=RSV
	Psalm 22.17 count=RSV
	Psalm 48.12 number=RSV
translate	2 Samuel 3.10 transfer=RSV
	Hebrews 11.5 RSV take up
unspeakable	2 Corinthians 9.15 RSV inexpressible
usury	Exodus 22.25 interest=RSV
	Leviticus 25.36 interest=RSV
	Matthew 25.27 interest=RSV
vain	Judges 9.4; 11.3 RSV worthless
vex	Exodus 22.21 wrong=RSV
	Numbers 25.17 RSV harass
	Acts 12.1 afflict; RSV lay violent hands upon

virtue	Mark 5.30 power=RSV
	Luke 6.19 power=RSV
volume	Psalm 40.7 roll=RSV
	Hebrews 10.7 roll=RSV
wealth	Ezra 9.12 prosperity=RSV
	Esther 10.3 good; RSV welfare
	1 Corinthians 10.24 good=RSV
wealthy	Psalm 66.12 RSV spacious
	Jeremiah 49.31 at ease=RSV
witty inventions	Proverbs 8.12 discretion=RSV

APPENDIX VI:

LISTS OF MEMBERS OF THE REVISION COMMITTEE AND OF THE ADVISORY BOARD FOR THE MAKING OF THE REVISED STANDARD VERSION [1]

In the following list of the members of the Committee, only those institutions are listed with which the men were connected at the time of their election to the Committee. Deaths are recorded only in the case of those who died while still in active membership. The Section to which each member has been assigned is indicated by O.T. (Old Testament) and N.T. (New Testament).

President Frederick C. Eiselen, Garrett Biblical Institute, 1929. Died May 5, 1937. O.T.

President John R. Sampey, Southern Baptist Theological Seminary, 1929-1938. O.T.

Dean Luther A. Weigle, Yale University Divinity School, 1929-. O.T. and N.T.

Professor William P. Armstrong, Princeton Theological Seminary, 1930-1937. N.T.

Professor Julius A. Bewer, Union Theological Seminary, 1930-. O.T.

Professor Henry J. Cadbury, Harvard University, 1930-. N.T.

[1] Reproduced from *An Introduction to the Revised Standard Version of the Old Testament* (New York, Nelson, 1952), by kind permission of the Division of Christian Education of the National Council of the Churches of Christ in the United States of America.

Professor Edgar J. Goodspeed, University of Chicago, 1930-. N.T.

Professor Alexander R. Gordon, United Theological College, Montreal, 1930. Died 1930. O.T.

Professor James Mo'*.tt, Union Theological Seminary, 1930. Died June 27, 1944. O.T. and N.T.

Professor James A. Montgomery, University of Pennsylvania, 1930-1937. O.T.

Professor Archibald T. Robertson, Southern Baptist Theological Seminary, 1930. Died Sept. 24, 1934. N.T.

Professor James Hardy Ropes, Harvard University, 1930-1932. N.T.

Professor Andrew Sledd, Emory University, 1930-1937. N.T.

Professor J. M. Powis Smith, University of Chicago, 1930. Died Sept. 26, 1932. O.T.

Professor Charles C. Torrey, Yale University, 1930-1937. O.T.

Professor William R. Taylor, University of Toronto, 1931. Died Feb. 24, 1951. O.T.

Reverend Walter Russell Bowie, Grace Church, New York, 1937-. N.T.

Professor George Dahl, Yale University, 1937-. O.T.

President Frederick C. Grant, Seabury-Western Theological Seminary, 1937-. N.T.

Professor William A. Irwin, University of Chicago, 1937-. O.T.

Dean Willard L. Sperry, Harvard University Divinity School, 1937-. O.T.

Professor Leroy Waterman, University of Michigan, 1937-. O.T.

Professor Millar Burrows, Yale University, 1938-. O.T. and N.T.

Professor Clarence T. Craig, Oberlin Graduate School of Theology, 1938-. N.T.

President Abdel R. Wentz, Lutheran Theological Seminary, Gettysburg, 1938-. N.T.

Professor Kyle M. Yates, Southern Baptist Theological Seminary, 1938-. O.T.

Professor William F. Albright, Johns Hopkins University, 1945-. O.T.

Professor J. Philip Hyatt, Vanderbilt University, 1945-. O.T.

Professor Herbert G. May, Oberlin Graduate School of Theology, 1945-. O.T.

Professor James Muilenburg, Pacific School of Religion, 1945-. O.T.

Professor Harry M. Orlinsky, Jewish Institute of Religion, New York, 1945-. O.T.

Dean Fleming James, University of the South, 1947-. O.T.

The Chairman and the General Secretary of the International Council of Religious Education are members ex officio of the American Standard Bible Committee, without assignment to Sections, but charged with a special responsibility for matters of general policy, finance, and public relations. The men who have thus served as members of the American Standard Bible Committee are:

Dr. Robert M. Hopkins, Chairman ICRE, General Secretary World's Sunday School Association, 1929-1931.

Dr. Hugh S. Magill, General Secretary ICRE, 1929-1936.

Dr. Harold McAfee Robinson, Chairman ICRE, General Secretary Presbyterian Board of Christian Education, 1931-1937.

Dr. Roy G. Ross, General Secretary ICRE, 1936.

Dr. Walter D. Howell, Chairman ICRE, Secretary Presbyterian Board of Christian Education, 1937-1938.

President Arlo A. Brown, Chairman ICRE, Drew University, 1938-1948.

Dr. Paul C. Payne, Chairman ICRE, General Secretary Presbyterian Board of Christian Education, 1948-.

With the Committee has been associated an Advisory Board made up of representatives from each of the denominations affiliated with the International Council of Religious Education. This Board has acted in an advisory capacity; its members have been consulted with respect to the principles underlying the revision, have reviewed drafts, and have made many valuable suggestions. The representatives of the denominations who have thus served on the Advisory Board are:

Advent Christian Church: President O. R. Jenks, Aurora College, Aurora, Ill.

African Methodist Episcopal Church: Rev. Charles W. Abington, Philadelphia, Pa.

African Methodist Episcopal Zion Church: Bishop John W. Martin, Chicago, Ill.

American Baptist Convention: Professor Charles N. Arbuckle, Andover-Newton Theological Seminary, Newton Center, Mass.

Dr. W. W. Adams, Central Baptist Theological Seminary, Kansas City, Kansas

American Lutheran Church: Dr. H. C. Leupold, Capitol University Theological Seminary, Columbus, Ohio

Associate Reformed Presbyterian Church: Professor G. G. Parkinson, Due West, S. C.

Augustana Evangelical Lutheran Synod of North America: Rev. J. Vincent Nordgren, Minneapolis, Minn.

Baptist Convention of Ontario and Quebec: Professor H. L. MacNeill, McMaster University, Hamilton, Ont.

Professor N. H. Parker, McMaster University, Hamilton, Ont.

Baptist Union of Western Canada: Rev. G. G. Harrop, Saskatchewan, Canada

Church of the Brethren: Rev. E. G. Hoff, Elgin, Ill.

Church of God: Rev. Otto F. Linn, Dundalk, Md.

Church of the Nazarene: Dr. Olive M. Winchester, Pasadena College, Pasadena, Calif.

Rev. Roy E. Swim, Kansas City, Mo.

Churches of Christ: Rev. H. Leo Boles, Nashville, Tenn.

Churches of God in North America: Rev. F. D. Rayle, Harrisburg, Pa.

Colored Methodist Church: Bishop William Y. Bell, Cordele, Ga.

Congregational and Christian Churches: Dr. Sidney A. Weston, Boston, Mass.

Disciples of Christ: Dean Stephen J. England, Phillips University, Enid, Okla.

Professor W. C. Morro, Texas Christian University, Fort Worth, Texas

Professor Henry Barton Robison, Culber-Stockton College, Canton, Mo.

Evangelical and Reformed Church: Professor Allen G. Wehrli, Eden Seminary, Webster Groves, Mo.

Evangelical United Brethren: Bishop John S. Stamm, Harrisburg, Pa.

Dr. J. Gordon Howard, Otterbein College, Westerville, Ohio

Five Years Meeting of Friends in America: Professor William E. Berry, Earlham College, Richmond, Ind.

Free Methodist Church of North America: Professor George E. Turner, Asbury Theological Seminary, Wilmore, Ky.

Mennonite Brethren in Christ: Dean J. A. Huffman, Taylor University, Upland, Ind.

Methodist Church: Dr. C. A. Bowen, Nashville, Tenn.

Dean B. Harvie Branscomb, Vanderbilt University, Nashville, Tenn.

Dr. Lucius Bugbee, Cincinnati, Ohio

President F. G. Holloway, Western Maryland College, Westminster, Md.

Missouri Lutheran Synod: Dr. George V. Schick, Concordia Seminary, St. Louis, Mo.

Moravian Church in America: Professor Raymond S. Haupert, Bethlehem, Pa.

National Baptist Convention of America: Rev. C. J. Gresham, Atlanta, Ga.

National Baptist Convention, U.S.A.: Dr. Marshall A. Talley, Nashville, Tenn.

Presbyterian Church, U.S.: Professor Donald W. Richardson, Union Theological Seminary, Richmond, Va.

Presbyterian Church in U.S.A.: Professor John W. Bowman, Western Theological Seminary, Pittsburgh, Pa.

Rev. Park Hays Miller, Philadelphia, Pa.

Protestant Episcopal Church: Rev. Cuthbert A. Simpson, New York, N. Y.

Reformed Church in America: President John W. Beardslee, Jr., New Brunswick Seminary, New Brunswick, N. J.

Southern Baptist Convention: Dr. T. L. Holcomb, Nashville, Tenn.

Dr. Hight C. Moore, Nashville, Tenn.

Dr. Clifton J. Allen, Nashville, Tenn.

United Baptists of the Maritime Provinces: Professor W. N. Hitchins, Wolfville, Nova Scotia

United Brethren in Christ (Old Constitution): Rev. J. Ralph Pfister, Huntington, Ind.

United Church of Canada: Rev. Frank Langford, Toronto, Ont.
Rev. C. A. Myers, Toronto, Ont.
Professor R. B. Y. Scott, Montreal, Canada

United Lutheran Church in America: Dean E. E. Flack, Hamma Divinity School, Springfield, Ohio

United Presbyterian Church in North America: President John McNaugher, Pittsburgh-Xenia Theological Seminary, Pittsburgh, Pa.
Professor James L. Kelso, Pittsburgh-Xenia Theological Seminary, Pittsburgh, Pa.

Scholars who have rendered aid at various points, in response to the request of the Committee, are Professor G. R. Driver, of Oxford University, who read and commented upon the drafts of many of the Old Testament books; Professor John F. Fulton and Dr. Henry E. Sigerist, of Yale University, who dealt with questions in the history of medicine; Professor Alexander M. Witherspoon, of Yale University, to whom were referred disputed issues with respect to English usage; and Professor John C. Trever, of Drake University, later Director of the Department of English Bible of the Division of Christian Education, National Council of Churches of Christ in the United States of America, who made a detailed study of the terms used in the Bible as names of trees.

APPENDIX VII:

PASSAGES FROM A MODERN VERSION
OF THE
NEW TESTAMENT IN LOWLAND SCOTS

Among the curiosities of the literature relating to our subject is a version of the New Testament arranged by William Wye Smith and entitled The New Testament in Braid Scots. *This is in no sense a scholarly work; it is not even a translation but merely a loose rendering of the King James Version into a Scottish dialect as this was recollected by an expatriate Scot in Canada. It was published by Alexander Gardner, Paisley, Scotland. A revised edition is dated 1904. Though, because of its nature, no mention of it has been made in the body of the present book, some excerpts are printed below, since these may interest and perhaps amuse readers of Scottish descent.*

Matthew vi.26-30. 'Look ye to the wee birdies i' the lift; for they naither saw nor shear, nor lead intil the barn; and yet yere Heevenlie Faither gies them meat. Are-ye-na a hantle better nor they? And what amang ye, be he nevir sae fain, could mak his sel a span heigher? And anent cleedin; why soud ye hae sae n..ckle cark and care? Look weel at the lilies o' the lea, hoo they growe; they toil-na, nor spin; And yet say I, that Solomon in a' his glorie was-na buskit braw like ane o' thae! Noo than, gin God sae cleed the foggage (the day on the lea, and the morn brunt i' the oven), hoo muckle mair you, O ye o' the sma' faith!'

Mark iv.1. And he begude again to teach by the Loch-side. And an unco thrang gather't till him, sae that he gaed intil a boat, and sat i' the Loch; and a' the folk war by the Loch, on the lan'.

Acts xix.1-2. And it cam aboot while Apollos was in Corinth, that Paul, gaun throwe the heigher pairts, cam intil Ephesus; and faund a wheen disciples, And to them quo' he, 'Gat ye the Holie Spirit whan ye believed?' But they said, 'On the contrar, we warna tell't thar was ony Holie Spirit!'

Romans xvi.20-24. But the God o' peace sal ding Sautan aneath yere feet sune! The tender-love o' oor Lord Jesus Christ be w'ye! Timothy, my marrow, salutes ye, and Lucius, and Jason, and Sosipater my kinsmen. I, Tertius, wha penned this Epistle, salute ye i' the Lord. Gaius, the enterteener o' mysel and o' the hail kirk, salutes ye. Erastus the City Treasurer salutes ye; and Quartus oor brither. The kindly love o' oor Lord Jesus Christ wi' ye a'! Amen!

I Thessalonians v.20-21. Geck-na at preachins, But pit a' things to the test; and what is bonnie haud fast.'

APPENDIX VIII:

NON-BIBLICAL SAYINGS OF JESUS

In 1897, fragments of papyri began to be collected at Oxyrhynchus, about ten miles west of the Nile, near the modern Behnesa. Oxyrhynchus had been a center of Christian culture in the fourth century. Thousands of these fragments eventually came to light and were translated and edited. Best known among them are those containing sayings attributed to Jesus. These sayings often recall similar sayings in the Gospels; but their form is different, and in some cases there is no strict counterpart in the Bible.

Much of the Greek text is conjectural restoration of lacunae. Another reconstruction of these sayings is now possible through a more recently discovered Coptic manuscript.

THE SAYINGS OF JESUS
from the Oxyrhynchus papyri

These are the life-giving Sayings which Jesus spake who liveth and was seen of the Ten and of Thomas. And He said to them: Whosoever heareth these Sayings shall not taste of death.

I
Jesus saith:
> Let not him who seeketh cease from seeking until he hath found;
> And when he hath found, he shall be amazed;
> And when he hath been amazed, he shall reign;
> And when he hath reigned he shall have rest.

II

Judas saith: "Who, then, are they who draw us? And when shall come the Kingdom which is in Heaven?" Jesus saith: "The birds of the air and, of the beasts, whatsoever is under the earth or upon the earth, and the fishes of the sea; these are they which draw you. And the Kingdom of Heaven is within you; and whosoever shall know himself shall find it. And when ye have found it, ye shall know that ye are sons and heirs of the almighty Father, and ye shall know that ye are in God and God in you. And ye are the city of God."

III

Jesus saith:

Shall a man who has found the way not fear to ask . . . determining all things concerning the place of his seat? Ye shall find that many first shall be last, and the last first, and they shall inherit eternal life.

IV

Jesus saith:

Everything that is not before thine eyes,
And that which is hidden from thee, shall be revealed unto thee;
For there is nothing hid that shall not become manifest,
And buried that shall not be raised up.

V

His disciples examine him and say: How shall we fast, and how shall we pray, and how shall we do alms, and what shall we keep of the traditions? Jesus saith: Ye shall not be as hypocrites. Do not these things openly, but cleave to the truth; and let your righteousness be concealed. For I say: Blessed is he that doeth these things in secret, for he shall be rewarded openly by the Father who is in Heaven.

VI

Jesus saith:

Cast out first the beam out of thine own eye,
And then thou shall see clearly to cast out the mote that is in thy brother's eye.

VII

Jesus saith:

Except ye fast toward the world, ye shall not find the Kingdom of God.
And unless ye sanctify the whole week, ye shall not see the Father.

VIII

Jesus saith:

I stood in the midst of the world, And in flesh was I seen of them;
And I found all men drunken, And none found I athirst among
them;
And my soul grieved over the sons of men,
Because they are blind in their heart, And see not with their
understanding.

IX

Jesus saith .. , ... to . . . . . . (their ?) poverty.

X

Jesus saith:

Wheresoever there be two, they are not without God.
And where there is one alone, I say, I am with him.
Lift up the stone, and there thou shalt find me;
Cleave the wood, and there I am.

XI

Jesus saith:

A prophet is not acceptable in his own country,
Neither doth a physician do healing upon them that know him.

XII

Jesus saith:

A city built upon the top of a high mountain and established
Can neither fall nor be hidden.

XIII

Jesus saith:

Thou hearest with one ear,
But the other thou hast closed.

APPENDIX IX:

SPECIMENS OF EARLY CHRISTIAN LITERATURE[1]

I: APOSTOLIC FATHERS

(a) Shepherd of Hermas (Vision I)

He who had bred me up sold a certain young maid at Rome; whom when I saw many years after, I remembered her, and began to love her as a sister. It happened sometime afterwards, that I saw her washing in the river Tiber; and I reached out my hand unto her, and brought her out of the river.

And when I saw her I thought with myself, saying, How happy should I be if I had such a wife, both for beauty and manners. This I thought with myself; nor did I think any more. But not long after, as I was walking and musing on these thoughts, I began to honour this creature of God, thinking with myself; how noble and beautiful she was.

And when I had walked a little, I fell asleep. And the spirit caught me away, and carried me through a certain place toward the right-hand, through which no man could pass. It was a place among rocks, very steep and unpassable for water.

When I was past this place, I came into a plain; and there falling down upon my knees, I began to pray unto the Lord, and to confess my sins.

And as I was praying, the heaven was opened, and I saw the woman

---

[1] This rendering is based on an old, English translation, compared with original texts. A good modern translation of the Apocryphal New Testament literature is available in: M. R. James, *The Apocryphal New Testament,* Oxford University Press, 1953.

which I had coveted, saluting me from heaven, and saying, Hermas, hail! and I looking upon her, answered, Lady, what doest thou here? She answered me, I am taken up hither to accuse thee of sin before the Lord.

Lady, said I, wilt thou convict me? No, she said: but hear the words which I am about to speak unto thee. God who dwelleth in heaven, and hath made all things out of nothing, and hath multiplied them for his holy church's sake, is angry with thee because thou hast sinned against me.

And I answering said unto her, Lady, if I have sinned against thee, tell me where, or in what place, or when did I ever speak an unseemly or dishonest word unto thee?

Have I not always esteemed thee as a lady? Have I not always reverenced thee as a sister? Why then dost thou imagine these wicked things against me?

Then she, smiling upon me, said: The desire of naughtiness has risen up in thy heart. Does it not seem to thee to be an ill thing for a righteous man to have an evil desire rise up in his heart?

[Hermas, overcome with sorrow, is then visited by the vision of an old lady, symbolizing the Church, who instructs and comforts him.]

(b) *Barnabas*

But the way of darkness is crooked and full of cursing. For it is the way of eternal death, with punishment; in which they that walk meet those things that destroy their own souls.

Such are: idolatry, confidence, pride of power, hypocrisy, double-mindedness, adultery, murder, rapine, pride, transgression, deceit, malice, arrogance, witchcraft, covetousness, and the want of the fear of God.

In this walk those who are the persecutors of them that are good; haters of truth; lovers of lies; who know not the reward of righteousness, nor cleave to anything that is good.

II: APOCRYPHAL NEW TESTAMENT

(c) *Gospel of Nicodemus (Acts of Pilate)*

Then the Lord holding Adam by the hand, delivered him to Michael the archangel; and he led them into Paradise, filled with mercy and glory;

And two very ancient men met them, and were asked by the saints,

Who are ye, who have not yet been with us in hell, and have had your bodies placed in Paradise?

One of them answering said, I am Enoch, who was translated by the word of God: and this man who is with me is Elijah the Tichbite, who was translated in a fiery chariot.

Here we have hitherto been, and have not tasted death, but are now about to return at the coming of Antichrist, being armed with divine signs and miracles, to engage with him in battle, and to be slain by him at Jerusalem, and to be taken up alive again into the clouds, after three days and a half.

(d) *Gospel of Thomas*

On a certain day also, when the Lord Jesus was playing with the boys, and running about, he passed by a dyer's shop, whose name was Salem.

And there were in his shop many pieces of cloth belonging to the people of that city, which they designed to dye of several colours.

Then the Lord Jesus going into the dyer's shop, took all the cloths, and threw them into the furnace.

When Salem came home and saw the cloths spoiled, he began to make a great noise, and to chide the Lord Jesus, saying,

What hast thou done to me, O thou Son of Mary? Thou hast injured both me and my neighbours; they all desired their cloths of a proper colour; but thou hast come and spoiled them all.

The Lord Jesus replied, I will change the colour of every cloth to what colour thou desirest;

And then he presently began to take the cloths out of the furnace, and they were all dyed of those same colours which the dyer desired.

And when the Jews saw this astonishing miracle, they praised God.

APPENDIX X:

SPECIMENS OF THE DRAFT VERSION OF THE REVISED TRANSLATION OF THE JEWISH PUBLICATION SOCIETY OF AMERICA [1]

Genesis i.1-5

[1] When God began to create the heaven and the earth— [2] the earth was unformed and void, with darkness on the face of the deep and the wind of God moving over the face of the water— [3] God said, "Let there be light"; and there was light. [4] God saw that the light was good, and God set the light apart from the darkness. [5] And God called the light Day, and the darkness He called Night. And there was evening and there was morning, the first day.

Genesis xxxii.23-33

[23] That same night he arose, and taking his two wives, his two maid-servants, and his eleven children, he crossed the ford of the Jabbok. [24] He took and sent them across the stream. After he had sent across that which he had, [25] Jacob remained all alone. And a man wrestled with him until the break of dawn. [26] When he saw that he had not prevailed against him, he wrenched Jacob's hip at its socket, so that the socket of his hip was strained as he wrestled with him. [27] Then he said,

---

[1] Reproduced from the proof sheets by kind permission of the publishers, The Jewish Publication Society of America. It is to be noted that this is only a *draft* translation and is subject to revision.

"Let me go, for dawn is breaking." But he answered, "I will not let you go, unless you bless me." 28 He said to him, "What is your name?" And he replied, "Jacob." 29 And he said, "Your name shall no longer be Jacob, but Israel, for you have striven with beings divine and human, and have prevailed." 30 Jacob then asked, "Pray tell me your name." But he said, "Why do you ask my name?" And he blessed him there. 31 So Jacob named the place Peniel: "For I have seen God face to face, yet my life has been preserved." 32 The sun rose upon him as he passed Penuel, limping on his thigh. 33 That is why the children of Israel to this day do not eat the sinew of the hip that is upon the socket of the thigh, for he wrenched the socket of Jacob's thigh, the sinew of the hip.

APPENDIX XI:

SPECIMENS OF THE DEAD SEA SCRIPTURES IN ENGLISH TRANSLATION

In 1947 began, in a cave seven and a half miles south of Jericho, in the cliff bordering the west side of the Dead Sea, the discovery of a collection of ancient manuscripts whose importance is now renowned throughout the world. They are commonly called the Dead Sea Scrolls. The cave lies about a thousand yards north of a ravine, the Wadi-Qumrān, which is dominated, a few miles northward, by a terrace with a large cemetery containing many tombs and some ruins, Khirbet-Qumrān. Since the discovery of the first manuscripts, extensive archaeological excavations have been undertaken over a large area, and as manuscripts have come to light they have been examined, and, since April 1951, the work of publishing them has been going on.

The value of these discoveries lies, in considerable measure, in the light they have cast on a little-known Jewish sect before the time of Christ, and the consequently important information they have provided for further study of the cultural background of Christianity. The writings fall very roughly in the same period as the Old Testament Apocrypha and Pseudepigrapha.

The following passages are provided by way of illustrating the kind of material that has come to light: [1]

[1] Square brackets indicate words that are obscure in the text. Parentheses indicate words inserted to clarify the meaning.

A: *The Omnipotence of God and the Nothingness of Man*
(1QS xi.15-22) [2]

Blessed art Thou, O my God,
Who hast opened the heart of thy servant to Knowledge!
Confirm in righteousness all his deeds,
And decide in favour of the son of Thy handmaid,
According to Thy kindness for the elected among men,
Which causes them to stand as a party before Thee for ever.
For without Thee no way is perfect
And without Thy will, nothing is done.
Thou hast taught all Knowledge,
And everything that has come to pass exists by Thy will.
And there is no other beside Thee
To gainsay Thy decision
And to understand all Thy Holy Thought
And to contemplate the depth of Thy Mysteries,
And to apprehend all Thy Marvels
Together with the force of Thy Might.

Who then is able to bear Thy Glory?
For what indeed is he, the son of man, among Thy
marvellous works?
And what is he that is born of woman, what is his worth
before Thee?
Yea, this man, he was kneaded from dust,
And to become the prey of worms, such is his destiny!
Yea, this man is but a frail image of potter's clay,
Whose return is to dust,
What will the clay reply, that which the hand fashioneth?
And what thought can it understand?

B: *Some Moral Maxims* (1QS x.17-xi.2)

I will repay no man with retribution of evil:
Only with good will I pursue a man;

---

[2] This passage and the following one (B) are reproduced in English translation by kind permission of Vallentine, Mitchell & Co. Ltd., London, from the translation by R. D. Barnett, published by them, of A. Dupont-Sommer's *The Jewish Sect of Qumrān and the Essenes*, which was first published in French by Editions Lassalle under the title: *Nouveaux Aperçus sur des Manuscrits de la Mer Morte*, 1953. Both passages are from the *Manual of Discipline*.

For with God is the judgment of every living thing,
And He will reward a man with his due.
I will not be envious from a spirit of wickedness,
And my soul shall not covet the riches of violence.
As for the multitude of the men of the Pit, I will not
          lay hold of them until the Day of Vengeance;
But my anger I will not turn back far from wicked men,
Nor will I be content until He inaugurates the Judgment.
I will be without rancour and without anger against those
          who are converted from rebellion.
But I will have no compassion on those who have turned
          aside from the way;
I will not console those who are chastised until their
          way becomes perfect.[3]

And I will not keep Belial in my heart;
And folly shall not be heard in my mouth,
Nor shall criminal deceit, nor falsehoods, nor lies be
          found on my lips.
But the fruit of holiness shall be on my tongue,
And abominations shall not be found in it.
With thanksgivings I will open my mouth,
And the acts of God shall my tongue relate,
Also the faithlessness of men until the annihilation
          of their transgression.
Vain words will I abolish from my lips,
Impurities and perfidies from the understanding of
          my heart.
With wise reflection I will conceal Knowledge;
And with prudent understanding I will protect [it] with
          a firm boundary,
So as to preserve faith and right strictly according to the
          righteousness of God.
I will [accomplish] the Ordinance with the measuring line
          of the times,
And . . . . righteousness;
To love the discouraged with piety,

[3] The translator here calls attention to the New Testament injunction (Matt. xviii.17): "And if he refuse to hear the Church also, let him be unto thee as the Gentile and the publican."

And to strengthen the hands of those whose [heart] is
    troubled;
[And to teach] understanding to those who stray in spirit,
And to instruct in teaching those who criticise,[4]
And to reply humbly before the haughty in spirit,
And [to respond] with a contrite spirit to men
    who use the stick,
Who point the finger and utter wounding words [5]
And possess wealth.

C: *A Hymn* (1QH v.5-20) [6]

I thank Thee, Lord, that Thou didst not leave me
    When I dwelt with a people [heavy with sin;
For not according to my transgression
    Nor] according to my guilt hast Thou judged me,
And Thou didst not leave me in the abominations of my thoughts,
    But Thou hast saved my life from the pit.

For Thou didst appoint [thy servant a fugitiv]e in the midst of lions
    Ready for the sons of guilt—
Lions that break the bones of the noble
    And drink the blood of the strong;
And Thou hast put me in terror with many fishermen
    Who spread the net upon the face of the waters,
    And (with) hunters for the sons of evil.
And there for judgment Thou didst establish me,
    And a foundation of truth Thou didst strengthen in my heart
    And waters of a covenant for those who seek it.
But Thou hast closed the mouth of lions
    Whose teeth are like a sword
    And their fangs like sharp spears;
    Poison of serpents! Their only thought to seize prey.
But though they lie in wait
    They do not open their mouth against me,
For Thou, my God, hast hidden me
    (From) the presence of the sons of man,

4 Cf. Isaiah xxix.24.
5 Cf. Isaiah lviii.9.
6 This translation and the following one, *D*, both hitherto unpublished,
are by Professor S. LaSor, by whose kind permission they are here reproduced.

And Thy Torah is hidden in m[e
    Unti]l the time of the revelation of Thy salvation to me.

For in the distress of my soul Thou didst not leave me,
    And my cry Thou didst hear in the bitterness of my soul;
And the judgment of my sorrow Thou didst cut off when I wept,—
    So Thou deliverest the soul of the afflicted.
In the den of lions
    That sharpened their tongue like a sword
Thou, my God, didst close on my behalf their teeth
    Lest they tear the soul of the afflicted and poor,
And Thou hast gathered their tongue
    Like a sword into its scabbard,
        So as not [to cut o]ff the soul of Thy servant.

And so that Thou mightest make me strong
    Before the sons of man,
    Thou hast done wondrously with the poor.
Thou hast brought him into the crucibl[e
    Like go]ld in the workings of fire,
        And like silver being purified in the silversmiths' furnace,
            To purify (it) seven times.
So they rushed upon me, the wicked mighty men with their torments,
    And all the day they crush my spirit;
But Thou, my God shalt turn the storm to a whisper,
    And the soul of the poor Thou hast saved by Thy r[ighteousness,
    And hast snatched the one t]orn by the jaw of lions.
Blessed art Thou!

D: *The Rule* (1QS v.1—vi.4) [7]

5:1   This is the rule for the men of the Community who volunteer
        to turn from all evil and to hold to all that He commanded for
  :2   His good pleasure: To be separated from the congregation of the
        men of unrighteousness; To become a community in doctrine
        and in property; To reply at the command of the Sons of Zadok,
  :3   the priests who keep the covenant, and at the command of the
        majority of the men of the covenant who hold to the covenant,
        (for) at their command shall proceed the lot for every matter: for
  :4   doctrine, for property, and for judgment; To perform true unity
        and humility, righteousness and justice, and the love of mercy

[7] From the *Manual of Discipline*.

APPENDIX XII:

THE ROMAN CATHOLIC CHURCH AND THE BIBLE IN WESTERN EUROPE TODAY

by E. H. Robertson [1]

The Roman Catholic Church in France and Belgium, and to a certain extent also in Germany, has recently shown a remarkable interest in the Bible. This return to the Bible, or perhaps better, return of the Bible, is closely connected with an equally important liturgical revival, which is changing the Church in these countries. Indeed, the principal domestic dispute between Dominicans and Benedictines, wherever you meet them, seems to be whether the Biblical revival produced the liturgical revival or vice versa, or whether both are not due to a return to the sources. The Dominicans tend to see the whole movement as flowing from the masterly work of Père Lagrange, who opened the School of Jerusalem in 1890 and dealt with "modernism" in the Roman Catholic Church. The Benedictines tend to look to the Rhineland monastery of Maria Laach, where a group of scholarly monks working on ancient manuscripts have discovered certain early forms of the liturgy and experimented with them. Both see scholarly beginnings in the twin movement and both resent fiercely the suggestion that it is caused by Protestant influences.

[1] Reproduced by kind permission of the Reverend E. H. Robertson of the United Bible Societies, Geneva. It is a hitherto unpublished report.

The Dominicans seem to have the stronger case chronologically. 1890 is a very early date and there is no denying the immense influence of the School of Jerusalem which was opened in that year, nor the stature of the Dominican, Père Lagrange. The immediate irritant was "modernism." Roman Catholics have never wavered in their adherence to the Bible as the inerrant Word of God. When Alfred Loisy tried to appropriate the work of Harnack for the Catholic understanding of the Bible, he was branded with the name of "modernist" and thrown out of the Church. A papal encyclical first used the word and as a term of abuse. The great work of Lagrange was to set up a school of Roman Catholic scholars to study the Bible, as Roman Catholics, and to match their scholarship against the growing liberal schools of Europe. They did not choose the way of *Lux Mundi*,[2] which accepted the results of modern scholarship into the Catholic position and gave the Church of England a leading place. Rome was more reactionary, but it certainly produced scholars of high calibre to serve in Jerusalem. Throughout the years since 1890 a translation of the Bible, from the original languages, has been appearing, book by book with comments and notes. The high quality of this French translation and of its notes has put the Jerusalem Bible into the first rank. More than forty of these little paper-covered volumes have appeared and you can see them, complete now, on the shelves of any well-instructed French priest. Of course in the forty-volume form it was for priests and scholars only, not for the general public. More recently, popular editions of the Jerusalem Bible have appeared with fewer notes and bound in a single volume. Prices are still too high to make it a common possession, but nearly every Roman Catholic in France knows that this translation exists, that it is a good thing to read and that it might be quoted in any sermon. There are other modern translations but it is the Jerusalem Bible that has the prestige value and is best known.

The change in atmosphere is quite remarkable. Only a few years ago, if you talked to French Roman Catholics about Bible reading, you would get the reply quoted by a leading Roman Catholic scholar: "Read the Bible? But that's a Protestant book," or "That's not permitted, it's on the index," or zealous priests might have said: "You will lose your faith if you read the Bible. It has such bad examples and is therefore not permitted." (Quoted from *La Lecture chrétienne de la*

[2] An important series of Oxford studies, published in 1889, which, by recognizing in principle modern Biblical criticism, distressed some of the older Tractarians.

Bible, Dom Célestin Charlier.) The best Catholics never believed that, but there is no doubt that—much as it was deplored by some—it was the common attitude, so completely had the papal encyclicals of the nineteenth century against the Protestant Bible societies done their work.[3] The twentieth century saw the beginning of the change in high places; but of course it will be a long time before they hear about it in the parish churches even of the larger towns where old priests often cling to old ways. But two papal encyclicals this century are very revealing: Benedict XV, in the encyclical *Spiritus paraclitus* of the 15th September 1920, recommended the faithful to read every day from the books of the New Testament and from certain selected books of the Old Testament. Pius XII, in the encyclical *Divino afflante spiritu* of the 30th September 1943, gave his approval to those Catholic scholars who are translating the Bible into the common tongue from the original texts, and laid upon all priests the duty of encouraging among Roman Catholics "a knowledge and love of the Holy Books."

It is in this way that the Bible is beginning to replace Thomas à Kempis as the principal devotional book among French-speaking Roman Catholics.

Every faithful Roman Catholic in France today, who may feel that the Segond or Synodale translations are too Protestant, has a good choice of recommended Roman Catholic translations. The translation of the Abbé Crampon, made thirty years ago, has been revised; the Benedictines of Belgium have produced the very colloquial Maredsous translation; these, in addition to the Jerusalem Bible, give a choice. Now, there is appearing a translation which cannot be condemned as Protestant and will undoubtedly make its appeal to Roman Catholic and Protestant intellectuals. It is the Dhorme version, being prepared in three splendid and expensive volumes by one of the best publishing houses in Paris, Gallimard, and appearing in a celebrated series of French classics, *La collection de la Pléiade.* Dhorme is an ex-Roman Catholic, but his team of translators include the best men from the Roman Catholic and Protestant faculties. The first volume has already appeared and has been well received. Here is the scholar's Bible, and it may prove one of the most important pieces of common ground between the Roman Catholics and Protestants of France.

The liturgy of the Roman Catholic Church has suffered from a confusion of two elements, and every reform has tried to deal with this.

[3] The *Syllabus of Errors* promulgated by Pius IX in 1864 classed the Bible Societies with communism as among the condemned "pests" *(pestes).*

The two elements, which can be traced from a very early period, are sometimes called the temporal and the sanctoral. The temporal follows closely the ecclesiastical year and is based upon six events all firmly grounded in the Bible: Advent, Christmas, Septuagesima, Lent, Easter and Pentecost. In this part of the liturgy there were ample readings from the Bible supplemented by commentaries taken from the Fathers.

The other part, however—the sanctoral—is based on the lives of the saints and has a large place in it for the worship of the Virgin Mary.[4] The Bible has very little to say about the Virgin and of course practically nothing about the saints, who mostly came after it was written. It was therefore necessary to supplement the sanctoral part of the liturgy from traditional legends, and this is particularly true in the worship of the Virgin Mary. The Gospels tell us nothing of the birth of the Virgin, but legend has supplied the names of her parents, the date of her birth and the date of her presentation in the Temple. Of course this legend took a long time to grow into tradition, and the first celebration of the presentation of the Virgin in the Temple was on the 21st September 1372, under Pope Gregory XI. Thus the worship of the Virgin has grown until in recent years we have seen added to it the Feast of the Assumption of the Blessed Virgin. The same applies to the growth of legends of the saints in the liturgy. The medieval taste for the miraculous was satisfied in this way, but it so cluttered up the liturgy that there was constant need for reform. Despite all the efforts of Charlemagne and several popes, confusion reigned in the Latin liturgy until the end of the Middle Ages. At the Council of Basle in 1435 Martin de Senging could report: "The divine office is recited with confusion, in haste, without piety and with only one purpose, that of getting to the end as soon as possible."

There were three efforts at reform during the sixteenth century. First by Pope Leo X, who was a humanist and greatly offended by the style of the Latin liturgy. He put into the hands of Zacharie Ferreri, Bishop of Guardia, the task of writing the liturgy nearer to the style of Cicero and Vergil. This literary reform was ended by the sack of Rome in 1527. The second attempt was by Pope Clement VII, who was less concerned with pure Latin than with a return to primitive Christianity. He gave the task to a Spanish Franciscan, Francisco Quignonez, who

4 [Note by G. MacG.:] "Worship" is misleading in this context. The Roman Church does not permit the worship (latria) of the Virgin as God: what is encouraged is a special honor and devotion to her (hyperdoulia). The difference is infinite.

maintained that the earliest function of the divine office was to instruct by the daily reading of the Bible and of Church history. This reform is of special importance because it has been revived in recent years by the Benedictines and has led to the liturgical reform of our own day. Quignonez broke through the jungle of the existing liturgy and created order. He arranged the Psalter in such a way that it was recited regularly in its entirety. The office included each day three lessons, one from the Old Testament, one from the New Testament and on saints' days a legend of the saint, or on other days a homily on the Gospel for the day. This plan included the more important chapters of the Old Testament and the entire New Testament except for the Apocalypse, of which only the early chapters were read. This was not a reform, it was a revolution. The liturgy became principally a reading of the Bible supplemented by Church history. Quignonez's breviary went well in Germany, Italy and France, but it led to riots in Spain. It was severely criticized at the Council of Trent by John of Arz, who maintained that it was dangerous to expose ordinary people to so much of the Bible without comment. The Council of Trent, under the influence of Pope Paul IV, abandoned the breviary of Quignonez and opted for the old Roman breviary.

Thus the third reform of the liturgy was initiated: it was an attempt to change as little as possible, and in fact learned very little from the two previous reforms. So disappointing did this seem to Roman Catholics, particularly in France, that there was rebellion and disobedience. France carried out its own reform, but of course the extent of its deviation was limited.

In the seventeenth century, under the influence of Gallicanism and the opposition of Protestantism, it became necessary to remove all superstitious material. The breviary of François de Harley appeared in 1680 with more than forty doubtful legends of the saints removed. They were replaced by homilies from the Fathers. Among his many reforms was the removal of the legend of the Assumption of the Virgin. Harley planned not only to return to the primitive liturgy but in fact to make a breviary almost entirely in the words of Scripture. Yet even this was not enough. In the midst of an anti-Roman feeling that then ran through France, a feeling which was roused by the publication of the Bull *Unigenitus* in 1713, Grancolas and Foinard reduced the sanctoral even further. This revised breviary, published as late as 1736, had the support of the Archbishop of Paris, and remained in use until the nineteenth century. It contained hymns which were largely scriptural paraphrases. The breviary was finally disposed of by Dom Guéranger, Abbot of Solesmes (1805-1875).

Thus, as one scholar has said, "A century of Christian poetry was sacrificed to ultramontanism, and the Roman Catholic liturgy was unified throughout the world." Largely under the influence of this active Abbot of Solesmes the nineteenth century saw a renewed interest in the liturgy. It was a kind of Roman Catholic renaissance in France. The Abbot sought to go back to the thirteenth century; but Solesmes was not always a place of enlightenment, and incredible explanations were given to the function and office of the priest that had no Biblical foundation, except in allegories of passages from the Bible.

Today something of the hopes and aspirations of men who were condemned are being realized in France. Centuries of effort to get the Mass into the vernacular—effort which was opposed at every point by the ecclesiastical authorities—are now bearing fruit. Today devotional books abound and prayers can be read in the mother tongue, although vernacular Masses are not yet common outside certain monasteries. There is very little happening today in the liturgical revival which was not attempted in an earlier century; the difference is that now it is approved of.

The day before yesterday these translations of the Canon [of the Mass] hunted by the priests and the police; these oratories and chapels ransacked; these pages which had committed no other crime than that of making available to those who had not read Latin the most holy and certainly the most inoffensive of prayers, these pages torn out, destroyed, trampled, thrown into the fire like obscene books; today this same . . . Mass translated into all the known languages, printed in tens of thousands of copies, warmly recommended to all, by the bishops and by the Holy See. (Henri Bremond)

What is now happening in France and Belgium, and to a certain extent also in Germany, is part of an attempt to make the liturgy play a major part in Roman Catholic devotion. It is a kind of protest against the neglect of the liturgy. The story of its beginning is a very simple one. Scholars, searching through the manuscripts to find what were the primitive forms, and monks given permission to experiment in revived forms of worship, discovered that they were in touch with a living thing that must be made available to the people. It was out of this, mostly among Benedictines, that the great cry came that the function of the liturgy is to teach. The relation of the liturgy to personal devotional life is best summed up in the words of Antoine de Seurent:

> To live liturgically, that is to conform as far as possible his own spiritual life to that of the Church expressed in the official books of its worship. . . . The liturgy is at one and the same time source and method of prayer.

The reform has not yet fully done its work and it is still possible to go into Roman Catholic churches in France where the confusion is as bad as the Middle Ages and the language no more intelligible. Mauriac can still talk of "the sleep of stupor" or of "spiritual lethargy we die of through our religious offices." There is, however, throughout Europe a sense of the need for this reform, not by reversing tradition but by returning to the ancient forms. Part of this return is a rediscovery of the Biblical basis of the whole liturgy, and of one of its great purposes: to teach the people by the constant reading of passages from the Bible, readings which obviously should be understood.

Both the Biblical and liturgical lines lead to exciting developments this century in France, Belgium and Germany, with notable experiments in England, and the question arises: How is all this working out in practice in the village churches? The answer must be that not very much is evident, but much is promised. The Bible is being read more by Roman Catholics, but the readers are still a minority. The liturgy of the Easter Vigil has been restored and the Bible can be heard in the vernacular, but in the great majority of the Roman Catholic churches the services are as unintelligible as ever. Despite the energies of the Dominicans and the Benedictines, ably supported by many Franciscans, the movement has not yet become a landslide. I was therefore not surprised when visiting Lyon to find Mass as disorderly and as meaningless as in the days of Martin Luther.

But now there is another side to the picture, mostly to be seen in the monastic churches. The one I know best is at Sanary, in Provence, where you will find much superstition but very little genuine religion: the churches are hung with pictures of outlandish miracles but they are empty of people. Provence is not de-Christianized, it is simply pagan. In this setting, where the parish churches are hardly ever visited, the Benedictines have taken over a ninth-century church, restored it and made it their monastic church, and have also bought a large old house which they are rebuilding to form a small monastery. When I visited, the reconstruction was still in progress and there was only one monk, together with a novice.

While staying at the house I visited the church several times: on Saturday evening it was to attend None with the monk and his novice. This was conducted simply, in Latin, and the long history of the Church was evident as this ancient service was repeated.

Sunday morning was a very different picture. There at Mass peasants from the neighborhood and visitors from the towns thronged in. There was not a place to be found. It contrasted so markedly with the empty parish churches that one had to look for a reason. The monk simply said, "I am not the parish priest and I do not visit these people in their homes; I simply ring a bell and they come." You needed to attend the service to see why they came. There was a typical country choir made up of simple people, some of whom could sing. The music was below the average but there was a tremendous enthusiasm as all the people felt that they had a part to play in the singing of the liturgy and of the hymns. The earlier part of the service, the ante-communion, was conducted simply, slowly and in French. The simplest peasant could understand what was being said. The Gospel was read by the novice, in the modern Maredsous translation, and read in a way that would improve many an [English] broadcast of Evensong. The sermon was clear and a simple Bible exposition of Mark 13. Then as we moved towards the Ordinary of the Mass the monk and his novice approached the altar, which was clearly a table set away from the wall, and laid a cloth upon it, setting it as for an evening meal. The priest stood behind the altar. Much of what followed was in Latin, but there was a surprising amount in French. Whenever the Latin seemed obscure or the action of the Mass might be unintelligible the priest described what was happening and what the words meant. As often as possible there were responses from the congregation. These were usually sung, and a simple duplicated copy of the music was given to every person present. It was the Mass and there was no departure from the normal form, except that it was completely explained and as far as possible put into a language that could be understood by peasants. At the communion the Element [Host] was received standing, not kneeling.

The two things that impressed me as I took part in that worship were, first, that the Mass was clearly intelligible, and second, that the Bible was understood. This constitutes a revolution in Roman Catholic practice.

My principal concern, of course, is with the Bible, and I have tried to show how there is a Biblical revival in the Roman Catholic Church. If you were to discuss this with a Benedictine or a Dominican, I think you would find three plain warnings given about assuming too much from this revival. They would be in the form of definitions of the Roman Catholic attitude to the Bible. First, the Bible cannot be taken as a single unit; it must be regarded as a collection of books, inspired by God but having different parts and showing a development. Second, the Bible is not the norm of faith but it reveals what were the norms of faith of past saints and patriarchs. It tells us of the faith of Ezekiel and Jeremiah, of Elijah and of Moses; it is not the norm of faith for the Church today. Third, the Bible is to be read, and now it is encouraged; but it must not be read as a personal activity. It must be read with the Church. When the Roman Catholic reads the Bible he is not able to read it alone, he reads it "Catholicly" with all his brethren. He must take to his reading of it all the richness that the Spirit has deposited in the Church. Tradition still holds a powerful place in the reading of the Bible.

APPENDIX XIII:

TABLE SHOWING THE NUMBER OF CHAPTERS, VERSES, AND WORDS IN THE BIBLE [1]

Book	Chapters	Verses	Words (KJV)
Genesis	50	1,533	32,267
Exodus	40	1,213	32,692
Leviticus	27	859	24,546
Numbers	36	1,288	32,902
Deuteronomy	34	958	28,461
Joshua	24	658	18,858
Judges	21	618	18,976
Ruth	4	85	2,578
I Samuel	31	810	25,061
II Samuel	24	695	20,612
I Kings	22	816	24,524
II Kings	25	719	23,532
I Chronicles	29	941	20,369
II Chronicles	36	822	26,074
Ezra	10	280	7,441
Nehemiah	13	406	10,483
Esther	10	167	5,637
Job	42	1,070	10,102
Psalms	150	2,461	43,743
Proverbs	31	915	15,043

[1] As computed by the Gideons.

Book	Chapters	Verses	Words (KJV)
Ecclesiastes	12	222	5,584
Song of Solomon	8	117	2,661
Isaiah	66	1,292	37,044
Jeremiah	52	1,364	42,659
Lamentations	5	154	3,415
Ezekiel	48	1,273	39,407
Daniel	12	357	11,606
Hosea	14	197	5,175
Joel	3	73	2,034
Amos	9	146	4,217
Obadiah	1	21	670
Jonah	4	48	1,321
Micah	7	105	3,153
Nahum	3	47	1,285
Habakkuk	3	56	1,476
Zephaniah	3	53	1,617
Haggai	2	38	1,131
Zechariah	14	211	6,444
Malachi	4	55	1,782
Matthew	28	1,071	23,684
Mark	16	678	15,171
Luke	24	1,151	25,944
John	21	879	19,099
Acts	28	1,007	24,250
Romans	16	433	9,447
I Corinthians	16	437	9,489
II Corinthians	13	257	6,092
Galatians	6	149	3,098
Ephesians	6	155	3,039
Philippians	4	104	2,002
Colossians	4	95	1,998
I Thessalonians	5	89	1,857
II Thessalonians	3	47	1,042
I Timothy	6	113	2,269
II Timothy	4	83	1,703
Titus	3	46	921

Book	Chapters	Verses	Words (KJV)
Philemon	1	25	445
Hebrews	13	303	6,913
James	5	108	2,309
I Peter	5	105	2,482
II Peter	3	61	1,559
I John	5	105	2,523
II John	1	13	303
III John	1	14	299
Jude	1	25	613
Revelation	22	404	12,000

APPENDIX XIV:

COMPARATIVE CONSPECTUS OF THE HEBREW BIBLE AND THE SEPTUAGINTAL GREEK VERSION

The Hebrew or Palestinian canon was fixed at the Synod of Jamnia, about A.D. 90. The Alexandrian canon or Septuagintal Greek Version was less rigidly defined, but it always included apocryphal books. The Latin Vulgate followed the general pattern of the Septuagint, while the Reformers, though they held many of the apocryphal books in respect, insisted on distinguishing these from the books included in the Hebrew Bible which alone they acknowledged as properly belonging to the Old Testament canon. Nevertheless, the King James and other English versions depart from the *order* of the Hebrew canon.

Hebrew Bible	*Septuagintal Greek Version*
THE PENTATEUCH:	THE PENTATEUCH:
Genesis	Genesis
Exodus	Exodus
Leviticus	Leviticus
Numbers	Numbers
Deuteronomy	Deuteronomy
THE FORMER PROPHETS:	HISTORICAL BOOKS:
Joshua	Joshua
Judges	Judges

Hebrew Bible	*Septuagintal Greek Version*
I and II Samuel	Ruth
I and II Kings	I and II Kings (= I and II Samuel)
THE LATTER PROPHETS:	III and IV Kings (= I and II Kings)
Isaiah	I and II Chronicles
Jeremiah	*†I Esdras
Ezekiel	†II Esdras (= Ezra-Nehemiah)
The Twelve Prophets (Hosea, Joel, Amos, Obadiah, Jonah, Micah, Nahum, Habakkuk, Zephaniah, Haggai, Zechariah, Malachi)	**POETICAL AND DIDACTIC BOOKS:**
	Psalms
	Proverbs
	Ecclesiastes
POETICAL BOOKS:	Song of Solomon
Psalms	Job
Job	*Wisdom of Solomon
Proverbs	*Ecclesiasticus (or Wisdom of Sirach)
THE FIVE SCROLLS:	
Ruth	**STORY BOOKS:**
Song of Solomon	Esther (containing additions)
Ecclesiastes	*Judith
Lamentations	*Tobit
Esther	
	PROPHETICAL BOOKS:
PROPHECY:	The Twelve Prophets (Hosea, Amos, Micah, Joel, Obadiah, Jonah, Nahum, Habakkuk, Zephaniah, Haggai, Zechariah, Malachi)
Daniel	
HISTORY:	Isaiah
Ezra-Nehemiah	Jeremiah
I and II Chronicles	*Baruch

* These books are not found in the Hebrew Bible.

† I Esdras is sometimes called "Greek Esdras." II Esdras in the Septuagint is to be distinguished from another work sometimes called II Esdras (the Ezra Apocalypse). The usage of the Vulgate adds to the confusion: here I and II Esdras = Ezra-Nehemiah (found in the Hebrew Bible), III Esdras = "Greek Esdras" (I Esdras of the Septuagint), and IV Esdras = the Esdras Apocalypse (sometimes called II Esdras).

Septuagintal Greek Version

Lamentations
*Epistle of Jeremiah
Ezekiel
Daniel (including *The Song of
the Three Children, *The His-
tory of Susanna, *Bel and the
Dragon)

THE BOOKS OF THE MACCABEES:

*I and II Maccabees (to which
were sometimes added III and
IV Maccabees)

Note 1: The traditional threefold division of the Hebrew canon is as follows: (a) The Torah or Law (Pentateuch); (b) The Prophets (Former and Latter); (c) The Writings (all other books).

Note 2: Some manuscripts of the Septuagint also have the *Psalms of Solomon (placed after Psalms) and the *Prayer of Manasseh.

Note 3: According to the official reckoning of the Roman Church (declared in the Council of Trent in the sixteenth century and confirmed in the Vatican Council in 1870), the canon includes the apocryphal books with the exception of the Prayer of Manasseh and III and IV Esdras (Vulgate reckoning), which, however, are placed in an appendix at the end of the New Testament.

Note 4: In the King James Version of 1611 the Apocrypha was included between the Old Testament and the New.

* These books are not found in the Hebrew Bible.

INDEX